A History of Masculinity

IVAN JABLONKA

A History of Masculinity

From Patriarchy to Gender Justice

Translated by Nathan Bracher

ALLEN LANE
an imprint of
PENGUIN BOOKS

ALLEN LANE

UK | USA | Canada | Ireland | Australia
India | New Zealand | South Africa

Penguin Books is part of the Penguin Random House group of companies
whose addresses can be found at global.penguinrandomhouse.com.

First published in France as *Des hommes justes:
Du patriarcat aux nouvelles masculinités* by Éditions du Seuil 2019
First published in Great Britain as *A History of Masculinity* by Allen Lane 2022
001

Copyright © Ivan Jablonka, 2019
Translation copyright © Nathan Bracher, 2022

The moral right of the author has been asserted

Set in 10.5/14pt Sabon LT Std
Typeset by Jouve (UK), Milton Keynes
Printed and bound in Great Britain by Clays Ltd, Elcograf S.p.A.

The authorized representative in the EEA is Penguin Random House Ireland,
Morrison Chambers, 32 Nassau Street, Dublin D02 YH68

A CIP catalogue record for this book is available from the British Library

ISBN: 978–0–241–45879–2

Table of Contents

Introduction:
Revolutionizing the Masculine

Men have been at the forefront of every battle, except for the battle for equality of the sexes. Their dreams have spearheaded every liberation, except for the emancipation of women. With few exceptions, they have grown comfortable with the patriarchal workings of society. They have gained from it. Today, as before, gender privileges are endemic throughout the world.

Although it has been shaped by millennia of stereotypes and institutions, the traditional model of masculinity is outdated. It is both old-fashioned and harmful because it is a mechanism for dominating not only women, but also men whose masculinity is deemed illegitimate. Our dream for the future is to invent new masculinities so that they mesh with the rights of women and undo patriarchal hierarchies. This has the potential to transform everything: the family, religion, politics, business, the city, seduction and even language.

In every country, whatever the situation may be for women, it is urgent to define an ethics of masculinity for the entire range of social behaviour. How can we prevent men from trampling on the rights of women? What does it mean to be a 'good guy' with respect to equality between the sexes? This is a real challenge both psychologically and socially. Creating new models of masculinity requires goodwill and personal effort, but it must stem chiefly from a political rationale. Opposing patriarchy is much like fighting against climate change: it is important to do one's part individually, but collective action and systemic reforms are absolutely required. Today, we need egalitarian men who care more about respect than power. Just men, but men who are just.

DEMOCRACY'S BLIND SPOT

In 1791, Olympe de Gouges opened her *Declaration of the Rights of Woman and the Female Citizen* with this bold challenge: 'Men, are you able to act with justice? This is a woman's question to you.' More than two centuries after her death, looking at the make-up of governments, unequal pay, the distribution of domestic chores, and gender violence throughout the world, we still wonder whether men are 'able to act with justice'. Neither the invention of democracy, nor the Industrial Revolution, nor twentieth-century socialism and decolonization have changed things: our modernity has yet to truly address these issues – and hence it remains unsound.

Numerous institutions far and wide speak of equality of the sexes. And yet the rights of women are still overlooked even within our most democratic societies. From Aristotle to Rawls, from Descartes to Rousseau, philosophers have shown little interest in the question. Their reflections on justice did not include gender justice. As for the revolutionaries of France, they sacrificed themselves for freedom, except when that freedom benefited women. By taking note of these shortcomings and reconstructing the masculine around rights for all women and all men, we can all get closer to the ideal of equality.

Where to begin? Let's take two examples: sharing chores and sexual violence. In the twentieth century, society changed more rapidly than men did. Nowadays in Western societies, most women work, pursue careers, choose their sexuality, but men have not accepted all the necessary consequences of those realities. Women's perspectives have widened tremendously. Not so for men, who have not parted ways with their habits of giving orders and being served. Within each couple, we can see that the reality of progressive social upheavals runs up against entrenched resistance to change. Gender inequalities tend to crystallize around (not) sharing chores, an issue that demonstrates the relationship between individual experience and collective transformations.

Similarly, the #MeToo movement has shown that the definition of the masculine requires a thoroughgoing debate. The movement has led some men to ask hard questions about sexual violence. This has not led to significant change yet, but such questions are the first step. Why are there so many instances of abuse, harassment and rape, in a climate of indifference or latent tolerance? At what point does one become a Harvey Weinstein? And to what extent? Am I a flirt or a creep?

Such disquieting questions are healthy, but so much remains to be discussed. With respect to gender justice, what is a good father, good partner, good colleague, good manager, good lover, good believer, good leader or good citizen? All of this must lead to us asking ourselves, individually and collectively, what it truly means to be a man today.

It is no longer up to women to torture themselves with questions about their life choices, justify themselves at every moment, exhaust themselves reconciling work with motherhood, family life and leisure. It is up to men to catch up with a world that has changed. The onus is on them to question themselves about the masculine, without buying into the mythology of the hero of modern times who deserves a medal because he has programmed the washing machine. Such introspection would be meaningless and totally ineffective if it did not involve all areas of society: legislation, fiscal policy, the welfare state, the organization of labour, corporate culture, the etiquette of romance, parenting, pedagogy, schooling and codes of sociability.

Our governments claim to value equality and justice, but are severely lacking in men passionate about equality and justice. Our democracies have a blind spot: gender justice, which demands that we put an end to inequalities between the sexes. The challenge for men is not to 'help' women become independent, but to transform the very reality of masculinity so that it is no longer a tyranny.

NEW MASCULINITIES

Unlike other revolutions – the rise of the Neolithic, monotheism, the Age of Exploration, modern science, human rights, decolonization – the feminist revolution has not garnered the active support of many men. Why is that? Men feel targeted and threatened, but they are above all unable to see it as the truly revolutionary development that it is. Indeed, many have viewed it as mere agitation: at best, as 'changing old practices', at worst, merely 'girls' stuff'.

This explains why feminists have often been on their own – leading to a sense that there is a war between the sexes. On the one hand, many men feel attacked by feminist demands, while on the other, some women refuse to collaborate with their 'oppressors'. These two positions stem from the same premise: that equality between the sexes does not concern men. That is not true. In 1966, the anthropologist Germaine Tillion wrote that nowhere do we find 'an isolated, uniquely feminine adversity, nor a degradation that hurts daughters without tarnishing fathers'.* As she and many others have pointed out, the rights of women are simply part of human rights. This is the fight that men have shunned. Can we imagine a common front, an inclusive feminism?

Throughout history, men such as Nicolas de Condorcet, Charles Fourier, William Thompson, John Stuart Mill, Léon Richer, Jin Tianhe and Tahar Haddad have supported the emancipation of women. They defended women's physical integrity, liberty of movement, and intellectual, civil and political equality. They demanded that women have the right to learn, work, vote, love and be autonomous. Their commitment shows that the problem is not one of sex, but of gender; it is not about biology but rather about culture. As such, everyone can fight against it: feminism is a political choice.

However, while these bold thinkers had the ambition of putting women's rights on the same footing as men's, they did not intend to change men's lives or challenge their social authority, nor to confront their own dominance. Their position was generous, but inconsistent, seeking to remedy effects without tackling the causes. That is why implementing a feminism that puts women on the same footing as men does not go far enough. Prohibiting female genital mutilation, sharing chores within a couple, establishing gender parity in politics and business, and so on, are obviously necessary, but nevertheless insufficient goals.

This model of parity, which focuses on making women 'men's equals', has inspired feminism since the end of the eighteenth century. But it has left men's prerogatives pretty much intact, since women have had to demand and secure rights that men already had. This relation has to be reversed. The dynamics of gender require a model

* Germaine Tillion, *Le Harem et les cousins* (Paris: Seuil/Points, 1982/1966), p. 14.

in which the masculine should be redefined with respect to the rights of women. Because they have gained freedom and equality, women embody the norm of a democratic society: it's up to men to adapt to this legal and empirical reality.

All activism must begin with soul-searching. Such self-examination concerns first of all those in power: politicians, top officials, business leaders, managers, advertisers, urban planners, police officers, judges, doctors, journalists, teachers and researchers. All must reflect on masculinity in general and, for men, their own in particular. Are there situations where I take advantage of my status as a man, without even intending to, without even knowing it? Is the masculine defined by force, aggressiveness, the drive for power and money, putting others down? Why do men who scorn women also despise certain men, perceiving them to be 'degenerate' or 'traitors' to their sex?

There are a thousand ways of being a man: hence the idea of 'masculinities'. We can conceive of a man who is a feminist, but also of a man who accepts his share of the feminine, a man utterly offended by violence and misogyny, a man who abandons the roles he is compelled to take on, a man without authority, arrogance, privilege and the pretension of representing all humankind. The new masculinities can cure the masculine of its superiority complex.

GENDER JUSTICE
AND COLLECTIVE PROGRESS

A revolution of the masculine presupposes a theory of gender justice which aims for a *redistribution of gender*, just as social justice demands the redistribution of wealth. However, before considering the social, institutional, political, cultural and sexual implications of such a project, we have to understand the world we live in, with its two seemingly contradictory traits: longstanding patriarchy and the flaws of the masculine.

One of the reasons why progress has been so slow is that we have ignored the history of masculine domination. Many of us see day after day that men hold all the power, but do not know for how long this has been true, nor how it came to be. So we must talk about the Palaeolithic and Neolithic periods, and about the Classical era, all those times when the masculine ceased being a point of view and became the embodiment of the superior and universal. That is how we will get to the roots of the problem. If we want to act now, we have to adopt a long perspective, in order to take stock of the work that needs to be done. So we should begin by calling the masculine into question.

The masculine ideal of chivalry supposedly requires men to act in a certain way. That explains why they are always on the verge of a crisis, alienated by their own domination. Since the nineteenth century, feminism's victories and women's access to positions of responsibility, as well as the redefinition of family roles, have shaken up the hierarchy of the sexes. In the last quarter of the twentieth century, manufacturing jobs disappeared and service sector employment became predominant, creating upheaval for the status of men. At university, as in the job market, young men face ever stiffer competition from young women, who are better adapted to the economy of knowledge.

Everlasting patriarchy, on the one hand, increases doubts even further. How can we explain this paradox? The fact of the matter is that men are worried about no longer being dominant. Let's take advantage of that. The time has come to lay out a new project for society: gender justice. That implies *criteria of justice* (non-domination, respect, equality), an *ethics of gender* (maxims to guide the masculine) and subversive action (dismantling patriarchy), in order 'to live with equals', as John Stuart Mill puts it. That is how we can redistribute gender. This is therefore about signing up to a 'new deal' that would create an equal division of public and private powers, responsibilities, activities and roles.

My proposals are laid out here in four parts. The first retraces the formation of patriarchal societies; the second focuses on the agents of feminism and their struggles; the third analyses the transformations creating deeper fault lines in the idea of masculinity. Together, they shed light on how men's power has been constructed, then challenged. The fourth part shows that, thanks to these challenges, the masculine can be redefined. Men have a history other than patriarchy, and thus another future: new masculinities – masculinities that recognize the rights of women, but also those of all men.

Underlying my thought are two interconnected preoccupations:

how men behave and how they should behave. It is best first to understand how the current situation came to be, before laying out an ethical path forward. To conceptualize what exists before desiring what should be. To what end? Collective progress.

As an essay in social science and a political manifesto, this book speaks about our happiness. This quest follows in the footsteps of the philosophers of the Enlightenment, who discovered the idea of happiness, and of the champions of American independence, who wanted to translate it into a reality. The founders of the French Republic in 1793 stated, 'The end of society is common happiness.' They failed to consider that one of the components of a happy society is equality between the sexes. However, this fight cannot be won without the participation of men.

It may seem surprising to refer to revolutions led by men in the eighteenth century when all speeches began, 'Gentlemen.' But they created a new world. We might hope to accomplish for the sake of gender justice what they dared to do for social justice. Could we imagine a new 4 August 1789, in the very first months of the French Revolution, when the aristocrats collectively gave up their privileges? This would mean that today's men were capable of acknowledging and abandoning theirs. What for? In order to create a happier world, founded on the rights of all women and all men, with free women and just men.

PART ONE

The Rule of Man

I

The Globalization of Patriarchy

What do the Catholic Church, the New York Stock Exchange and a Baruya ritual in New Guinea have in common? In each case, men rule. Masculine domination is one of the most universal characteristics of human societies. Like money, it is a language all humans understand.

MASCULINE DOMINATION IS UNIVERSAL

There is no known society in which women as a group exercise the entire range of moral, political and economic power, by codifying social life (what is permissible for both sexes, for example) or making the decisions that involve the whole community (such as whether to go to war). Everywhere, men are the ones giving the orders as leaders or legislators, generals or bosses, husbands or fathers, even if they lead lives of frugal celibacy as priests. In the 1860s, jurist Johann-Jakob Bachofen believed he had identified the existence of an ancient society led by women, but what he described as 'maternal law' was in fact a Romantic femininity, one that meshed well with the power of men. In this society the maternal uncle raises his nephews and leaves them his possessions. There was similar disappointment with the Chambri of New Guinea: contrary to what was long believed, men dominate women in that society.*

* Joan Bamberger, 'The Myth of Matriarchy: Why Men Rule in Primitive Society' in Michelle Rosaldo and Louise Lamphère (eds.), *Women, Culture, and Society* (Stanford:

However, women play an important role among the Native American Iroquois, the Mosuo in Southern China, the Khasi in India and the Akan in Africa. In these societies, property can be handed down from mother to daughter (matrilinearity). In certain cases, the husband joins his wife's family after marriage (matrilocality). Among the Igbo of Nigeria, women grouped into *umuada* (collectives) watch over the villagers' health and oversee the settlement of conflicts. However, these isolated groups ruled by women nevertheless coexist with masculine power and, on a wider level, fit into patriarchal states. Meanwhile, truly matrilinear societies are in the process of disappearing. The Mosuo community, in which women are heads of the family and sexually autonomous, has become little more than a tourist attraction.*

Where does patriarchy come from, and what explains its incredible stability in all eras, all spiritualities and all political regimes? No one is able to provide an unequivocal answer to this a complex question, one that involves biological, social and economic factors, as well as religious, legal and cultural considerations.

In order to understand how men's domination over women has been institutionalized, we have to begin by defining the forces of oppression by means of a 'deep history' that borrows from biology and evolutionary psychology. We must therefore approach the question with the full scope of human history in mind – an approach that requires caution, as many of these epochs have left no writing, and some very little material trace. The first source available to us is ourselves: the anatomically modern human, *Homo sapiens*, that appeared about 300,000 years ago.

Stanford University Press, 1974), pp. 263–280; and Deborah Gewertz, 'A Historical Reconsideration of Female Dominance Among the Chambri of Papua New Guinea', *American Ethnologist*, Vol. 8, No. 1, 1981, pp. 94–106.
* Choo Waihong, *The Kingdom of Women: Life, Love, and Death in China's Hidden Mountains* (London: Tauris, 2017).

SEXUAL DIMORPHISM

All societies, without exception, have recognized the binary character of the human species, which they divide into two distinct groups: men and women. However, from a biological standpoint, there are very few differences between them.

Women and men share the same physiology – skeleton, organs, blood circulation, breathing, digestion, excretion, aging, death – with a cranium holding a brain, two legs adapted for walking on two feet, two arms that bend, two hands with opposable thumbs. They have five sensory perceptions. As beings endowed with reason, they are capable of learning, feeling emotions and making moral judgments; they have the same physiological, affective and social needs, and the same intelligence. In the field of mathematics, for example, girls and boys have the same aptitudes and the same results: this equality of performance suggests that scientific reasoning has a biological basis.* Between man and woman, there are simply many more similarities than differences.

It is on the sexual level that they are distinguished. The genetic sex of humans is determined at the moment of fertilization. Women possess two X chromosomes; men, an X chromosome and a Y chromosome. Beginning in the seventh week of gestation, the embryonic genital organs start to differentiate, with the gonads becoming either ovaries or testicles. In the male, the Y chromosome triggers the differentiation of the testicles, which secrete testosterone, causing the appearance of the prostate and the penis. In the female, certain passages develop into the uterus, Fallopian tubes and vagina. The clitoris and the labia probably appear from the process activated by the ovaries and the placenta. At birth, the infant's sex can normally be discerned by the visual appearance of the sexual organs.

At puberty, bodies are differentiated further. In girls, the breasts develop and the pelvis widens before the beginning of menstruation, while in boys there is an increase in muscle mass, a widening of the

---

* Elizabeth Spelke (with Stephen Pinker), 'The Science of Gender and Science', The Mind Brain and Behavior Inter-Faculty Initiative, available at https://www.edge. org/3rd_culture/debate05/debate05_index.html

shoulders, growth of hair on the face and chest, and a visible enlargement of the Adam's apple. The transformation of the vocal cords generally makes masculine voices deeper than feminine voices.

Besides the pathologies affecting the respective organs of women and men (breast cancer, prostate cancer), the symptoms of some illnesses can vary according to sex, as seen for example in coronary thrombosis. There are also some illnesses that afflict one sex more than the other. Since boys only have one X chromosome, they will more be more affected than girls by certain genetic anomalies situated within this chromosome, such as type A or B haemophilia or Duchenne muscular dystrophy. Researchers have also measured minor cognitive differences between the sexes: on average, men succeed better in throwing for accuracy and in tests of mental rotation, whereas women have greater dexterity, and are also better at calculations and verbal expression.*

THE ORDER OF GENDER

Societies assign a code of conduct to each sex, a combination of rights and duties called gender. On the level of the individual, this determines first names, physical appearances, manners of dress, behaviours and, at times, the manner of speaking. Gender is everywhere: in education, advertising, language, public restrooms, and in the fact that Juliette paints her nails while Paul has short hair.

From the moment of birth, gender interprets and exaggerates biological sex. Societies devote a lot of energy to disassociating the sexes, by plunging them into a 'feminine' or 'masculine' culture that becomes a set of incorporated arrangements, a second nature. Human beings learn to assume their gendered condition through the entire set of attitudes prescribed to them depending on whether they are boys or girls. In a given society, the *order of gender* is what reminds each and every one of their obligations based on their sex. A man can come to the workplace in a skirt, but he risks being greeted with surprise or

* See for example Diane Halpern, *Sex Differences in Cognitive Abilities* (New York: Psychology Press, 2012 (4th edn).

disapproval. As social animals, human beings find it difficult to escape their gender: it is now part of the human condition.

We can therefore define women historically as human females who are taught to be feminine, and men as human males taught to be masculine. There are now, fortunately, a number of spaces allowing freedom from these binary strictures, where both sexes can adjust or even reject these gender prescriptions.

The existence of gender was perceived quite early: Aeschylus describes a 'virile', insufficiently feminine Clytemnestra, and Saint Paul denounces

Man and woman according to NASA

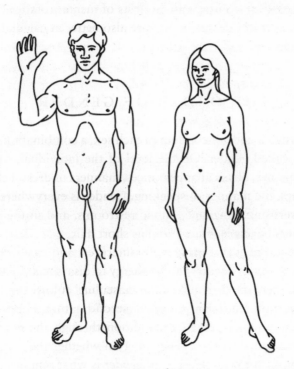

In the early 1970s, two Pioneer space probes were sent into space carrying a metallic plaque representing two human beings, one male, the other female. These two biological figures are gender coded: the woman has long hair, a graceful posture, and her vulva has been discreetly made invisible. Most significantly, it is the man who raises his hand in a greeting from all humanity. Extraterrestrials will know who rules on Earth.

'effeminate', insufficiently masculine men. Yet the concept was only theorized over the course of the twentieth century. In his *Intermediate Types Among Primitive Folk* (1914), the homosexual, feminist, libertarian vegetarian Edward Carpenter shows how, as opposed to the 'super virile' men and 'ultra-feminine women', 'more or less feminine men' and 'more or less masculine women' shuffle the array of gendered behaviours. In the 1930s, anthropologists Margaret Mead and Gregory Bateson observed gender shifts among certain peoples in New Guinea, when women behaved like men, and vice versa.

Gender has become an indispensable tool in the social sciences, and some have gone so far as to believe it to be the basis of everything: the division of the sexes is understood to be a social construction; the categories of 'woman' and 'man' artificial, or even fictitious. One to two per cent of children in the world are born intersexual, that is to say not corresponding to the conventional binary standard: for example, an XY girl without a uterus, an XX boy with small testicles, an XXY boy suffering from various disorders (Klinefelter syndrome), an XXX girl or an XXXY boy. There are many people – often referred to as transgender – who feel themselves to be a woman in a man's body, or vice versa. With the aid of hormonal and surgical treatment, it is now possible for them to change their sex.

Although the determination of sex involves complex matters of genes, hormones and anatomy, it seems hard to deny that there are only two biological designations, particularly from the standpoint of evolution, since most alternative genetic profiles are sterile. There is, then, a certain natural basis that makes it possible to identify males and females in humans. Indeed, the division between XX and XY has been characteristic of mammals for 250 million years, well before *Homo sapiens*. Granted, factors other than sex set human beings apart, but it is a fact that societies have never classified their members according to the form of their ears or the length of their feet. The binary character of the sexes remains an invariable in human thought.

Since sex precedes gender, it might be tempting to attribute the male good fortune of patriarchy to biology. Men have an interest in having multiple sexual partners to disseminate their genes: in humans, just as in chimpanzees and baboons, the male has a propensity to fight to beat his rivals for mating rights. As a consequence of evolution, men are on average taller and stronger than women. In his list of universals, Donald Brown includes men's tendency towards aggressive behaviour, theft and deadly violence. The biology of the *Homo sapiens* male may have something to do with that: androgenic hormones (such as testosterone) can serve as stimulants.* Scientists have shown that testosterone plays a role in the development of muscles and in the arousal of the brain centres involved in aggression. Testosterone levels increase during the offensive phases in sports games.†

Despite men's physical advantages in these areas, women are better at withstanding pain and fatigue, and their supposed weaknesses have not prevented them from historically being assigned the most onerous tasks. While it is important to note actual disparities between the sexes, as well as the propensity for aggression in men, patriarchies are not defined by 'might makes right': they rely less on the use of violence than on the power of laws, institutions and customs. One could imagine a world where female cooperation leads to their domination of men. Among bonobo chimpanzees, for example, the females are not as tall and muscular as the males, but their bonding together brings about a clearly gynaecocratic society. Even though male *sapiens* have genetic and hormonal characteristics that provide some physical advantages, we have to differentiate between human biology and patriarchal institutions, since it is clear that the latter are not based on the former. How, then, did the binary character of the sexes lead to social inequality?

THE MATERNAL EXPENDITURE

At a simple biological level, reproduction requires the sexual encounter of a male and a female. The female then takes on three tasks: gestation, during which a fetus (or several) develops inside her body; delivery, representing a critical moment for both mother and baby;

* Frans de Waal, *Le Singe en nous* (Paris: Fayard, 2006), p. 62 ff; and Donald Brown, *Human Universals* (Philadelphia: Temple University Press, 1991), last table.
† See for example Menelaos Batrinos, 'Testosterone and Aggressive Behavior in Man', *International Journal of Endocrinology and Metabolism*, Vol. 10, No. 3, 2012 pp. 563–568.

and lactation, where the child is fed with maternal milk for as long as its digestive system is incapable of handling solid food (no substitute for the milk of the mother or wet-nurse was possible before the development of pasteurization in the nineteenth century).

It takes a lot of time and energy for women to produce a living being. Adding together the nine months of pregnancy and the period of breast-feeding, 'maternal expenditure' can span two or three years for every child. The bond between the mother and her baby is strengthened by oxytocin, a neuropeptide synthesized by the hypothalamus and secreted during and after childbirth. Oxytocin is conducive to caring behaviours (contact, gazes, smiles, games), even if these also depend on the context and the mother's past experiences.* This physical bond explains why the biological mother is most of the time the social mother (another universal from Brown's list). Women therefore have an essential role in transmitting the earliest knowledge to children: they provide their first learning experiences and their first experience of language, as well as a general sense of comfort in the world.

What is the man's role, then? In the animal realm, parents' educative strategies often depend on the role they have played in reproduction: the investment prior to the birth determines the investment subsequent to the birth. In fish and amphibians, parenthood is thus egalitarian, consonant with external fertilization. Many bird species mobilize both parents after the laying of the eggs. The male phalarope incubates the eggs and raises the chicks; the male pigeon secretes milk in its crop.

Among 95 per cent of mammals, however, it is the mother that takes care of the offspring, with the male only taking on the job of insemination. This desertion by the father has various causes: the profusion of male gametes, internal fertilization, the uncertainty of paternity, the interest in going to fertilize other partners. In order to maximize his chances of reproducing elsewhere, the male indulges in a 'blackmail' of sorts. He will leave the female to watch over their offspring alone, knowing that she will do so; she has already provided the biggest physiological investment. Along with the wolf, marmoset and tamarin, however, the human male is an exception to this general rule: he

* See for example Ruth Feldman et al., 'Evidence for a Neuroendocrinological Foundation of Human Affiliation', *Psychological Science*, Vol. 18, No. 11, 2007, pp. 965–970.

assumes his paternal responsibilities by protecting his companion and their progeny or by bringing them food, though always with the possibility of abandoning them, since the mother has invested too much to leave. In the end, the father 'stays', but on his terms.*

Unlike other primates, humans live in couples, with (supposedly) exclusive sexual relations that take place privately. In comparison to sexual promiscuity, monogamy presents a certain number of advantages. It reduces the efforts required by polygamy, diminishes rivalry among males, involves both parents in teaching social rules and behaviours, and constitutes much larger social networks through the alliance of the maternal family with the paternal family. This aptitude for cooperation between the sexes partly explains the success of the genus *Homo*. The pre-eminence of pleasure in human sexuality, linked to woman's receptivity outside her time of fertility, is also a factor in monogamy, since in a way sex serves to cement the couple together.†

Sexual pleasure and the convenience of raising children together explain why the two parents do not separate. But this cooperation comes at the cost of maternalizing the woman, whose social value stems from her biological monopoly: in order to reproduce, the man needs a woman's body. Like wounded pride, this inferiority can be repaired by the belief that, with his seed, the man 'puts' the child in the woman's womb. Given the amount of time needed to make a little human being, from gestation until the first learning experiences, the man has to appropriate the body of the woman for himself if he wants to avoid having his 'fruit' retrieved by someone else.‡ Hence the belief that he possesses the mother along with the child.

He carries out this appropriation in exchange for his presence: within the monogamous family, the mother and children belong to him. In giving life, a woman loses her autonomy not only to the child that she

* Jared Diamond, *Why Is Sex Fun? The Evolution of Human Sexuality* (New York: Basic Books, 1997); and Jean-Baptiste Pingault and Jacques Goldberg, 'Stratégies reproductives, soin parental et lien parent-progeniture dans le monde animal', *Devenir*, Vol. 20, No. 3, 2008, pp. 249–274.
† Blake Edgar, 'Powers of Two' in *Evolution: The Human Odyssey* (New York: Scientific American, 2017), section 2.4.
‡ Françoise Héritier, *Masculin/Féminin*, Vol. 2, *Dissoudre la hiérarchie* (Paris: Odile Jacob, 2002), p. 20 ff.

carries and nourishes, but also to the man who dwells with them. Men's confiscation of women's childbearing capacity constitutes the key to the reproduction of the species, and explains why the two universals – stable conjugal unions and masculine domination – are so frequently associated. Women specialize in maternity, freeing up men for other tasks: that is the starting point of a sexual division of labour, with men producing and women reproducing.

Women seem to be 'objectively' superior to men, because they are capable of both giving life and nourishing the baby with their body. But the opposite, the subordination of women as mothers, has prevailed.

A DIVISION OF LABOUR

The Upper Palaeolithic was an ice age extending from 45,000 to 10,000 BCE in Europe. Humans were hunter-gatherer nomads who carved elaborate tools, killed large herbivores, harvested wild plants and decorated caves.

None of the animals and objects (horses, swords, chariots) that masculinity would later appropriate existed among human groups at that time, with the dog and the bow only attested with certainty towards the end of the period, between 14,000 and 10,000 BCE. Thanks to ethnological comparisons, we can nevertheless advance the hypothesis of a sexual division of labour. The Standard Cross-Cultural Sample, a representative group of cultures existing in Africa, the Mediterranean perimeter, Eurasia, the Pacific and the Americas, is a notion originally crafted by Murdock and White in 1969 to offer scholars a 'sample of the world's known and well-described cultures', 186 in number.* In all these societies, the domains of the masculine and the feminine are distinct. Big-game hunting, butchering and the transformation of hard raw materials are strictly the responsibility of men, while women are in charge of the children, food preparation and working with soft materials (spinning, weaving, basketry). Women

* George P. Murdock and Douglas R. White, 'Standard Cross-Cultural Sample', *Ethnology*, Vol. 8, No. 4 (Oct. 1969), pp. 329–369.

can also contribute to the production of food by gathering berries or capturing small game.*

Several arguments have been used to explain this distribution of tasks: men are supposedly more robust, while women are kept 'out of harm's way' in order to ensure the survival of the species; or, on a symbolical level, men supposedly chose toughness and death, while women were associated with life. Did men's monopoly over hunting give them the power to distribute meat to the women, children and elderly? Did men take over the prestigious but less strictly necessary duties, while in fact it was women who supplied daily nutritional needs? We can also imagine that the hunting of 'big game' – rhinoceros, mammoths, reindeer, buffalo – required male and female cooperation in order to kill the animal and carve it up.

If we accept this hypothesis of a division of labour, we can suppose that hand axes were mainly used by men, while women used scrapers, needles, awls and grindstones. In the Ohalo II site (circa 20,000 BCE) in Israel, the cutting of flintstone and the grinding of grain corresponded to two very distinct areas, near the bright entrance of the hut in daylight and in its darkest part, respectively.† It is nevertheless likely that the women had to master fire, as well as the tools for cutting and artistry. In several caves in Spain and France, 75 per cent of hands traced with a stencil belong to women.‡ In the twentieth century, rock cutting was conducted by women among the Arawe of New Guinea and the Koryaks of Siberia.

The culture of the Upper Palaeolithic is characterized by a large number of figurines representing women. The most ancient, dating from 35,000 BCE, was found at Hohle Fels in the Swabian Jura in Germany. Others were sculpted during the Gravettian era from 24,000 to 20,000 BCE, and were discovered at Laussel and Lespugue in southwestern France, Weinberg in Bavaria, Willendorf in Austria, Avdeevo

* Peggy Reeves Sunday, *Female Power and Male Dominance: On the Origins of Sexual Inequality* (Cambridge: Cambridge University Press, 1981), ch. 4.
† Ehud Weiss, Mordechai Kislev, et al., 'Plant-Food Preparation Area on an Upper Paleolithic Brush Hut Floor at Ohalo II, Israel', *Journal of Archaeological Science*, No. 35, August 2008, pp. 2400–2414.
‡ Dean Snow, 'Sexual Dimorphism in European Upper Paleolithic Cave Art', *American Antiquity*, Vol. 78, No. 4, pp. 746–761.

in Ukraine, and Gagarino, Kostenki and Zaraysk in Russia. In all, there are about 250 figurines carved in ivory, bone, stone or clay. From Siberia to the Atlantic, they are a testimony to the same canons of beauty: nude, very corpulent and perhaps pregnant women, with voluminous breasts, a protrusive abdomen, wide hips, large buttocks and a prominently visible vulva. The sculptors are focused on the sexual characteristics, exaggerating them to the detriment of facial expressions and limbs (the Venus of Brassempouy, whose face is finely outlined, and the figurines in Maltese ivory in Siberia, with their dressed haired and fur clothes, are exceptions). From the Gravettian era to the end of the Magdalenian era, circa 12,000 BCE, the figuration of the feminine corresponds to a well-defined genre, with prominently visible sexual attributes, and with representations of the vulva serving as a synecdoche of the feminine body, as in the caves of the Aquitaine and Cantabria regions.*

The meaning of these statuettes has been widely debated. One interpretation sees the power of woman as genitor, as a source of all life. For Marija Gimbutas, these artistic forms belong to a 'civilization of the goddess', a society of a matriarchal, egalitarian sort founded on peace and respect for life, which supposedly triumphed in Europe before being destroyed by invaders bringing the culture of war.† But one can also see them as reducing women to their sex. These statuettes could therefore correspond to a sexualization of women as viewed through the eyes of men. The goddesses' nudity is certainly compatible with masculine domination.

We can suppose, then, that around 20,000 BCE there was a division of human labour, with big-game hunting allotted to men, and childbearing to women. At the very least, Palaeolithic art proves that the feminine was assigned a 'specialized domain' connected to sex. Such assertions will of course spark debate. The absence of written sources and the scarcity of material documentation make it tricky to

---

* Jean-Paul Demoule, *Naissance de la figure: L'art du Paléolithique à l'Âge du fer* (Paris: Gallimard, 2007), p. 33 ff; Raphaelle Bourrillon et al., 'La thématique féminine au cours du Paléolithic supérieur européen', *Bulletin de la Société préhistorique française*, Vol. 109, No. 1, 2012, pp. 85–103.

† Marija Gimbutas, *The Civilisation of the Goddess: The World of Old Europe* (San Francisco: Harper, 1991).

The Venus of Willendorf
(dating to circa 25,000 years ago)

Fetish of daily life, talisman favouring fertility, goddess of maternity or love? The Venus of Willendorf is also a sex without a face.

advance hypotheses about such a vast area of time and space. But it is important to take epistemological risks.

LANDS AND WEAPONS

At the outset of our geological epoch, the Holocene, the climate warmed. The invention of human agriculture – and the subsequent move towards more sedentary behaviour – that began in the Fertile Crescent during the Neolithic period radically changed societies. The transformations became the crucible of masculinity. At the Turkish site of Göbekli Tepe, the masculine seems to have become predominant as early as the tenth millennium BCE: the bas-reliefs represent men and threatening animals like leopards, foxes and wild boar. At La Valltorta in the Spanish Levante, cave paintings dating from 10,000 to 9,000 BCE show dozens of male archers, sometimes nude, raining down arrows on herds of deer. Women are depicted harvesting honey. In this era, societies were still semi-nomadic.

The transformations of the Neolithic period deepened the sexual division of labour traced out in the Palaeolithic period. Men monopolized the tasks of clearing the land, ploughing, using draught animals and building habitatation; women took care of gathering berries, mushrooms and wood, making clothes and cooking food, all while watching over children. Many of these tasks were carried out in dwellings, or close by, such that the domestic sphere gradually became the feminine domain. Women's specialization in textile crafts could be found in all agrarian societies, at Suse, among the Hittites, at Mycena, in Classical Greece, in Rome, in the works of Homer as well as in the Bible. This sexual division of labour was perpetuated throughout Medieval Europe, from Spain to the Scandinavia of the Vikings, and continues today.

That does not mean that the easiest work has fallen to women. It is rather the opposite: in the fields of ancient Egypt as in the rice paddies of China, women took care of agricultural work with only rudimentary tools. This reality has been confirmed by ethnological observations in tribes whose way of live is closely related to that of the Neolithic period. Among the Nambikwara of Brazil, for example, woman play a fundamental role in daily life – although their gathering of food and their childcare is still seen as an 'inferior' type of activity. When they travel, the women carry the heavy sack containing the family wealth, while the husband walks ahead with his bow. Similarly, among the Baruya of New Guinea, the routine, monotonous tasks relegated to women are considered undignified.*

---

* Claude Lévi-Strauss, *Tristes Tropiques* (Paris: Plon/'Terre humaine poche', 1955/2001, p. 331 ff; and Maurice Godelier, *La Production des grands hommes: Pouvoir et domination masculine chez les Baruya de Nouvelle*-Guinée (Paris: Flammarion/'Champs', 1982/2003. See also Jean-Paul Demoule, *Les Dix Millénaires oubliés qui ont fait l'histoire: Quand on inventa l'agriculture, la guerre et les chefs* (Paris: Fayard, 2017), ch. 9.

Once they had developed to the stage that they could sustain large populations, agriculture and the raising of livestock brought about an increase in the birth rate. Unlike nomadic life, which obliged women to carry their small children, necessarily limiting them in number, sedentary society made possible a more rapid succession of births. Population growth can be seen as early as the seventh millennium BCE at Çatalhöyük in Anatolia, and it constituted a major transition in the history of humanity, radically changing the life of women, who were now more and more often mothers. Women became assets, both because they worked and because they produced children. Their offspring underwent social selection: the sons were able to succeed their fathers. In Mesopotamia as in China, the development of agriculture was correlative to the emergence of patrilinear systems, with possessions handed down from father to son, masculine primogeniture, patrilocal residence and technical training reserved for boys.*

The transformations of the Neolithic period resulted in the split of the sexes' respective social destinies. Women experienced even greater pressure from sedentism: higher birth rates led to domestic confinement, which in turn increased the time they spent pregnant and caring for children. Meanwhile, men gained new sources of power, possessing new land and livestock, mastering new tools and food stocks.

In the Neolithic as in the Paleolithic period, it is difficult to distinguish between a tool and an arm, or between a hunting weapon and an instrument of war. As far as we can tell, masculinity incorporated the use and symbolism of violence from early on. In the agricultural communities of the Cerny culture in the middle Neolithic period (circa 4500 BCE), tombs of men contain bows and arrows. Ötzi, who died around 3,300 BCE in the Tyrolean Alps, carried with him an unfinished bow, arrows, a copper battle-axe, and a bloodied flintstone knife (he himself had an arrow in his back).

In the second millennium BCE, bronze metallurgy was used to create the first known weapons of war, tools whose explicit function was to

---

* Margaret Ehrenberg, *Women in Prehistory* (London: British Museum Press, 1989), pp. 99–105; and Maxine Margolis, 'The Relative Status of Men and Women', in Carol Ember et al. (eds.), *Encyclopedia of Sex and Gender*, Vol. 2 (New York: Springer, 2003), pp. 137–145.

kill other humans: swords (around 1700 BCE), daggers, halberds and lances, as well as defensive weapons such as shields, breastplates and helmets. From this time, the figure of the warrior can be found throughout the world: in Corsica on the Filitosa menhirs, in Sardinia on bronze statuettes, in Scandinavia on the Tanum engravings and in Sanxingdui, China, where jade and bronze daggers accompanied massive, impressive masculine heads with square jaws and thick eyebrows.

Once invented, the weapons of war immediately became a masculine prerogative. Men took arms along with them even to the grave, as in the case of the man who died at Ponte San Pietro in the third millennium BCE and the one at Leubingen around 1900 BCE. Both were buried with an arsenal of daggers and battle-axes, and were accompanied by a young woman who was probably sacrificed. As the privilege of male elites, arms conveyed new meanings: while woman is endowed with the ability to create life, man has the capacity to take it away.*

The warrior's array of weapons was completed by the horse, domesticated in the sixth millennium BCE by the Botai peoples of Kazakhstan, then by the Mongols, and adopted in Europe beginning in 4000 BCE.† Coupled with the bow, the horse proved to be a fearsome military asset. Certain peoples such as the Scythians in the steppes of Eurasia and the Parthians on the Iranian plateau soon specialized in cavalry or mounted archery. In Egypt, the horse and the chariot facilitated the New Empire's conquests from 1500 BCE on. Whether it was used for war, racing or ceremonial display, the chariot was an object of masculine prestige, often associated with commanders and nobility. We find it in Homer in the eighth century BCE, in the tomb of the Prince of Hochdorf in Germany around 500 BCE, as well as in Philip of Macedonia's gold staters around 330 BCE.

Male supremacy in the area of war is qualified by two exceptions: the female warriors of Central Asia, armed with arrows and battle-axes, to whom the Greeks pay homage in the legend of the Amazons,

---

* Jean Giulaine and Jean Zammit, *Le Sentier de la guerre: Visages de la violence préhistorique* (Paris: Seuil, 2001); and Anne Lehoërff, *Par les armes: Le jour où l'homme inventa la guerre* (Paris: Belin, 2018).
† Ludovic Orlando et al., 'Ancient Genomes Revisit the Ancestry of Domestic and Przewalski's Horses', *Science*, Vol. 360, No. 6384, April 2018, pp. 111–114.

and the 'princesses' in South East Asia and among the Celts, who took tremendous riches with them into the other world.* The young woman buried in Thailand with 120,000 seashell pearls, earrings and bracelets may merely have been a rich heiress, but the Lady of Vix, who died in Burgundy, France, in the sixth century BCE, seems to have held real political power, since she possessed a chariot, threw banquets with special vessels for serving wine, and maintained relations, at least on a commercial level, with the Greeks.

We must nevertheless differentiate between the domination of men, which favours a sex, and the model of virility, which celebrates a gender. In this light, we can see that women can in special cases appropriate for themselves the codes of masculinity, founded on the horse, the chariot or alcohol. Not one of them was buried with arms, however. The sword is male.

THE SELF-EVIDENT MAN-KING

Beginning in the fifth millennium BCE, group burials declined in Europe, with leaders beginning to be interred in rich private burial places, as at Varna in Bulgaria. The first dynasties appeared in Egypt and Mesopotamia at the end of the fourth millennium BCE. At Uruk, an alabaster statuette was found dating from 3000 BCE, representing a 'priest-king' with a long beard and well-formed muscles. Masculine characters started to appear in ancient narratives. Gilgamesh, the hero of one of the most famous Mesopotamian legends, is supposed to have reigned at Uruk around 2700 BCE. Among the reigns that we know of are those of Pharaoh Kheops, around 2500 BCE, and Sargon, founder of the Akkad empire, around 2,300.

The first monarchs were almost always men, even if queens could occasionally rule in association with a husband or a son, as in the case of Pharaoh Hatshepsut, or with a durably obscure status, like that of

---

* Adrienne Mayor, *Les Amazones: Quand les femmes étaient les égales des hommes* (Paris: La Découverte, 2017), chs. 11 and 13; and Charles Higham, *The Archaeology of Mainland Southeast Asia From 10,000 BC to the Fall of Angkor* (Cambridge: Cambridge University Press, 1989), pp. 77–78.

'Man', 'king', and 'woman' in cuneiform

  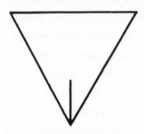

In Mesopotamia at the end of the fourth millennium BCE, *the first system of writing in the world asserts the superiority of the masculine over the feminine. A woman is simply identified with her vulva, whereas a man is represented as an individual, with a body, a head and eyes. As for the king, he is literally a crowned man.*

Puabi in Mesopotamia. Fashioned around 2500 BCE, the Standard of Ur is a wooden chest to the glory of a Sumerian king: on one side, he is depicted admiring his soldiers and slaves, and on the other, presiding over a religious banquet as both war chief and interlocutor of the gods. From around the same time, a large number of coins bear the effigy of a crowned king with a laurelled head, the reverse side depicting an archer or a charioteer. State patriarchy was born along with the self-evident man-king.

The position of man as chief of state confers unprecedented power. From its origins, the state has been patriarchal, led by masculine elites whose prerogatives are sovereignty, administration and war. In Egypt, men held all of the civil occupations: vizier, chamberlain, treasurer, architect, priest, scribe. Many of these responsibilities were inherited, handed down from father to son. The pharaoh had power over the thousands of workers in his service: that is why he was buried under a pyramid, whereas a European leader had only a mound. The pyramid displays the power of the pharaoh, who was able to mobilize thousands of male workers for his personal service.

Compared with the beginning of the Neolithic period, the state made it possible for men to gain even greater power. The appropriation of land was transformed into territorial conquest. Violence turned into war. Empires arose. From antiquity on, conquerors would always be men: Sargon, Rameses II, Cyrus II, Alexander, Scipio, Caesar, not to mention their innumerable generals.

Even if women had rights at the civil level, the law of the Mesopotamian states was strictly patriarchal, as much in the Babylonian South as in the Assyrian North. In the code of the Babylonian king Hammurabi (circa 1750 BCE), men set women's obligations. A husband could exploit or repudiate his wife and forgive or punish adultery, as well as possess – and produce offspring with – concubines and slaves. A debtor could pawn his wife and children, and the daughter of a murderer could be killed as a punishment for her father's

The Victory Stele of Naram-Sin (circa 2250 BCE)

Naram-Sin, king of Akkad, grandson of Sargon, is seen at the summit of a pyramid illumined by the stars. Bearing arms and wearing a helmet, he triumphs over his enemies (one of them has taken an arrow in the throat; another pleads for mercy). With the mastery of arms, the conquest of power, the expression of being all-powerful and divine election, masculine royalty is in place.

crime. Assyrian law (circa 1400 BCE) devoted an entire section to the status of women, and was even harsher.

Similar discriminations were operative in the Athens of the fifth century BCE, where sexual segregation was mandatory. Women were excluded from public life and intellectual activities. The agora, the banquet and the market were masculine areas; women, minors for life, were just bodies destined to produce male heirs and remain cloistered in the home (except at times of celebration). The strategist, orator, hoplite, charioteer and philosopher were by definition men; the great sages were Thales, Empedocles, Hippocrates, Hipparchus, Euclid, Archimedes and Strabo. For Aristotle, writing from 340 to 320 BCE, women were passive, incomplete creatures, a sort of defective male. The same misogyny can be found in Rome, although less systematically. The emperor, *pater familias* and soldier are the three figures on which Roman power was constructed.

GOD IS NO LONGER A WOMAN

In Europe, as in the Middle East, dominant men easily accepted representations of women, which in any case remained quite marginal. The statuettes found at Çatalhöyük, particularly the Seated Woman, conform to the same canons of beauty as the Gravettian goddesses. In the Cyclades of the third millennium BCE, a new kind of figuration appeared: an elongated woman with a slender figure, angular shoulders, an oval face, pointed chin and arms tightly crossed around the waist, between her thin chest and triangular, slitted pubis. As goddess miniatures, propitiatory objects, symbols of deceased women or companions of deceased men, these statuettes do not seem to attest a feminine role fundamentally different from what had gone before: woman always appears in her sexualized nudity.

Except for Arinna among the Hittites or Amaterasu in Japan, who were both sun goddesses, women lent their face to nurturing deities, always linked to childbearing, fertility and harvests: Astarte throughout the Middle East; Aruru (or Ninmah) for the Sumerians; Isis for the Egyptians; Hera, Demeter and Persephone in Greece. Certain goddesses drew their power from their womb, such as Lajja Gauri in

India, who is often represented with her legs spread wide apart, or as the 'princess with the flamboyant uterus' in one of Java's legends.

These goddesses were often subordinate to the gods, and to masculinity in general. Such was the case of Inanna/Ishtar, the Mesopotamian goddess of love and war. Although equipped with weapons and sometimes decked out with a beard, she was tied to Dumuzi, who symbolizes the king, by a sacred marriage.* Generally, the high priestesses moved about very little, and often remained in their sanctuaries. Among them, Enheduanna, the daughter of Sargon, known for her hymns to the goddess Inanna, was a pawn in the political strategy of her father. Beginning in the second millennium BCE, the pantheon of early civilizations became dominated by a single god, seen as the creator of the universe, master of the heavens, the sun and lightning: Enlil in Mesopotamia, Baal in the Levant, Tarhuna among the Hittites, Viracocha among the Incas, Zeus in Greece, Jupiter in Rome, Taranis in the Celtic world, Thor for the Vikings. Feminine divinities were now relegated to the rank of spouses or sisters. The power of creation had been transferred to the hands of men.†

The ascension of the masculine culminated in monotheism. At the end of the second millennium BCE, when Egypt had conquered the tribe of Israel, YHWH appeared as a warrior god of the desert. In the eighth century BCE in Samaria, he became the first of the gods, venerated as a bull or as Baal, god of the storm who rides on the clouds. In the kingdom of Judah, he armed kings, first Saul against the Philistines and then David when he seized control of Jerusalem. After the destruction of the Temple in 587 BCE, the 'Deuteronomists' insisted that the Babylonian gods had not vanquished YHWH. On the contrary, it was he who had used them to chastise his disobedient people. God was born. Though unique and transcendent, he nevertheless kept his titles masculine: 'lord', 'king' and 'master'.‡

Whether they were founded by Moses, Confucius, Buddha, Jesus

---

* Yağmur Heffron, 'Inanna/Ištar', *Ancient Mesopotamian Gods and Goddesses* (Oracc and the UK Higher Education Academy, 2016).
† Gerda Lerner, *The Creation of Patriarchy* (Oxford: Oxford University Press, 1986), chs. 8–10.
‡ Thomas Römer, *L'Invention de Dieu* (Paris: Éditions du Seuil, 2014).

(along with his twelve disciples) or Mohammed, the origins of religions and spiritualities can be found in the message of a man. How do they manage to reconcile a universal message with their masculine origin? It is easy to show that monotheisms posit the equality of all human beings and exhort them to justice. The Torah and the Gospels command all to love their fellow human beings. In the seventh century CE, the Quran included both men and women in the Ummah, the community of the faithful, as well as in the mercy of God. Responding to a question from his wife Oum Salama, the Prophet replies that grace is not determined by sex, but by faith, sincerity, kindness towards the poor and obedience to God.

Now all religions and spiritualities were skewed toward patriarchy. In the Hellenistic period, Judaism established the religion of the Almighty God based on the exclusion of women. The divine covenant was sealed with males: Abraham, Moses, David, the patriarchs, kings, priests, circumcized boys, men forming the minyan. The Ten Commandments were addressed to men, who must not covet their neighbour's wives. The female creature was the source of sin and death, excluded from the divine pact, except when she worked for the propagation of the species: the act of creation, the metaphysical elevation of the masculine, won out against the act of procreation, the redemptive punishment of the feminine. After their menstrual period, women had to purify themselves before being allowed into the sanctuary, giving themselves to their husbands or touching food.

According to the mainstream interpretation, Eve was created after Adam, from one of his ribs. She let herself be tempted by the devil before becoming a seductress: Adam ate the forbidden fruit in order to please her.* In continuation of the Aristotelian and biblical misogyny, Saint Paul refuses to let women speak, teach or lead the liturgy. The Catholic Church must have no woman pope, cardinal, archbishop, bishop or priest. Man has monopolized the sacred and monotheism is a patriarchal covenant: God chose the king to rule over men, and men to rule over women.

Despite the message of justice and respect conveyed by Confucius

* 'Ève', *Dictionnaire de théologie catholique* (Paris, Letouzey and Ané, 1911–1913), Vol. V, Part 2, p. 1640 ff.

around 500 BCE, Confucianism as a state religion imposed on women the rule of the 'three obediences': the triple submission to the father (during youth), to the husband (in adulthood) and to the oldest son (if widowed). The rule of the 'four virtues' recommends that women be good housewives, maintain a serious countenance, speak with deference and remain chaste. In the lands of Islam, the egalitarian spirit of the Prophet was replaced by misogynistic had-iths: 'The people that entrusts its affairs to a woman will never know prosperity,' or 'Dogs, donkeys and women interrupt prayer when they pass in front of the believer.'* From one region to another, the law (*sharia*) and jurisprudence (*fiqh*) justify the submission of women in the areas of sexuality, education, employment and divorce, as well as the inferiority of daughters in inheritance and the stoning of adulterous women.

For countless Jewish, Christian, Muslim and Hindu exegetes, women represent nothing but pride, laziness, lust. As the curse of the species, they must be kept in check. Because of their supposedly natural inferi-ority, or else for the sake of social harmony, they have to obey men, who will decide for them. The inequality of the sexes unites religions beyond their differences: their generous principles have not prevailed over the social structures already in existence.

From this point on, patriarchy was spread from its origins in the Mesopotamian states, Greek city-states, the Roman Empire, Middle Eastern monotheisms and Chinese civilization. China, for example, transmitted its patriarchal model to Japan and Korea. With its rules of obedience and virtue, Confucianism penetrated into Japan at the end of the fifth century CE. The Tang legal codes in particular transformed the condition of women from the sixth century on: total submission of the wife to her husband (she must consider him 'like heaven'), patrilocal marriage, permission for the man to beat or repudiate his spouse, meas-ures against feminine adultery, and so on. Shōmu, the first Chinese-style emperor of Japan, contributed to the 'Tang-ification' of the country from 720–740 CE. The crises stemming from the mistrust of his daughter Kōken when she took the throne preceded the decline of the

---

* Fatima Mernissi, *Le Harem politique: Le prophète et les femmes* (Paris: Albin Michel, 1987), p. 150 ff.

status of women at court and their exclusion from official capacities. The *danson johi* principle in force in feudal society taught that it was necessary 'to respect men, despise women'. Similarly, the neo Confucianism of the seventeenth century exhorted the husband to command, the spouse to obey. Such was the message of the *Onna Daigaku* (The Great Learning for Women), an influential education manual in the Japan of the Edo period. The same phenomenon of the masculinization of society can be observed from the fifteenth century onwards under the Joseon dynasty in Korea.*

From the construction of modern states to the coming of fascist regimes, various phenomena have contributed to the extension of masculine domination: Christian and Muslim monotheism and divine right monarchy (with three masculine figures of leadership – God, the king and the clergyman), but also market capitalism, the rise of the bourgeoisie and colonial imperialism. The three Latin works most often read in Europe between the sixth and the fifteenth centuries were written by men: Gregory the Great, Pierre Lombard and Isidore of Seville (not counting three Church Fathers prior to the Middle Ages).†

The encounter of the Inca emperor and the conquistador Pizarro at Cajamarca, Peru, in 1532, pitted against each other two men unequally equipped with the attributes of masculinity. On one side, the Son of the Sun, recently victorious in a fratricidal war, carried on a litter by the princes of his empire and capable of raising an extraordinary ransom in gold. On the other, the bearded Spaniard, knighted by Charles V, Holy Roman Emperor, with his God, his henchmen, his horses, his swords and his guns. The last three assets ensured his victory. All we have to do is contemplate the Dutch art of the seventeenth century, from Rembrandt to Vermeer, including Gérard Dou and Pieter de Hooch, to see to what extent gendered roles had become immovable:

---

* Dorothy Ko, JaHyun Kim Haboush and Joan Piggott (eds.), *Women and Confucian Cultures in Premodern China, Korea, and Japan* (Berkeley and Los Angeles: University of California Press, 2003).
† Francesco Siri, 'Les best-sellers au Moyen Âge,' *L'Histoire*, No. 445, March 2018 (according to the FAMA database of popular works written in Medieval Latin).

armed men, surgeons, sages, with women staying inside as housewives – mothers preparing meals or taking care of their children.

Such is the world that we have inherited.

THE ORIGINS OF PATRIARCHY

Today, we are capable of landing on the moon, destroying the planet and reimplanting oocytes, but we are not able to reproduce outside a uterus, and the little human is still made within a woman's womb. For millions of years, a baby has needed a physical bond with its mother in order to exist, that is to say, to grow, be born and survive. The maternal expenditure, encouraged by internal fertilization and oxytocin, weighs on women. Just as pregnancy and lactation can be considered 'handicaps' for women, so men's stature, strength and aggressive behaviour can appear as 'assets' for them. But that does not mean that masculine domination is inscribed in our genes.

In fact, patriarchy proceeds from an interpretation of bodies: it transforms female biology into destiny, subjecting women to one function. If they are 'by nature' genitors, then men are at leisure to take over other spheres: the economy, war, power, and so on. For women, maternity and its corollaries, for men, the rest of human activity. Patriarchy therefore reposes on an essentialization of women's reproductive capacities. Instead of saying that women *have* a womb, it states that women *are* a womb. Rather than observing that certain women give birth at certain times in their lives, it proclaims that the existence of all humans of the female sex must be organized around their aptitude for procreation. Hence the sophism: certain women can be mothers, and since motherhood is a service for men, therefore all the women will be assigned to servitude.

The deficiency of males, their inability to create children, was converted into an all-powerful status. Deprived of the power that women have, men reserved all the others for themselves, including that of controlling feminine sexuality. This was the revenge of males: their biological inferiority led to their social hegemony. Even now in the twenty-first century, men dominate the political, religious and economic spheres on all continents, and ethnological observations among hunter-gatherers also indicate situations of feminine subordination: genital cutting, premature marriage of girls, exchanges of sisters and nieces, patrilocality, the possibility of exerting rights over one's spouse, forcing women to work.* We might thus suppose that, since masculine domination exists on a planetary level today as before, it has always existed, stemming from a *universal interpretation of universal biological phenomena*. A very plausible scenario, but not proven.

Let's focus on what can be taken for granted thanks to archaeological sources. The Gravettian statuettes from around 20,000 BCE and the La Valltorta paintings from around 10,000 BCE suggest that men were hunting while women bore children. This differentiated distribution of tasks in a context of global poverty then gives way to the masculine prerogative characterized by the accumulation of agricultural capital and the monopoly of armed force. Patriarchy becomes the rule once there is something to monopolize (land, herds, food stocks, raw materials, power over women and certain men). At a minimum, we can conclude that the human groups of the Palaeolithic era instituted a *division between the sexes*, while Neolithic societies imposed an *inequality between the sexes*.

While patriarchal societies probably appeared as early as the Upper Palaeolithic period, they were certainly in place in the fourth millennium BCE in Europe, during the Neolithic period, and in Mesopotamia at the dawn of the first dynasties, as attested by the masculine figures of the leader, the archer and the ploughman. Male rule was founded on a threefold functionality: the king, the warrior, the farmer. These three types respectively correspond to political and religious sovereignty, the skills of warfare and agricultural production. Together, they are the three pillars of ancient society.

Masculine domination accounts for men's immediate hold over writing in the fourth millennium BCE, over the state in the third millennium BCE, over arms in the second millennium BCE and over religions in the first millennium BCE. As societies become increasingly complex, inequality between the sexes produces a number of multiplier effects: sedentism, the invention of agriculture and animal husbandry, social hierarchy,

* See for example Alain Testart, 'Manières de prendre femme en Australie', *L'Homme*, Vol. 36, No. 139, 1996, pp. 7–57.

territorial conquests, and political and spiritual powers all conspire to subordinate women. What is commonly called 'civilization' (agriculture, writing, metallurgy, state, empire) is indissociable not only from masculine agency, but also from masculine culture. There are, then, several convergent universals: recognition of gender binarity, division of labour according to sex and men's social superiority over women.

There are, however, two factors adding more nuance. First, masculine domination is not the only inequality on earth. It is often the case that other hierarchies prevail: the free versus the enslaved, rich versus poor, natives versus foreigners. Conversely, there is an equality of the sexes 'from the bottom': millions of human beings before the arrival of modern medicine and social welfare all suffered the same servitudes, the same dire poverty and the same physical suffering (except for the huge number of women dying in childbirth).

Second, patriarchy is not anchored in human nature: it does not stem from biological determinism, nor from any intrinsic precedence, such as parent/child or firstborn/younger child. That is why we need not be fearful of our biological dissimilarities: even though humans differ in some ways (most men have no uterus, most women secrete less testosterone), their de facto non-equality does not entail any rightful inequality. Believing in the equality of the sexes is not a matter of empirical observation: it is a moral position and as such, represents a non-negotiable absolute.*

It is precisely because all these realities get confused that patriarchy seems natural to so many people, both men and women. Distinguishing de facto differences from rightful equality, however, is a way of securing the entire set of human rights. And assuming responsibility for the long history of patriarchy constitutes the first step in reconciling justice with masculinity.

---

* Stephen Pinker, *The Blank Slate* (New York: Viking, 2002/2016).

2

The Woman Function

In Plato's *Timaeus*, it is said that women's wombs are like a 'little animal' living inside them. The First Epistle to Timothy (attributed to Saint Paul) states that woman will be 'saved through childbearing'. For Rousseau, author of *Émile*, 'The male is only a male at certain moments; the female all her life.' For George Sand herself, a French female writer in the nineteenth century who lived as men's equal, woman is 'forever a slave to her own heart and to her womb'.

We could keep on giving citation after citation stating that women's destiny is to perpetuate the species. Women are not only reduced to their bodies, but they are also seen merely as sexual organs. In order to understand why this belief has fared so well century after century, we must dissect patriarchy as a *megastructure of thought* producing a social system.

ON WOMAN AS SERVICE

Patriarchal thought considers women in a utilitarian mode. Their bodies, made available for men, are assigned several functions: giving pleasure, making children, and then nurturing these children in a household. Three organs implement this multifunctional conception of women: the vagina, the uterus and the breasts.

The sexual function of woman is manifest in institutions designed to provide men with numerous sexual partners: polygamy, concubinage, seraglio, brothel. The harem is seen in the Palace of Mari in Syria at the beginning of the second millennium BCE, then in the Chinese, Mughal and Ottoman empires. These places of pleasure, which also serve political and educative purposes, should not make us forget the less extreme forms of sexualization, such as the duty to please at every instant and the countless aesthetic rules imposed on women: epilation, make-up, dieting, and so on.* Western tourists seek suntans and watch their weight while on the island of Djerba in Tunisa. Meanwhile, the local ritual of *hanjba* confines the fiancée indoors and makes sure she is stuffed with dates and honey; all so that she will be as pale and as fat as possible by the time of the wedding.

Second, women serve to produce children. In the Middle Ages, a good queen is, above all else, one who supplies her husband with descendants. Her pregnancies are eagerly scrutinized. Wives who are sterile or unsuited to carrying out their 'duty' run the risk of being repudiated, as were Ingeborg of Denmark in 1193, Jeanne of France in 1498 and Josephine de Beauharnais in 1809. In Song-dynasty China of the twelfth and thirteenth centuries CE, women were instruments marked for the continuation of the male lineage: early marriages were favoured in order to increase the number of births, with the possibility of repudiation if the woman did not engender a boy.† In the nineteenth century, Pierre Larousse's *Grand Dictionnaire* defined woman as the 'female of the man, a human being organized for the conception and birth of children'. This use for procreation explains the abundance of laws forbidding or limiting abortion, even to this day. Men – politicians, doctors, clerics – are the ones controlling women's childbirth.

When not eroticized to stir men's desire, the breast corresponds to the third feminine function: lactation. Women nurse their children (and sometimes the children of others), but also feed their families and an entire people. In a figurative sense, the bare breast embodies religious and patriotic causes: the Madonna in Renaissance Italy, the good wet nurse in the Netherlands of the seventeenth century, Delacroix's *Liberty Guiding the People* in post-Revolutionary France.‡

---

* François Laplantine, 'La *hajba* de la fiancée à Djerba (Tunisie)', *Revue de l'Occident musulman et de la Mediterranée*, No. 31, 1981, pp. 105–118.

† Jian Zang, 'Women and the Transmission of Confucian Culture in Song China', in Dorothy Ko et al., *Women and Confucian Cultures*, pp. 123–141.

‡ Marilyn Yalom, *History of the Breast* (HarperCollins, 1997).

Pleasure, reproduction, nursing: women 'serve'. These functions are integrated into a life cycle: the young girl to be kept as a virgin (she is going to be useful); the married woman (she is useful), the post-menopausal woman (she no longer is useful, which gives her a certain autonomy). She serves a purpose, while also serving the husband, the children, the sick and the elderly, in a private or semi-private setting. These practices have sometimes been adopted by different categories of women: in the nineteenth century, bourgeois morality distinguished the mistress and the prostitute, who were used for sensual pleasure, from the legitimate spouse, who was reserved for the making of descendants. We can therefore define the 'woman function' as the entire set of sexual, reproductive and ancillary practices that women must engage in for the satisfaction of men.

While women 'serve' a purpose, men for their part do not 'serve' at all. This single difference is enough to doom the former to domestic servitude, while freeing the latter for a life of the mind or for action. Such an inequality of functions has not only political, but also cultural and medical consequences. The female body has been studied to the extent that it is useful. That explains the overinvestment in obstetrics and lactation, to the detriment of knowledge in other fields. Around 1330, the Milanese doctor Maino de Maineri's book on health guide-lines mentioned women only with respect to four things: menstruation, conception, pregnancy and lactation. In the Poggi Museum in Bologna, the anatomical wax figures from the eighteenth century provide a graphic representation of the female reproductive system, with realistic, removable fetuses and internal organs. Seeking to group mammals together in the 1750s, Linné chose the Latin term *mammalia,* in refer-ence to the mammae of females: the nurturing mother was an iconic figure in that era. Meanwhile, other words (the German *Säugetiere,* 'suckling animals'), as well as other criteria (viviparity, the presence of fur, the form of the heart), were equally plausible.*

Unlike the breasts and the womb, the clitoris has been a neglected organ: it is only useful for women's pleasure. Two Italian doctors, including one Gabriel Fallope, 'discovered' it in the mid-sixteenth

---

* Londa Schiebinger, *Nature's Body: Gender in the Making of Modern Science* (Bos-ton: Beacon Press, 1993), ch. 2.

century, without arousing much interest. From 1940 to 1970 in the United States, the clitoris was simply omitted from drawings representing the feminine genital organs.* It was not before the very end of the twentieth century that an Australian urologist, Helen O'Connell, gave a complete physiological description of the clitoris, working from the dissection of corpses before obtaining three dimensional images in 2005 thanks to MRI. In another area, feminine homosexuality was systematically denounced or ridiculed since, again, it 'served' no purpose.

Reducing women to their biology (the 'absurdity of immanence', as Simone de Beauvoir put it) justified both their exclusion from intellectual activities and their status as transferable or exchangeable means of production. The book of Exodus authorized the sale of girls, as was the case in China before the practice was banned under the Yuan dynasty in the sixteenth century.† The exchange of women is even more frequent in the context of a marriage. Claude Lévi-Strauss has shown that the prohibition of incest, which requires a man to 'give' his daughter or sister to other men, brings about the circulation of women. The direct exchange of women (with cross-marriages) differs from the exchange of a woman for possessions (a dowry understood to be the price of the fiancée). Marriages can seal alliances between families or states, with the fiancée being in that case nothing more than the mode of the agreement. In a large number of Christian ceremonies, the bride comes into the church clutching her father's arm and exits on her husband's arm: she has been 'transferred'. Conversely, in the Maghreb as studied by Germaine Tillion, endogamy makes it possible to keep women and property within the family.

Women are conceived to be objects in several systems of law. In Mesopotamia, the rape of a woman wronged her owner, the father or the husband, who suffers the 'damage'. Assyrian law held that a father could rape the wife of the one who had assaulted his daughter. As for

* Nancy Tuana, 'Coming to Understand: Orgasm and the Epistemology of Ignorance' in Robert Proctor and Londa Schiebinger (eds.) *Agnotology: The Making and Unmaking of Ignorance* (Stanford: Stanford University Press, 2008), pp. 108–145.
† Mary Keng Mun Chung, *Chinese Women in Christian Ministry: An Intercultural Study* (New York: Peter Lang, 2005), p. 52.

the victim, she was given in marriage to her rapist, who thus received the 'damaged' goods.* Women have also been sent into newly colonized territories, where the presence of numerous soldiers made for a highly imbalanced ratio of men to women. In the eighteenth century, the Russian government sent prostitutes and criminals to Siberia for them to become wives for the Cossacks. Officers chose first, with the rank and file soldiers having to content themselves with those suffering from tuberculosis and syphilis.†

CONTROLLING WOMEN'S BODIES

The use of the 'woman function' is based on a set of constraints aiming to control women's bodies in order to put them to optimum use. The first of these constraints involves menstruation. One could fill an entire volume with the negative superstitions associated with it. According to Pliny the Elder, author of *Natural History*, menstrual blood makes wine turn into vinegar, crops wither and die, fruit fall from the tree, bees perish and iron rust. In numerous cultures, a menstruating woman is considered taboo: she was declared 'impure' (*musukkatu*) in the ancient Middle East, isolated in a 'house of impurity' among the Hebrews, banned from activities in Islam and according to the Hindu custom of *chaupadi*, condemned to spend a week without eating in a 'menstrual hut' among the Baruya. Various purification rituals follow these segregations. Menstruation is the justification for excluding women from all activities involving bloodshed: big-game hunting, carving up the carcass, slaughtering swine, and more generally, the professions of war, as well as the priesthood when it involves animal sacrifice.‡ Women are supposed to be ashamed of the blood

---

* Godfrey Driver and John Miles, *The Assyrian Laws* (Oxford: The Clarendon Press, 1935), particularly tablet A, article 55.
† Yuriy Malikov, *Tsars, Cossacks, and Nomads: The Formation of a Borderland Culture in Northern Kazakhstan in the 18th and 19th Centuries* (Berlin: Klaus Schwarz, 2011), pp. 81–82.
‡ Alain Testart, *L'Amazone et la cuisinière: Anthropologie de la division sexuelle du travail* (Paris: Gallimard, 2014).

periodically flowing out of their vagina. Their organs and humours are in themselves pathological.

These traditions are incorporated into an economy of disgust inspired by the 'nature' of women, a hodge-podge of masculine fears and aversions tying the feminine body to the slimy, membranous, humid, uncontrolled and demonic, from the witches' sabbath to hysterical fits. Jean Bodin's pamphlet, *On the Demon-Mania of Witches* (1580), supplied persecutors with numerous arguments. In the 1870s, Pierre Larousse, albeit rather misogynistic himself, has to recall that 'menstrual blood is just as pure as the blood from the rest of the body,' so that periods are nothing degrading for women.

Virgin purity is the counterpart of menstrual impurity. Deuteronomy includes a passage on the 'integrity' of the woman: a girl who has lied about her virginity will be stoned. The obsession with girls' virginity, which the family honours and the fiancée's price depends on, can be observed in most religions and societies, at least until the twentieth century. It is integrated into a moral double standard: while a young man's sexual experiments are tolerated or even encouraged, everything must be done to 'protect' the young girl, by means of confinement, parental surveillance, vigilant chaperoning and a heavy silence surrounding sexuality. In nineteenth-century bourgeois Vienna, young girls were kept in a 'completely sterilized atmosphere' from birth until marriage: they did not spend one minute alone and did not leave the house without being accompanied.* In rural Maghreb, magic sexual rites based on tattooing and incision made it possible to preserve a girl's virginity by 'closing' her.† Young brides were so unprepared for their first sexual relation that the wedding night was sometimes transformed into a traumatizing rape.

---

* Stefan Zweig, *The World of Yesterday: An Autobiography* (New York: Viking, 1943), pp. 64–66.
† Fatima Moussa et al., 'Du tabou de la virginité au mythe de "l'inviolabilité": Le rite du *r'bit* chez la fillette dans l'Est algérien', *Dialogue*, Vol. 185, No. 3, 2009, pp. 91–102.

On defloration as rape

This ignorant young girl is given over to this eager young man ... This young, eloquent, well-heeled, tender young man is suddenly transformed. Right where the young girl was dreaming of a beaming god, she sees some sort of hairy, pulsating beast muttering raucous sounds, famished for her flesh, thirsty for her blood. This is no longer love, it is legal, customary rape.

Alexandre Dumas *fils*,
preface to *L'Ami des femmes* (1864)

He took hold of her body furiously with both arms, as if famished for her, and laid quick, biting, wild kisses all over her face and upper chest, smothering her with his caresses. She had opened her hands and remained motionless under his movements, no longer knowing what she was doing, what he was doing, in a confusion of the mind that no longer let her understand anything. But a sharp pain suddenly tore through her, and she began to moan, twisting in his arms, while he possessed her violently.

Guy de Maupassant, *A Woman's Life* (1883)

In any case, however deferential and courteous a man might be, the first penetration is always a rape. While she desires caresses on her lips and breasts and perhaps yearns for a familiar or anticipated orgasm, here is a male sex organ tearing the young girl and introducing itself into regions where it was not invited ... love takes on the appearance of a surgical operation.

Simone de Beauvoir,
The Second Sex (1949)*

* From the translation by Constance Borde and Sheila Malovany-Chevallier: *The Second Sex*, by Simone de Beauviour (New York: Vintage Books, 2011), p. 453.

Women have also been subject to a morality of modesty and discretion. This control takes several forms: *pudicitia* in Rome, *tsniout* in Judaism, submissive deference in Confucianism, the 'ideal of the young girl who looks down, keeps her mouth tightly shut, and her sexual organ closed', in the Maghreb.* In the middle of the second millennium BCE, Assyrian law stipulated that girls of the family, married women and widows had to veil their heads when going out in the street, whereas prostitutes and slaves were required to go bare-headed, or else risk suffering fifty blows of a rod and having their ears cut off.† The veil was consequently prescribed for 'virtuous' women throughout the Middle East, in Greece and Rome, as well as in respectable Jewish and Christian families (Saint Paul and Tertullian recommend it). In the environment of insecurity wreaking havoc in Medina in the 620s, the hijab protected women of high social standing, while slaves were left to their aggressors.‡

The veil hides and protects. The idea that 'a woman's voice is a nudity', as were her hair, face and chest (whose exposure was by nature indecent), prevailed in the Babylonian Talmud: a woman was 'in her birthday suit' the moment she stepped out of her house.§ The notion of *awra* refers to provocative nudity in Islam. Christian culture was also intent on veiling the 'obscenity' of the feminine body: statues in the garden of Versailles were clothed under Louis XV, bodily hair and nipples were concealed in the Neoclassical sculpture of the nineteenth century, and so on.

In addition to the mutilations punishing women in Assyrian law, as related in Deuteronomy, the feminine body was subject to enslavement, constraints and 'shaping' for aesthetic and social reasons. In China, foot-binding consisted of rolling up the four toes inwards, putting the heel bone in a vertical position and thus making it painful and precarious for young girls to walk. The practice first began under the

---

* Daniel Rivet, *Le Maghreb à l'épreuve de la colonisation* (Paris: Hachette littératures, 2002), p. 76.
† Sophie Démare-Lafont, 'À cause des anges: Le voile dans la culture juridique du Proche-Orient ancien' in Olivier Vernier et al., (eds.), *Études d'histoire du droit privé en souvenir de Maryse Carlin* (Paris: La Mémoire du droit, 2008), pp. 234–253.
‡ Fatima Mernissi, *Le Harem politique*, p. 231 ff.
§ Delphine Horvilleur, *En tenue d'Ève: Féminin, pudeur et judaïsme* (Paris: Grasset, 2013).

Song dynasty in the middle of the tenth century; from the imperial court, it spread down to the wealthy classes before becoming a general practice under the Ming in the fourteenth century.* The Kayan, an ethnic minority living in the region between Myanmar and Thailand, place spiralled rings on their young girls' necks, deforming their ribs and clavicles. Then there are the practices of excision (ablation of the clitoris and labia minora) and infibulation, which aim to preserve a young girl's virginity, discourage her from masturbating and prepare her to be a faithful spouse by depriving her of sexual pleasure. At the beginning of the twenty-first century, the genital mutilation of 200 million women took place throughout the world, particularly in sub-Saharan Africa, East Africa, India and Indonesia.

It has been claimed that foot-binding and excision were carried out for the 'good' of girls, under the pretext that it ensures their beauty and prestige, and thus increases their marriageability. In reality, these mutilations transform women into ornaments, precious objects or maternal wombs. They prepare women for a life of servitude.

What the aversion to menstruation, the obsession with virginity, the requirement of the veil and the practice of mutilation all have in common is that they create a dichotomy between groups of women according to the criteria of men. If a woman does not carry out her ablutions after her period or after childbirth, if she has sexual relations before marriage, if she goes out bareheaded, if she has a 'natural' vulva or toes, she falls into disrepute: filthy, repulsive, fallen. If on the contrary she complies with tradition, she remains respectable and virtuous, with the benefit of being protected by her father or chosen for marriage.

The prohibitions weighing on women's bodies make it possible to reserve them for their authorized use: conjugal intercourse and the production of legitimate children, an ideal of 'the good life' to the advantage of males. In patriarchal systems, women render themselves worthy of men through exclusions and sufferings conforming to male desire, all while humbly striving to undo the negative norms that men have imposed on them.

---

* Li-Hsiang Lisa Rosenlee, *Confucianism and Women: A Philosophical Interpretation* (Albany: SUNY Press, 2006), pp. 139–141.

SILENCE AND EVENTS

Masculine prerogatives include liberty of action and thought, access to knowledge and discourse, the direction of sacred liturgy and military vocation, as well as the right to make decisions for both sexes. Women's domain is restricted to the economy of daily life: bearing children, feeding, clothing.

This domestication of woman (from the Latin *domus*, 'home') has long been fully incorporated into society. The activities prescribed according to gender that were first put in place in the Neolithic period were still perpetuated in rural areas in the twentieth century. From the 1920s to the 1950s in the Burgundy region of France, a woman successively played the role of seamstress (before marriage), cook (with the arrival of children), and then had to assist with childbirth and washing of the dead (after menopause).* During the same era in the Beauce region, near Paris, the male farmer ploughed the earth with his companions, bought land and livestock, built a home, invested in a tractor, acquired an automobile, got involved in politics and went to war. His wife, meanwhile, did the housework, cooking, washing and child-raising, as well as taking care of the farmyard and the milking.† Even in our modern urban world, laundry often falls on the shoulders of women.

The relegation of women to the domestic sphere is of a piece with their exclusion from places of power. One half of humanity told the other half to keep quiet. In the *Odyssey*, Telemachus sends his mother back to her spinning, along with the servants: 'Men are the ones who do the talking.' In *Ajax*, Sophocles mentions 'these few words that we constantly repeat: "Woman, silence is women's ornament." Saint Paul states in the First Epistle to Timothy: 'The woman must keep silent, in complete submission.' At a time when England and Scotland were ruled by women, preacher John Knox blared out with his *First Blast*

---

* Yvonne Verdier, *Façons de dire, façons de faire: La laveuse, la couturière, la cuisinière* (Paris: Gallimard, 1979).
† Ephraim Grenadou, Alain Prévost, *Grenadou, paysan français* (Paris: Seuil, Points/Histoire, 1966/1978).

of the Trumpet Against the Monstruous Regiment of Women (1558); a century later, Robert Filmer asserted in *Patriarcha* (1680) that power naturally falls on the shoulders of men. The gendered division of responsibilities resulted in the great leaders being Pericles and Hadrian, Charlemagne and Napoleon, Metternich and Roosevelt. Men make events happen, while women remain silent.

Even France's queens suffered from this disqualification. From the tenth to the twelfth century they exercised partial power, playing a certain part in diplomacy and in working out royal strategy, but their power was severely weakened at the end of the twelfth century under the influence of both clerical misogyny and the rediscovery of Aristotle: their names subsequently disappeared from royal charters and diplomas. After the two dynastic crises of 1316 and 1328, during which daughters were excluded from the French crown, jurists resorted to the gender argument and reserved kingship for men, the only ones worthy of sacred functions. Resurrected from an ancient custom of German origin, Salic law excluded women from the throne, condemning queens to be nothing more than the king's spouse.*

The dispossession of women can be observed in other domains. They were excluded from assuming responsibilities under the Ancien Régime, with no possibility of exercising a public charge, of being guardians of any children other than their own, of entering into a contract or of testifying on notarized documents. They were excluded from public debate: as Talleyrand explains in his *Report on Public Education* (1791), men are destined to live on the 'stage of the world', while the 'domestic asylum' is better suited for women. Jules Simon, partisan of the Republic, would repeat the same thing seventy years later, writing, 'Women are made to hide their lives ... to govern the small world of the family in peace.'† In Mediterranean society, they were excluded from public places: streets, plazas, cafés, souks, mosques. The 'invisible harem', as Fatimi Mernissi (born in Fez 1940 in a real harem) refers to it, is defined by the prohibitions – a variation on the

---

* Murielle Gaude-Ferragu, *La Reine au Moyen Âge: Le pouvoir au féminin, XIVᵉ–XVᵉ siècle* (Paris: Tallandier/ Texto, 2014), p. 113 ff. See also Mary Beard, *Women & Power. A Manifesto* (New York: Liveright/Norton, 2017).
† Jules Simon, *L'Ouvrière* (Paris: Hachette, 1861/1871), p. 88.

word *haram* – that one has internalized: women do not have the right to penetrate into the 'exterior' space, which belongs to the masculine. Men enjoy the tumult of the public area, speaking and taking risks; women are relegated to self-effacement in the beneficent shadows.

Patriarchy is defined as much by masculine domination and the subordination of women as by the inviolable assignment of qualities. Hence these perennial dualities: men make laws, women determine the mores; the man governs the state, the woman her household; the man rules by arms, a woman by love; he sheds his blood for the home-land, she offers her children; one is cut out to be tough, the other is gracious; one is abstract and individualistic, the other concrete and relational; or to put it like a bestseller of the 1990s, *Men Are from Mars, Women Are from Venus*. Certain pairings are a different way of saying the same thing: knight/lady, poet/muse, painter/model, film-maker/actress, boss/secretary, Head of State/First Lady, and so on.

To each, his/her 'power' – that's the order of nature. Thus formu-lated, such a distribution no longer conveys the prison of gender, but rather suggests the equilibrium of the world; no longer masculine domination, but the miraculous harmony between the sexes.

CONJUGAL ABSORPTION

Although it does grant the wife certain rights, monogamous Christian marriage, a 'domestic society' formed by a man and a woman with a view to raising their children, gives precedence to the husband-father. In his First Epistle to the Corinthians, Saint Paul proclaims that the man is the head of the woman, since she had been created from him for his benefit. Over the course of its long history, the Church has varied in its strictness about conjugality, but the spirit of marriage has scarcely var-ied at all: indissolubility, authority of the husband, subordination of the wife. In an encyclical from 1930, Pope Pius XI asserted that 'the wife's submission to her husband can vary in degree,' but no variation was allowed to shake up 'the very structure of the family' willed by God.*

---

* 'Femme', *Dictionnaire de théologie catholique: Tables générales* (Paris: Letouzey and Ané, 1951), p. 1508.

Civil law says the same thing. The Prussian Civil Code of 1750 was influenced by Roman law: it affirms that the husband is 'by nature' the head of his family. In marrying, the woman leaves her own family and enters into that of her spouse; she goes to live in his home and acknowledges his rights over her body, in consideration of having children with him that will perpetuate the lineage.* According to the doctrine of coverture inscribed into English common law, the wife is 'covered over' by her husband, who subsumes her. As the jurist Blackstone wrote in his *Commentaries on the Laws of England* (1765), the 'legal existence of the woman is suspended during the marriage, or at least is incorporated and consolidated into that of the husband'.†

Under the influence of French legal experts such as Jean Bodin and Charles Dumoulin in the sixteenth century, followed by Philippe de Renusson in his *Traité de la communauté des biens* (Treatise on the Community of Property, 1692), the husband is the 'head and master of the community', which includes his spouse's movable property and real estate. This principle is also found in the customary law of Paris (article 233), the customary law of the Bourbonnais region (article 135) and most of the French reformed customary legal codes. Under the Ancien Régime, the husband represented his wife and conjugal family, since all its members were supposed to have the same interests. During the Revolution and the beginning of the nineteenth century, the *cens* (householder franchise) giving men the right to vote could include taxes paid by their wives. Thus an idle man with no property, but married to a florist, was authorized to have the tax paid by his spouse count as qualifying him to vote.‡ Democracy remained a masculine monarchy.

As for the civil code of 1804, it further solidified the husband-father's rights. While men and women were in most cases equal before

* Susan Bell and Karen Offen (eds.), *Women, the Family, and Freedom: The Debate in Documents*, Vol. 1, *1750–1880* (Stanford: Stanford University Press, 1983), p. 31 ff.
† William Blackstone, *Commentaries on the Laws of England*. Vol. I (1765), p. 442. Available at http://www.kentlaw.edu/faculty/fbatlan/classes/BatlanGender&LawS2007/CourseDocs/coursedoc07/Blackstone.pdf
‡ Anne Verjus, *Le Cens de la famille: Les femmes et le vote, 1789–1848* (Paris: Belin, 2002), ch. 2 in particular.

the civil law (in matters of inheritance, possessions, commerce and trials, for example), that equality disappeared completely in marriage. As laid down by article 213, the wife owed 'obedience to her husband' in exchange for his protection. Obliged to live with him, she could not without his agreement buy, sell, exercise any paid activity, keep her own salary, appear before a tribunal either as plaintiff or defendant, or exercise authority over her children. At the debates over the civil code, Napoleon stated that the husband must have 'absolute power' over his wife, watching closely over her outings and frequentations. During his exile on the island of Saint Helena, the emperor echoed Saint Paul, again recalling that woman 'gives us children and the man does not give her any. She is therefore his property, like the fruit tree is the gardener's property.'* Underlying the civil code is the reasoning that, in getting married, the woman agrees to submit herself to her husband *by contract*. She therefore ceases to belong to herself, resulting in her civil incapacity. She becomes like a child, as if her status of spouse reduced her to the legal status of a minor, like that of the children she is tasked with raising.

In the patriarchal mindset, a woman is first of all someone belonging or related to someone else: her father's daughter, then her husband's spouse. In French law, it is said that the woman 'follows her husband's condition'. Indeed, under the Ancien Régime, she took on the rank and social credentials of her husband; the noble woman marrying a commoner is stripped of her privileges. Following the same logic, the civil code of 1804 held that the foreign woman marrying a male French citizen would become French, whereas the female French citizen marrying a foreigner would lose her citizenship. The wife also takes her husband's name, changing her identity. People commonly say 'Mr and Mrs Smith', in that firmly set order, and they even say 'Mrs John Doe' or 'Mrs Admiral Peter Johnson'. Women are systematically tied to their matrimonial situation, 'Miss X', or 'Mrs Y', or 'Widow Z'.

The man personifies the family unit into which the woman has been dissolved; the masculine as universal subsumes the feminine as

---

* Cited by Jean-Joseph Damas-Hinard, *Napoléon, ses opinions et jugements sur les hommes et sur les choses*, Vol. 1 (Paris: Dufey, 1838), pp. 477–478.

particular. We can understand why legislators have been neither anxious nor able to crack down on physical violence between spouses (as long as it remained 'reasonable'). In France, the penal code of 1810 punished infanticide and parricide, but not conjugal assaults, which were simply relegated into the catchall of 'assault and battery'. Only at the end of the nineteenth century did violence begin to serve as a reason for separating spouses.* In most countries, and up until the end of the twentieth century, marriage implied that the woman was sexually at the husband's disposal: the notion of 'conjugal rape' therefore had no meaning. The principle of absorption also explains the condition of widows in Asia. For when the husband dies, the spouse is no longer worth anything beyond her fidelity to the deceased, by means of mourning (encouraged in China and Vietnam beginning in the thirteenth century) or committing suicide (the *sati* in India).

The first argument for defenders of the patriarchal family is not that of might makes right, but of collective utility, the benefits brought about by conjugal cooperation. In the France of the nineteenth century, thinkers of all sensibilities recommend that the traditional roles be maintained in the family. In *La Réforme sociale* (1864), the conservative Catholic Frédéric Le Play affirmed that woman was an agent of moral progress when she remained in the 'providence of the family hearth'. The eminent thinkers of the French Republic – Alfred Fouillée, Henri Marion, Émile Durkheim – considered the family to be conducive to individual integration and social progress. In *Psychologie de la femme* (1900), Henri Marion asserted that if the wife threw herself into political struggles, she would risk shattering the unity of her family. Proudhon, the theorist of anarchism and a virulent misogynist, in *La Pornocratie ou les Femmes dans les temps modernes* (1875), set out to define the modalities of conjugal bliss. Husband and wife form 'a complete whole', but happiness is ensured only when each spouse fulfils their part according to the age-old division: 'One for the outside, the other for the inside.'

The linchpin of this reasoning is the wife's domestic specialization under the husband's authority, a partial solidarity that constitutes the

* Victoria Vanneau, *La Paix des ménages: Histoire des violences conjugales, XIXe–XXIe siecle* (Paris: Anamosa, 2016), chs. 1–2.

'hierarchical complementarity of the sexes'.* In this framework, it is not possible to conceptualize inequality as such: the man-subject and the woman-object are inseparable, forming one organic unit. Not masculine domination, but an intelligent distribution of tasks; not the subjection of the wife, but an asymmetry of genders, for their mutual benefit. This hypocrisy is the reason for all these false verbs (the wife 'reigns' in her household, the man 'obeys' his charming wife), while in reality such thinkers legitimate masculine pre-eminence in the name of nature and morality.

One could just say that man and woman are each meant to reign over their respective domains: outside and inside, master of the world and ruler of the household, Mars and Venus, and so on, and leave it at that. But the reality is that the husband is the 'head of the family' while his spouse is 'the soul of the hearth' because men have willed it so. Men devote themselves to the public sphere with their political, military and professional responsibilities, but they also supervise the private realm. In France, the civil code authorizes them to make all the important decisions concerning the life of the couple and the family: the woman therefore rules over the household only by delegation. Le Play praises the English for the 'judicious sharing of responsibilities', which corresponds to the natural order of things, whereby the husband accepts the 'unreserved delegation of his authority' to his wife in domestic matters.† This delegation can, however, be suspended, even in its smallest details. In twentieth-century Japan and the Mediterranean regions of Europe, the wife sometimes did not dine at the same table when there were guests: she served them the meal and afterwards ate alone in the kitchen like a servant.

* Irène Théry, *Mariage et filiation pour tous: Une métamorphose inachevée* (Paris: Seuil, 2016), p. 68. See also Judith Surkis, *Sexing the Citizen: Morality and Masculinity in France, 1870–1920* (Ithaca: Cornell University Press, 2006).
† Frédéric Le Play, *La Réforme sociale en France déduite de l'observation comparée des peuples européens*, Vol. 1 (Paris: Dentu, 1866, 2nd edn.), pp. 265–267.

THE AURA OF THE WOMAN

In the division of labour over which the masculine presides, patriarchy recognizes a special role for women. Certain tasks have been the special domain attributed to women ever since the Neolithic period, if not earlier: food preparation, textile crafts, minding the hearth, raising children. A wife who keeps her household in good order, and who is mindful of her own demeanour is gladly deemed worthy of respect. Her conduct determines her own personal value, but also that of the entire family. In the end, *masculine honour depends on feminine compliance.*

In many societies in Latin America, the Maghreb and Southern Europe, women govern the domestic domain, holding authority and prestige. Among the Romani of Andalusia, women must stay at home, but in return they embody moral values, as well as commitment to the household and to the community, which everyone considers to be essential values.* In Malta, women are the ones who maintain ties with parents, friends and neighbours, but also with the dead: their frequenting of grocery stores and churches thus serves several purposes, and this social undertaking takes place outside the house.† From the nineteenth century to the first part of the twentieth, it was not unusual in France for a worker to automatically turn his pay over to his wife, who was in charge of providing for household needs and keeping the budget: she not only laid down household rules, but also worked as the 'cashier of current accounts'.‡ Among shopkeepers, 'The husband acts like the errand and delivery boy, and it's the lady of the house sitting at the counter who makes all the decisions,' as French

---

* Caterina Pasqualino, *Dire le chant: Les Gitans flamencos d'Andalousie* (Paris: CNRS, 1998), pp. 262–263.
† Jon Mitchell, 'Performances of Masculinity in a Maltese Festa' in Felicia Hughes-Freeland and Mary Crain (eds.), *Recasting Ritual: Performance, Media, Identity* (London: Routledge, 1998), pp. 68–94.
‡ Paul Lerebours-Pigeonnière, 'La famille et le Code civil' in *Le Code Civil, 1804–1904: Livre du centenaire* (Paris: Dalloz, 1904/2004), pp. 263–294.

writer Marguerite Yourcenar, when asked about the condition of women, mischievously observed.*

The woman function therefore confers upon the wife a positively valued role, coupled with decision-making capacity. Within the zone of autonomy that patriarchal society recognizes, women exercise a certain power, even to the detriment of men. Now, these responsibilities are not unrelated to the maternal figure central to various cultures: the Italian *mamma*, the 'Jewish mother', and so on. As the guardian of traditions mindful of the wellbeing of all, this sacrificial mother self-lessly imparts the lavish benefits of her love, her culinary talent and her medical competence.

Feeding children imposes a heavy responsibility on mothers and, paradoxically, confers upon them a public role. In the France of the Ancien Régime, it was common for plebeian women to troop together, shouting their protests against hunger. Washerwomen, shopkeepers, street peddlers and fishwives, along with the wives of soldiers, crafts-men or workers: all these 'she-devils', as the authorities would say, assailed wheat lofts and threatened magistrates, sometimes when they were pregnant or with their children. In Nemours, during the Flour War of 1775, a woman looter shoved her husband aside: 'Get back, this is women's business.'† The nurturing function of women obliges them to act.

The imposing moral authority of the family mother is of a piece with the cult of the evanescent young girl worshipped by an adoring admirer. The idealization of the 'lady' whose person inspires both Platonic veneration and amorous passion runs throughout Western poetry: tales of chivalry, songs of the Troubadours, and *Minnesänger* from the twelfth century; the *Canzoniere* of Petrarch devoted to Laura in the mid-fourteenth century; poems and oratory competing at the Cour Amoureuse, founded in 1401; Honoré d'Urfé's pastorale *L'Astrée* at the beginning of the seventeenth century; and later

---

* Marguerite Yourcenar, 'La condition féminine' (1981), available at www.youtube.com/watch?v=FoN3EofaqkM
† Jean Nicolas, *La Rébellion française: Mouvements populaires et conscience sociale, 1661–1789* (Paris: Seuil, 2002).

neo-Petrarchan sonnets and rondos. The idolization of the young woman led to a rhetorical inversion of gender relations, illustrated around 1640 by the poetry of Vincent Voiture, with his themes of the 'slavery of love,' love as a prison, the lover enchained by passion, suffering the cruelty of his lady, bearing the yoke of feminine tyranny. These metaphors transform the man into a vassal, the lady into his overlord. In the nineteenth century, Victorian artists celebrate the purity and innocence of young girls, who with their delicate traits, their delightful spontaneity and naive *joie de vivre* are placed on a pedestal of virginity. Such is Rose La Touche, transfigured by Ruskin, along with the twelve delightfully incomprehensible young girls found in *Praeterita*. The same goes for Ophelia in Pre-Raphaelite painting, in which nature serves as the setting for her lily-like beauty. The same figure also appears as the 'muse' inspiring the creative genius of poets.

The worship of the sacrificial mother and that of the adorable young girl are merged in the figure of the Virgin Mary, a saint by her virtue as well as by her abnegation, *mater dolorosa* who had not, however, known a man. In a slightly debased manner, there is the young mother of a family, the fairy enchanting the life of her husband and children, but whose charms still prove to be captivating: Julie in *The New Heloise* by Rousseau, Madame de Mortsauf in *The Lily of the Valley* by Balzac, the ideal woman touted by Ruskin in his lecture 'Of Queens' Gardens', and by Coventry Patmore in his poem 'The Angel in the House'. She is the one who transforms the house into a home for her overworked husband, burdened by professional demands. Beside the hearth, she serves as a guide for the man and a model for the whole society.

Courtly love, the poetry of gallantry and hymns to women constitute a masculine art in which men determine feminine value, define the codes of seduction, express their pride as protectors and reveal their ability to sublimate their passion through poetic creation. It is clear that the mythification of woman in the form of a perfect, ethereal creature fits perfectly into masculine domination. The patriarchal feelings of disgust with menstruation, prostitutes, and all things 'impure' are converted into fascination for the 'mysteries' of women, the 'purity' of young girls, the dominion of her beauty, the 'sacred' devotion of the nursing mother. The praise of women elevates them to a determined place. Similarly, the worship of the Virgin and the aggressivity of the macho join together in two closely linked stereotypes: the moral superiority of the holy mother of the family justifies and excuses the faults of the man who remains a little boy, with his intemperance, his infidelity and his excesses of all sorts.*

As can be seen, feminine perfection reveals perfect masculine domination. The praise of women is the self-glorification of patriarchy. In 1869, John Stuart Mill was one of the rare men to denounce 'silly panegyrics on the moral nature of woman', which in fact signal her intellectual inferiority. Granted, the novels of Jane Austen and the Brontë sisters do feature intrepid heroines who know what they want, particularly when it comes to love, but they are always struggling within stifling gender norms. It was only decades later that Virginia Woolf would decide to 'kill the Angel in the House'.†

THE PATRIARCHAL CIRCLE

We are now poised to return to the longevity of patriarchy, which, throughout every era and every regime on every continent, has managed to survive. In order to explain this extraordinary durability, should we invoke the physical superiority of men, the fatigue of the pregnant or nursing mother, women's resignation, the poverty and ignorance that has often been their lot in life, the progressive interiorization of their incapacity? In order to perpetuate their power, have men used force, fear, loyalty, the inertia of established ways?

It is fundamentally important to distinguish patriarchy from individuals who either take advantage of it or who are subjected to it, depending on their sex. Patriarchy is first of all a *system of thought*,

---

* Evelyn Stevens, 'Marianismo: The Other Face of Machismo in Latin America' in Ann Pescatello (ed.), *Female and Male in Latin America* (Pittsburgh: University of Pittsburgh Press, 1973), pp. 90–101.
† Sandra Gilbert, Susan Gubar, *The Madwoman in the Attic: The Woman Writer and the Nineteenth-Century Literary Imagination* (New Haven: Yale University Press, 1980), p. 17.

founded on laws, norms, beliefs, traditions, practices – and this system holds up on its own. It involves institutions as complex as the
state, religion or the family, borrowing from each arguments that all
come together to justify the subordination of women. As a result, this
subordination appears as something 'normal', anchored in nature,
based on reason, consistent with what has 'always been done'.

From their very birth, women are caught up in a *patriarchal circle*.
This circle postulates their maternal nature, tying them to the woman
function, a common practice that confines them to the domestic
realm, where they are glorified for their altruism, the foundation of
their maternal nature and so on.

Within the patriarchal scheme of things, each sex finds its destiny.
'Nature' falls to women, associated with the only function recognized for them: the woman function, meaning service for the body,
procreation and the home. For their part, men are assigned to 'civilization,' with the risks and challenges that it involves. They are the
outside conquerors, while women are the good fairies of daily comfort. Patriarchy therefore reposes on collaboration between the
sexes – in other words, the opposite of the war of the sexes, but a
highly skewed collaboration. For women are neither as free nor as
valued as men: asymmetrical complementarity is cooperation without equality.

Within this circle, the virtues justify the obligations, and the obligations reinforce the virtues. What results is the 'obvious' nature of its
functioning, which is precisely the system's strength: not only does
each find his or her place, but they are also each at their place. The
model's stability stems from its implacable logic, which no single individual is capable of shaking. The patriarchal system provides women
with a certain role within a reassuringly ordered world: there they
find a status, respectability, possible prestige, as 'the lady of the house',
'keeper of family traditions', 'saintly woman', and so on. The woman's
aura is a compensation for her subordinate role.

Patriarchal society offers each woman a deal, with an array of constraints and rewards if she complies: masculine protection in exchange
for feminine obedience. Such is the philosophy of this agreement, formulated in almost identical terms in texts that are otherwise very
different: the Epistle to the Ephesians attributed to Saint Paul, the

The patriarchal circle

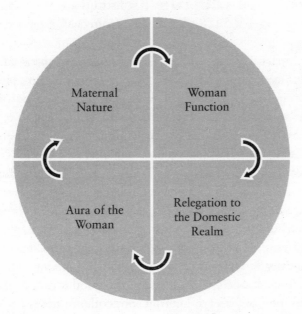

Maternal nature, woman function, relegation to the domestic realm, aura of the woman.

Quran's sura on women (with its notion of *qiwâma*, the husband's responsibility and authority) and article 213 of the Napoleonic civil code. The man provides for the needs of the family, and in exchange is the undisputed head.

And hundreds of millions of women say 'yes', either because it's their choice, or because, on the contrary, they have no choice. At the end of *The Creation of Patriarchy* (1986), Gerda Lerner offers this troubling conclusion: 'The patriarchal system can only function with the cooperation of women.' Such cooperation has been acquired not only by indoctrination, lack of education, coercion and discrimination, but also by the consent of those concerned, to the benefit of a system of social regulation. The incredible strength of patriarchy is that it has in the long run proved to be comfortable for everybody, and one can understand that it will take a similarly incredible strength to challenge it.

VIRTUOUS PRISONERS
VERSUS FALLEN WOMEN

Has this apparently peaceful and harmonious arrangement between the sexes traced out a sort of best of all possible worlds, millennium after millennium? Of course not. Such a notion leaves out the essentialization of women, the takeover of their childbearing capacity, their uncompensated domestic work, their infantilization by the legal system, the negation of all their rights.

The biological predestination of women, with all its attendant functions, has collectively benefited men. In the nineteenth century, men were able to earn a salary outside the home, found political parties and labour unions, acquire democratic rights. Women's invisible labour allowed men to become abstract subjects and free citizens, as well as politically committed intellectuals. For example, the wife of the great French sociologist Émile Durkheim was 'extraordinarily devoted' to her husband, providing support over the years, comforting him, tidying up his manuscripts, correcting his proofs, attending his courses and taking care of his correspondence.* Thanks to the discreet collaboration of their secretary-wives, thousands of scholars and writers were able to study, create, conceive new ideas, free from all material concerns. Men's self-realization has depended on the exploitation of women.

Does that necessarily mean that women are oppressed? In Rome, a patrician woman was better off than a male slave. But if the patrician woman had the better life, it was not as a woman: it was as the spouse of a patrician man. The patriarchal circle does not so much oppress as it subordinates. It does not deprive women of love or riches (although these situations may happen), but of freedom. In the nineteenth century, the upper-class woman surrounded by her servants, the miner's wife busying herself with her household, the woman shopkeeper stationed behind the counter were perhaps happy, and maybe more so than their husbands. A great number of women have decided to

* Christophe Charle, 'Le beau mariage d'Émile Durkheim,' *Actes de la recherche en sciences sociales*, Vol. 55, November 1984, pp. 45–49.

concern themselves exclusively with their children and their home, and some of them have found it rewarding. But before finding out whether the patriarchal circle has its virtues, we must find out if it is possible to get out of it, and, above all, at what price.

At the end of Henrik Ibsen's *A Doll's House* (1879), the charming, cheerful, submissive Nora, a model wife, decides to leave her household, disgusted with her husband's selfishness. This conclusion stirred up a scandal throughout the world: a mother of a family who 'had it all' abandons her husband and children to go and live her own life. How dare she? What will become of her? In the Western literature of the eighteenth and nineteenth centuries, emancipated women with an independent lifestyle and sexual freedom are almost always punished by illness and death: Manon Lescaut, la Traviata in Verdi's opera, Carmen in Bizet's opera, Nana in Zola's novel.

Patriarchal thinking divides women into two groups: the 'virtuous', under either paternal or marital masculine protection, and the 'fallen', who belong to everyone. This is the same logic as the Assyrian law in which the veil made it possible to distinguish spouses from prostitutes. The same dichotomy was laid down by the Romans: the matron to whom the man entrusts his household enjoys dignity, while the slaves he turns to for sexual pleasure are debased. In his *Fable of the Bees* (1714), Mandeville admits the necessity of 'sacrificing part of the fair sex for the conservation of the other'. The same alternative is described by Proudhon: 'Courtesan or housewife.'

Losing masculine protection is synonymous with exclusion. The society of the nineteenth century was extremely harsh on women outside the patriarchal circle: single women and lesbians, but also single mothers, prostitutes, delinquents. These women who had 'fallen' were women in excess, and the nickname attached to them points to their unworthiness: the *fille-mère* in French (literally 'girl-mother') whose pregnancy dooms her to shame and poverty; the *grisette*, the young working-class woman who prostitutes herself from time to time in order to survive; the *demi-mondaine*, a kept woman for rich lovers; the 'spinster', mocked because she is still not married at the age of thirty. Their exclusion underscores by contrast the enviable status of the family mother, linchpin of the institution of marriage. A woman outside masculine authority is a lost girl.

The criterion of patriarchal affiliation structures not only societies, but also urban spaces. Until the second half of the twentieth century, Vienna had an incalculable number of brothels, houses of prostitution, nightclubs, cabarets and dance halls: a whole array of 'feminine merchandise' available at any time and at the entire range of prices, in filthy streets as in luxury establishments. English prisons had the objective of reforming criminals who had not only broken the law, but also transgressed the norms of gender: a wash house, a laundry service and knitting were supposed to transform these demons into 'true women'.* Such is the alternative to the patriarchal circle: if the woman refuses her honourable reclusion, she becomes a potential prostitute. Between service to the family and degradation outside a household, feminine liberty is unthinkable.

---

* Stefan Zweig, *The World of Yesterday*, and Alice Bonzom, 'A Crash-Course in Femininity? Female Criminals in the Victorian and Edwardian Era', *Books and Ideas*, 23 October 2017, at https://booksandideas.net/A-Crash-Course-in-Femininity.html

3

Masculinities of Domination

Patriarchal thought believes man to be superior by virtue of his sex, but it also values masculine gender, which is the manner of formulating a 'male self'. Since masculinity takes concrete form in bodies, rites and institutions, it is possible to draw up an anthropological table outlining different ways of being a man, to which English devotes no less than five words: virility, manhood, manliness, maleness and masculinity, which in French are all blended together in *virilité et masculinité*. Virility is a notion much narrower in scope than masculinity, however. The former touts itself as a supposedly desirable quality, while the latter represents an array of cultures. Among these figures the masculinity of domination, or the manner in which a man imposes his authority: a patriarchal masculinity, ultimately.

The domination of men is a constant in history. However, the masculinity of domination is relatively malleable: Frederick Barbarossa differs from Julius Caesar, and a Teutonic knight differs from the dancer Louis XIV. It is therefore important to bring to light how masculine power manifests itself concretely: in objects and attributes, rites and institutions, discourses and practices, but also in self-confidence, feelings of native legitimacy and superiority complexes.

VIRILITY AS A QUALITY

The sovereign expresses both the masculinity of power and the power of masculinity. Whether he be pharaoh, king, emperor, sultan, Negus, shah, tsar, Tenno or kaiser, he is the one who commands others. He has several ways of coming to power, including heredity, violence, charisma and prodigality, each compatible with the others. In the thirteenth century, what was claimed to be the 'law of the Turks' designated the regicide by which, in the absence of a rightful heir, the throne falls upon the king's murderer. The 'baraka', the benediction of Allah, is a gift held by men of God, the Prophet, saints and marabouts, as well as by sultans and kings. Like the Melanesian 'big men', Viking kings of the tenth century (Haakon the Good and Eric Bloodaxe) set up a system of loyalty by means of gifts offered to beholden supporters.

Obviously, men in power are not limited to the figure of the king. Heads of state can borrow from the monarchic tradition (as in the France of the Fifth Republic). Or they can play the role of the providential saviour: the young, spirited captain (Napoleon in 1795), the prophet leading his people (Lenin, Mussolini, Hitler), the old sage called back into service in times of adversity (Pétain in 1940, De Gaulle in 1958).* But the masculinity of domination extends well beyond the political and military order. It characterizes the explorer, aviator, athlete, self-made man, scholar and even the poet. From the revolutionary to top corporate executive, from the foreman to the master thinker, the male has embodied all the primary roles.

Masculinity in glory is demonstrated and displayed via a set of objects that confer virile qualities on those who possess them. They are not very different from the monopolies of the Palaeolithic era (facial hair, meat), with a few new contributions from the Neolithic period (arms, horses and other means of locomotion).

The beard and the moustache gave rise to an art of facial hair: the neatly combed beard on the statue of the intendant Ebih-Il of the kingdom of Mari around 2300 BCE, the curly beards of the soldiers of Darius in the frieze of the archers around 500 BCE, the oiled beard of the high priest Aron in the Psalms, the serpentine moustache and long, pointed beard of the Chinese Emperor Yongle, the tumultuous grey beard of God painted by Michelangelo on the ceiling of the Sistine Chapel, the infantryman's moustache or well-trimmed goatee. All

---

* Raoul Girardet, *Mythes et mythologies politiques* (Paris: Seuil/Points. Histoire, 1986), p. 70 ff.

the many forms recall the 'majesty of the man'.* A whole array of masculine sociability is organized around meat: duck hunts, hunting with hounds, other forms of venery, North American barbecues, South American *asado* and the French *bifteck*. The latter partakes of the same 'mythology of blood' as wine: savouring the scarcely cooked meat at the centre makes it possible to take in its taurine strength.†
Alcohol and tobacco enable other occasions for fraternizing.

Ever since the invention of the sword in the Bronze Age, the masculine has seized hold of every new weapon, particularly firearms: the Chinese cannon, the Spanish musket, the Colt of the cowboy, the machine gun of the World War I soldier. In Medieval Japan, the break-up of the state incited lords to recruit men of arms, capable of protecting the population and waging private wars. The first Samurai fought only for their renown, even if they resorted to treachery. In the eleventh century, they perfected training techniques for achieving their ends: the way of the man at arms, the way of the horse and bow. However, it was only in the sixteenth century that the *bushidô* (way of the warrior) incorporated moral values such as loyalty or the sense of honour.‡

Horsemanship is another mark of virility, as much in Western statues as in Kazakh nomadic life and Arab civility. From the thir-teenth to the fifteenth century, the Mamelukes received elite military training. Given in Turkish with the aid of Arab treatises, the education of young soldiers included the handling of the sabre, lance and bow, as well as equestrian skills (*furusiyya*). All Mamelukes owned their own arms and horses, sometimes given to them by the sovereign in person. The combination of the indomitable horse and the bellicose male gave rise to the 'myth of the stud', a Muslim political construction of virility that has run from Al-Jahiz (died in 868) to the present.§

---

* Jacques-Antoine Dulaure, *Pogonologie ou Histoire philosophique de la barbe* (Paris: Lejay, 1786), p. 189.
† Roland Barthes, 'Le bifteck et les frites', in *Mythologies* (Paris: Seuil/Point essais, 1957/1970), pp. 77–79.
‡ Saeki Shin'Ichi, and Pierre-François Souyri, *Samouraïs: Du dit des Heiké à l'invention du Bushidô* (Paris: Arkhê, 2017).
§ Julien Loiseau, *Les Mamelouks, XIIIᵉ–XVIᵉ siècle: Une expérience du pouvoir dans l'Islam médiéval* (Paris: Seuil, 2014); and Raja Ben Slama, 'Le mythe de l'étalon' in

Beginning in the twentieth century, the passion for cars holds the place that the declining art of horsemanship yielded to it. Except for its industrial origin, this passion is basically no different: the same love of speed and of smooth, streamlined contours, the same feeling of physical domination and the same display of wealth. Porsches, Ferraris and Lamborghinis, along with Harley-Davidsons and Triumph Thunderbirds, offered the same dangerous thrills. Car racing constitutes one of the great masculine myths, portrayed on the screen by actors such as James Dean and Steve McQueen.

In the United States, during the twenty-first century, huge pickups with suggestive names (Ford King Ranch, Ford Ranger Raptor, Nissan Texas Titan, Chevy Avalanche, Jeep Gladiator, Dodge Viper) are racking up record sales. As symbols of hyper-masculinity offering the consumer the ultimate macho experience, pickups are feature attractions in fairs and festivals that are also celebrations of virility. Such is the case of the Texas Truck rodeo, organized over two days in the presence of the specialized press, where an award for the Truck of Texas is announced at the end of the activities.* Capitalism has discovered ways of glorifying the accessories of virility: Borsalino or Stetson hats, Zippo lighters, Marlboro cigarettes, and so on.

NATIONAL MODELS

In *Masculinities* (1995), the Australian sociologist Raewyn Connell theorized the notion of 'hegemonic' masculinity, borrowing from Antonio Gramsci the idea that domination is imposed by a total cultural hold over beliefs and values in the raising of children. Connell refuses essentialist or normative definitions of masculinity (the 'eternal masculine'), defining it instead as a position within a given configuration of gender. Hegemonic masculinity is that which dominates the order of gender, legitimating patriarchy at the top of governments, armies and businesses, while subordinating other masculinities. In the West, for

---

Fethi Benslama and Nadia Tazi (eds.), *La Virilité en Islam* (La Tour d'Aigues: L'Aube, 2004), pp. 205–219.
* 'The Politics of Very Big Trucks', *The Economist*, 6 October 2012.

Horseman and biker

So similar . . . Nevertheless, four centuries separate Velasquez's Equestrian Portrait of the Count-Duke Olivares *(1638) and the photo of a biker mounted on his Harley (2013). Can the art of horsemanship and the biker mindset be explained by biological factors such as the role of testosterone and adrenaline, or social factors such as equating virility with exaltation of speed and risk-taking?*

example, this position belongs to the rich white heterosexual man, aged forty to sixty-five.

Unfortunately, this notion of hegemonic masculinity proves to be rather vague, and, most importantly, poorly adapted to time periods and societies outside the contemporary anglophone world, as Connell herself has admitted.* Not only are there many versions of hegemonic masculinity, but also their cultural and institutional modes of expression are quite different, depending on the contexts in which they are rooted. From the nineteenth century on, nation-states developed their own masculinity, inspired by religion and imperialism.

British stoicism teaches self-mastery, unblinking endurance and coolness in the face of adversity: 'Keep a stiff upper lip.' That is the message conveyed in public schools, as well as by poets such as Henley in 'Invictus' and Kipling in 'If'. Such self-discipline can also be combined with the virtues of a 'muscular Christianity' in the manner of Thomas Hughes. While the English value fair play in team sports, Germans appreciate exercise that instils endurance: they prepare for war with gymnastics, as well as with fencing and swimming. Modern gymnastics (*Turnen*) was invented by Friedrich Ludwig Jahn after the Prussian defeat at Jena, and saw a revival in the 1860s and 1870s, parallel to the construction of a national German identity.†

Can we speak of a Mediterranean masculinity, shaped by the legal right of *pater familias* and the Catholic Church? In the eighteenth century, the army of Piedmont reorganized its discipline to follow the Prussian model. From 1820 to 1870, Italian unification was the business of men that played out among the Carbonari – Victor-Emmanuel II, Cavour and Garibaldi's Thousand (whose ranks included only two women). On the occasion of the annual celebration on the island of Malta, eight *reffiegha* share the honour of carrying a statue of Saint Paul on their bruised shoulders in a

* R. W. Connell and James W. Messerschmidt, 'Hegemonic Masculinity: Rethinking the Concept', *Gender and Society*, Vol. 19, No. 6 (Dec., 2005), pp. 829–859.
† George Mosse, *The Image of Man: The Creation of Modern Masculinity* (New York and Oxford: Oxford University Press, 1998).

procession glorifying national identity, the grandeur of the Church and gender identity.*

The conquistadors, colonialism, monarchy and Catholicism transplanted the Spanish model of virility into the New World. It shaped Argentine history, both in the bloody Conquest of the Desert and in the myth of the gaucho, the horseman of the pampas – rough-rider and military guide. The folklore of the violent and generous Mexican macho was drawn from the Porfiriato revolts after 1876 and in the 1910 revolution, before being transformed into chauvinistic virility (*hombrismo*) in the 1930s.

Over the course of the nineteenth century, the Mexican *vaquero* was imported into the United States, where he became the cowboy. Fierce masculinities clashed together in the Far West: the ranch hand herding cattle on horseback, the farmer cultivating his land, the outlaw, the lieutenant colonel leading a cavalry regiment, the buffalo hunter and even the great Indian chief (Buffalo Bill and Sitting Bull posed for a photo together in Montreal in 1885). The myth of the western is filled with violence and has exalted the American nation in the apotheosis of the white man, from John Wayne, the invincible hero ill at ease with his feelings, to Clint Eastwood, 'The Man With No Name', identifiable by his poncho and his hat, mysterious, laconic, wild and terribly handsome.

Farther north, the world of ice and snow put the trapper, the woodcutter and the gold digger to the test, fighting hand to hand with the elements that make it possible to know how one measures up against nature. The novellas of Jack London, inspired by his experience in the Klondike, express the solitude of the adventurer with his sledge dogs in the snow-covered landscape, struggling for survival; the last man in Cormac McCarthy's *The Road* is on a similar quest. Man strives to overcome nature, as well as his fears and enemies.

As we can see, the masculinity of domination has been diffracted into a multitude of collective stereotypes. Even ridiculous or tragicomic heroes such as Spain's Don Quixote, Germany's Michael Kohlhaas and Portugal's Bernardo Soares can become national symbols in which every man can recognize himself.

* Jon Mitchell, 'Performances of Masculinity in a Maltese Festa' pp. 68–94.

THE FOUR TRIUMPHS
OF THE MASCULINE

It is important to understand how these forms of masculine domination have been constructed to exercise power: the capacity to impose one's authority as a man.

The *masculinity of ostentation* asserts itself by displaying its vigour, desire, courage and prodigality: boasting, swaggering, speaking loudly, always being ready to fight, taking mindless risks in order to show what one is made of. At the beginning of the narrative that bears his name, Gilgamesh, the young king of Uruk, conducts himself with arrogance: sure of himself and his strength, eager to brandish his arms, he kidnaps his subjects' daughters.

From one era and country to another, men become braggarts, cocky smooth talkers, daredevils. Virile peacocks, they call attention to themselves by the folly of their largesse (a knight or a king is supposed to offer his guests a feast) or by the irascibility that leads them to shed blood in response to the slightest offense (thereby obeying a 'culture of honour'). In Spain, and later in France, the characters of El Cid and Don Juan demonstrate a highly phallic and completely excessive culture of challenge and duel. This brings together the display of masculinity with the cult of performance: their nobility is indistinguishable from male pride. In Great Britain, the members of the Bullingdon Club of Oxford exhibit their scorn for moral, financial and sexual limits by indulging in all sorts of mischief.

Contrary to this garishness, the *masculinity of control* lauds the inner strength by which a man reins in his passions, tames his appetite and tempers his violence. As Norbert Elias's 'civilizing process' resulting in an overall reduction in war and violence, the masculinity of control constitutes the ideal of a good number of philosophies: Buddha's renunciation of desire, Stoic conscience for Epictetus and Marcus Aurelius, the struggle against lust in Christianity and Sufism, the restraint of the Confucian man of letters, the gentleman's 'self-government' in its imperial version (according to Kipling) or as embodied by Baden-Powell's Scouts. Military parades require bodily discipline and precise gestures, as in the silent drill in the United

States, when a platoon of Marines executes a precisely choreographed exhibition with guns.

In this case, masculine power holds back masculine power. The man dominates to such an extent that he even dominates himself: his own power is able to yield to itself, to obey his injunction in order to attain a higher degree of power. 'I am the master of myself as of the universe,' states Augustus in Corneille's *Cinna*. From the Middle Ages to the Classical era, various codes recommend that the 'good king' should control himself in his anger as well as in his pleasures. Around 1600, as Henri IV spent his time hunting and waging war in France, the Malaysian treatise *Taj Us-Salatin* defined the rules of royal civility: shun pride, engage in the exercise of piety, respect limits in eating and drinking, fight against carnal impulses. It was this ideal of the 'perfect man' that became mandatory for the *priyayi* gentlemen of Java beginning in the seventeenth century: unbridled confrontation must be go hand in hand with a rigorous conduct, a sense of duty and a refinement of mores.* Similarly, certain rich bourgeois men in the Protestant Netherlands of the seventeenth century and northern Catholic France of the nineteenth century practised a culture of austerity, consisting of living meagrely, dressing simply and consuming quietly – far from the aristocrat who makes a show of his ostentatious masculinity.

The *masculinity of sacrifice* is grandiose and horrifying: it consists of intentionally doing away with oneself. It is less a question of losing one's life, and more a matter of immolating one's life out of fidelity to a transcendent cause or principle. The man is prepared to die for another – his God, his king, his lord, his country, his lady, his family or even all of humanity. He loses his life in his commitment, like the assassinated prophets – Lincoln, Jaurès, Gandhi, Martin Luther King and Yitzhak Rabin. Or like all soldiers who wanted to die and made it known – the French writers Péguy and Psichari cut down in 1914; the French sociologist Robert Hertz, who considered war to be 'something sublime'; and the US veteran John Wheeler, whose determination

---

* Romain Bertrand, *L'Histoire à parts égales: Récits d'une rencontre Orient–Occident, XVIᵉ–XVIIᵉ siècle* (Paris: Seuil, 2011), chs. 12–13.

was unaltered by the war in Vietnam. Wheeler stated, 'Masculinity is the idea that there are things that are worth dying for.'*

The hero combines abnegation and saintliness, identifying with his own ideal, remaining steadfast until martyrdom, like the first Christians. He chooses to plunge into the absolute. In Corneille's tragedy, Polyeucte seeks death as a happy outcome: 'I consent, or rather I aspire to my ruin.' But the soldier of his faith closely resembles the crusader or the false messiah. Malraux's characters are both revolutionaries and terrorists. In the Second World War, the Japanese kamikazes also believed in something. How to distinguish between courage, pride and fanaticism?

Last but not least, the *masculinity of ambiguity* offers a superior form of domination, because it is capable of integrating the feminine. Father and mother of Israel, YHWH takes on the former functions of his spouse Asherah. Metaphorically, he gives life, as in the book of Isaiah (42:14), where he cries out 'like a woman in childbirth'. The demi-god Gilgamesh trembles before the giant Humbaba and weeps for his friend Enkidu. In archaic Greece, the heroes are not ashamed of the tears flowing down their cheeks: Achilles weeps at the death of Patroclus, Agamemnon sheds tears after the Trojans' success, Ulysses cries in contemplating the sea.† From the century of Pericles on, tears are reserved for women. From Mackenzie to Lamartine, however, Romanticism was to give rebirth to the tradition of the 'sensitive man'.

From antiquity to the eighteenth century, men of high society shared their attributes with women: robes, stockings, heels, wigs, powders, diadems, rings. Sukeroku, a traditional character in Japanese Kabuki theatre, is a samurai wearing make-up, carrying a parasol and wearing a violet headband (tied to the right as for women), and performing a long dance when entering on to the stage. His charm, poses, nonchalance and panache of a roguish dandy make him wildly appealing to female spectators. The geisha are even

---

* Nicolas Mariot, *Histoire d'un sacrifice: Robert, Alice et la guerre, 1914–1917* (Paris: Seuil, 2017), p. 98; and John Wheeler, *Touched With Fire: The Future of the Vietnam Generation* (New York: Watts, 1984), pp. 140–141.
† Hélène Monsacré, *Les Larmes d'Achille: Le héros, la femme et la souffrance dans la poésie d'Homère* (Paris: Albin Michel, 1984).

instructed to learn femininity from him.* In the second half of the twentieth century, the biggest masculine stars have also played on these ambivalences: Elvis Presley and Marlon Brando in the United States, Patrick Dewaere and Gérard Depardieu in France, as well as 'metrosexual' soccer players like David Beckham. A woman is tied to her sex, but for the true male, anything goes: he can be gentle or violent, armed or bejewelled, tearful or insensitive.

MAKING MEN

Masculinity is learned. First comes an individual and private initiation with a paternal figure. The most interesting thing here is not the father-son fishing expedition, but the learning process of the body, into which the laws of masculinity are inscribed from early childhood. Such is the activation of the penis: Herodotus was surprised that Egyptian men squatted down to urinate, which proves that Greek men stood to urinate. Has that habit changed twenty-five centuries later? The fact is that a man is often someone who 'pisses on two feet' with no little pride. The penis is also the instrument of sexual affirmation. A young Quebecois tells of the sexual education he received from his father at the end of the twentieth century:

> For him, guys were guys, he was proud to be a man and have sons. I was nine or ten years old, he showed me a *Playboy*. The girls were nude, all spread out. My father showed them to me, saying, 'That's what a girl is, you caress the girl, you penetrate her with your penis and you impregnate her.' But he never told me that two guys or two girls could do that together.†

Masculinity is also learned in a collective and public manner, through rites of passage that transmit gender codes to the young. Initiation among males is one of the major principles of the masculinity of

---

* Agnès Giard, *Les Histoires d'amour au Japon: Des mythes fondateurs aux fables contemporaines* (Grenoble: Glénat, 2012), pp. 303–304.
† Cited by Michel Dorais, *Mort ou fif: La face cachée du suicide chez les garçons* (Montréal: VLB, 2001), p. 76.

domination. It is based on the idea that men come from men, not from women. Power is handed down by a masculine 'reproduction', miming and surpassing that of women, who have the biological monopoly of the process.

Certain ceremonies are aimed at appropriating the capacities of the feminine body. Among Jews and Muslims, circumcision makes boys' sexual organ bleed, like that of women. Young Makonde in Tanzania have to wear a wooden abdominal apparatus that reproduces the form of a pregnant woman. In masculine societies, including the Mamelukes in Egypt, Japanese warriors before Meiji, the Kayapo of Brazil and the Hopi of Arizona, young boys are brutally torn away from the feminine world in which they have grown up. Among the Baruya, boys are secluded in the 'house of men', the biggest of the village, where for several years they are subjected to an initiation made of mocking, humiliation, blows and abuse, and designed to extricate them from the feminine world. In the end, the 'true' man is born, without the intervention of his superfluous mother. A male does not come from a woman's childbirth, but rather is co-opted by his peers. That is what explains the exclusive friendships – sometimes of a homoerotic nature – between the heroes in numerous myths: Gilgamesh and Enkidu, Achilles and Patroclus, the Knights of the Round Table, and so on.

Up until the end of the twentieth century, military life in all its forms – conscription, barracks, trenches, warships – provided the principal collective initiation in the Western world. In the military, men are shaped by learning discipline, the brotherhood of arms and teamwork. They acquire a 'new somatic culture': standing at attention, marching in step, aiming, firing, maintaining their arms and personal effects, making their bed neatly. All these highly structured gestures shape the body and mind of the soldier.*

Once acquired, masculinity can be maintained individually or collectively. In the nineteenth century, almost all gathering places were reserved for the masculine: mines and bistros, secondary schools and clubs, smoke rooms and assemblies, meetings of the editorial board and of the board of administration. Each nation has its gender sociability:

* Odile Roynette, *Bons pour le service: La caserne à la fin du XIXe siècle* (Paris: Belin, 2017), p. 340 ff.

secret meetings of Italian Carbonari, cock fights and cantinas in Mexico, baseball and posses in the United States, not to mention the campus fraternities (there were more than 500 of them at the end of the nineteenth century). On the Greek island of Lesbos, the café is an enclave of close masculine friendship and cordiality; far from their wives, men develop friendships over card games, songs, drinks, business and even siestas.*

MASCULINE UNIVERSALISM

Even though they are at odds with each other, these forms of masculine domination aim to distinguish 'real' men from the others; the wimps, cowards, chickens, quitters and sissies. That is why the triumph of the masculinities of domination (including the masculinity of ambiguity) is of a piece with demeaning the feminine as an inferior gender. As Françoise Héritier has shown, the masculine/feminine couple is constructed on the positive/negative model. Other binary couples are juxtaposed in accordance with it: superior and inferior, high and low, strong and weak, hard and soft, rational and irrational, logical and illogical, glorious and vile, trustworthy and suspect, active and passive for Aristotle, the sublime and the beautiful for Burke.

These mental categories are so widespread that they are no longer noticed. In the *Iliad*, Menelaus calls his soldiers 'Achaean women' to make them feel ashamed. In the middle of the twelfth century CE, the German abbess Hildegard of Bingen glorifies the 'virility' of the Holy Spirit, who prevents the Church from sinking into weakness and corruption. Around 1550, the theologian Jean Viguier states that in the carnal relation, the man is active and the woman passive. Mozart's *Magic Flute* (1791) pits Sarastro, the sagacious initiator and giver of laws, against the fanatical, hate-filled Queen of the Night. As the French writer Ernest Legouvé explained in 1848, the Republic needs

---

* Evthymios Paptaxiarchis, 'Friends of the Heart: Male Commensal Solidarity, Gender, Kinship in Aegean Greece' in Peter Loizos and Evthymios Paptaxiarchis (eds.), *Contested Identities. Gender and Kinship in Modern Greece* (Princeton: Princeton University Press, 1991), pp. 156–179.

to complement the 'virile' principles of liberty and equality with the 'feminine' qualities of fraternity. For the linguist Otto Jespersen, the English language is masculine, with its clearly audible consonants, whereas the Hawaiian language (*'I kona hiki ana aku ilaila ua hook-ipa . . .'*) is effeminate and ridiculous.

This binary paradigm shows up in domains far removed from issues of gender. From the eighteenth century on, academic traditions set the aridity of mathematics above the pleasure of belles-lettres, the hard sciences above the human sciences. In the 1870s, historian and philosopher Ernest Renan judged that Europeans were a 'race of masters and soldiers'. Besides the fact that the colonial heroes – Kitchener, Rhodes, Bugeaud, Faidherbe, Gallieni, Lyautey were all men, imperialism was presented as a resistance to the decadence and weakness engendered by peace. To conquer was a virile act, the taking of possession, a penetration of some by others.* In the twentieth century, diplomacy staged couple-like relations between 'strong' and 'weak' countries: the United States and Mexico, Germany and Greece, France and Italy, and so on. Politics also adopted this dichotomy, as in the United States, where Republicans like to feminize their Democratic opponents, the elite of the East Coast or the unproductive welfare state (with its 'welfare queens'): 'real' men do not vote Democratic.†

This hierarchy of gender explains why masculine women are generally tolerated (they 'raise' themselves up to the level of men), whereas effeminate men are generally despised (they 'fall' down to the level of women). Similarly, professions tend to be devalued when they are associated with or are accessible to women, in education, for instance, or in personal care. In any case, the masculine is perceived as a notable achievement, while the feminine is understood as a failure.

The inherent inferiority of the feminine authorizes the masculine to represent it. As Simone de Beauvoir points out, the official forms used for records of civil status present symmetrical rubrics (masculine or

---

* Christelle Taraud, 'La virilité en situation coloniale' in Alain Corbin (ed.), *Histoire de la virilité*, Vol. 2, *Le Triomphe de la virilité: Le XIXᵉ siècle* (Paris: Seuil, 2011), pp. 331–347.
† Anna Greenberg, 'Do Real Men Vote Democratic?' *The American Prospect*, 19 December 2001. See also Thomas Frank, *What's the Matter with Kansas?*, 2004, ch. 1.

feminine), but in reality the masculine constitutes both the positive and the neutral, while the feminine appears only as the negative.* The man embodies not so much the first sex as the abstract subject, the principle of reference, the valid norm for all humanity, unlike the bodies of women and children, locked within their organic particularity.

Masculine universalism is reinforced by the confusion in many languages of the human being in general with the human being of masculine sex. Such is the case in English, Spanish, French, Italian and Portuguese – in other words, almost all of Western Europe and the Americas (although not in German, Russian and Japanese, nor in the Scandinavian languages). As, with unwitting humour, the French *Encyclopédie* put it in the mid eighteenth century, 'All women and girls are sometimes included under the term men.' In French, the masculine is what is used in the absence of semantic content.

In most cases, the feminine only refers back to itself. As is the case with the French *femme*, the German *frau* refers both to the human being of feminine sex and a man's spouse. Moreover, the German record of a woman's civil status refers back to her biology (*Frau Schmidt ist eine Frau*), while the men have their own social title (*Herr Schmidt ist ein Mann*), which connotes power and authority, as in *Herrschaft*. The adjective for delicious and the magnificent (*herrlich*) also refers back to the masculine, whereas there exists only one word derived from *Dame*: *dämlich*, which means 'stupid'.

Language proclaims the nobility of the masculine and the debasement of the feminine. In Romance languages, words for 'patriot' and 'patrimony' stem from *pater* (the father), and 'virtue' from *vir* (the male). Testicles (from *testis*, 'witness') denote reliability and courage, as in 'to have balls'. A word can change its meaning according to its gender. In Italian and French, the courtier, as in a Baldassare Castiglione, is a model of well-heeled sophistication, whereas the courtesan is a prostitute. In French, *le médecin* ('doctor') has no feminine equivalent, since *la médecine* designates the field of knowledge. *Le couturier* (fashion designer) creates, *la couturière* (seamstress) carries out the task. *L'esthéticien* (aesthetician) meditates on beauty, *l'esthéticienne* (beautician) performs

---

* Simone de Beauvoir, *Le Deuxième Sexe*, Vol. 1, *Les Faits et les mythes* (Paris: Gallimard/Folio essais, 1949/1976), p. 16.

Man and woman in signage

	General Information		Restrooms (men)	Restrooms (women)
Man with legs straight	Car park	Airport	Airport	Airport
	Waste bin	Museum (*)	Street (**)	Street (**)
Man with legs apart	Red light	Ski lift	University	University
	Monument	Pedestrian tunnel	Monument	Monument
Man moving	Public transport	Public transport	Public transport	Public transport
	Hotel	Theatre	Theatre	Theatre
The woman-function	Swimming pool	Hotel	Airport (**)	
	Car park	Lift	Plane	
	Street (*)	Street	Train station	

On the left, general information: car-park ticket machines, throwing rubbish in waste bins, emergency rendezvous and so on. On the right, silhouettes indicating restrooms for men or women. The abstract, universal character of masculinity appears forcefully: the generic pedestrian is symbolized in the same way as the man-with-penis in the restrooms. While the male represents the human being par excellence, the woman is always referred to by her gender: dress, hair, legs closed or maternal care.

[The photos were taken in France, except * in Germany and ** in China.]

beauty treatments. Conversely, *maîtresse* (mistress) in the sense of lover has no masculine equivalent, just as *klatschtante* in German (chatterbox, literally 'gossipy aunt') only exists in the feminine.*

The feminine is degraded in numerous languages. The words 'cunt' and 'pussy' in English, *Fotze* and *Möse* in German, *pizda* in Russian, and *con* in French can be used both to describe the anatomy and to

* See Luise Pusch, *Das Deutsche als Männersprache: Aufsätze und Glossen zur feministischen Linguistik* (Frankfurt: Suhrkamp, 1984).

insult. In Chinese, the character 女, which designates the feminine, represents a young girl on her knees. The good 好 is represented by a woman with a baby, security 安 by a woman under a roof, the mother 母 by her breasts and nipples. As for wife 妻, it is a woman holding a broom. In Japanese, one adds the word 愚 (*gu*, 'stupid') to the name of loved ones: the expression 愚妻 (*gusai*, 'dumb woman') often designates one's own wife, while the expression 愚夫 (*gufu*, 'dumb husband') is virtually never used. The adjective 女々しい (*memeshii*, 'girl-like') refers to a crybaby, but the adjective 雄々しい (*ooshii*, 'man-like') means courageous.

Grammar also tends to privilege the masculine. Since the middle of the seventeenth century, the masculine in French has taken precedence over the feminine, under the guise of being the nobler gender. In Japanese, linguistic rules do not apply to men and to women in the same way: masculine language is neutral, while feminine language is clearly 'feminized'. Women are therefore obliged to alter their manner of speaking, using neutral language at work and feminine language at home. Men have several forms available for 'I' (*watashi*, *boku* and *ore*). By contrast, women are constrained by the norm of femininity, which requires them to use only the most polite expression, *watashi* (and its variant form *atashi*), in order to be modest.

WHAT IS PATRIARCHY?

All forms of masculine domination prosper in patriarchy: the world is recreated among men. Women are destined for specialized roles of procreation, maternity, nurturing and nursing, while men maintain that women are of no use in the making of boys into men. How can we explain this paradox?

Demeaning women by assigning them to domestic roles under the trappings of a magic aura enables heads of families to absorb them as if they were inessential beings. Hence men's pretension to represent humanity in its entirety. Masculinity summarily takes hold of moral authority, abstract norms and self-evidence, abandoning the domain of corporeal, day-to-day utility to women. The symbolic power of the masculine is used to justify social domination by men.

By means of a history, a body of thought, its cultures, rites, words and institutions, patriarchy lays the foundation of masculine privilege. However, this is not for the benefit of all men, nor to the detriment of all women. Not only do the masculinities of domination hate inferior masculinities, seen as just as illegitimate and deficient as the feminine, but the mechanism that produces males can equally devour its own children. Such are the men who were humiliated by the rites of Sparta and New Guinea, or the men who perished by the tens of thousands on 1 July 1916, the first day of the Battle of the Somme. Patriarchy is therefore not a machination, but a machinery, and not all men are its evil agents, nor are all women its victims.

The masculinities of domination nevertheless believe they represent the quintessence of the masculine, even the masculine per se, as if it only existed via its will to power, the summit of virility. Exerting its hold over the order of gender, patriarchy is *a system in which the masculine embodies both the superior and the universal, to the benefit of the majority of men and a minority of women.* It is institutionalized sexism in the form of prestige and transcendence; its culture is the masculinity of domination. The feminist revolution has challenged this entire system.

PART TWO

The Revolution of Rights

4

The First Age of Emancipation

In the Babylonia of 1900 BCE, female religious devotees in Sippar, near Baghdad, reconciled spiritual life and financial operations: they bought, sold, made loans, invested in real estate, undertook lawsuits. In order to manage their domains, the businesswomen employed an army of intendants, irrigation managers, cowherds, winnowers, harvesters and agricultural workers – all seconded by a large number of slaves. For their part, the wives of Assyrian merchants were weavers and often exported their work to Anatolia. When their husband was absent, they represented his interests in dealing with colleagues or authorities, signed contracts and wrote letters, all the while overseeing daily activities in the household: looking after children and managing servants, slaves, purchases, religious offerings, and so on.*

These women can be seen as symbols of emancipation or as exceptions that confirmed the rule. It is true that Assyria was governed by a king assisted by a male council and that, unlike the men, women were not entitled to engage in bigamy (not to mention the misogyny codified by the Assyrian legislation a few centuries later). But these examples raise an important question: can a woman be free in a patriarchal society?

---

* Sophie Démare-Lafont, 'Quelques femmes d'affaires au Proche-Orient ancien' in Anne Girollet (ed.), *Le Droit, les affaires et l'argent* (Dijon: Mémoires de la SHDB, Vol. 65, 2008), pp. 25–36; and Cécile Michel, 'Femmes au foyer et femmes en voyage: Le cas des épouses des marchands assyriens au début du IIᵉ millénaire av. J.–C.', *Clio: Histoire, femmes et société*, No. 28, 2008, pp. 17–38.

THE PROTECTION OF THE
PATRIARCHAL CIRCLE

Patriarchy grants women a certain liberty, a kind of paternalist autonomy. The Mesopotamian codes did indeed implement the rudimentary
law of an eye for an eye, yet they also provided a legal framework: the
state ensured a minimal protection of its subjects, including women.
There is a difference between the rule of law, even if it is misogynous,
and criminal anarchy, with trafficking, abductions and slavery transforming women into human livestock. The patriarchal family guarantees
protection to legitimate wives as well as their daughters. This can be
seen in the status of the mother of the family: the Hammurabi code and
the Bible command that she be honoured on an equal basis with the
father. The patriarchal circle therefore grants certain rights to 'virtuous'
women, merely by distinguishing them from 'fallen' women such as servants, slaves and prostitutes.

In Rome, society was so centred on men that women were even
absent from flour riots: food was a matter too serious to be left to
women.* Yet the revolt against the Oppian law (*Lex Oppia*) testifies
to the room for manoeuvre enjoyed by rich patrician women. Adopted
in 215 BCE during the second Punic war, the law prohibited women
from wearing shimmering clothes or gold jewels, under punishment
of having them confiscated. This war tax, which turned into a sump-
tuary (luxury) tax, aroused the anger of Roman women, who laid
siege to the forum and succeeded in having it abrogated in 195 BCE,
much to the annoyance of Roman senator Cato the Elder.

Within the Roman family, the *patria potestas* conferred practically
unlimited power on the man. Marriage confined the woman within a
regimen of legal servitude, in the hand (*manus*) of her husband. Still,
it was a union of two free wills, since the husband and the wife had
the same legal status in the eyes of gods and mortals (the consent of

---

* Christophe Badel, 'Les femmes dans les émeutes frumentaires à Rome' in Marc
Bergère and Luc Capdevila (eds.), *Genre et événement: Du masculin et du féminin en
histoire des crises et des conflits* (Rennes: Presses Universitaires de Rennes, 2006), pp.
39–51.

the wife was, however, not required by the Greeks). Over time, Roman marriage proved to be a rather flexible institution. A 'free' marriage (*sine manu*) allowed the woman to depend only on a fictitious guardian, with mothers of three children even liberated from that control under Augustus. Divorce was more and more common towards the end of the Republic and ensured almost total liberty for certain women. Under the Empire, some women had the right to repudiate their husbands.* Referring to an edict from Augustus, the Consul Velleius Tutor issued a decree forbidding women from being liable for their husbands. This 'Velleian law' formalized the legal incapacity of Roman women, but also served to protect their possessions from the greed of spendthrift husbands or those hounded by creditors.

The Christianity of the first few centuries did not hesitate to acclaim women, female martyrs or queens who converted their husbands. Most importantly, monogamous marriage posited an intimate relationship between the man and the woman, even if the man headed the family. The immortality of the soul and the recognition of the importance of love in Christianity gave marriage a spiritual aura that transcended the mere reproduction of the species. 'Husbands, love your wives as Christ has loved the Church,' recommends Saint Paul in his Epistle to the Ephesians. Woman is not man's slave, but his partner. The husband does not own his wife, since the spouses belong to each other, even in carnal relations: each has exclusive rights over the body of the other. For his entire life, the man will have to be content with his wife, and vice versa.†

Most of these principles can also be found in the Quran: the innate equality of all human beings (sura on the Inner Apartments), a husband's responsibility towards his wife, a woman's right to inherit and own property (sura on women), a rule forbidding the husband from maligning his wife (sura An-Nur, on light). Moreover, the wives of the Prophet were themselves assertive women: sometimes educated, often divorced from their first husband or widowed, they go about freely, reasoning, questioning, contesting. The first among them, Khadija, was in

* Pierre Grimal, *L'Amour à Rome* (Paris: Payot, 1988/2002), ch. 3.
† 'Mariage', *Dictionnaire de théologie catholique*, Vol. IX, 2nd part (Paris: Letouzey & Ané, 1927), pp. 2075–2077.

possession of a great fortune that she used to yield a profit. Being older than Mohammed, she was the one who asked for his hand. As in Christianity, between man and wife there exists a reciprocity of sexual rights. Islam does authorize divorce, but the husband must then give the dowry back to his wife.

Certain patriarchal societies have recognized the property rights of women's inheritances or their possessions. In the Japan of the seventh century, women could have debts and claims, buy and sell land and own slaves. In eighteenth-century Constantine, Algeria, women oversaw the property received as a dowry themselves, invested in property and had recourse to the justice of the qadi (judge) in case of a conjugal dispute.* Under the Ancien Régime in France, the right of succession became more and more egalitarian and testamentary capacity was more and more regulated, except in the south, which was under Roman law. Women who were owners of a fief voted in the assemblies of the States Provincial and States General. In the nineteenth century, women sometimes resorted to a marriage contract in order to protect their inheritance against their husbands, who otherwise could have seized it.†

INDEPENDENT WOMEN

In a world dominated by men, women only begin to enjoy a semblance of freedom when they manage to escape from the bonds of marriage or if they succeed in staying at the top of a hierarchy. They are emancipated by widowhood, or by life in a convent, or else by occupying a throne, taking up arms or exercising extraordinary talent.

'Free' women are in the first place those who live by themselves, without a husband, protected by their virginity or their widowhood. Historically, widows have often enjoyed a special status: in Sumer, thanks to the Code of Ur-Nammu; in Medieval Europe (even in

* Isabelle Grangaud, *La Ville imprenable: Une histoire sociale de Constantine au XVIIIe siècle* (Paris: EHESS, 2002).
† Nicholas Frémeaux and Marion Leturcq, 'Prenuptial Agreements and Matrimonial Property Regimes in France, 1855–2010', *Explorations in Economic History*, Vol. 68, April 2018, pp. 132–142.

Viking Scandinavia); and in the China of the Song dynasty, where, even when remarried, the widow was officially considered the head of the family. In modern Europe, the best-known example is that of Glückel von Hameln (1646–1724). After the death of two successive husbands, this mother of fourteen children (twelve of whom survived childhood) handled the family business, which dealt in precious stones, alone. From Hamburg, she obtained credit, travelled throughout Europe and brokered lucrative marriages for her children. Under the Ancien Régime in France, the rare instances of women being accepted into corporations before the reform of 1776 were always those involving the widows of deceased masters. At the beginning of the nineteenth century, the young widow Clicquot became the first women to head a champagne-producing business.

In these cases, the woman was independent because she was seen 'as a man': widowhood brought about a transfer of virility. Those women who were sterile, or had been repudiated or undergone menopause, could also take on a man's role: such was the case, for example, among the Pikuni and Iroquois native peoples of America, as well as among the Nuer in Eastern Africa.

The opposite is true for religious women devotees: they are 'free' because they have already been 'taken'; they are either dedicated to a divinity (like the high priestesses and vestals) or spiritually united with God (like the cloistered monastic women in Christianity). In the early twelfth century, in the mixed abbey of Fontevraud, France, monks were subordinate to women: the powerful Petronille de Chemillé directed the spiritual and temporal matters of the abbey and its eighty-five priories. Heloise was placed at the head of the abbey of Argenteuil before becoming the abbess of Le Paraclet, an exclusively feminine monastery. Hildegard of Bingen was also elected abbess in 1136.

It would be excessive, however, to see these situations as cases of a liberty won by women. At Fontevraud, Pétronille was appointed by a man intentionally: for the monks, living among women (sometimes former prostitutes) was a form of humiliation. Moreover, each sex had its dedicated occupations: physical work for the men, psalmody and contemplation for the women. As for Heloise, she asked Abelard to provide the rules of life for her abbey. Similarly, the beguines (women who lived in communities next to monasteries in Flanders,

Paris and Cologne) were restricted by the Church in the second half of the thirteenth century. They had to join a religious community, or else be accused of collusion with heretics. In 1312, the Council of Vienne abolished the status of beguine.*

If religious women and widows escape from the woman function, it is because they have no earthly husband, at least not any more. Replacing men in the exercise of power, as did Cleopatra in Egypt, Himiko in Japan, Wu Zetian in China, Isabel I of Castile in Spain, Elizabeth I in England, Catherine II in Russia and Maria Theresa in Austria (who had sixteen children), is another matter. We should not have too many illusions about the power of queens. Female monarchs do not rule as women: they embody the continuity of the state, only owing their power to the random chance of birth, succession, death or regency. They often rule by delegation, in the name of their deceased husband, as Blanche of Castile did during the minority of her son, Louis IX of France. Moreover, it is the masculine that dominates in the woman king. Crowned in 1384, Hedwig of Poland was officially deemed 'king'. In England, Elizabeth's father had her mother executed three years after her birth. Once in power, Elizabeth had her rival, Mary Stuart, beheaded, thereby adopting the symbolism of *imperium*: a solemn pose for paintings, an austere lifestyle, an explicit chastity, a masculine entourage and the 'heart and stomach of a king', as she said in her famous Tilbury speech of 1588.

At the time of the Renaissance, thirty-three queens, princesses and regents governed some of Europe's most consolidated states (France, England, Spain, the Netherlands), but their power was by its very nature contested, since the authority of the nobles and the clergy remained in the hands of men.† In France, Salic law condemned women to little influence, with the exception of a few favourites of future kings: Gabrielle d'Estrées, Madame de Montespan, Madame de Maintenon and Madame de Pompadour.

---

* Jacques Dalarun, '*Dieu changea de sexe, pour ainsi dire*': La religion faite femme, *XIᵉ–XVᵉ siècle* (Paris: Fayard, 2008), pp. 117–119; and Didier Lett, *Hommes et femmes au Moyen Âge: Histoire du genre, XIIe–XVe siècles* (Paris: Armand Colin, 2013), pp. 109, 180.
† Thierry Wanegffelen, *Le Pouvoir contesté: Souveraines d'Europe à la Renaissance* (Paris: Payot, 2008).

The Seal of Joan of Burgundy (circa 1328)

The seal's circular form and wealth of symbols place the queen on the same level as a king: Joan is represented standing, crowned, holding two sceptres and surrounded by lions. Since her husband Philippe VI had to go away to wage battle in the Hundred Years War, he entrusted the government of the kingdom to her in 1338. Joan corresponded with the Pope and was surrounded by artists and writers, yet she would fall victim to a dark legend stigmatizing the 'lame evil queen'.

Women's energy and talent ensured them a certain form of autonomy, however. Such was the case for women of war in France: Joan of Arc, Jeanne Hachette and the Grande Mademoiselle, cousin of Louis XIV, who ordered her troops to fire on the royal soldiers from the Bastille in 1652. Such was also the case for women of letters. Owing to her meticulous education and her mastery of Mandarin (usually reserved for men), Murasaki Shikibu became the poetess of the imperial court of Japan, before writing *The Tale of Genji*, one of the masterpieces of Japanese literature, in the early eleventh century. In France, Christine de Pisan wrote *The Book of the City of Ladies* (1405), which made the case that women were as intelligent and capable as men. However, she had to adopt strategies of masculinization in order to be accepted.

Beginning in the Renaissance, female poets and intellectuals made a name for themselves on the Italian peninsula: Laura Terracina, to whom we owe a *Discourse on Ariosto* in 1550, and Elena Cornaro Piscopia, who was accepted for a doctorate in philosophy in Padua in 1678, and was the first woman to hold a university degree. A few artists achieved distinction, too: Catherine van Hemessen was a Flemish painter of the sixteenth century, and Artemisia Gentileschi, recognized in 1610 for painting *Susanna and the Elders* at the age of 17, was the first woman admitted to the Florence Academy of the Arts of Drawing. Marie Sibylle Merian, who died in 1717, was a German naturalist and artist, and one of the rare scientists of the period.

Within the extremely rigid intellectual and legal context of the time, these women constituted exceptions. In spite or because of their talent, they often appear to have been in socially precarious positions, sometimes facing violence (Artemisia Gentileschi was raped by her tutor and subjected to humiliating questions from the court), sometimes rejected by the authorities (after having overcome the Bishop of Padua's opposition, Elena Cornaro Piscopia was still forbidden from teaching). In France, out of the six royal academies founded in the seventeenth century, only the Academy of Painting (1648) admitted women. Catherine Duchemin entered it in 1663, followed by the Boullogne sisters, Sophie Chéron and Catherine Perrot. No woman belonged to the Royal Academy of Dance. As for the French Academy (1635), it remained a male bastion until the end of the twentieth century.*

Women did actively participate in economic life. In France, Henri IV abolished Velleian law in 1606, consequently allowing women to sign contracts, transfer their financial dowry, and also to be despoiled by their

---

* Marie-Jo Bonnet and Christine Fauré, 'Femmes' in Lucien Bély (ed.), *Dictionnaire de l'Ancien Régime: Royaume de France, XVIe–XVIIIe siècle* (Paris: PUF, 1996), pp. 536–540.

husbands. Women were able to practise several trades, as laundresses, hairdressers, fashion merchants, milliners and midwives. Textile production was highly feminized in the region of Lyon. Following Turgot's reforms of 1776, women could join new guilds and become butchers, grocers or hosiers. The fact that numerous trades refused women, especially if they were married, did not prevent them from working, either alongside their husbands or as 'independent' laundresses, ironing maids, used clothes dealers or merchants of second-hand goods. Their work and their leisure-time activities required a certain mobility: they were present in markets, fairs, covered food markets and cabarets.*

'THE WOMAN QUESTION'

After Roman *sine manu* marriage, Christian humanism and the entry into the world of work, the fourth factor favouring the autonomy of women in Europe was literacy. In the Germanic countries, the Reformation encouraged the education of girls as well as boys, so that all might have access to the Bible. In the wake of the Catholic Reformation in France, a large number of initiatives were undertaken in the early seventeenth century: boarding houses and convents for upper-class young ladies, as well as free schools for girls from poor backgrounds. In most cases, instruction was limited to needlework and the catechism. The curriculum sketched out by Fénelon in *The Education of Girls* (1687) was more ambitious: in spite of their 'natural weakness,' he was in favour of teaching them history, poetry, music and basic economic and legal concepts, but was against their learning Latin. Fénelon exerted a certain influence on Madame de Maintenon, who founded the Royal House of Saint-Cyr, intended for young girls from penniless aristocratic families.†

* Nicole Dufournaud, 'Rôles et pouvoirs des femmes au XVIe siècle dans la France de l'Ouest', history thesis, EHESS, 2007, ch. 3 in particular; and Cynthia Truant, 'La maîtrise d'une identité? Corporations féminines à Paris aux XVIIᵉ et XVIIIᵉ siècles', *Clio: Histoire, femmes, sociétés*, No. 3, 1996.
† Patricia Touboul, 'Le statut des femmes: Nature et condition sociale dans le traité *De l'éducation des filles* de Fénelon', *Revue d'histoire littéraire de la France*, Vol. 104, No. 2, 2004, pp. 325–342.

The education of women constituted a major issue, with their future role in society depending on it. That is the meaning of the struggle led, in Venice, by Lucrezia Marinella in *The Nobility and Excellence of Women* (1591) and Modesta Pozzo in *The Merit of Women* (1600); in France, by Marie de Gournay in *The Equality of Men and Women* (1622); and, in England, by Mary Astell in *Serious Proposal to the Ladies* (1694), which traces out the project of a university for women. In the eighteenth century, several dozen treatises praising women were published in France, as well as dictionaries recalling their historical importance, such as Mademoiselle de Scudéry's *Illustrious Women* (1642) and Jacquette Guillaume's *Les Dames illustres* (Illustrious Ladies, 1665). Several female authors state their certainty of being equal to men and even superior to them in certain domains. For Marguerite Buffet, men can go ahead and 'glory in their tall bodies and their fat heads, for that's what they have in common with very stupid animals and very big heavy beasts': for their part, she argued that women possess more piety and fidelity, as well as a livelier mind.*

The affirmation of women had consequences for religious as well as literary life. In Great Britain, liberal Protestants recognized the equality of both spouses before God and even accepted the possibility of divorce, as did John Milton in 1643. Among the Quakers and Baptists, women took the floor to speak in public, coming out of the silence that Saint Paul had prescribed for them. This spiritual equality soon developed a political dimension.

At the time of the Levellers in the 1640s, women joined men in the drafting of petitions and pamphlets. In France, women preachers created a feminine mysticism in the manner of Madame Guyon, a wealthy widow central to Quietism, who was eventually imprisoned in the Bastille several years after being driven out of Saint-Cyr.

Women were increasingly in the public limelight. For instance, Madame de Rambouillet's Blue Room hosted men of letters such as Honoré d'Urfé, Voiture and Guez de Balzac; the Précieuses were arbiters of linguistic elegance who distinguished themselves by the purism of their style and the refinement of their manners. There were also some fifteen

---

* Marguerite Buffet, *Nouvelles observations sur la langue française* (Paris: Cusson, 1668), pp. 228–232.

women from the highest echelons of nobility active during the Fronde under the regency of Anne of Austria, who insisted on their ability to play a role in political, diplomatic and military matters. Among them, the Duchess of Longueville, sister of the royal princes of the Fronde, was to become the patroness of the Port-Royal abbey.*

However, these groups only involved a micro-elite of cultivated women, few enough to be quickly reduced to silence. The 'learned ladies' were ridiculed among the circles of the French Academy and by writers such as Molière and La Fontaine, and traditional order was rapidly re-established under the reign of Louis XIV. As for Mademoiselle de Scudéry, a mainstay of the Blue Room and pivotal figure on the Parisian literary scene in the 1640s and 1650s, she had to publish under her brother's name, and she would later be criticized for learned pretensions and her salon for being in bad taste.

Each of these groups nevertheless gave women collective visibility. Through the power of speaking, the passion for poetic creation or the drive to act and engage in controversy, the involvement of women in the debates of their time compensated for their inferior civic status. Among the *Précieuses*, the love of language, the effort to achieve distinction, the cult of heroism and the solidarity with other women constituted the first steps toward the assertion of a feminine voice.† Women mattered more and more in intellectual life. In 1637, Descartes chose to write his *Discourse on the Method* in French in order to also be read by women, who were not taught Latin.

It was above all literature that was constructed as a feminine space. A high society pastime consisting of 'talking literature' was developing in ladies' bedrooms. It involved the writing and reading of poems, novels, diaries and an incredible amount of correspondence. Love, which these women heavily favoured, opened them to interior life, a prelude to the discovery of other sentiments, melancholy or enthusiasm. After writers of novels such as Mademoiselle de Scudéry or Madame de La Fayette, the rise of women as readers enabled them to share their tastes or escape into moments of close friendship, livening

---

* Sophie Vergnes, *Les Frondeuses: Une révolte au féminin, 1643–1661* (Seyssel: Champ Vallon, 2013).
† Benedetta Craveri, *L'Âge de la conversation* (Paris: Gallimard, 2002), ch. 9.

up the idleness to which they were doomed in marriage. The women of elite society were consumers as well as producers of culture, though that did not prevent them from ensuring the success of novels written by men, from *L'Astrée* to *The New Heloise*.

In China, *tanci* was being developed in the same era as a literary genre based on examples of Confucian virtue and piety. Women in the wealthy echelons of society, who were cloistered in their reserved quarters, had raconteurs come to their homes. Originally a form of entertainment, *tanci* was adopted and reinterpreted by women, becoming a true literature in which they spoke of themselves, their sufferings and their hopes.*

The seventeenth century was therefore one of emancipation for women around the world. Increasingly schooled and literate, they could assume cultural, social, economic and even religious or political roles. They exercised power not only in Europe (with Marie de Medici and Anne of Austria regent rulers of the kingdom of France), but also in Africa (Anna Nzinga fought against the Portuguese in present-day Angola) and in the Islamic world (the sultans of Aceh were patronesses of arts and letters who ruled for half a century on the island of Sumatra). They also played a role in the conquest of the New World. Pocahontas was the daughter of a great Native American chief who brought the indigenous tribes of Virginia closer to the settlers before marrying a planter and converting to Christianity; in the previous century, La Malinche had been a valuable intermediary for Cortés in Mexico.

SALONNIÈRES AND NEW MOTHERS

The sparkling high society life so prominent in eighteenth-century France was inconceivable without women: they hosted gatherings, set the rules of the social game and contributed wit and gaiety to conversation, along with polite manners and refinement. A good many salons were associated with a feminine figure, the 'hostess' who transformed her dwelling into a space of fashionable hospitality: Madame de

---

* Catherine Gipoulon, 'Naissance d'un mouvement d'émancipation' in Qiu Jin, *Pierres de l'oiseau Jingwei* (Paris: Des Femmes, 1976), p. 19.

Tencin, Madame de Lespinasse and Madame de Luxembourg hosted an elite group of men of the royal court, men of letters, artists, ambassadors and notable women. Their influence was so palpable that, for foreign observers, France was the country of women.* The comedies of Marivaux and Beaumarchais featured men fooled by clever women, both servants and countesses, who seemed to impose their will.

Nobility guaranteed women a certain equality. With social rank prevailing over sex, a duchess had a higher standing than a male baronet, and of course she loomed over a commoner. In the upper echelons of the Parisian aristocracy, women enjoyed real autonomy, with a social and love life parallel to that of their husbands. But a woman's role also played out in her household, with her children. Under the influence of Rousseau in the second half of the eighteenth century, several noble women took an interest in pedagogy and methods of raising small children. Madame d'Épinay expressed her wish to raise her children herself instead of entrusting them to a wet nurse. After she gave birth in 1746, her husband rudely refused: 'You, nurse your child? I thought I would die laughing. Even if you were strong enough to do that, do you think that I would consent to such a ridiculous thing?' In 1759, she published the *Lettres à mon fils* (Letters to my son), in which she urges him to embrace a life of honour and sincerity guided by conscience. She became friends with Rousseau, Grimm, Diderot and d'Holbach, but, separated from her husband and exasperated by her son's escapades, she found happiness only with her granddaughter, for whom she wrote her *Conversations d'Émilie* in 1774.†

So it was that in addition to their civilizing role as *salonnières* (ladies who hosted salons), women had a recognized civic role as educators This was a citizenship of sorts, one that lay somewhere between being an intellectual accompaniment to their philosopher friends and providing enlightened motherhood for their children. The Age of Enlightenment would grant them nothing more, but for the readers of

---

* Mona Ozouf, *Les Mots des femmes: Essai sur la singularité française* (Paris: Gallimard, 1999), pp. 325–327 in particular; and Antoine Lilti, *Le Monde des salons: Sociabilité et mondanité à Paris au XVIIIᵉ siècle* (Paris: Fayard, 2005), p. 111 ff.
† Sabine Melchior-Bonnet, *Les Grands Hommes et leur mère: Louis XIV, Napoléon, Staline et les autres* (Paris: Odile Jacob, 2017), p. 156 ff.

Rousseau, this was a social, and almost political status; these women refined the mores of their contemporaries and trained the minds of future citizens. This motherhood of the Enlightenment would have an influence in Prussia, Russia, Poland and even in the Japan of Emperor Meiji at the end of the nineteenth century, where the adage 'good wife, wise mother' (*ryōsai kenbo*) entrusted mothers with a certain responsibility in the work of national recovery.

The campaign for the literacy of girls was pursued in the eighteenth century, particularly in Paris, where new schools blossomed. These came in private or charitable forms, but were almost always associated with religious orders. In 1760, the city held more than 250 educational establishments, which taught around 11,000 schoolgirls. There was clearly significant progress: within a century the proportion of Parisian women capable of signing their will went from 60 to 80 per cent (as opposed to 85 to 91 per cent of men). The gap between regions remained enormous, however: the female literacy rate languished at only 12 per cent in the south of France. During the 1780s, in the northern and eastern parts of France 44 per cent of women could sign their names, compared to 27 per cent in France as a whole. In England, the figure stood at 40 per cent, while it was 37 per cent in Belgium. *

Among the richest in society – a group still legally and politically dominated by men – women were able to achieve some degree of autonomy. Central to this was their increasing literacy and their subsequent role in the creation of 'literature', a move toward political activity and the claim of equality, and an important role in high society life. If this was an emancipation of women, what were its limits?

In the 1760s, young Geneviève Randon de Malboissière received instruction in mathematics, Spanish, Italian, German, English, drawing, dance and natural history. In this wealthy, noble family won over to Enlightenment ideas, the education of girls was important, but it remained 'gratuitous', without giving access to any profession or status. Feminine knowledge was intended uniquely for pleasure: it was only tolerable if it was not in competition with the social position of

* Martine Sonnet, 'L'éducation des filles à l'époque moderne', *Historiens et géographes*, No. 393, February 2006, pp. 255–268; and Roger Chartier, 'L'analphabétisation en Belgique (XVIIIᵉ–XIXᵉ siècle)', *Annales ESC*, No. 1, 1980, pp. 106–108.

men.* Élisabeth Vigée was a talented and renowned painter who came to the Royal Academy of Painting in 1783 with the backing of the queen, but she suffered criticism because she had the same legal status as her husband, Monsieur Lebrun, an art merchant. By inscribing her name on her paintings with a pocketknife, she managed to put her personal mark on them, displaying an 'authorship devoid of authority'.† As for Rousseau, idolized by so many women readers, he stated in *Émile* that 'all women's education should be relative to men': the duty of a woman was to be pleasing and useful to men.

Maternal lactation and high society life are sometimes placed in opposition to each other: so how can they serve as evidence of feminine emancipation? In both cases, women were confirmed in their domestic roles of devotion to others: nursing children and the art of hosting guests are two 'natural' talents that patriarchy affirms in the behaviour of women. There was moreover a difference in nature between *salonnières* like Madame Geoffrin, who humbly acknowledged their ignorance, and the tiny minority of learned women, such as Émilie du Châtelet, who translated Newton, and Laura Bassi, who taught physics at the University of Bologna, where she had Spallanzani and Volta as her pupils. The *salonnières* doubtless suffered from their lack of education, as Madame d'Épinay, who was nevertheless a prolific writer, admitted in 1771: 'The fact is that I am very ignorant. My entire education was oriented toward the pleasurable talents.'‡ And Madame de Staël, a first-class intellectual who authored novels and essays, wrote in *Germany* (1813): 'They are right to exclude women from political and civil matters; nothing is more contrary to their natural vocation as is all that would create for them relations of rivalry with men.'

Nevertheless, this first age of emancipation at the heart of patriarchy prepared women for the fights for equality that they were to wage beginning with the French Revolution.

---

* Martine Sonnet, 'Le Savoir d'une demoiselle de qualité: Geneviève Randon de Malboissière (1746–1766)', *Memorie dell'Academia delle scienze di Torino, classe di scienze morali, storichi et filologiche*, Vol. 24, No. 3, 2000, pp. 167–185.
† Charlotte Guichard, *La Griffe du peintre: La valeur de l'art (1730–1820)* (Paris: Seuil, 2014), ch. 6.
‡ Cited by Benedetta Craveri, *L'Âge de la conversation*, p. 43.

5

The Victories of Feminism

Today, women are at the head of multinational corporations and nation-states around the world. All professions are open to them; they can dress as they want; they have the right to maternity leave. The complaint of a woman who has been sexually assaulted is taken seriously; her attacker, if arrested, is prosecuted. Such was not the case anywhere in 1850. Between the latter part of the eighteenth century and the end of the twentieth century, something incredible took place: a revolution whose effects on our daily life are felt every day. Under the strain of this revolution, this ongoing battle, the patriarchy has started to crack.

WOMEN IN REVOLUTION

Women actively participated in the Atlantic revolutions from 1776 to 1804, though not on the same level as men, which is hardly surprising, given their exclusion from the political sphere. As early as 1760 in the American colonies, the Daughters of Liberty were on the move, organizing the boycott of English goods; in this respect, Martha Washington was active alongside her husband. The 'Founding Fathers' of the United States were nevertheless all men, as were the members of the Continental Congresses, the signatories of the Declaration of Independence, and the first presidents and vice-presidents.

In the Caribbean, enslaved women fled (sometimes with their children), but they comprised only 20 per cent of runaways. Women participated in the Haitian revolution beginning with the Bois Caiman ceremony of 14 August 1791 in Saint-Domingue; they took on a mainly ritual function, with chants and dances, while the men led the movement and held the guns. Several women combatants fought in the War of Independence: one was Catherine Flon, who invented the Haitian flag, and another, Sanité Belair, who demanded to be executed as a uniformed soldier. In 1802, in Guadeloupe, women took part in combat by relaying orders, preparing bullets, comforting the wounded and carrying the dead. It was in this context that Solitude, a pregnant mulatto woman, was infamously executed.*

We find politically active women throughout Revolutionary France, too. They were involved in a wide range of action, from helping to draw up the *Cahiers de Doléances* (Lists of Grievances), to submitting petitions to the king and the National Assembly, and – once the Revolution was in full swing – took part in physical confrontations, political clubs and in the writing of polemical publications. As was the case elsewhere, however, political and military functions were monopolized by men. For this reason, the French Revolution has been variously interpreted both as a time of feminine emancipation and, on the contrary, as a reaffirmation of masculine supremacy. There are in fact arguments supporting both theses.

What can we conclude? We should observe in the first place that women immediately joined the Revolution, from its very outset in the year 1789, not only because of their anger over the price of flour, but also for deeply political reasons. Generally speaking, the Revolution was a struggle against despotism and unearned social privilege. However, for women, the Revolution was concerned not only with the status and roles of the king and aristocrats *in particular*, but also of men *in general*; whereas men were thinking only of the king and aristocrats, and not at all of their own despotism and privileges.

Feminism was born out of two events: the abolition of privileges on 4 August 1789, and the passage of the Declaration of the Rights of Man and the Citizen on 26 August 1789. These two closely connected changes issuing from an assembly of men opened a new horizon: the end of (masculine) privileges and the demand for equality (between

---

* Arlette Gautier, *Les Soeurs de Solitude: Femmes et esclavage aux Antilles du XVIIᵉ au XIXᵉ siècle* (Rennes: Presses Universitaires de Rennes, 2010), p. 205 ff; and Jasmine Narcisse and Pierre-Richard Narcisse, *Mémoire de femmes* (Port-au-Prince: UNICEF, 1997).

Two interpretations of the French Revolution

	The 'feminist' revolution	The 'patriarchal' revolution
Origins in the Age of Enlightenment (before 1789)	Literacy and education for women	The 'homosocial' virtue of the Republic (Montesquieu, Diderot, Rousseau)
	Increased number of women authors	All the authors of the *Encyclopédie* are men, except for one anonymous woman
	Representation of women among painters (Vigée-Lebrun)	Glorification of neoclassical virility (David)
1789	The 'Petition of Women of the Third Estate to the King' (January)	Pornographic libel aimed at Marie-Antoinette
	Women's march to Versailles (5–6 October)	The rioters, guards and militiamen are mostly men
Laws, measures, ideas (1789–1792)	Equality of inherited succession; disinheritance prohibited	Confirmation of the Salic law
	Civil equality between the sexes; women as witnesses to civil status	Women as 'passive citizens'
	Marriage as a civil contract; right to divorce	Man as head of the family
	Abolition of the *lettres de cachet* peremptorily consigning individuals to prison, and of paternal power over adult children	Paternal right to jail wayward children; paternal power over under age children

	The 'feminist' revolution	The 'patriarchal' revolution
	Olympe de Gouges, *Declaration of the Rights of Woman*; Etta Palm founds Société patriotique et de bienfaisance des Amies de la Vérité (Patriotic Society for the Protection of Women Promoting the Truth)	All government ministers and representatives elected to the National Assembly are men; decree 'To great men, from a grateful nation'
	Louise de Kéralio's activity in journalism and politics	Louise de Kérialo's republican sexism
War (1792)	Roles played by Anne-Josephe Théroigne de Méricourt and Claire Lacombe	Men declare and wage war
	Influence of Manon Roland	Danton's speech on 'Audacity'
1793	Execution of Louis XVI, 'royal parricide'	Execution of Marie-Antoinette
	Reduction of the freedom to witness for the fathers of families (7 March)	Arbitrary power of the father over his natural children
	Society of revolutionary republican women (May); female sans-culottes	Women are excluded from the Convention's tribunes (20 May)
	Women's right to vote on the sharing of common lands (10 June)	Women's clubs and societies prohibited (30 October)

	The 'feminist' revolution	The 'patriarchal' revolution
Effects of the Revolution (after 1799)	Challenge to masculine authority (king, fathers)	Virile nature of power; masculine suffrage until the middle of the twentieth century
	Shaking of the patriarchal family	Napoleon's Civil Code (1804); prohibition of divorce (1816); single mothers rejected
	Girls' right to schooling	School inequalities to the detriment of girls
	Human rights	Rights of man only

women and men). The Women's Petition to the National Assembly was presented at the end of 1789 and very clearly articulated this demand: it consisted of abolishing 'all privileges' of the masculine sex and liberating women from 'thirteen million despots' who embodied the 'masculine aristocracy,' so that women might finally enjoy the same liberty and rights as men.* Thirteen years earlier, in 1776, Abigail Adams had entreated her husband John, a member of the Continental Congress and future President of the United States, not to place unlimited power in the hands of men, those potential 'tyrants'.

Hence the question: were the men of the French Revolution defending human universalism, the Promethean ideal of emancipation; or was it masculine universalism, yet another patriarchal project? The Declaration of the Rights of Man had the inherent ambiguity characteristic of the French language, of making human beings in general indistinguishable from human beings of masculine sex. Two days after the vote, the French National Assembly reaffirmed Salic law: like the 'Declaration of the Rights of Man and Citizens', the 'Declaration of

* *Les Femmes dans la Révolution française*, Vol. 1 (Paris: EDHIS, 1982), facsimile No. 19. See also Karen Offen, *European Feminisms, 1700–1950: A Political History* (Stanford: Stanford University Press, 2000), ch. 3.

the Rights of Man Concerning Powers' favoured males.* In the Constitution of 1791, women were classified as passive citizens, along with domestic servants, criminal defendants and the bankrupt. The widow and woman of letters Olympe de Gouges published her *Declaration of the Rights of Woman and the Female Citizen* in the same year: by feminizing the title of the original Declaration, she ironically underscored its incomplete nature. After she had been guillotined for collusion with the Girondins in 1793, the prosecutor for the Commune of Paris lambasted 'this manlike woman' who 'marched to her death for her crimes': her sad example reminded French women that nature had 'entrusted domestic tasks' to them and 'given [them] teats for nursing'.†

But one can also judge that, in addition to active citizens, the Declaration of Rights included the 'other' men (Jewish men, Black men, indigent men), as well as women and children. It announced the end of dominations, particularly in articles 1 and 4 on liberty. Because it carried within it an unlimited claim to dignity and equality, it promised all the oppressed that their day would come.‡ As early as 1791, the Constituants emancipated Jews and, less than three years later, the Conventionnels abolished slavery (citizenship had already been granted to free persons of colour). A century later, in 1878, the Italian feminist Salvatore Morelli was invited to the International Conference for the Rights of Women held in Paris: she wrote that the meeting completed the work of the Encyclopédistes and French revolutionaries.

RIGHTS FOR WOMEN

What is in fact important in the Declaration of 1789 is not the word 'man', but 'rights'. Everything follows: liberty, equality, security, suffrage, education, independence. For, however we interpret the statement

---

* Auguste Amic, Étienne Mouttet, *La Tribune française: Choix des discours et des rapports les plus remarquables*, Vol. 1 (Paris: La Tribune française, 1840), p. 72. About this interpretation, see Joan Scott, *Only Paradoxes to Offer: French Feminists and the Rights of Man* (Cambridge, MA: Harvard University Press, 1997).

† Cited by Alphonse de Lamartine, *Histoire des Girondins*, Vol. 4 (Brussels: Muquardt, 1847), pp. 202–203.

‡ About this opposite interpretation, see Mona Ozouf, *Les Mots des femmes*.

'All men are born and remain free and equal,' we cannot avoid wondering: what about women? The end of privilege implies the end of those held by men. The equality of rights contains the equality of the sexes. Of course, Christine de Pisan, Marie de Gournay and Mary Astell had in their time already defended the principle of the equality of the sexes. But in a society of orders in which no one holds rights, in which the powerful themselves only have ranks and titles, women's claims could only ever be metaphysical. That is why the rights of women are indissociable from the first stirrings of modernity: individual autonomy, the rule of law, civil society – the 'coming out of the state of minority', as Kant put it.

Beyond their social differences and political divergence, the women of the French Enlightenment took part in the public debate, and not only on the subject of equality between the sexes. Between 1777 and 1788, female authors in France numbered 78; between 1789 and 1800 it was 329, that is, four times more. Paris was the epicentre of the literary awakening of French women, but it was also taking place in cities such as Lyon, Toulouse, Caen, Dijon and Avignon, and even in small towns.* It was not only the number that is important, but also the tone, the ardour: women entered into politics with violence, resorting to controversy, polemics, demands and indictments, all of which were discursive modes reserved for men.

Even in England, where the number of women authors was much lower, the French Revolution incited Catharine Macaulay and Mary Wollstonecraft to take a stance in favour of liberty, against privileges, despotism and the traditionalism of Burke, whom both of them attacked. In her pamphlet of 1790, Wollstonecraft defended the 'rights of men' (as opposed to the 'rights of man') in the name of reason and justice. In the same vein, she rehabilitated the women who demonstrated on 5 October 1789, whom Burke had treated with scorn. Expanding the scope of her reflection in *A Vindication of the Rights of Woman: with Strictures on Political and Moral Subjects* (1792), she demanded the equality of the sexes within marriage as well as in social life. Women were not sweet flowers, perpetual minors flourishing in the

* Carla Hesse, *The Other Enlightenment: How French Women Became Modern* (Princeton: Princeton University Press, 2001), p. 37 ff and p. 55.

shadow of men, but 'creatures of reason,' endowed with intelligence, eager to learn, capable of energy and strength. In her posthumously published novel *Maria* (1798), Wollstonecraft denounced the 'wrongs' that society inflicts on women, who spend their lives being sold, betrayed, stolen and raped.

What defines a woman is not her uterus or her breasts, but her faculty of reason, with two corollaries: rights and liberty. In order for *woman as subject* to exist, it is enough to say that human reason is inherent in women: this recognizes them as individuals endowed with inalienable rights, common to all human beings. This new model – based on reason, rights, liberty, equality and the ability to speak out and inhabit a public role – doomed in its very principle the hierarchy of the sexes. This is why the Declaration of 1789 enabled women to escape from the patriarchal circle, enabled them to work or be active in politics, to write or command – in other words, to live their own lives. In coming out of the masculine orbit, woman would lose her aura of grace and mystery. Women do not need to be placed under glass or venerated as angels of the house: they just need rights.

However ambiguous the Atlantic Revolutions may have been, they are what gave the first feminists their most powerful weapons. Half a century later, at the convention of Seneca Falls in 1848, Elizabeth Cady Stanton used the Declaration of Independence as a model to bring accusations against men (as the Americans had done with the English) and proclaim the equality of women in a 'Declaration of Sentiments'. Feminism was invented at the end of the eighteenth century by women and men who understood what lessons were to be learned from the new political era. Among them, the mulatto woman Solitude, Manon Roland, Olympe de Gouges and Mary Wollstonecraft.

Once revolutions set the fight against despotism and privilege in motion, feminism was born. It sought the emancipation of all women in order to resolve this untenable contradiction: proclamations of rights for some, but slavery for others. Subsequently, feminism would consist of closing the gap between the promise of universal ideals and the reality of inequalities. And it matters little what we call it – 'feminism' in France and in all of Europe at the end of the nineteenth century, 'the cause of women' in Swedish, and the 'new doctrine of woman' in the words of Japanese writer Takamure Itsue – feminism is not a word, but a struggle for the recognition of rights in a socio-political configuration that renders them conceivable and possible. Today, the French Revolution is over, but the feminist revolution to which it gave rise is not.

CIVIL EQUALITY

The first battle dealt with civil rights, which enabled women to escape from the authority of their fathers and husbands and gain access to all professions. In Norway in 1845, then in Sweden and Denmark in the 1850s, single women ceased to be dependent on their fathers. In Great Britain, Caroline Norton campaigned for the Custody of Children Act (1839), which authorized separated mothers to request custody of their children under the age of seven; the Matrimonial Causes Act of 1857 allowed women to divorce more easily. In the United States, women could receive a plot of land by virtue of the Homestead Act of 1862. In all these cases, legislators did not encroach directly on the rights of men, since the laws only concerned single or separated women. The Married Woman's Property Act (1882), on the other hand, gave the married woman the control of her own possessions and marked a break not only in England, but also in Ireland and the Australian states, where it influenced legislation. At the beginning of the twentieth century, Germany, Brazil and Nicaragua recognized the civil competence of wives, allowing them to administer their own possessions and enter into contracts, although husbands retained their status as heads of the family.*

In France, the issue of civil equality was particularly acute, since the Napoleonic civil code worsened the condition of married women. In this domain, French feminists did not obtain their first victories until the end of the nineteenth century: the right to open a savings account (1881), reinstatement of the right to divorce with symmetrical status for the wife and the husband in the matter of adultery (1884), civil

---

* Arlette Gautier, 'Travail et droits du mariage dans les Amériques et les Caraïbes' in Gérard Gomez and Donna Kesselman (eds.), *Les Femmes dans le monde du travail dans les Amériques* (Aix-en-Provence: Presses Universitaires de Provence, 2016), pp. 31–32.

capacity of the wife in case of separation (1893), the possibility of serving as a witness in acts of civil status (1897), freedom to dispose of her own salary (1907), elimination of the duty to obey (1938), the right to work and open a bank account without the husband's permission (1965), joint parental authority (1970), divorce by mutual consent (1975) and equality between spouses (1985). This was the end of paternal and marital power. It had taken a century for marriage to no longer be the tomb of feminine liberty.

On the professional level, equality is less a matter of authorizing women to exercise an activity than of allowing them access to every employment. From the very beginning women have worked – in the fields, rice paddies, farms, at home, in shops, or in certain sectors such as domestic service, retail, and so on. Even when women were gainfully employed outside their own family sphere, their remuneration was often meagre, considered to be a supplement in a survival economy. Globally, women therefore did subalternate, manual and poorly paid work.

We can distinguish several steps in the emancipation of women by means of work. The first is industrialization, which made it possible for them to get out of the household and acquire a certain autonomy, while at the same time offering the possibility of acting collectively. A female working class appeared at the very beginning of the nineteenth century in the United States, Great Britain and France, then at the beginning of the twentieth century in Egypt, India, Japan and China. Disputes often broke out in the most feminized sector, that is the textile industry: demands from the Lowell Mill Girls in Massachusetts in the 1830s, action by the woman workers in Lancashire, the silk mill workers' strike in Lyon in 1869, and those in the Shanghai silk factories in the early 1920s. The match factory workers of the Bryant & May plant went on strike in 1888, backed by the socialist feminist Annie Besant, who denounced a 'white slavery' in the heart of London. The mobilization of the match factory workers successfully paved the way for the changes of the Second International and the new unionism, which were now more open to women. The First International and the labour unions had previously responded with a 'virilist' model in the 1860s and 1870s. At the same time, feminine labour unions such as the Women's Trade League (1874) and the National Federation of

Women Workers (1906) were forming in Great Britain in the early twentieth century, and also in France in Christian worker circles, around the figure of Marie-Louise Rochebillard.

In the second half of the nineteenth century, the postal and telegraphic services, department stores, lower administrative offices and teaching were sectors employing large numbers of women. These positions offered a certain social recognition, particularly for single women, who often paid a price by sacrificing their private life. In Denmark, Mathilde Fibiger (a future telegraphist) published her highly popular 1851 novel *Clara Raphael*, the story of a woman who refuses marriage in order to fulfil her intellectual and professional ambitions.

The employment of women further developed during and after the First World War, and became widespread in the second half of the twentieth century. The feminization of work, mainly in the tertiary sector, was a revolution observable in most Western countries: the whole structure of society was significantly altered. At the beginning of the twenty-first century, women's rate of employment exceeded 75 per cent in most countries of the OECD (OCDE), as opposed to about 45 per cent in the 1960s and 90 per cent for men. In France, four out of five blue-collar workers are men, while four out of five white-collar workers are women.*

ACCESS TO THE PRESTIGIOUS PROFESSIONS

True equality for women means the ability to get out of the woman-function sectors (domestic services, care providers, teaching) and access positions of power, for it is only thus that they can compete with men. The emancipation of women is achieved not only by access to salaried employment, but also from the exercising of responsibility over the course of a career. In this regard, it is clear that gaining the necessary qualifications is crucial.

* Sylvie Schweitzer, *Les Femmes ont toujours travaillé: Une histoire de leurs métiers, XIXᵉ and XXᵉ siècle* (Paris: Odile Jacob, 2002); and Olivier Marchand, '50 ans de mutations de l'emploi', *INSEE Première*, No. 1312, September 2010.

In France, women obtained the *baccalauréat* (for the completion of secondary education) for the first time in 1861, the bachelor of science in 1868, the medical doctor's degree in 1870, the law diploma in 1887, the *agrégation* (degree conferring the status of a tenured lycée teacher) in philosophy in 1905, the doctorate in letters in 1914 and the *agrégation* in medicine in 1923.* Beginning in 1924, the curriculum for girls and boys became identical in secondary schools, and both now had to take the same *baccalauréat* exam. Within this movement, Marguerite Thibert earned her doctorate in letters in 1926 and Simone de Beauvoir ranked second in the *agrégation* for philosophy in 1929. The Paris Technical Institute of Chemistry was one of the first engineering institutes to open to women.

It took determined endeavour to gain access to professions of prestige: positions in medicine, law, university faculty, upper administration and international organizations. Depending on the specific masculine monopoly that she toppled in various fields of knowledge, each pioneer became a symbol of power or of the sacred: Isala Van Diest, the first female doctor in Belgium at the end of the nineteenth century; Jeanne Chauvin, who earned a doctorate in law with a thesis on the 'professions accessible to women' and in 1901 became the first woman lawyer to plead a case in court; Marie Curie, the first female scientist to receive the Nobel Prize in 1903 (she would receive a second one in 1911); Katharine Davis, the first woman to head a major governmental administration (the Bureau of Social Hygiene in New York City) in 1914; Pauline Chaponnière-Chaix, the first woman to have a seat on the International Committee of the Red Cross in 1922; Paulette Nardal, the first Black student enrolled in the Sorbonne, in the early 1920s; Regina Jones, the first woman rabbi, in the Germany of the 1930s. The career of Simone Veil in the second half of the twentieth century in France was no less remarkable. A magistrate by training, she first officiated over the penitentiary administration, and then the Office de Radiodiffusion-Télévision Française (the government-sponsored radio and television broadcasting service). She then served as a government minister in both the European Parliament and on the

* Carole Christen–Lécuyer, 'Les premières étudiantes de l'Université de Paris', *Travail, genre et sociétés*, Vol. 4, No. 2, 2000, pp. 35–50.

Constitutional Council, before going on to be elected to the French Academy. She was 'a woman in a world of men'.*

One of the last bastions is the world of business. A few multinational corporations, such as Hewlett-Packard, Lockheed Martin, PepsiCo, eBay, General Motors, UPS and YouTube have been headed by women. In France, the royal decree of 1724 denying women access to the Paris Stock Exchange (now Euronext Paris) was only abrogated in the 1960s, and it took two more decades for there to be female traders. Among the twenty-seven countries of the European Union, only 25 per cent of owners of businesses employing workers are women. The domains of military command and space exploration, as well as surgery, are still largely masculine. According to an executive order of 2002, women can serve in all capacities within the French army, except aboard submarines and in certain training positions. Valentina Terechkova of the Soviet Union and Sally Ride of the United States figure among the rare women to have carried out a space flight. In 2012 Liu Yang became the first Chinese woman astronaut. Will the first human being to set foot on Mars be a woman? The march towards equality is far from being completed.

THE VOICE OF WOMEN

From publicly taking the floor to electoral eligibility, the revolutions at the end of the eighteenth century reserved the benefits of democracy for men. Deprived of rights, reduced to a glorious symbolism (the busts of Marianne in France, the Statue of Liberty in New York), women nevertheless engaged in civic and political action.

Women snatched the victory of citizenship in various forms. There was Rousseau's idea of maternity in the 1760s, and the production of ideas and collective actions during the revolutions. Beginning in the nineteenth century, women participated in charitable undertakings

* Anne Chemin, 'Simone Veil, la parole libre d'une femme dans un monde d'hommes', *Le Monde*, 30 June 2017. See also Juliette Rennes, *Le Mérite et la Nature: Une controverse républicaine: l'accès des femmes aux professions de prestige, 1880–1940* (Paris: Fayard, 2007).

and strikes, and then, in the Great War, they served as nurses, sponsors and munitions factory workers. During the Second World War, women played a crucial role in the resistance against Nazi occupation. In the United States, the Grimke sisters, close to Quaker circles, defended both the rights of slaves and of women: in the 1830s, they appealed to Southern Christians and had 20,000 Northern women sign an abolitionist petition. There were even those who spilt blood: Charlotte Corday, who stabbed Marat in 1793; Sofia Perovskaia, who helped organize the assassination of Tsar Alexander II in 1881; and the anarchist Germaine Berton, who executed the leader of the extreme right-wing movement Les Camelots du Roi in 1923. Though excluded by law, women have been able to become 'citizens' by their social and political action.

True citizenship, however, is founded on the civil rights that feminists demanded after the unilateral gains made by men, such the Reform Act of 1832 in Great Britain and universal male suffrage in France in 1848. As soon as the government of the new French Republic declared that 'every Frenchman of virile age is a political citizen', and that 'the right is equal and absolute for all', women protested with petitions and press articles. In *La Voix des femmes* (The Voice of Women), Eugénie Niboyet emphasized the contradiction between democracy and masculine privilege, while Jeanne Deroin attempted to run as a candidate for the Constituent Assembly. The year 1848 was therefore an important moment in feminist consciousness, since there were henceforth two political classes: men and women. Sex had become the principal criterion for civic inclusion (or exclusion).

Like the French Revolution, the Springtime of the Peoples represented both an upheaval and a reinforcement of the patriarchal order. In 1848 and 1849, feminist initiatives (by the Vésuviennes in Paris, Karoline von Perin in Vienna, Mathilde Anneke in Cologne, Louise Dittmar in Leipzig) met with failure, with their newspapers banned after only a few issues. The only one to hold up for a time was the *Journal des femmes* (The Women's Journal) founded by Louise Otto. This was despite the fact that the Parliament of Saxony had quickly passed a measure requiring all newspapers to be headed by men. In Prussia, women were forbidden from belonging to political associations and participating in meetings – which amounted to an exclusion from public life (one that lasted until the beginning of the twentieth century). For its part, the Hamburg university for young women closed its doors after two years. In the United States, however, the convention of Seneca Falls marked only the beginning of struggles for recognition.

Feminists were divided over what path to follow. In Great Britain, Millicent Fawcett's 'suffragists' adhered to a line of peaceful legality, spreading their ideas through rallies, articles, manifestos and petitions (in contrast to the 'radical suffragists', who often came from working class backgrounds). Emmeline Pankhurst's 'suffragettes', however,

A poster for La Fronde, by Clémentine-Hélène Dufau (1898)

The newspaper La Fronde *(The Sling) was founded in 1897 by Marguerite Durand and written entirely by women. Feminist, republican, secular, and defending Dreyfus, the paper campaigned stridently for professional and civic equality. In this advertisement, Clémentine-Hélène Dufau, the former pupil of Bouguereau and a recognized artist, depicted a woman of the bourgeoisie, a female worker and a farming woman, all in solidarity.*

opted for direct, sometimes violent action, harassing government ministers, causing fires and organizing hunger strikes.* In France, the feminist movement was less powerful, but the range of actions undertaken was still considerable. There were female candidates running for election (Léonie Rouzade and Marie-Rose Astié de Valsayre in the 1880s), newspapers founded (*La Citoyenne* in 1881, *La Fronde* in 1897), associations created (the French Union for Women Suffrage in 1909), highly publicized scenes (Hubertine Auclert overturned a ballot box in a voting station in 1908) and also demonstrations (the march of 5 July 1914 in Paris). In *Le Vote des femmes* (Women's Vote) published in 1908, Hubertine Auclert marshalled arguments of various types: women pay their taxes as do men; they are good at managing savings and household budgets; they are presently reduced to the status of colonial subjects and criminals stripped of their rights; women who are single and educated should be able to vote immediately. Her efforts were in vain.

WOMEN CITIZENS

Globally, feminine suffrage was disseminated in three waves. It happened first on a local level in the 1860s, when women were allowed to vote in Bohemia, Sweden, Russia and the state of New South Wales in Australia, as well as in Great Britain and Ireland. Subsequently, British and French women could vote in certain collective or institutional bodies (boards of guardians, school committees, public welfare councils). Whether it was municipal or professional, this right to vote sanctioned the inclusion of women, not their sovereignty. They were recognized as 'citizens' on the basis of domestic competence, which qualified them for handling social matters (schools, hygiene, protection of childhood). This 'domestic citizenship' was the demand of many feminists in Great Britain and in the United States, as well as in Germany and France.

---

* Béatrice Bijon and Claire Delahaye (eds.), *Suffragistes et suffragettes: La conquête du droit de vote des femmes au Royaume-Uni et aux États-Unis* (Lyon: École Normale Supérieure, 2017).

At the end of the nineteenth century, women won the right to vote in the peripheral areas of the anglophone world (in the territories and states of the American West, and in English colonies and dominions): in Wyoming as early as 1869 and in Utah the following year; in New Zealand and Colorado in 1893; in several Australian states beginning in 1894; in Idaho in 1896 and in all of Australia (except for the Aborigines) in 1902. Although New Zealand women were the first to vote at the national level, they had to wait until 1919 to run as candidates.* These victories were due to several factors: not only the political activism of educated feminists, at work on several fronts of social reform, but also the example of the English suffragists and suffragettes, as well as the capacity of these frontier territories for experimentation. In the American states, laws aiming to provide better protection of children and to promote equality within the family and the workplace were passed with the assistance of women.

The third wave occurred in Europe and North America at the beginning of the twentieth century. Women voted at the national level in Finland in 1906, in Norway in 1913, in Denmark in 1915, in Canada in 1917, in Poland, Russia and Great Britain (those 30 and older) in 1918, in Germany in 1919 and in the United States in 1920, followed by almost all of the other nations of the world. In Portugal, suffrage only became universal in 1976, whereas educated women had obtained the right to vote in the 1930s. In Switzerland, women did not become electors at the federal level until 1971, and in the Appenzell cantons, only towards the end of the 1980s. To summarize, we can say that the vast majority of women still did not have the right to vote at the end of the nineteenth century, but secured that right by the end of the twentieth.

In Great Britain and France, the cradles of feminism, women became fully-fledged citizens only in 1928 and 1944, respectively. But the belated character of these two victories conceals some important disparities. The leaders of the Third Republic felt that women were

* Rebecca Rogers, '1893: Le suffrage des femmes en Nouvelle-Zélande' in Pierre Singaravéloui and Sylvain Venayre (eds.), *Histoire du monde au XIXᵉ siècle* (Paris: Fayard, 2017), pp. 356–359.

not autonomous subjects. Under the thumb of priests or already represented by their husbands, they were bound to their physical or mental particularities, prisoners of their sex, far from the abstract individualism required for universal suffrage.* Whereas the French conceived of democracy in a radical 'all or nothing' mode, the British agreed to gradually grant women the right to vote according to their age, marital status and the type of election. In both countries, however, the men in power tended to minimize the role of the feminists and presented suffrage as a 'reward' granted to women for their domestic virtues or their participation in the war effort.

Once they had become citizens, women were slowly integrated into political life because men were not ready to make a place for them within the government, and also because they had a hard time getting elected, as shown by the failure of the lists of women in Sweden during the interwar years. The first women to serve as government ministers were Margaret Bondfield in Great Britain in 1929 and Frances Perkins in the United States in 1933: both were put in charge of Labour ministries. In France, the governmental team of the Popular Front included three female undersecretaries of state (in National Education, Scientific Research and Protection of Childhood) in 1936, even though they could not even vote. In 1974, Simone Veil entered the government as Minister of Health, with Françoise Giroud in charge of the Ministry of the Feminine Condition. But even when they became government ministers, women remained for the most part confined to their habitual specialized domains, in Europe as well as in Africa and India: social welfare, rights of women, water, environment. It was only at the end of the twentieth century that elected legislative bodies began to be feminized.

The most revealing factor is the exercise of sovereign power. Aside from queens, several women served as their country's leader in the second half of the twentieth century: Sri Lanka's Sirimavo Bandaranaike in 1950, India's Indira Gandhi in 1966 and again in 1980, Israel's Golda Meir in 1969, the United Kingdom's Margaret Thatcher in 1979, the Philippines' Cory Aquino in 1986, Pakistan's Benazir Bhutto in

* Pierre Rosanvallon, *Le Sacre du citoyen: Histoire du suffrage universel en France* (Paris: Gallimard/Folio histoire, 1992), pp. 519–545.

Proportion of seats occupied by women in national legislative assemblies (1990–2014).

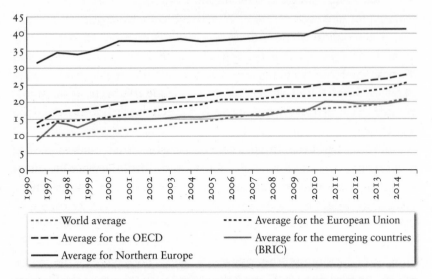

Worldwide, the proportion of women occupying a seat in a legislative assembly doubled, going from 9 per cent to 20 per cent in twenty-five years. Only the Northern European countries, however, are approaching parity. Progress has therefore been undeniable, but limited, particularly in the emerging countries (Brazil, Russia, India and China).*

1988, Turkey's Tansu Çiller in 1993. The movement accelerated in the twenty-first century in countries as different as Indonesia, Finland, Germany, Chile, Liberia, Iceland, Kyrgyzstan, South Korea and New Zealand. Women have served as ministers for the army in Sweden, the Netherlands, Germany and France.

There is a tradition of women as head of state in two regions of the world: Northern Europe and the Indian subcontinent (although this is almost always in the context of dynastic families remaining in power for decades). Nevertheless, between the 1950s and the beginning of the 2010s, less than 5 per cent of the planet's national leaders were women, and among them, one third came to power at the death

* United Nations MDG (Millennium Development Goals) indicators, 2014.

of their husband or as an interim.* No woman has served as minister of defence or finance in Great Britain. The United States and France have never had a woman president.

BODILY LIBERTY

After civil rights and citizenship, the struggle has focused on sexual rights, which give women control over their bodies. From the nineteenth century on, feminists have led the struggle against the double standard that has the liberty of men coexisting with the subjugation of women. Between 1869 and 1886, in Great Britain, Josephine Butler and more than two million petitioners demanded the abrogation of laws on contagious diseases, which authorized the control and incarceration of prostitutes in view of protecting the health of sailors.

In the nineteenth century, rape was seldom punished: police suspicions focused more on the victim than on the aggressor. In the United States, the rape of a slave or a Black woman was not prosecuted. If the victim was a white woman, however, the attacker theoretically risked the death penalty (until the ruling on *Coker* vs *Georgia* in 1977). In France, the penal code of 1810 sanctioned the 'crime of rape,' but without defining it, and many sexual assaults were considered as acts of lewdness and put aside. In 1857, the Dubas integrated the notions of constraint or surprise into jurisprudence. It was only from the 1970s onward that rape was seen as a particularly serious crime, thanks to the struggle of feminists such as Gisèle Halimi (parallel to the work of Susan Brownmiller and Kate Millett in the United States). After the 1978 trial of three men (first prosecuted for 'assault and battery', before finally being brought before a criminal trial court), who were accused of having raped two female campers in the Marseille Calanques area, the law of 1980 finally defined the crime of rape with precision.

Bodily rights go far beyond protection against violence. In the nineteenth century, clothing constituted a daily reminder of the stark inequality between the sexes. In the well-to-do bourgeoisie, men could

* Kathleen Phillips et al., 'Ethnic Diversity, Gender, and National Leaders', *Journal of International Affairs*, Vol. 67, No. 1, 2013, pp. 85—104.

be content with the austerity of plain black attire, while women were shackled to highly complex manners of dress, often requiring long preparation – not only for clothing, but for jewellery and hairstyles. Petticoats, crinolines, hoop skirts, corsets and trains put pressure on the feminine body and bent in sometimes unbearable ways. The vast disparity between men and women in the area of clothing only gradually began to disappear from the late nineteenth century onwards.

Sport justifies the wearing of adapted outfits that free the body, a physical deliverance symbolized by tennis player Suzanne Lenglen and

Annette Kellermann (1916)

Born in Australia in 1887, Annette Kellermann learned how to swim as a child because of health concerns. She became a swimming and diving champion, pioneered synchronized swimming, and created a scandal in 1907 by wearing a one-piece bathing suit. She became a movie star, and shocked the public again by appearing nude in A Daughter of the Gods *(1916).*

swimming champion Annette Kellermann. In Germany, gymnastics was cautiously opened to women; the theorist Moritz Kloss recommended that they be given constant care however, in view of their supposed fragility. There were nevertheless a million women practising *Turnen* (gymnastics) in the early twentieth century. At the sports contest of the 1900 World's Fair (officially recognized by the Olympic Games), women only made up 2 per cent of athletes, and were limited to a few competitions such as swimming, tennis and croquet. It would not be until the Olympic Games of 1928 that they were authorized to compete in track and field events.

Women liberated themselves not only by wearing clothing that relaxes the body, easing its contours, but also by adopting simpler and more practical masculine clothing. In 1851, Amelia Bloomer borrowed from a friend the idea of baggy pants tightened at the ankles, partially covered by a skirt: the bloomer style, which provided freedom of movement while concealing the legs, and became wildly fashionable in the United States, thanks to the newspaper *The Lily*. Eager to fight taboos and prohibitions (in 1800, a Parisian woman could be arrested for dressing as a man), avant-garde feminists in France hailed the wearing of trousers. This was the challenge offered by George Sand, by the writer and duellist Gisèle d'Estoc, as well as by the socialist Madeleine Pelletier, who put on black trousers with a cane and top hat: 'My suit tells men: I am your equal.'*

Over the course of the twentieth century, women's dress drew nearer to that of men. Certain women workers took to wearing men's clothes during the First World War. In the 1920s, the style of the flappers (*la mode garçonne* in France, *Bubikopf* in Austria), which combined androgynous contours with short hair, ties and trouser suits, went well beyond physical appearance: it challenged the order of gender by committing to a new lifestyle, one that suggested sexual choice and freedom of expression. In this sense, fashion designers such as Coco Chanel and actors such as Louise Brooks worked for the emancipation of women.

After the Second World War, trousers became a part of the feminine wardrobe in Europe. They came in the form of the *frac*, the tailcoat

* Christine Bard, *Une histoire politique du pantalon* (Paris: Seuil, 2010), pp. 112 ff and 237.

style created by Christian Dior; the trouser suit of Yves Saint Laurent; and jeans imported from the United States. This was despite the fact that trousers were still forbidden in many lycées up until the 1970s. Parallel to this masculinization of outfits, dresses and skirts became shorter at the instigation of Courrèges, among others. For some, ready-to-wear clothing and cosmetics were instruments of self-affirmation. As Helena Rubinstein, a Jewish émigré from Poland who created an industrial empire in the early twentieth century, loved to say, 'Beauty is power.'

SEXUAL REVOLUTIONS

The end of the moral double standard was predicated on women taking charge of their sexuality, instead of letting men (from Fallope to Freud) appropriate it for themselves through their learning and their morality (as in the Victorian era).

In the early twentieth century, a first revolution took place in the United States, Germany and Sweden. It featured several components. The progress of sexual education and the normalization of masturbation, recommended first by the American gynaecologist Alice Stockham, was key, as was the spreading practice of 'erotic play' – which consisted of reciprocal kissing and caressing. The struggle for the recognition of lesbians, born from the initiative of Helene Stöcker and Anna Rüling, was also a vital aspect of this revolution. Out of the 2,200 American women that Katherine Davis questioned at the end of the 'flapper decade' in 1929, 90 per cent approved of contraception, 85 per cent were in favour of non-procreative sexual pleasure, while 65 per cent of single women and 40 per cent of those married accepted the idea of masturbation. Sex had become an integral part of a happy marriage.*

A second revolution occurring in those same countries made it possible to bring down censorship and taboos in the 1960s. The works of William Masters and Virginia Johnson, summarized in their bestselling *Human Sexual Response* (1966) and extended by Anne Koedt

* 'Katherine Davis' in Jerrold Greenberg et al. (eds.), *Exploring the Dimensions of Human Sexuality*, Sixth Edition (Burlington: Johnes & Bartlett Learning, 2017), p. 41.

in *The Myth of the Vaginal Orgasm* (1970) revolutionized the understanding of feminine pleasure by demonstrating its clitoral basis, which made it possible to correct Freud's mistakes. In 1962, the German pilot Beate Uhse opened the first sex shop in the world, specializing in products for 'the hygiene of the couple', in Flensburg.

Progress in contraception was conducive to these revolutions in sexual pleasure. In Sweden, feminist activist Elise Ottesen-Jensen taught lower-class women to use diaphragms and condoms, and then founded the Swedish Association for Sexuality Education, which disseminated advice on health, hygiene and birth control. Birth control was developed in Great Britain and the United States from the 1920s on the initiative of Helena Rosa Wright and Margaret Sanger. For these pioneers, it was not so much about democratizing the orgasm as allowing women to conceive their children intentionally and in love, within a happy marriage: all so that women's sex lives might cause them less anxiety. Their action, which ran up against numerous types of opposition, was based in private clinics and organizations such as the American Birth Control League, founded in 1921. They became organized into a worldwide network, the International Planned Parenthood Federation, founded in 1952 by Elise Ottesen-Jensen.

The right to abortion was one of the great feminist struggles of the second half of the twentieth century. In Germany, abortion was formerly punished by a heavy prison sentence, as it was in France following the enactment of the penal code of 1791, worsened by a law of 1920 (a backstreet abortionist was even guillotined under the Occupation). Since abortions were illegal, they were carried out in conditions dangerous to women's lives: only the wealthiest could afford to go abroad. In 1956, the former member of the Resistance Évelyne Sullerot and the gynaecologist Marie-Andrée Lagroua Weill-Hallé founded La Maternité Heureuse (Happy Maternity), predecessor of the French Movement for Family Planning, in order to 'fight against clandestine abortions, ensure the psychological equilibrium of the couple and improve the health of mothers and children'.

Abortion was legalized in Soviet Russia then prohibited under Stalin, then once again authorized in the USSR in 1955. Bulgaria, Hungary, Poland, Romania and Czechoslovakia followed suit shortly after, well before Great Britain (1967) and the United States (1973).

In France, the law decriminalizing abortion was promulgated in 1975, as the result of an intensive mobilization. This included the Manifesto of the 343 (women admitting to having had an abortion), Choisir la Cause des Femmes (Choose the Women's Cause), the Mouvement pour la Liberté de l'Avortement et de la Contraception (Movement for the Freedom of Abortion and Contraception), depositions by eminent personalities and Gisèle Halimi's argument for the defence in the Bobigny trial (a teenager who aborted after being raped), as well as the courage and political acumen of Simone Veil in the National Assembly. The debate was just as heated in the Federal Republic of Germany, marked by the appeal of 193 members of parliament and five Länder to block the law of 1974, thereby bringing about its provisional suspension by the Constitutional Court.*

The right to work, to a career, to get out of the patriarchal circle without being despised, to participate in the affairs of the body politic, to vote, to physical integrity, to freedom of movement: feminism concretely enacted the 1789 revolution of rights. Among them, the sexual and reproductive rights won in the second half of the twentieth century constituted not only a social revolution, but also an anthropological break. Women's control over childbirth restored to them the property of their bodies. This victory proclaimed the equality of the sexes even more loudly than the Declaration of the Rights of Man. With contraception and abortion, women finally had their habeas corpus.†

---

* Christina Ottomeyer-Hervieu, 'L'avortement en RFA', *Les Cahiers du CEDREF*, Nos. 4–5, 1995, pp. 103–109.
† Geneviève Fraisse, 'L'habeas corpus des femmes: une double révolution?' in Étienne-Émile Baulieu, Françoise Héritier and Henri Léridon (eds.), *Contraception, contrainte ou liberté?* (Paris: Odile Jacob, 1999), pp. 53–60.

6

What Is Emancipation?

In 1970, feminist activists published an issue of the French journal *Partisans* titled 'The Year Zero of the Liberation of Women', wiping two centuries of reflections and struggles off the slate. The politically committed folk singer Joan Baez celebrated women's sexual freedom in 'Love Song to a Stranger' (1972) and the combativity of women workers in 'Bread and Roses' (1974). When asked 'Are you a feminist?' almost half a century later, she replied: 'Not really. I never had to fight as a woman.'*

To say that feminists do not always agree with each other is an understatement. There is nothing surprising about that: feminism was an immense undertaking that sought to overcome numerous challenges. It was only natural that it should split up into different, sometimes rival factions. On a deeper level, these antagonisms reveal an ambiguity and an uncertainty. The ambiguity stems from the fact that feminism is not an organization, but a loose network made up of a great number of movements, strains of thought, and personalities: no single one can embody feminism by itself. The uncertainty exists because it is not easy to determine feminism's ultimate goal. Does it seek to promote the status and dignity of women, equality between the sexes, parity at every level, the destruction of patriarchy, the dissolution of gender? As important as the debate may be, it is not vital: the fragmentation of the various strains of feminism has not prevented the solidarity of women in any country.

* Interview with Joan Baez, 'Trump m'inspire', *Le Point*, No. 2374, 1 March 2018.

THE TWO FAMILIES OF FEMINISM

The history of feminism is commonly divided into three successive 'waves', according to Frances Power Cobbe's marine metaphor. The first wave extended from the nineteenth to the first part of the twentieth century, ushering in the right to work along with civil and political equality. The second stretched from the 1960s to the 1980s, sweeping away social inequity and the skewed distribution of household chores, the denial of sexual rights, the machismo that kills. The third wave supposedly began in the late twentieth century, raising the issue of gender and the demands of minorities. With the #MeToo movement, we have presumably entered into the fourth wave.

It is not hard to expose the flaws of that chronology. Most eighteenth-century feminists denounced the tyranny of marriage and educational discrimination: Olympe de Gouges demanded that women have the right to divorce and obtain access to all positions of employment. In the early twentieth century, Madeleine Pelletier had already raised the question of gender identities, while Nelly Roussel had demanded the right to contraception. The scourges of sexual violence, unequal pay, menstrual exclusion and denial of the right to abortion continue to mobilize women throughout the world. On many points, Simone de Beauvoir remains our contemporary. The supposed opposition between the French 'universalist' feminists and the American 'radical' feminists is incapable of giving a just account of the thought of Monique Wittig, Luce Irigaray and Hélène Cixous, whose influence has been enormous in the United States. Rather than speaking of waves, we might, following Karen Offen, describe the history of feminism in volcanic terms, with the patriarchal crust being regularly fissured by irruptions and lava flows.

It is more stimulating to let the polarities structuring feminism stand out. Simplifying complex, evolving systems of thought, we can distinguish a *feminism of equality*, which postulates the fundamental identity between men and women on the basis of their common humanity, from a *feminism of difference*, which emphasizes the specificity of women, the feminine and the maternal. While both feminisms agree on fighting against injustices and discrimination, the former seeks to bring about the emancipation of all women and men in the tradition of the Enlightenment, while the latter organizes the resistance of a group in the face of masculine domination. Harmony and understanding between the sexes grounded in the thirst for justice, or struggle between the sexes as a response to oppression? A society of equals or the separatism of combat?

The first approach posits not only that women are equal to men, but also that, regardless of their biological specificity, they are identical in intelligence, rights and duties. Women should not always be reduced to their 'condition': except for certain very precise situations, they do not lead their lives as women, but as individuals. This feminism places its hopes in cooperation between the sexes within a democratic society, and in the context of a mutually beneficial heterosexuality, on the explicit condition that women and men hold equal rights in an atmosphere of reciprocal respect.

The Second Sex ends with a call to 'fraternity' between men and women: what makes equality possible is the relative unimportance of sex ('one is not born a woman'). For her part, Moroccan sociologist Fatima Mernissi declares: 'Only if men and women work together, and if men use women's brains, can they succeed.'* American feminist Nancy Fraser argues for a 'parity in participation,' in which all members of a society could interact as pairs, because they would enjoy the same recognition and an equal distribution of wealth.

At the beginning of the twentieth century, socialist feminists fought alongside men for the emancipation of the working class. Clara Zetkin headed the newspaper *Die Gleichheit* (Equality) and in 1907 organized the first International Conference of Women Socialists, in Stuttgart, on the fringes of the conference of the Second International. In 1910, she succeeded in establishing the principle of an International Day of Women (generally set for 8 March).† In keeping with Marxist materialism, Christine Delphy and Colette Guillaumin considered sex to be only a social category produced by patriarchal economy and 'relations of sexage'. Because of masculine exploitation, women were

---

* Undated interview available at www.francetvinfo.fr/societe/religion/fatima-memissi-sociologue-et-feministe-marocaine_2568461.html
† Nicole Gabriel, 'L'International des femmes socialistes', *Matériaux pour l'histoire de notre temps*, No. 16, 1989, pp. 34–41.

prisoners of class destiny, and it was up to the oppressed to put an end to their oppression. Regardless of its 'bourgeois' or 'revolutionary' character, the force of this strain of feminism is in the universality of its moral position and its egalitarian radicality.

The second approach, that of differentialist feminism, posits the physiological and moral specificity of women as ontologically distinct from men. Women have their own perspective on the world, diffracted through a feminine experience, consciousness, solidarity, sexuality, writing, and even, for Carol Gilligan and Nel Noddings, a feminine ethic.

The 'laugh of the medusa', as Hélène Cixous put it, makes it possible to escape the patriarchal logos. Imbued with psychoanalysis, Antoinette Fouque's feminism marvels at women's capacity to give life: there are two opposite sexes, and this split allows a break from the male subject's 'monos', which are always expressed in oppressive forms: monotheism, monarchy, humanism, the Republic one and indivisible, and so on. Andrea Dworkin speaks of women and men as if they belonged to two different species: prey and predators. Man uses woman, the mother of a family or a prostitute, through her vagina, in a degrading sexual relation that reflects his hate for her. Masculine power has several weapons available for terrorizing women: pornography, rape, the penis, the sexuality of pleasure or reproduction, in a 'continuum of phallic control' aiming to objectivize women.

In this feminism, feminine essence precedes the existence of women. The identity of each sex is by nature: the biological predestination of women is redeemed by a new combative femininity. Feminine positivity must resist masculine negativity, which is bred in the 'culture of rape' or 'uterus envy'. Male oppressors and female victims: two barricaded universes. In this sense, one cannot escape one's condition. This feminism draws its strength from its critical power and intransigence in the face of all forms of domination.

MATERNALIST FEMINISM

One might think this 'identity-based' approach to be characteristic of an extreme left-wing radical feminism. Viewed over the centuries, however, this current is in fact not only in the majority, but also compatible with the bourgeoisie of the right, which posits the exceptional biological and moral status of women as the basis of their citizenship. Between the gift of life and love for others, their aptitude for caring justifies women's participation in public affairs, and it is primarily due to their maternal, nurturing and social virtues that they deserve rights: without women, the definition of the public good would be incomplete.

In Germany, the notion of *Mütterlichkeit*, women's spiritual sentiment of maternity, tied together the various feminist movements throughout the nineteenth century up until the aftermath of the First World War. It inspired, for example, Henriette Schrader-Breymann, a pedagogue involved in the kindergarten movement and the education of girls after 1848, and also Louise Otto, who defended the 'true femininity' in her newspaper *Neue Bahnen* (New Ways). Founded in 1865, this publication of the National Association of German Women became the crucible of modern feminism, although Louise Otto never failed to praise the family mother.*

We find the same tendency in the English-speaking world: one of the great struggles of American, Australian and New Zealand feminists was the fight against alcohol, as shown by the worldwide ramifications of the Women's Christian Temperance Union from 1874 on. Other causes also mobilized women. In 1909, the campaign for the regulation of the milk industry in Massachusetts was led by Elizabeth Putnam, who mourned the death of her infant after it had ingested tainted milk. Women engaged in civic action not only as spouses and mothers, but also as consumers. Their social rights had to be complemented by economic rights, which meant defending their purchasing power, activating associations and favouring ethical commerce. In the United States of the first part of the twentieth century, women citizens invented the politics of public-minded consumers.†

In the same era, French women were availing themselves of

---

* Ann Taylor Allen, *Feminism and Motherhood in Germany, 1800–1914* (New Brunswick: Rutgers University Press, 1991); and Alice Primi, 'Le journal Neue Bahnen entre 1866 et 1870' in Patrick Farges and Anne-Marie Saint-Gille (eds.), *Le Premier Féminisme allemand, 1848–1933* (Villeneuve d'Ascq: Presses Universitaires de Septentrion, 2013), pp. 19–32.

† Lizabeth Cohen, *A Consumers' Republic: The Politics of Mass Consumption in Postwar America* (New York: Knopf, 2003).

differentialist arguments: engaged in tasks that men were incapable of carrying out, they were both worthy of public affairs and capable of contributing to progress in society. For Jeanne Deroin, the mother fulfilled sacred functions, ensuring the future of her children and the general imparting of love: the state was a 'great household' that she would administer like her own. Léonie Rouzade, the socialist, pacifist, and member of the Solidarity of Women, defended the idea that maternity should be subsidized by the state, since it was 'the first of social functions'.*

For French upper-class women, religious and charitable activities served as a substitute for voting and salaried employment, and offered them more than citizenship in society: the role of representing France before God. Led by priests who claimed a political role for themselves in the manner of Queen Clotilde and Joan of Arc, numerous feminine associations took on the project of the construction of the Sacré-Coeur Basilica in Paris in the 1870s. This conservative Catholic feminism ensured a civic function for women in the domains neglected by the young Republic: the education of girls and care for the poor. These ladies extended their patronage in view of having everyone benefit from the care that they lavished on their own families: it was an apolitical way of engaging in politics. In the early twentieth century, the League of French Women and the Patriotic League of Frenchwomen figured among the most powerful organizations in the country, with several hundred thousand members.†

These women reformers were transforming the woman function from private responsibility into public policy. Hygiene, temperance, home values, kindergarten, care for the poor, social welfare and consumer goods that nurture: maternalism has been one of the main vectors of feminism throughout the world, and it has proved to be

* Anne Cova, *Maternité et droits des femmes en France (XIXᵉ–XXᵉ siècle)* (Paris: Anthropos, 1997), p. 78.
† Jacques Benoist, *Le Sacré-Coeur des femmes de 1870 à 1960: Contribution à l'histoire du féminisme, de l'urbanisme et du tourisme* (Paris: Éditions ouvrières, 2000); and Bruno Dumons, 'Mobilisation politique et ligues féminines dans la France catholique du début du siècle', *Vingtième Siècle. Revue d'histoire*, No. 73, 2002, pp. 39–50.

Tract of the French Union for Women's Suffrage (1935)

WHAT SHOULD THE AGENDA FOR FRENCH WOMEN BE?

On the municipal level

France must become a totally clean, healthy, and beautiful country thanks to women...

A model urban district must be clean. It must have:

1. Water in sufficient quantity for every household, and a monitored garbage dump.
2. A covered wash house.
3. A covered market.
4. A dispensary.
5. A nursery school.
6. Social workers charged with tracing infectious diseases...
7. Kindergarten.

On a general level

– For women:

Certain reforms in the Civil Code, such as:

1. The modification of Article 213, which does not give the wife her rightful place.
2. The elimination of Article 215, in order to allow her to testify freely in court, to the extent that the interests of the family are being neglected...
4. The equality of morality that would make the commercialization of vice disappear.
5. The employment of women in certain services of the police...

– For the family:

1. The fight against social evils [immorality, alcoholism, shanty towns, tuberculosis, syphilis].
2. The improvement of housing for workers in urban and rural areas.
3. An application of Sunday off made as wide as possible.
4. A practical organization of the social welfare and hygiene.

Archives of the Aube Department, 21 J 931

crucial in opening civic action to women. These new roles did more to get women out of the house than did the right to vote.*

MATERNALISM, PACIFISM AND ECOFEMINISM

National controversies led to international struggles. At the beginning of the twentieth century, feminism was associated with pacifism, driven by mothers not wanting to see their children become cannon fodder. In France, Gabrielle Petit founded the paper *La Femme affranchie* (The Emancipated Woman) in 1904, and was convicted of anti-militarism. After her break with the suffragists in Great Britain, from 1915 Helena Swanwick led the activities of the British section of the International League of Women for Peace and Liberty. In the early 1980s, women activists from the Greenham Common camp in England and from Seneca, New York, protested as women and mothers against the presence of nuclear weapons, which they framed as symbols of patriarchal militarism.

In Sweden, the theme of the 'life-woman', a guardian of the great equilibriums of nature, inspired the Fogelstad group in the 1930s. Elin Wägner proposed a synthesis of feminism, respect for the environment and ancient matriarchal cultures. On the eve of the Second World War, her political activity took an anti-fascist turn in *Peace With the Earth* (1940), co-authored with Elisabeth Tamm.† The thought of Ellen Key (the social centrality of maternity, the strength of the mother–child relationship, love as a moral ideal) influenced Japanese feminists in the first half of the twentieth century. For the poet Hiratsuka Raichō, as for the female historian Takamure Itsue, the mother maintained intimate ties not only with her child, but also with nature: this proximity nourished the dream of a return to the original matriarchy, purified of

---

* Seth Koven and Sonya Michel, 'Womanly Duties: Maternalist Politics and the Origins of Welfare States in France, Germany, Great Britain, and the United States, 1880–1920', *The American Historical Review*, Vol. 95, No. 4, October 1990, pp. 1076–1108.
† Carolyn Merchant and Abby Peterson, '"Peace with the Earth": Women and the Environmental Movement in Sweden', *Women's Studies International Forum*, Vol. 9, No. 5–6, 1986, pp. 465–479.

all Chinese influence. After 1931, in accordance with these beliefs, Itsue withdrew to a house deep in the woods.*

In sub-Saharan Africa, 'survival' feminism consists of ensuring the supply of food, securing property, winning better working conditions, and seeking peace and interethnic understanding, in order to face the economic crises and dysfunctions of the state, from which women are the first to suffer. In the Ivory Coast, women from the middle class and the lower middle class, in 1977, founded the Cocody Group for the Promotion of Cultural Activities. Their goal was to improve everyday life, by creating better public transport systems and by lowering local prices, through the use of neighbourhood networks. Similarly, in urban areas of Zambia, the 'feminization of poverty' drove family mothers to take action in order to earn money, feed their children, obtain credit, and so on.†

In the last quarter of the twentieth century, maternalism evolved into 'ecofeminism', to use the expression formulated by Maria Mies and Vandana Shiva in 1993. Charged with guaranteeing the survival of the group by cultivating the earth, searching for water and firewood, cooking, raising children and forming emotional bonds, women preserve life against the destruction caused by masculine capitalism. Ecofeminism makes it possible, then, to resist the dual oppression of both nature and women by men. Several actions demonstrated the efficacy of feminine mobilization: the Chipko movement in India and the Green Belt Movement in Kenya in the 1970s aimed to protect local forests, and the Collective of Women's Groups for the Protection of Nature was formed in Senegal. In 1992, the Earth Summit in Rio de Janeiro recognized the competence of women in preserving natural resources and implementing sustainable development.‡

Maternalism was therefore not consigned to oblivion by the arrival

---

* Pierre-François Souyri, 'Takamure Itsue (1894–1964), une pionnière de l'histoire des femmes au Japon' in André Burguière and Bernard Vincent (eds.), *Un siècle d'historiennes* (Paris: Des Femmes, 2014), pp. 281–293.

† Gwendolyn Mikell (ed.), *African Feminism: The Politics of Survival in Sub-Saharan Africa* (Philadelphia: University of Pennsylvania Press, 1997), pp. 142 and 206 ff in particular.

‡ Édith Sizoo, *Par-delà le féminisme* (Paris: ECLM, 2003); and Laura Pérez Prieto, 'Contre le capitalisme hétéropatriarcal et destructeur de l'environnement: l'écoféminisme critique,' *Passerelle*, No. 17, June 2017, pp. 68–74.

of Simone de Beauvoir's egalitarian views. It has in fact been maternalism that has provided the link between feminisms of the North and those of the South, and between the movements in the Americas and those of the Far East, disproving the frequently heard notion that emancipation is supposedly the privilege of Western women. From Christian altruism to the struggles of ecofeminism, maternalism has won for women what men had refused them. To that extent, it is one of the most stable structures of feminism on a worldwide level.

But this progress may conceal a regression. Being peaceful and peacemaking, driven by their empathy and their closeness to nature, women have been essentialized. At that point, there is a problem that differentialist feminism does not solve: the perennial character of the patriarchal circle. Although it is true that the experience of maternity and the family can open social horizons for women, they nevertheless remain stuck in the woman function, where patriarchy dreams of forever assigning them according to the 'duties of their sex'. How, then, is it possible to know whether the politicization of the mothering function does not simply conform to the logic of the system, which accepts these activities outside the household simply because women continue to tend and nourish the collective? The ambiguity remains: women's aptitude for nurturing can indeed qualify women for dealing with public affairs, but it can just as well limit their lives to forever caring for men and children.

Since the feminism of difference grows out of feminine and maternal elements consistent with patriarchal thought, where women are supposed to have a 'natural' inclination towards caring for others, it is less disruptive to the overall structure of gender. Egalitarian feminism, however, leads women to assail bastions held by men, quite simply because they are equally capable. What is at stake here is the chance to follow one's ambition by taking on such leadership roles in the pursuit of knowledge or creativity. Better to live as a human being than rule as a woman.

THE UNITY OF FEMINISMS

Simone de Beauvoir does not think like Carol Gilligan. In France, the MLF (Mouvement de Libération des Femmes, or Women's Liberation

Movement) split up in the late 1970s. Feminists in Africa and Asia could understandably feel abandoned by Western feminists who depict them as more or less backward 'women of the Third World'.* In order to prevent feminism from weakening itself with sisterly hatred, and to avoid giving the impression that there would be as many fights as there are cultures and religions, we must emphasize what women activists all over the planet have in common. Beyond centuries and borders, a *unity of feminists* exists: they engage in a universal struggle for equality and justice.

The first thing they have in common is the affirmation of the woman as a free, autonomous person in charge of herself. Whether they live in a metropolis in India, a village in Kenya or on a college campus in the United States, women have the same dignity, aptitudes and rights as men, and no one has the authority to silence them on the pretext that they are supposedly biologically or intellectually inferior.

In the Chinese province of Guangdong, there was a wave of protests against marriage in the early nineteenth century: refusing submission to a husband, peasant and working-class women preferred to live in homes for young girls. A century later, the young woman poet Qiu Jin opposed the Manchu regime, and left her husband and children because the revolution had to begin in households. Having gone to Japan in 1904, she returned to her country and became a teacher in an elementary school for girls. As a local leader of Sun Yat-Sen's party, she was executed in 1907 for plotting against the government. In her *Stones of the Jingwei Bird*, published fifty years after her death, Qiu Jin exhorts women to refuse submission, get out of their homes, find a profession and be independent though in solidarity with other women, making the 'commitment to save those among our sisters who are suffering'. Feminism consists of choosing the life that one wants to lead.

The second thing feminists have in common is their persistence in voicing demands. At the basis of all activism is the observation that 'this is not right', a feeling of iniquity that produces a revolt and sparks conflict, calls to action and the demand for rights. This struggle

---

* Chandra Mohanty, 'Under Western Eyes: Feminist Scholarship and Colonial Discourses', *Feminist Review*, No. 30, Autumn 1988, pp. 61–88.

consists of calling attention to both women and the injustices they have endured. For this reason, it shakes up the established order, and that is one more difference between the feminism that arose out of the Atlantic revolutions and the friendly cordiality among male and female socialites in the salons of the Ancien Régime. Feminism consists of refusing to 'play the game'.

This refusal necessarily causes a scandal: Amelia Bloomer making trousers for herself in 1851; Huda Sharawi, founder of the Egyptian Feminist Union, publicly taking off her veil in 1923 ; Manoubia Ouertani, who went up to the podium bare-headed and denounced the oppression of Tunisian women at a conference on feminism in 1924; Christine Delphy, Christiane Rochefort, Monique Wittig and the others who in 1970 went to place flowers on the tomb of the unknown soldier in Paris in honour of his wife; the 'Femen' showing their bare breasts inscribed with slogans defending the rights of women.

Once a woman refuses to 'remain in her place,' in the shadow of men, within a timeless tradition, she commits an act of insubordination. All feminism is an attack on the gendered order of the family, a threat to the stability of society. Every feminist is a rebel, the term that Angelica Balabanoff (a social-democrat activist close to Clara Zetzkin and a member of the Women Socialists International at the beginning of the twentieth century) chose for her autobiography. That is the reason why one cannot set reformist feminism against revolutionary feminism, in the same way that one cannot oppose maternalism and egalitarianism. All feminism is radical. Every feminist is scandalous.

The third thing feminists have in common is their collective dimension. Since the end of the eighteenth century, feminism has been expressed through petitions, newspapers, journals, demonstrations, associations and hashtags: the Seneca Falls convention in 1848, International Women's Rights Conventions beginning in 1878, the International Council of Women created in the United States in 1888, the International Woman Suffrage Alliance in the early twentieth century, the London suffragist Mud March in 1907, the Union of French Women created in 1944 (which grew to reach the Antilles), the magazine Ms. founded by Dorothy Pitman Hughes and Gloria Steinem in New York in 1974, the Ni Una Menos (Not One Less) campaign in several Latin American countries after 2015, the #MeToo movement from 2017.

This public, federative expression is obviously not uniquely Western. As early as the beginning of the twentieth century, the press was the weapon of feminism in Egypt (with *Al Fatah* in 1892), in Turkey (*The Women's Journal* in 1895), in Iran (*Knowledge* in 1910), as well as in China, where three or four newspapers were created each year between 1903 and 1907 at the initiative of woman intellectuals such as Chen Xiefen and Chen Qin. In Japan, the journal *Seitō* (Bluestocking) was created in 1911 by former students of Japan Women's University, and denounced patriarchal oppression, voicing the aspirations of the 'new woman' in themes such as love, sexuality and literature.*

All these examples show why feminism is joyful. The feminism of the 1960s and 1970s cannot be reduced to slogans, and certainly not to personal conflicts. Its finest success was the collective liberation that it enabled and that can be seen in the itineraries of the feminists' daughters, who have become economists, documentary film-makers, teachers and lawyers. The daughter of Swiss film director Carole Roussopoulos thinks back on her childhood:

> Much laughter, conversation. All these women of the MLF were after all loudmouths, but they were very nice to me, showering me with compliments. My mother is someone who takes up a lot of space: she is exuberant, she has charisma, but she is also someone who is very generous. That is my vision of feminism.†

The theoretical quarrels among the various currents of feminism are therefore less interesting than the emancipation to which, together, they lead. Is ecologist senator Larissa Waters, who was the first legislator to nurse her child during a session of the Australian Federal Parliament on 9 May 2017, a symbol for the feminism of equality or the feminism of difference? The same question applies to the French writer Virginie Despentes, whose neo-warrior feminism is capable of turning male violence against its perpetrators. Her denunciation of

---

* Jacqueline Nivard, 'L'évolution de la presse féminine chinoise de 1898 à 1949', *Études chinoises*, Vol. 5, Nos. 1–2, 1896, pp. 157–184; and Christine Lévy, 'Féminisme et genre au Japon', *Ebisu*, No. 48, Fall–Winter 2012, pp. 7–27.
† Cited by Virginie Linhart, *Le jour où mon père s'est tu* (Paris: Seuil. 'Points', 2008), p. 137.

rape, her affirmation of sexual liberty, her use of radical language and her mix of pessimism and humour blur boundary lines, and contribute to her work's liberating sense of strength.

A pragmatic approach consists in fighting against all conditions of subordination and discrimination. There is a clear feminist practice in gaining equality of the sexes in education, employment and public affairs, and in the normalization of the feminine body, especially in regard to pregnancy and maternal health, as well as in the validation of female sexual choice and expression.

Emancipation consists in gaining rights for oneself and for others – not only the right to work, to vote, to love, to have or not have children, but also the right to lead one's life as one wants, to be free without this freedom coming at the cost of violence. In a context of subordination, feminism aims to *obtain the greatest extent of rights for women, including the right to get out of the patriarchal circle.* This universal quest rises above cultures, traditions and religions: it projects the feminine toward a horizon of freedom and equality.

7

Feminist Men

Since the late eighteenth century, women who dare to call themselves feminists have been a minority in many countries around the world. Feminist men are an ultra-minority. Why? Is it out of prudence, or because of indifference, blindness, scorn or misogyny? Or is it a fear of betraying the established order of gender? It must be said that a feminist man is often exposed to women's disbelief, and to men's hostility. In the late nineteenth century, when the French activist Hubertine Auclert asked Alexandre Dumas *fils* if he would preside over the Women's Suffrage Society, his response was pitiful: 'I will be of greater assistance to you by remaining independent. If I accepted the presidency that you offer me, they would say to me, "You are with Hubertine Auclert," and no one would listen to me at the French Academy any more.'*

REASONS FOR BEING
A FEMINIST ALLY

What people might say is not the main thing. Because ultimately, it is not easy to know what a feminist man is or could be: a 'nice' husband, an 'enlightened' father, a man who speaks to women without contempt, who fights alongside them? But women do not need to be assisted in the struggles that they have carried out very well by themselves. As for praise ('my wife is a real fairy of the house'), we know what they can conceal.

* Cited by Hubertine Auclert, *Le Vote des femmes* (Paris: Giard et Brière, 1908), p. 107.

For Raewyn Connell, middle-class egalitarian husbands are complicit with hegemonic masculinity because they conveniently adapt their attitude without forgoing their 'patriarchal dividend'. For her part, Christine Delphy considers masculine feminism to be a 'neo-sexism': men involved in the movement speak in women's place, as usual. The feminism of men, the highest form of machismo? In *Le Féminism au masculin* (Masculine Feminism, 1977), Benoîte Groult on the contrary salutes the courage of certain male thinkers who were ahead of their time.

In order to go beyond polemics, let us begin by taking a closer look at the reasons that drive a man to become a feminist (or at least to defend the rights of women). First, there are the ties of affection. Men of letters maintained friendships with women of letters, as in the case of Montaigne and Marie de Gournay, or Descartes and his correspondence with princesses. Certain intellectuals, such as Madame de Staël, the Brontë sisters, Takamure Itsue, Gloria Steinem and Michelle Perrot were raised by passionately egalitarian fathers. Such was also the case of the young American woman Theodosia Burr, whose father was Vice-President of the United States: he supervised her education. Dozens of women activists – Amelia Bloomer, Millicent Fawcett, Emmeline Pankhurst, Lucretia Mott, Ursula Bright, Ida Rauh and Hubertine Auclert, for example, had the support of their husbands. In the early twentieth century, British suffragist Selina Cooper's husband was a member of the Men's League for Women's Suffrage.

Did these husbands and fathers simply love their wives and daughters, or did they apply to their private lives the principles of equality they held dear? Both. In 1797, William Godwin married Mary Wollstonecraft, pregnant with his child and already mother of a little girl born out of wedlock. He admired her for her intelligence and independence of mind. In *An Enquiry Concerning Political Justice* (1793), he had lashed out at marriage as a 'monopoly' and a 'system of hoaxes'. When Mary died in childbirth at the age of 38, he was inconsolable, and set out immediately to write her biography, all the while devoting himself to raising his two little girls, one of whom would become Mary Shelley, the author of *Frankenstein*. In this case, it was love that united a woman and a man who were already feminists.

Empathetic identification, activated by 'mirror neurons' in our brain, thanks to which we are capable of feeling the hurt of others, offers another lead. In China, it was men who denounced foot-binding and the frightful suffering inflicted on five-year-old girls: Che Ruoshui in the late Song dynasty and Yuan Mei in the eighteenth century became the first to defend the cause of women. In the 1890s, Kang Youwei founded in Canton the first association to fight against this practice and for the education of girls.

This empathy is the basis of the humanitarian feminism prominent in the literature of the nineteenth century. Nguyên Du's *Truyên Kiêu* is a masterpiece of Vietnamese literature that tells the story of the sacrifice of a young girl who was molested by men and who then resigned herself to the fate of prostitution and servitude. In Europe, writers stood up for the victims of upper-middle-class selfishness: orphans, teenage mothers, prostitutes, disgraced courtesans. Such is the case of Alexandre Dumas in his plays and his novel *La Dame aux camélias* (the model for Verdi's *La Traviata*), as well as for Victor Hugo, who becomes the symbolic father of Fantine and Cosette in *Les Misérables*.

The rights of women can also be defended for the sake of social utility: the future of the nation demands that no talent nor energy be wasted. That is the reason why Plato makes a place for women in his Republic, a utopia conceived within one of the most misogynist societies of all antiquity: with good training, elite women will be able to become guardians of the city state and serve the common good, instead of wasting their talents by staying at home. In the second half of the nineteenth century, several American reformers voiced their commitment to feminism because, in their view, women achieve a higher degree of morality than men. Accustomed to taming the beasts who share their lives, women will know how to rid society of its masculine evils: alcoholism, exploitation, corruption. Under their feminism lay the hope for social redemption.

The plight of women interested the 'modernizers' who professed their visionary views. Such conceptions guided Arab, Japanese and Chinese intellectuals in the nineteenth century: they were convinced that the success of the West was based on the emancipation of women and the promotion of the nuclear family. That was the position defended in Japan by Tokutomi Sohō, an influential liberal writer, and by Fukuzawa Yukichi, who returned from a mission in Europe in 1862 converted to the ideal of equality between the sexes, contrary to Confucian traditions. Jin Tianhe published an essay titled *The Women's Bell* in Shanghai at the age of 29: in it, he advocated women's right to education, work, property, travel, friendship, love and the vote. He did so out of respect for human dignity, but also to transform China into a 'civilized' nation.*

The fight against the oppression of women intersected with the agenda of the social revolutions: abolitionists, socialists and feminists met in a convergence of struggles. At the World Anti-Slavery Convention of 1840, held in London, the exclusion of American women delegates stirred an awareness of feminism among both men and women.† Some thirty men attended the Seneca Falls Convention of 1848. Among them were the journalist William Garrison, the Quaker James Mott and the militant former slave Frederick Douglass. As abolitionists, they denounced all forms of slavery, that of women as well as of Black people, and demanded that they have the right to vote. In *The Origin of the Family, Private Property and the State* (published in 1884, one year after Marx's death), Engels strove to show that the domestic servitude of women stemmed from private property. Referring to Johann-Jakob Bachofen's *Mother Right* and Lewis Morgan's *Ancient Society*, he writes that at the outset of 'civilization'– let's say the Neolithic period – monogamy and the accumulation of wealth brought an end to the predominance of women. This seizure of power by men was the 'great historical defeat of the feminine sex': from it resulted all other inequalities. Engels concluded that in the family 'the woman plays the role of the proletariat'. Consequently, the collapse of capitalism and the abolition of private property will emancipate both workers and women.‡

---

* Lydia Liu et al., *The Birth of Chinese Feminism: Essential Texts in Transnational Theory* (New York: Columbia University Press, 2013), p. 205 ff.
† Hélène Quanquin, '"No shilly-shallying: Be brave as a lion": Les abolitionnistes américains à la Convention mondiale contre l'esclavage in 1840' in Florence Rocherfort and Éliane Viennot (eds.), *L'Engagement des hommes pour l'égalité des sexes, XIVᵉ–XXIᵉ siècle* (Saint-Étienne: Publications de l'université de Saint-Étienne, 2013), pp. 73–84.
‡ Josette Trat, 'Engels et l'émancipation des femmes' in Georges Labica and Mireille Delbraccio (eds.), *Friedrich Engels, savant et révolutionnaire* (Paris: PUF, 1997), pp. 175–192.

The feminism of men can be explained by love, empathy, interest, utility or strategy, but that does not detract from the quest for justice. There is therefore no reason to omit one last motive: the respect for human rights. The act of mutilating women, leaving them in ignorance, subjugating them to a husband or depriving them of the right to vote is quite simply unjust and immoral. Feminism is an ethic. In this domain as in others, it is not surprising that men were the first to go into action, certainly not because, as might be supposed, they have a monopoly on moral inclinations, but because they most definitly did have a monopoly on·education, speaking out and entering into the public sphere. All these factors combined to give rise to this strange species: feminist men.

THE HEROINE, THE WOMAN OF LETTERS AND THE SIBYL

Given a society in which the sexes' roles are set in stone, doing away with customary practices can seem a utopia. The vision of women who would live like men has inspired writers and artists. Three figures tell the story of that imaginary emancipation: the heroine, the woman of letters and the sibyl.

The Greeks were fascinated by the Amazons, the armed women on horseback who, Herodotus reported, refused to do the work assigned to their sex. Achilles even fell in love with their queen, Penthesilea, whom he fatally wounded. The Bible gives a few examples of courageous women – some matriarchs, others resistors: Sarah, Rebecca, Rachel, Judith decapitating Holofernes. Judith was particularly admired by Caravaggio and his disciples in the early seventeenth century: they depicted her as determined and fierce, her traits intensified by the effort needed to carry out her crime. In the same era, the figure of the bold (sometimes dangerous) woman appeared in Thomas Heywood's *Gynaikeion* (1624) and the Jesuit father Le Moyne's *La Gallerie des femmes fortes* (The Gallery of Strong Women, 1647). One Chinese legend tells the tale of the heroic deeds of the young Mulan, who disguises herself as a man and fights in the place of her father, who is too old. Ceramics from the Tang period in the seventh and eighth centuries represent female polo players or musicians mounted on their horses.

From the Renaissance on, humanists recognized women's right to have access to learning and knowledge. Educated women populate not only the Abbey of Thelema imagined by Rabelais, but also treatises such as the Spaniard Juan-Luis Vives' *Education of a Christian Woman* (1523), the Englishman Thomas Elyot's *Defence of Good Women* (1540), and the Czech Comenius' *Great Didactic* (1627). In the France of the 1670s, Poullain de la Barre wrote that 'the mind has no sex', while Fénelon was in favour of giving girls a more thorough domestic education. In the eighteenth century, Chinese reformer Chen Hongmou also advocated educating women.

Then there is the prophetess who reveals man's future: she relays the words of the divinity, such as with the Pythia of Delphi, or, as does the sibyl, renders oracles thanks to the predictions of obscure books. In the sixteenth century, Michelangelo painted sibyls as muscular as Hercules on the ceiling of the Sistine Chapel. In the midst of the upheavals of the industrial revolution in the 1820s and 1830s, Saint-Simon and his disciples announced the coming of the Woman, a 'sibyl of the future,' a promise of love and regeneration for an entire civilization. According to Émile Barrault, founder of the Companions of Woman, the sibyl softens the ferocity of the warrior and brings down social and national barriers: 'The prophecy of women is perpetual.'* This hopeful vein in Saint-Simon's thought continues up to the French poet Aragon, for whom 'woman is the future of man'.

It would clearly be wrong to present Plato or Father Le Moyne as feminists. Only men who actively work for the rights of women deserve that title. Like the pioneers of feminism, their struggle is indissociable from the Enlightenment and the revolutions of the late eighteenth century. In the *Encyclopédie*, for example, Jaucourt writes that the wife's legal subordination to her husband is contrary to the equality of nature and that man does not necessarily have more strength or wisdom than woman. Like all human rights, the rights of women partake of the invention of a democratic society.

---

* Émile Barrault, 'Les femmes' in Claude-Henri de Saint-Simon and Prosper Enfantin, *Religion saint-simonienne: Prédications* (Paris: Leroux, 1878, p. 182 ff.

THE THINKERS OF EQUALITY

In his *Letters from a Freeman of New Haven to a Citizen of Virginia* (1787), the Marquis de Condorcet denounced the oppressive laws that refused to consider women as sensible, moral and rational beings. A free state, he argued, must grant them the right to vote and the eligibility to assume public capacities.

Condorcet laid out his line of reasoning with *On the Admission of Women to the Rights of Citizenship* (1790), which provided a powerful corrective to the Declaration of the Rights of Man passed the preceding year by the Constituent Assembly in France. The fact of the matter was that the legal exclusion of women violated the equality of rights: in addition to the injustice of aristocratic privilege, depriving women of rights was an act of tyranny. There were several pretexts: women's pregnancies, their occasional indispositions, their household duties, their weak contribution to the arts, sciences and letters. But what was really to blame was male oppression, the force of habit and the ill effects of inequitable education. Condorcet articulated several arguments in view of putting an end to this state of affairs: the example of women of state (Catherine the Great) and intellectuals (Madame du Châtelet), the natural right of both sexes, the rational and moral nature of every human being, and democratic coherence.

Condorcet established a link between *liberty, equality and the rights of the person*: that was a conceptual break from Poullain de la Barre, whose egalitarianism only led to a reform of marriage and education among women. Condorcet's objective was not a humanist rehabilitation of women, but rather an emancipation: in both private matters and politics, he wished them to be sovereign over their own lives. Even though his *Principles of the Constitutional Plan* of 1793 still restricted citizenship to men, Condorcet was, if not the first, one of the very first feminists in the world. His audacity can be measured by other male and female reformers of that time. In addition to the right to vote and eligibility for public office, he advocated universal education for girls, while in 1791 Talleyrand was content to stop with domestic education.

Condorcet's ideas were taken up again by Pierre Guyomar, a representative elected to the Assembly, who in 1793 authored *The Partisan of*

Political Equality between Individuals. In this pamphlet, he proposed to abandon the 'prejudice of sex' (as shocking as the 'prejudice of colour') and to found a true democracy against the 'aristocracy of men'. The same year, another representative, Gilbert Romme, declared that 'every man of one or the other sex' must receive political rights.

Theodor Gottlieb von Hippel, a high-ranking government official in Königsberg, was one of the rare German feminists of his time, as one can see when comparing his positions to those of his friend Immanuel Kant. In his book *On Improving the Status of Women* (1792), Hippel argued for equality and individual liberty. However, his project was less focused on emancipation than on a reform of civic institutions and society, as much as treatmnet of the 'Jewish question' by Wilhelm von Dohm had been a few years before. It was aimed at integrating into society those beings characterized by their proximity to nature, their mild temperament and their rich affectivity.

Echoing personalities such as Wieland and Goethe, German newspapers took an interest in the ideas set forth by the Englishman James Lawrence, first in a *Mercure Allemand* article of 1793, then in a novel translated into several languages. Using the matrilinear society of the Nayar in India as an example, Lawrence advocated the abolition of marriage and paternity. Such a step would result in women being liberated from the yoke of men: they would be remunerated by the state to take care of children, while men could devote themselves to activities of the mind.* Was this a defence of free love, a gendered division of labour or a feminist utopia? In any case, James Lawrence was one of the first to reflect on the economic independence of women, who in his scheme of things would hold the power of money and filiation, prerequisites for a happy life outside marriage, far from the patriarchal family. Moreover, that was the vision defended by feminists in their novels, Mary Hays in *Memoirs of Emma Courtney* (1796) and Mary Wollstonecraft in *Maria* (1798).

The harmony theorized by the first socialists ran directly counter to

---

* First published in German as *Das Paradies der Liebe* (1800), it was translated into English as *The Empire of the Nairs* (1811). See Anne Verjus, 'Une société sans pères peut-elle être féministe? *L'Empire des Nairs* de James H. Lawrence', *French Historical Studies*, Vol. 42, No. 3, July 2019.

the society in which they were living. They dreamed of a society without oppression in which everyone would fulfil themselves and thrive according to their talents and inclinations, freed from the servitudes of their time. As an architect of an ideal world, Charles Fourier denounced the servitude of women in *The Theory of the Four Movements* (1808). Beyond the power of his style and rich imagination, the originality of his approach consisted of combining historical analysis, economics and social progress. For Fourier, the rights of women constituted the touchstone for assessing a society's advances. The passage between the eight periods of time that he points to, from Edenism to Harmony, is 'due to women's progression toward liberty', while instances of social decadence stem from regression in that area. As a passionate advocate of equality, Fourier showed that the flaws attributed to women were nothing but the reflection of the 'inherent defects of the social system': economic exploitation, subjugation in marriage, oppression in love. He went so far as to imagine the tyranny of a 'third sex' for a century, which would finally make men understand the iniquity of 'might makes right'.

The influence of this feminism is discernible in Zoé de Gamond, an enthusiastic exponent of Fourier's thought (that she prefers to Saint-Simon's) and first woman inspector of primary schools in Belgium. When universal male suffrage was proclaimed in 1848, Victor Considerant, one of Fourier's disciples, was one of the only men to protest, pointing out that women had always been deprived of the right to vote, even though that right had been granted to domestic servants and beggars.

In Great Britain, socialist theorist Robert Owen defended the equality of the sexes and the right to divorce. William Thompson, a rich Irish landowner close to the partisans of both Owen and Saint-Simon, published a feminist manifesto, *Appeal of One Half of the Human Race, Women, Against the Pretensions of the Other Half, Men* (1825). In it, he demonstrated that, since daughters did not have the same interests as their father, nor wives those of their husband, they could not legitimately be represented by them and therefore had to be given the right to vote. As was the case for slavery to another degree, marriage constituted violence against the wife, who in it lost her personality, rights and possessions, and became a procreation machine.

John Stuart Mill acquired an exceptional range of cultural knowledge, admired by his contemporaries, in the company of his father. Though his liberal and utilitarian views were an integral part of his paternal heritage, he nevertheless had to break with the patriarchal tradition that he was perpetuating. It was indeed precisely in order to refute the position of Mill's father that William Thomson had published his *Appeal of One Half of the Human Race*. Just as Thompson had been influenced by his friend Anna Wheeler, so John Stuart Mill constantly recalled what his books owed to his wife, Harriet Taylor. In *The Enfranchisement of Women* (1851), she had criticized the 'sentimental priesthood' to which women were doomed as victims not only of bourgeois society's disregard, but also of the worker movement's sexism. Her ideas inspired George Holyoake, also an Owenist, instigator of the *English Woman's Journal* in the 1850s.

However, Harriet Taylor's influence can be seen most importantly in *The Subjection of Women* (1869), published by John Stuart Mill eleven years after the death of his beloved wife. Following her example, he denounced all the injustices suffered by women: the asinine prejudices, the prison of marriage, the inaccessibility of careers, the exclusion from civic activity. Men were indicted as a group, since their despotism resembled that of the monarchy of the Ancien Régime and slavery in the United States. However, unlike those institutions that benefited a small minority, the abuse of power in this case stemmed from an entire sex. After the fall of absolutism and the abolition of slavery, the subjugation of women was the last vestige of the old world: 'Marriage is the only form of servitude recognized by our laws.'

But even though John Stuart Mill regretted that society would deprive itself of so many talented women, he did not challenge the traditional distribution of tasks, with women having to remain with their children. On that point, Harriet Taylor, who was insistent on their intellectual self-realization and their civic engagement, proved to be much bolder.

As an elected member, John Stuart Mill had already presented to Parliament the petition for women's right to vote from 1,499 women activists in 1866, three years before *The Subjection of Women*. The following year, his amendment was rejected, despite the support of 73 members of Parliament.

After his successor Jacob Bright succeeded in having women gain access to universal suffrage in municipal elections in 1869, dozens of bills in favour of women's right to vote were introduced by British members of Parliament, including Leonard Courtney, Hugh Mason and Faithfull Begg. In the early twentieth century, several masculine associations took up the baton, such as the Male Electors' League for Women Suffrage (1897), the Men's Committee for Justice to Women (1909), and most importantly, the Men's League for Women's Suffrage (1907), whose members included intellectuals, jurists, men of the Church, doctors and industrialists. From the latter came the most radical organization, Men's Political Union for Women's Suffrage (1910). Frederick Pethick Lawrence, a Protestant Unitarian like John Stuart Mill and Harriet Taylor, was force-fed in prison during his hunger strike, and was bankrupted after having to reimburse the damages caused by the suffragettes that he had supported.*

Three feminist thinkers

Have they [philosophers and legislators] not all violated the principle of the equality of rights in tranquilly depriving one-half of the human race of the right to take part in the formation of laws by the exclusion of women from the rights of citizenship? Could there be a stronger proof of the power of habit, even among enlightened men, than to hear invoked the principle of equal rights in favour of perhaps some 300 or 400 men, who had been deprived of it by an absurd prejudice, and forget it when it concerns some 12,000,000 women?... Either no individual of the human species has any true rights, or all have the same; and he who votes against the rights of another, whatever may be his or her religion, colour, or sex, has by that fact abjured his own.

Nicolas de Condorcet,
On the Admission of Women to the Rights of Citizenship (1790)†

---

* Martine Monacelli and Michel Prum (eds.), *Ces hommes qui épousèrent la cause des femmes: Dix pionniers britanniques* (Paris: L'Atelier, 2010).
† Available at https://link.springer.com/chapter/10.1007%2F978-1-4612-5304-4_24

And would not you, the oppressive sex, outdo women in shortcomings if a servile education had brought you up, like them, to think of yourselves as automata designed to submit to prejudice and to grovel to the master that chance has brought you? [...] I have provided a basis for saying that women, in a state of liberty, will outdo men in all mental and physical functions which are not dependent on bodily strength. [...] Women should have been producing liberators, not writers, political leaders like Spartacus, geniuses who could plan ways of leading their sex out of degradation. It is women who suffer most under Civilisation, and it is women who should be attacking it.*

Charles Fourier, *The Theory of the Four Movements*

But on women this sentence is imposed by actual law, and by customs equivalent to law. What in unenlightened societies colour, race, religion, or nationality are to some men, sex is to all women – an abrupt exclusion from almost all honourable occupations except ones that others can't perform or aren't willing to perform. Sufferings arising from this cause usually meet with so little sympathy that few people realize how much unhappiness is produced, even now, by the feeling of a wasted life.

John Stuart Mill, *The Subjection of Women* (1869)

Even though he was not, strictly speaking, an activist, John Stuart Mill made a considerable impact on posterity. With ties to the suffragist Millicent Fawcett, and accompanied up until the end of his life by his stepdaughter Helen, he gave rise to a line of male feminists throughout the world: August Bebel in Germany, Georg Brandes in Denmark, Fukuzawa Yukichi in Japan and certain liberals of the Third Republic in France.

---

* Gareth Stedman Jones and Ian Patterson (eds.), *Charles Fourier, The Theory of the Four Movements: Reader in the History of Social Thought* (Cambridge: Cambridge University Press, 1966, pp. 147–148. Available at https://libcom.org/files/Fourier%20-%20 The%20Theory%20of%20the%20Four%20Movements.pdf

THE SCANDAL OF
MASCULINE FEMINISM

The only other writer to have exerted such an influence on a global scale was the Norwegian Henrik Ibsen, who himself was won over by the female feminist intellectuals in his country. *A Doll's House* was published in 1879, translated into English and German by 1880, into French in 1889, Japanese in 1893 and Chinese in 1918. Nehru mentioned it in his Allahabad Address in 1928, at the inauguration of a university for women. The play caused an uproar and stirred up controversies everywhere. It was truncated in Germany, banned in Great Britain and attacked in Japan when it was staged at the imperial theatre of Tokyo in 1911. In the wake of all that, the magazine *Seitō* (Bluestocking) devoted an entire supplement to the character of Nora, symbol of the 'new woman'.* Ellen Key, Simone de Beauvoir and Betty Friedan would pay homage to her in their works.

The itinerary of Salvatore Morelli, from the South of Italy, is emblematic of the difficulties encountered by men actively committed to the rights of women. As a follower of Saint-Simon, he was imprisoned as an opponent of the Bourbons. In 1861, he published *Women and Science, or the Solution to the Social Problem*, which was translated into French and English in the following years. As an elected representative from 1867 to 1880, he submitted a series of bills to the Italian Parliament: the abolition of spousal servitude, the sharing of parental authority, civic equality between the sexes, the right to divorce, the authorization to track paternity, the possibility of handing down the mother's name to children and the opening of professions to women. Not only were these bills not placed on the agenda (except for when women were authorized to witness legal actions in 1877), but his colleagues in Parliament greeted him with laughter whenever he took the floor to speak. Despite his ties to other feminists such as John Stuart Mill in England

* Christine Lévy, 'Le premier débat public de *Seitō*: autour d'*Une maison de poupée*', *Ebisu*, No. 48, Fall–Winter 2012, pp. 29–58.

and Léon Richer in France, Morelli died in 1880 amid widespread indifference.*

In France, it was mainly in the areas of civil rights and academic instruction that men took part in the feminist struggle. In 1869, Léon Richer founded the paper *Le Droit des femmes* (The Right of Women), and then the Association for the Rights of Women, before organizing an international congress in Paris on the question in 1878. Greeted favourably by activists such as Julie-Victoire Daubié (the first woman to earn the *baccalauréat*), Maria Deraismes and Hubertine Auclert, he was jeered by his peers as the 'women's man'. Speaking before the select public who attended the lectures at La Bodinière in the mid-1890s, Léopold Lacour defended the equality of the sexes, as well as women's political and sexual rights: however, his humanist feminism was written off as eccentricity.†

However, the active commitment of men was marked by ambiguity. In the first place, their numbers in France remained very modest, only a few dozen in the last three decades of the nineteenth century. In the Association for the Rights of Women, their portion fell to one fifth in 1875, and they only represented one fourth in Women's Suffrage in the 1900s. Second, female feminist activists often had to seek out participation on the part of men, even if they were lukewarm: they could contribute finances and respectability to women's initiatives, not to mention the fact that a political publication had to be headed by a man. Lastly, men's arguments often tended to cut both ways, as when Jules Bois, the editor of the Parisian literary periodical *Gil Blas* and a regular at the La Bodinière lectures, celebrated the 'new Eve' with mystical overtones. In his book *L'Homme et la Femme* (The Man and the Woman), the press magnate Émile de Girardin responded to the taunt of Alexandre Dumas *fils*, who in 1872 had labelled his detractors 'feminists' (which was one of the first occurrences of the word): 'Feminist! So be it. I am honoured to

---

* Ginevra Conti-Odorisio (ed.), *Salavatore Morelli (1824–1880): Emancipazionismo e democrazia nell'Ottocento europeo* (Naples: ESI, 1992).
† Alban Jacquemart, *Les Hommes dans les mouvements féministes: Socio-histoire d'un engagement improbable* (Rennes: PUR, 2015), p. 34 ff, and Laurence Klejman and Florence Rochefort, *L'Égalité en marche: Le féminisme sous la Troisième République* (Paris: FNSP, 1989), p. 117 ff.

be with men and thinkers such as sirs Gladstone, Jacob Bright, Stuart Mill'. That did not prevent him from praising the housewife, however.

In 1870, at La Salle Molière in Paris, the advocate of the Republic Jules Ferry delivered a speech on the education of girls, referring to Condorcet. Ten years later, to the great dismay of the Right and the Catholics, the Camille Sée law instituted *lycées* (secondary schools) for young girls, though they were not aligned with programmes of instruction at *lycées* for boys, since they were destined to become family mothers. This feminism in education aimed to combat political feminism. The philosopher Henri Marion, also an advocate of the Republic, developed the notion of 'equality in difference' in order to counter the feminists' demands such as financial autonomy, access to careers and the right to vote.*

Unlike what was happening in Great Britain, the political world in France commonly deemed women's suffrage to be premature or downright laughable. Among the rare supporters of the suffragists was Marcel Sembat, who inserted the civil and political equality of women into his agenda as an elected representative to the National Assembly, and Ferdinand Buisson, a member of the Radical party and author of *Le Vote des femmes* (The Vote of Women, 1911), a comparative study of feminist victories in the world. René Viviani was one of the most faithful defenders of the feminist cause in the Belle Époque: as an editor for the periodical *Droit des femmes* (Right of Women) and someone close to the French League for the Rights of Women, beginning in the late 1880s, he took part in various conventions and associations, concern for without compromising his government career. Other expressions of masculine feminism caused a scandal: such was the case of the young Leon Blum's book *Du mariage* (On Marriage, 1907), in which he advocated sex education for young girls.

At the beginning of the twentieth century in New York, a group of intellectuals spoke out in favour of feminism as an instrument of liberation able to emancipate both men and women in their private as

* Nicole Mosconi, 'Henri Marion et "l'égalité dans la différence"', *Le Télémaque*, Vol. 41, No. 1, 2012, pp. 133–150.

well as public lives. Standing against capitalism and in favour of the economic and sexual independence of women, along with birth control, they led a bohemian life in Greenwich Village, not hesitating to shock their contemporaries with their stances. Among these radicals was Floyd Dell, who in 1917 penned the article 'Feminism for Men', and Max Eastman, co-founder in 1910 of the Men's League for Women's Suffrage, patterned after the English model. With branches throughout the United States, the association had thousands of members, including notably the philosopher John Dewey and Rabbi Stephen Wise. The activists who participated in demonstrations were mocked as 'milliners' or 'men in skirts', and reviled as traitors to their sex.*

In the nineteenth century, the thinkers of the Arab Enlightenment (Nahda) were advocates for the education of women, following the example of the Egyptian Al-Tahtawi, who with his in-depth knowledge of France had penned *The Honest Guide for Education of Girls and Boys*. After his studies in Cairo and Paris, his compatriot Qasim Amin followed in his footsteps, writing *The Liberation of Women* (1899), in which, for the sake of progress and civilization, he spoke out against the veil, polygamy, repudiation and forced marriage. The book caused a scandal, with its author forced out of the judiciary. In Tunisia, Tahar Haddad took the same path with *Our Women in the Sharia and Society* (1930). His basic point of departure was, 'In the East, woman continues to live under the veil.' She could get out of that shroud by engaging in physical exercise out in the open, going to school, having the right to choose her husband, to work, to enter into contracts and to witness in court. Bombarded with criticism from all sides, Tahar Haddad ended his life in dire poverty and solitude.†

---

* Michael Kimmel, Thomas Mosmiller, *Against the Tide: Pro-Feminist Men in the United States, 1776–1990* (Boston: Beacon Press, 1992), pp. 25–30.
† Alain Roussillon (ed.), *Entre réforme sociale et mouvement national: Identité et modernisation en Égypte (1882–1962)* (Cairo: CEDEJ, 1995), p. 58; and Souad Bakalti, *La Femme tunisienne au temps de la colonisation (1881–1956)* (Paris: L'Harmattan, 1996), p. 48 ff.

THE PHYSICIANS
OF THE EMANCIPATION

Although medicine has been a male monopoly ever since Hippocrates (with the elimination of 'witches' beginning in the fifteenth century), the practice of medicine has at times served the cause of women. In the first part of the nineteenth century, doctors, hygienists and psychiatrists sought to understand situations of feminine suffering, even if it was with the goal of implementing regulations and ensuring public order. In 1859, the French doctor Briquet demonstrated that hysteria was not an illness of the womb, but of the brain that disrupted the entire nervous system. How to help patients suffering from this disorder to feel better? 'Most commonly, these women are miserable, and quite happy to find in the person of the physician someone they can confide in.'* That paved the way for Charcot, and subsequently, Freud.

In 1832, Charles Knowlton published his *Fruits of Philosophy* in New York. In it, he dispensed all sorts of advice, replete with illustrations, for young married couples to control procreation. The book was a scandalous bestseller in England after its publishers were tried in 1877. Neo-Malthusianism was imported into France by Paul Robin, who discovered it during his exile in London in the 1870s. As a libertarian pedagogue and promoter of mixed education, he campaigned for birth control, as did Nelly Roussel and Gabrielle Petit at the same time: it was a right not to be a mother, and maternity was to remain a free choice. At the end of the century, English sexologist Havelock Ellis showed that, contrary to Victorian belief, women experience desire and that masturbation was a practice common to both sexes. His work, which was pursued after the Second World War by the Kinsey reports in the United States and those of Pierre Simon in France, led to a widespread abandonment of guilty feelings: the 'normal' woman has a sexuality. The rehabilitation of feminine pleasure contributed to women's liberty, and, quite simply, to their happiness.

For their part, the French disciples of Pasteur pioneered spectacular

---

* Pierre Briquet, *Traité clinique et thérapeutique de l'hystérie* (Paris: Baillière, 1859), p. 634.

progress in obstetrics, disseminating the principle of asepsis and perfecting the sterilization of milk, which the first childcare institutions distributed in baby bottles, with the Gouttes de Lait (Drops of Milk) opening in Paris and Fécamp in the early 1890s. These improvements occurred in a context of demographic anxiety, spurred by the spirit of revenge against Germany. The emancipation of women probably did not figure among the intentions of the first paediatrists Gaston Variot and Pierre Budin, but that was in effect the result of their action: reducing the number of women dying in childbirth and creating the possibility of feeding one's child by the bottle removed one of the main obstacles to salaried work for women.

In the United States, certain men looked into the matter of menstruation. The tampon, invented by Earle Haas in 1931, and the menstrual cup, patented in 1932 by Lester Goddard, were bought by women under the respective brand names of Tampax and Tassette. In 1919, the Austrian physician Ludwig Haberlandt had the intuition of a temporary hormonal means of contraception. With the aid of the Richter firm, he develop Infecundin, a hormonal preparation, before going on to commit suicide two years later, in the face of widespread hostility. After the Second World War, chemists and doctors invented oral contraception. One of them, George Pincus, was funded by Katharine McCormick, a philanthropical feminist and former suffragist close to Margaret Sanger, the pioneer of birth control. The pill was commercialized in 1960 in the United States, then in Australia, West Germany and Great Britain.*

This example shows that one must differentiate between doctors whose discoveries lent themselves to furthering a feminist end and those who strive to extend the rights of women through their active involvement with the feminist cause. The objective of the latter is to give back to women the control of their own bodies by making pregnancy a deliberate choice and a time of happiness. Certain gynaecologists tried to liberate mothers from the ancient curse 'In pain you shall bring forth children.' Dick-Read in England in the 1930s, and Nikolaiev in the USSR in the 1950s, developed a method of obstetrics based on exercises

---

* Jonathan Eig, *The Birth of the Pill: How Four Crusaders Reinvented Sex and Launched a Revolution* (New York, W. W. Norton & Company, 2014).

of relaxation and breathing. 'Painless' delivery was practised at the Bluets clinic in Paris by Fernand Lamaze, who was won over to the principle when he travelled to the USSR to study. Up until the 1980s, his method enjoyed wide popularity in France and the United States.*

In France, the communists accepted this Soviet-inspired feminism, but not the right to abortion. When the journalist Jacques Derogy published a book on the tragedy of clandestine abortions in 1956, Maurice Thorez, the leader of the French Communist Party, responded curtly in the columns of *L'Humanité*: 'The way to the liberation of women is led by social reforms, social revolution, and not by abortion clinics.' His wife, Jeannette Vermeersch, worried that with abortion and birth control imported from the United States, working women might 'have access to the vices of the bourgeoisie'.† The campaign for abortion rights was led without the support of the communists, but with that of the liberal right instead.

Pierre Simon played a key role in writing this page of history. As a gynaecologist, sexologist, practitioner of painless childbirth and activist for the right to contraception, he brought back diaphragms and condoms from London to family planning services, where they were distributed without charge. He lent his support to the elected representative at the National Assembly Lucien Neuwirth, who convinced General de Gaulle to legalize the contraceptive pill in 1967. Lastly, he helped write the Simone Veil law authorizing abortion, which was passed in 1974 under Giscard by a male National Assembly. In Great Britain, the men actively fighting in the Abortion Law Reform Association secured key positions in the government after the 1964 elections. Influenced by Alice Jenkins' book *Law for the Rich*, MP David Steel introduced a bill on medical termination of pregnancy, which was passed in 1967 by a 96 per cent male House of Commons.‡

In order to extend the sexual and reproductive rights of women

---

* Marianne Caron-Leulliez and Jocelyne George, *L'Accouchement sans douleur: Histoire d'une révolution oubliée* (Paris: L'Atelier, 2004)

† Annette Wieviorka, *Maurice et Jeannette: Biographie du couple Thorez* (Paris: Fayard, 2010), p. 566 ff.

‡ Claire Charlot, 'Les hommes et le combat pour le droit à l'avortement en Grande-Bretagne' in Florence Rochefort and Éliane Viennot (eds.), *L'Engagement des hommes*, pp. 99–113.

throughout the world, doctors have had to fight not only against habit and prejudice, but also against laws, churches and their fellow physicians, sometimes risking their lives and careers. In doing this, they have received the support of many male politicians, elected representatives in particular. In the United States, gynaecologists who practise abortion have had to face violence from 'pro-life' groups: from 1978 to 2015, a total of 11 murders, 26 attempted murders, 185 cases of arson, 42 bombings and more than 1,500 ransacked clinics had been registered.*

The struggle of gynaecologists since the 1930s

Country	Name	Period of activity	Cause engaged	Legacy
Great Britain	Grantly Dick-Read	1930s–1950s	Painless childbirth	Influence in the Western world
USSR	A. P. Nikolaiev	1950s	Painless childbirth	Influence in communist countries
France	Fernand Lamaze	1950s	Painless childbirth	Reimbursement by Social Security; international influence; approval of Pope Pius XII (1956)
	Pierre Simon	1950s–1980s	Painless childbirth, family planning	Political and moral influence
	Émile Papiernik	1960s–1980s	Family planning, abortion	Extension of maternity leave; the practice of abortion after the Veil law

* Karissa Haugeberg, *Women Against Abortion: Inside the Largest Moral Reform Movement of the Twentieth Century* (Urbana: University of Illinois Press, 2017).

Country	Name	Period of activity	Cause engaged	Legacy
France	331 doctors	1973 (manifesto in the news magazine *Le Nouvel Observateur*)	Abortion	Debate over the legalization of abortion
Germany	Horst Theissen	1970s–1980s	Abortion	Memmingen Trial (1988); conviction and prison sentence before appeal
United States	David Gunn	1980s–1990s	Abortion	Assassinated in 1993; passage of the bill of law protecting access to clinics (1994)
	John Britton	1960s–1990s	Abortion	Assassinated in 1994
	Barnett Slepian	1980s–1990s	Abortion	Assassinated in 1998
	George Tiller	1970s–2000	Abortion	Assassinated in 2009
Congo (DRC)	Denis Mukwege	1990s–2010	Reparation of victims of war rape	Attempted assassination in 2012; Nobel Peace Prize in 2018
	Gildo Byamungu	2010s	Obstetrics	Assassinated in 2017

Feminist women are rare; feminist men, even more so: but they do exist. Some men fight against patriarchy, while certain women are at ease with it. The real fault line therefore does not separate women from men (in the oppressed/oppressor mode), but feminists from non-feminists, on the subject of political commitment to the cause. It establishes a division between thinkers, jurists, doctors and activists of both sexes on one side, and on the other, a huge number of hostile males and a mass of indifferent citizens in favour of the established order of gender. In the 1860s, Anna-Maria Mozzoni, the great Italian feminist, honoured the names of Fourier, Saint-Simon, Leroux and Morelli: 'Thank you, generous men who defend every liberty and every liberation. . . and who, by speaking out, taking up your pens, and working, affirm the rights of women!'* Though scant in number, male allies have made some significant contributions.

This ratio of forces invalidates the *biologization of feminism*, the vein which consists of believing that any and every woman is a feminist by dint of being a woman. As the female French Rabbi Delphine Horvilleur – who knows what she is talking about – put it, feminism is not the discourse of a woman speaking from her tradition, but a critical manner of thinking, carried out by a woman or a man against a system that alienates women and the feminine.†

---

* Cited by Ginevra Conti-Odorisio, 'Salvatore Morelli: l'esprit européen de l'émancipation', *Les Cahiers du GRIF*, No. 48, 1994, pp. 151–163.
† Delphine Horvilleur, *En tenue d'Ève*, p. 181.

8

State Feminism

Feminism is not carried forward exclusively by either women or men, but by groups of women and men becoming actively involved in its cause. While the revolt against injustice often determines individual commitments, it would remain impotent without the existence of collectives to carry it through: associations, labour unions, and so on. Now the state is a super collective, implementing rights through legislation.

Since 1974, France has had a secretary of state charged with improving the condition of women and working for equality between the sexes, while in Great Britain, the position of Minister for Women and Equalities was created in the late 1990s with a similar purview. International organizations, states and numerous cities throughout the world practise 'gender mainstreaming', in other words, a systematic consideration of equality between women and men in public policy. However, this institutionalization of the struggle is more an outcome than a point of departure, for the feminist state, the 'woman-friendly state', arose in the nineteenth century.*

NATIONAL AND
INTERNATIONAL MATERNALISM

If a citizen is an individual holding rights over the collective, then women can avail themselves of this 'citizenship'. The first pieces of social legislation benefited women and children, because they were

---

* Helga Hernes, *Welfare State and Woman Power: Essays in State Feminism* (Oslo: Norwegian University Press, 1987).

deemed to be weaker than men. The French Revolution devoted intensive efforts on that level: the Committee on Mendicancy and the
Constitution of 1791 reformed support for abandoned children, the
decree of 28 June 1793 covered child poverty and single mothers, and
the Barère report of 1794 planned safety nets for widows and nursing
mothers. Society did not come to their assistance out of Christian
charity, as had been the case under the Ancien Régime, but by virtue
of the moral claim they had on the collective: protection is a right.

Throughout Europe in the nineteenth century, laws mitigated the
exploitation of female workers, reducing their working hours and
prohibiting work at night: such was the case in France in 1874, in
Switzerland in 1877, in Germany in 1883 and in Austria in 1885.
French women benefited from unpaid maternity leave beginning in
1909 and from a mandatory, compensated rest period with the Strauss
law of 1913. Of course, these pieces of legislation concealed all sorts
of ulterior motives (women had to be 'protected', they were at their
rightful place at home, and so on), and that's why certain feminists
like Maria Deraismes criticized them.

The state feminist approach consists of demanding rights for
women according to a conception of the social contract that ensures
the *protection of the most vulnerable*. That was one of the measures
in Hubertine Auclert's agenda of the 1880s: seeing to it that the
'maternal state' guarantee assistance to children, the elderly, the sick
and invalids, as well as monetary support to all mothers, married or
not. The 'maternal state' was to be an agency for protection and care,
as opposed to the 'Minotaur state', which was charged with policing
and military defence. Such social legislation stemmed from a supposed vulnerability: the unequal constitution of men (perceived to be
free and independent) and women (workers, mothers, widows) justified an infringement of liberalism.

In the twentieth century, women's rights were increasingly defended
by international organizations. The Berne Convention of 1906 banned
the use of the toxic chemical white phosphorus in the match industry,
in an extension of the struggle of the London match girls. After the
First World War, the Treaty of Versailles founded the International
Labour Office (ILO), composed of a General Conference and a Bureau. Right away, its charter laid down two feminist principles: equal

pay for equal work and the presence of at least one female advisor during discussions concerning women. At the first International Labour Conference in 1919, two of the six conventions adopted concerned women: the prohibition of night work and the definition of a standard maternity leave.

During the interwar period, tensions arose between the 'protective' stance (on maternity leave, the prohibition of night work and dangerous industrial substances, the material well-being of emigrating women and their children on ships) and the egalitarian position (pay equal to that of men, equal treatment, unemployment coverage). The protective position viewed women in their twofold difference with respect to men, that is, as potential mothers and participants in 'masculine' industries. The egalitarian position defended by Norwegian, English and American women emphasized women's inalienable right to work on an equal basis with men.*

The ILO also offered positions of responsibility to women such as Margaret Bondfield, Frances Perkins and Marguerite Thibert: in 1938, the feminization of these positions reached 41 per cent, with most occupied by single women. Maria Vérone, a lawyer and the president of the French League for Women's Rights, was happy to see that, thanks to its charter and the 'feminist sentiments' of its director, Albert Thomas, there were more women coming into the Bureau than there were coming into the League of Nations.†

THE WELFARE STATE AND THE EMANCIPATION OF WOMEN

As was the case at the ILO, maternalism played a decisive role in the first era of social safety nets: it helped fill the huge gaps in maternal

---

* Sandra Whitworth, 'Gender, International Relations and the Case of the ILO', *Review of International Studies*, Vol. 20, No. 4, October 1994, pp. 389–405; and Bureau for Gender Equality, 'Women's Empowerment: 90 Years of ILO Action' (Geneva: ILO, 2009).

† Françoise Thébaud, 'Les femmes au BIT: l'exemple de Marguerite Thibert' in Jean-Marc Delaunay and Yves Denéchère (eds.), *Femmes et relations internationales au XXe siècle* (Paris: Presses Sorbonne Nouvelle, 2007), pp. 177–187.

and infantile healthcare. As the welfare state gradually took shape over the course of the twentieth century, however, the various national contexts produced very different results, which is the best proof that the state can assume – or refuse to assume – responsibility for feminist policies. We can shed light on these processes by comparing the cases of Great Britain, Ireland and West Germany, on the one hand, with those of France and Sweden, on the other.

Great Britain adopted the model of the male breadwinner: the man provides the material needs for his family, while the woman remains at home, where she works (without remuneration), taking caring of her household. Social coverage and benefits depend on the man's salary, with the women and children as beneficiaries only. The government, employers and labour unions agreed to confine women to 'feminine' sectors of employment and dissuade them from working once they were married. Certain professions were closed to them by virtue of a 'marriage bar'. The powerful British feminist movement was not in a position to overturn this state of affairs. In the 1920s, Eleanor Rathbone's campaign for a financial subsidy for family mothers proved unsuccessful. As demonstrated by the 1931 Anomalies Act, which brutally deprived hundreds of thousands of wives of unemployment benefits, women were the predesignated victims of the various crises. These major orientations lasted into the Beveridge era after the war: for social security, married women were dependent on their husbands.*

Irish society reposed on the very same choices: a domestic role for women, a low level of unemployment protection for married women, prohibited professions and a joint tax declaration transforming the woman's salary into a supplement. As a result, Ireland had the lowest rate of professionally active women in all of Europe in the twentieth century. In 1990, its active population included only 32 per cent women, and only one in four married women were working.†

West Germany can be linked with this paradigm owing to the low number of women in the labour market, a situation worsened by the

* Sarah Pedersen, *Family, Dependence, and the Origins of the Welfare State: Britain and France, 1914–1945* (Cambridge: Cambridge University Press, 1993).
† Evelyn Mahon, 'L'accès des femmes au marché du travail: le cas irlandais', *Les Cahiers du GRIF*, No. 48, 1994, pp. 141–150.

virtual absence of preschool childcare, which created a reliance on women to bring up small children. While there was a spectacular increase in the number of women employed from the 1960s on in the United States and Sweden, it was negligible in West Germany. With a stagnant labour market, and without any augmentation of social services, the employment of German women could not develop: that is why they were over-represented in menial jobs, while men occupied the industrial sector. The obsessive fear of 'educative collectivism' (in reaction to both Nazism and to East German communism) also dissuaded parents from delegating child-raising chores to others. The demands of such private individual responsibilities weighed first of all on women: the bad mother, *Rabenmutter* (mother crow), is the woman who shirks her responsibilities by 'abandoning' her children to go to work. The domestic servitude that society imposed on women for the sake of the child was tied to the conservatism of the 'three Ks' – *Kinder, Küche, Kirche* (children, kitchen, church) – which persisted long after the Third Reich.*

The French and Swedish models were significantly different. In France, the elaboration of a policy favouring the birth rate was based on a compromise between the government, employers and social Catholicism. In the last few decades of the nineteenth century, businesses implemented family support on a local basis in order to retain their workforce. From 1932 on, the employees of industry and commerce who had more than two children received financial subsidies, mutualized by means of funding agencies to which employers had to subscribe. These family subsidies in the form of a salary premium were developed in the 1930s before being incorporated into the social security system after the war. This 'parental welfare state', to use Susan Pedersen's expression, did not confine women to their role as a mother, since the sum of money corresponding to the cost of children was distributed to the family. Moreover, the weight of the agricultural and artisanal sector, along with the growth of the industrial workforce,

---

* Gøsta Esping-Andersen, *Les Trois Mondes de l'État-providence: Essai sur le capitalisme moderne* (Paris: Presses Universitaires de France, 2007/1990), p. 240 ff; and Béatrice Durand, *Cousins par alliance: Les Allemands en notre miroir* (Paris: Autrement, 2002), p. 32 ff.

combined with the early development of childcare services (nursery schools and preschools), created a favourable environment for the employment of women, whether they were married or not.

The Swedish system was maternalist in its origins, following the example of Ellen Key. In 1934, the Myrdal spouses published a book devoted to Sweden's rampant demographic crisis. In order to remedy the situation, they advocated a series of social measures (maternity subsidies, tax incentives, housing assistance, school cafeterias), without challenging the principle of intentional parenthood or the professional activity of women. Several of these measures were adopted, as was the decriminalization of contraception in 1938. But it was only in the 1960s that the Social Democrats implemented this twofold model reconciling vigorous birth rates with economic redistribution, maternity and women's employment outside the home: the woman was both a family mother and an autonomous employee. The employment of women, be they single or married, childless, pregnant or mothers, was protected by law, while at the same time supported by the system of maternity leave, childcare for small children and infants, and a separate tax structure. The result was a clearly discernible rise in the percentage of women working in Sweden, which exceeded 80 per cent at the end of the twentieth century.*

The welfare state doubly benefited women by facilitating salaried work and creating new jobs, paving the way to the middle class. Not only in Sweden, but also in Finland, Iceland and France, it enabled women to combine family life with a professional career, all thanks to a feminist natalism. Even in the countries that have followed the model of the male breadwinner, the growth of the welfare state contributed directly to the feminization of work, with new activities absorbed by the sectors of healthcare, education and social services. In the 1980s, between 65 and 75 per cent of women with a university degree were employed in the social services sector in West Germany,

---

* Anne Pauti, 'La politique familiale en Suède', *Population*, No. 4, 1992, pp. 961–985; and Jane Lewis, 'Gender and the Development of Welfare Regimes', *Journal of European Social Policy*, No. 3, 1992, pp. 159–173.

the United States and Sweden. To that extent, the welfare state gave new sources of power to women.*

THE INFLUENCE OF COLONIAL EUROPE

In the nineteenth century, men in power in Europe cared little about the rights of women, but they referred to such rights to justify colonization, which would supposedly 'liberate' African and Asian women. The 'civilizing mission' therefore included the defence of women, by fighting against underage marriage, polygamy and repudiation: it was a way of justifying the subjugation of indigenous peoples, while at the same time idealizing the condition of European women. This sentiment of superiority that stigmatized the 'ferocity' of Africans and the 'debasement' of Orientals, the 'barbarity' of men and the 'passivity' of their wives, can be found in Julien-Joseph Virey, Pierre Larousse and many others. In the Maghreb, the French found the confinement of women and the separation of the sexes in public places to be particularly shocking. In French West Africa, the colonial powers accepted formal complaints from women, but ended up bolstering the authority of fathers, husbands and brothers in the name of tradition.†

The discourse of rights originating in Europe nevertheless did strengthen the feminist cause in the Middle East and Asia from the late nineteenth century on. Hubertine Auclert argued in favour of educating Algerian women; the actions of the English suffragettes had echoes in India, Sri Lanka and Egypt, beginning in the 1910s; Dutch socialists aided feminists in Indonesia; in Asia, the figures of Madame Roland, Madame de Staël, Harriet Beecher Stowe and Sofia Perovskaia became icons. In the 1930s, associations such as the Project for

---

* Martin Rein, 'Women, Employment, and Social Welfare' in Rudolph Klein and Michael O'Higgins (eds.), *The Future of Welfare* (Oxford: Basil Blackwell, 1985), pp. 35–57; and Jon Eivind Kolberg, 'The Gender Dimension of the Welfare State', *International Journal of Sociology*, Vol. 21, No. 2, summer 1991, pp. 119–148.

† Marie Rodet, 'Genre, coutumes et droit colonial au Soudan français (1918–1939)', *Cahiers d'études africaines*, No. 187–188, 2007, pp. 583–602.

the Protection of Indigenous Women fought against polygamy, the marriage of pre-adolescent girls and prostitution in Belgian Congo. At the 1931 Paris Colonial Exposition, the States General of Feminism took up the matter of the protection of mothers and the education of women in the Maghreb and in sub-Saharan Africa. In 1938, French feminist Denise Moran wrote a report on the condition of women in French West Africa.

The awakening of feminist consciousness in Africa and Asia was not due solely to Western influence. It also resulted from progress in schooling, increased numbers of employed women and the rise of a local bourgeoisie. It became essential for women to serve in a new function: being a 'presentable' wife, equipped with a minimum of learning, able to make a good impression in society, but without giving up her role of family guardian. In other words, they were expected to be both educated and discreet, at once 'modern' and 'traditional'. The wavering missionary intentions of the colonizers thus dovetailed with the agenda of local reformers, which were aligned with the desires of the bourgeoisie. It was in this way that sati in India was denounced both by Hindu intellectuals and the East India Company, which, when followed by some twenty princes and maharajahs in the mid nineteenth century, led the practice to be banned in 1929. In this case, it was only then that the rights of women were finally discussed among men.*

Can we speak of state feminism in the French colonies? As in France itself, 'feminine policy' was limited to the domain of education. In French West Africa, a decree of 1903 structured public schools on a pyramid-like system extending from village schools to institutions for training teachers. The result was quite modest: in the 1920s, secular schools took in 40,000 children, 9 per cent of whom were girls, while Catholic schools enrolled 6,500 with 33 per cent girls. In Dahomey, where fewer than 3 per cent of children were enrolled, a girls' school was added to the secular schools of Porto-Novo. In Senegal, girls'

---

* John Stratton Hawley (ed.), *Sati, the Blessing and the Curse: The Burning of Wives in India* (Oxford: Oxford University Press, 1994) pp. 101–102; and on a more general level, Kumari Jayawardena, *Feminism and Nationalism in the Third World* (London: Zed Books, 1986).

schools were opened in Saint-Louis, Dakar, Gorée and Rufisque, with instruction focusing on home economics – but the marabouts were opposed to them. At the start of the school year in 1939, there were 13,500 pupils attending primary schools in Senegal, with only about one hundred (1 per cent) being girls.* The results were equally medi-ocre in the Maghreb, especially since young girls were married at a very early age. In Tunis, the Louise-René Millet school, named after the French Resident General, was founded in 1900 for the daughters of the Muslim elite. There they learned good French manners and the prin-ciples of home economics.

The education of girls oscillated between emancipation and instru-mentalization. The French opened public schools to girls in Indochina, where, prior to colonization, only the daughters of wealthy families had access to instruction, and then only with a private tutor. At the start of the 1920s, girls represented 8 per cent of those enrolled. Twenty years later, the figure stood at 15 per cent, with clear progress in the Tonkin and Annam areas, and reached a high of 29 per cent in Cochinchina. One institution, which went by the name of the School of the Violet Tunics, admitted young girls from the indigenous popu-lation of Saigon: several of its pupils would go on to become teachers, school principals and physicians.† These schools were part of the colonizers' enterprise of moral conquest: the idea was to ingrain a love of France from within households via the 'indigenous woman'.

Schools in French West Africa trained several hundred female social workers (midwives and nurses) between 1918 and the 1950s: a teacher-training school opened in 1938. These 'pioneers of progress' were the tools of colonial power, which was intent on maintaining vigorous birth rates and controlling populations, all while educating future wives. The fact remains that these educated, employed and sometimes activist women contributed to the advancement of gender

---

* Marie-Laurence Bayet, 'L'enseignement primaire au Sénégal de 1903 à 1920', *Revue française de pédagogie*, Vol. 20, 1972, pp. 33–40; and Catherine Coquery-Vidrovitch (ed.), *L'Afrique Occidentale au temps des Français: Colonisateurs et colonisés, 1860–1960* (Paris: La Découverte, 1992), p. 26.
† Bui Tran Phuong, 'Viêt Nam, 1918–1945: Genre et modernité', doctoral thesis in history, the University of Lyon II, 2008, annex 3.

relations, even disseminating a type of maternalist feminism.* In Sierra Leone, the British named women as heads of hinterland chiefdoms under the protectorate, with the goal of eliminating the men involved in the insurrection of 1898. Madam Yoko, the chief of the Kpa Mende, thereby owed her rise in politics to her loyalty. The middle-class women of Freetown, however, had no right to vote in municipal elections.†

At the end of the nineteenth century, European countries enjoyed great prestige, with their aura of economic and military superiority. This is the reason why they were able to spread the model of their societies beyond the borders of their empires. In this context, the rights of women appeared to be a process of civilization to be urgently implemented.

In Japan, during the Meiji period, the minister of education criticized concubinage, and supported contractual marriage and education for girls, as well as the sending of female students to American universities in 1871. The women of the upper class changed their appearance, cutting their hair, abandoning the traditional kimono in favour of Victorian dress. In the early twentieth century, the number of girls attending school reached 97 per cent (as opposed to 15 per cent in 1873), university education was gradually becoming accessible, and women were employed at a higher rate. They nevertheless remained excluded from political life, since they could not vote, nor meet, nor even speak in public. According to the principle of *ryōsai kenbo*, they were responsible for managing the household and raising future male citizens, which still represented progress in comparison with Confucian tradition. In China, the Empress banned foot-binding by a decree in 1902, which had to be renewed in 1911. Between 1917 and 1922, a 'modernizing' movement in the Shanxi province condemned foot-binding as a barbaric practice to be eradicated by a system of fines and inspections.‡

* Pascale Barthélémy, *Africaines et diplômées à l'époque coloniale, 1918–1957* (Rennes: Presses Universitaires de Rennes, 2010).

† Odile Goerg, 'Femmes africaines et politique. Les colonisées au féminin en Afrique occidentale', *Clio: Histoire, femmes et sociétés*, No. 6, 1997.

‡ Dorothy Ko, *Cinderella's Sisters: A Revisionist History of Footbinding* (Los Angeles: University of California Press, 2005), p 50ff.

REVOLUTIONARY FEMINISM

Nationalist leaders granted women a real place, which did not mean that they defended the equality of the sexes. Gandhi did not break with the traditionally patriarchal context, but he did accept equality in certain domains: the personal fulfilment of women, sexual autonomy and the remarriage of widows. Most importantly, he held in high esteem the female *satyagrahi* activists who, by means of their peaceful attitude and their aptitude for sacrifice, contributed to the non-violent struggle, thus allowing a certain escape from household matters. It was a woman close to Gandhi, Sarojini Naidu, who presided over the Indian National Congress in 1920. For his part, Jawaharlal Nehru, India's first Prime Minister, had a more progressive position than Gandhi: sympathetic to the British suffragettes, he refused to let women limit their ambition to marriage.

South East Asia has a tradition of revolutionary feminism that can be traced back to the Trung sisters' resistance to the Chinese in first-century Vietnam. In the favourable context of anticolonial struggles, Vietnamese feminism rose up again at the beginning of the twentieth century, when men of letters were leading the nationalist movement, before it was taken over in the 1920s by young, Western-trained intellectuals. The equality of the sexes was accepted as a principle, and not only in view of mobilizing women. The refusal of a life determined by the family and the aspiration to individual liberty drove female *lycée* and university students, along with young women from the rural areas, to join the movement. Conversely, propaganda held up the young militia woman as a symbol of courage and devotion.*

In China, women participated in armed struggles, such as those which sought the Taiping Rebellion (1850–1864), to secure the redistribution of land, the equality of the sexes, and the possibility for women to take examinations and gain access to positions of responsibility. Qiu Jin joined in the anti-Manchu fight after the Boxer

---

* Bui Tran Phuong, 'Femmes vietnamiennes pendant et après la colonisation française et la guerre américaine' in Anne Hugon (ed.), *Histoire des femmes en situation coloniale: Afrique et Asie, XXᵉ siècle* (Paris: Khartala, 2004), pp. 71–94.

Rebellion at the turn of the century. Like Gandhi and Nehru, Mao was impressed by the potential of women for militancy. In the 1910s and 1920s, he published several articles against forced marriage and defended equal rights. He contested masculine hegemony by placing himself alongside the victims: 'Shameless men, wicked men transform us into toys and make us engage in endless prostitution for their benefit.' In 1927, he denounced the oppression of women in rural areas: peasants were enslaved by three systems of domination (political, clan-based, religious), but women were subject to a fourth (masculine tyranny). These were the 'four cords' binding Chinese women. At the beginning of the 1930s, the Soviet of Jiangxi, presided over by Mao, revolutionized women's lives: economic independence was extolled, alongside the right to be educated and politically active, freedom of marriage, the possibility to divorce, all along with opposition to footbinding and female infanticide.*

In Vietnam, as in China, women took part in revolution, which contributed to their emancipation. There was therefore a feminism that was endogenous to Asian societies and reactivated in the twentieth-century context of revolutionary and anti-colonial struggle.

Once in power, certain nationalist leaders implemented a state feminism. In Afghanistan, in the 1920s, the series of reforms enacted by Amanullah Khan reserved a place for the rights of women (prohibition of child marriage, abolition of the veil and polygamy, the right to vote), which provoked the anger of the orthodox Muslims and brought about tribal uprisings. In the same era, Turkey was engaging in a similar reform at the initiative of Mustafa Kemal Atatürk. In 1926, the new code of civil law prohibited polygamy and extended rights to women in matters of divorce, property and inheritance. Turkish women gained the right to vote and to be elected to the National Assembly in 1934 (ten years before French women), and, in the following year, the conference of the International Woman Suffrage Alliance was held in Istanbul. Similarly, Atatürk organized mixed secular schools. After studying in

---

* Hu Chi-Hsi, 'Mao Tsé-Toung, la révolution et la question sexuelle', *Revue française de science politique*, No. 1, 1973, pp. 59–85, and Kumari Jayawardena, *Feminism and Nationalism*, pp. 186–193.

Germany, the first Turkish woman doctor, Safiye Ali, opened an Istanbul clinic for mothers and children in 1923.

A commitment to women's rights can be observed at the highest levels of state power in the former French colonies. Bourguiba set out to emancipate women after Tunisia gained its independence. Inspired by the ideas of Haddad, the 1956 Code of Personal Status proclaimed the equality of the sexes, authorized divorce, and abolished polygamy, the repudiation of wives and forced marriages. Women gained access to higher education and the job market, with some becoming doctors and lawyers. In Guinea, women played an important role in the struggles for national liberation, as attested by support from the African Democratic Assembly and the martyrdom of M'Balia Camara, a pregnant woman killed in 1955. After independence in 1958, Sékou Touré undertook a policy of feminine emancipation with the help of the Democratic Party of Guinea (under the slogan 'Women support the Party – the Party emancipates women'). In spite of patriarchal institutions, the women of Guinea secured a certain number of rights: equality within marriage and in the courts of law, the freedom to manage personal possessions, indemnities in the case of repudiation, the right to divorce and to refuse the husband's desire for other wives. In 1968, one fourth of representatives elected to the national assembly were women.*

THE BETRAYAL OF WOMEN

Despite all these accomplishments, Kumari Jayawardena's conclusion is sombre: feminist demands were eclipsed by the priorities of national liberation, even though it had been won with the aid of women activists and combatants. The determination to create a 'modern' state did not diminish the domination of men.

After former colonies had gained independence, a return to patriarchal order occurred in Sri Lanka (beginning in 1946), India, the Maghreb and sub-Saharan Africa. Equality in civil society did not prevent women from remaining at the service of men as mothers in

* Claude Rivière, 'La promotion de la femme guinéenne', *Cahiers d'études africaines*, Vol. 8, No. 31, 1968, pp. 406–427.

the household, carriers of water, keepers of religious traditions and guardians of national authenticity. Even in Tunisia, the dictatorial rule of Bourguiba and Ben Ali resulted in decades of police violence directed against women in particular, whether they were activists in left political parties, labour unions, Islamist organizations, or simply relatives of political opponents: brutal physical abuse and rapes nullified the code of personal status.

African-American women, female students and family mothers played a crucial role in the civil rights movement in the United States, for example during the boycott of the Montgomery bus system in 1955 and the Great March on Washington in 1963. They were nevertheless confined in traditionally feminine functions: cooking, leading church singing, going from door to door, taking care of social work and charitable activities. For all that concerned political strategy, they remained in the background, and the ideal of masculine activism deteriorated into virile, militaristic rhetoric among the Black Panthers.* Civic equality did not include the equality of the sexes.

In Europe, during the nineteenth and twentieth centuries, socialists adhered to the same hierarchy of gender. They did not necessarily look down on women, but felt that their role and demands were clearly secondary. In First International circles, in about 1870, the 'family salary' conformed to the model of the male breadwinner, with women sent back to their households. As a German social-democratic thinker opposed to legal discriminations against women (in accordance with the 1891 Erfurt Programme), Eduard Bernstein nevertheless declared, 'The question of women's suffrage is not an issue of the first importance for socialism and the working class.'† In Austria-Hungary, social democrats declared their attachment to the equality of the sexes, but through their jokes and arguments for authority, they succeeded in limiting the influence of women. Anna Altmann, the only woman delegate from Cisleithania, and Adelheid Popp, editor in chief of the *Journal of Female Workers* for forty years, bore the brunt of this structural misogyny. For

---

* Vicki Crawford et al (eds.), *Women in the Civil Rights Movement: Trailblazers and Torchbearers, 1941–1965* (Bloomington: Indiana University Press, 1993).
† Cited in 'Le droit de suffrage pour les femmes', *La Revue socialiste*, Vol. 44, August 1906, p. 152.

Otto Bauer, one of Marxism's theorists, women fulfil their mission when they ensure their husband's comfort.*

In the USSR, the state emancipated women: they could work, actively engage in politics, live with their partners outside marriage, divorce and have abortions – in other words, escape from the woman function. Stalin executed an about-turn in 1935, immediately echoed by *Izvestia*: 'As full-fledged citizens in the freest country in the world our women have received from nature the gift of being mothers. May they safeguard and treasure it in order to give birth to Soviet heroes! Life-destroying abortion is unacceptable in our country.' Accordingly, the family was exalted and abortion forbidden (though it would be once again authorized after Stalin's death.)

The East German constitution promulgated in 1949 guaranteed the equality of the sexes. One year later, a law stipulated that marriage did not in the least diminish the rights of women: decisions concerning the place of residence and the raising of children were to be made conjointly; the wife had the right to be a student and a worker, even if that led to temporary separation. In the 1950s, women gained access to higher education and professional training. Abortion was legalized. Equal pay was ensured and in order for women to reconcile work and family life, beginning in the 1960s, each child was entitled to a place in a childcare centre. At the end of the Cold War, the number of East German women actively employed rose to 89 per cent, as opposed to only 56 per cent in West Germany.

As various testimonies recall, however, East German women shouldered the greatest burden of domestic chores. They were excluded from certain professions, particularly in the domain of technology, and no woman was at the head of a 'Publicly Owned Enterprise' (VEB). It is true that a good number of women held seats in the People's Chamber, under the tutelary figure of Clara Zetkin. These appearances were misleading, however: in 1950, women constituted only 15 per cent of the Central Committee of the Socialist Unity Party of Germany (SED), and that share even fell to 10 per cent in 1986.

* Paul Pasteur, 'Le semeur, la semence et le fidèle combattant de l'avenir, ou la masculinité dans la social-démocratie autrichienne (1888–1934)', *Le Mouvement social*, No. 198, 2002, pp. 35–53.

The masculine communist dictatorship was particularly visible within the Politburo's central committee holding most of the power: no woman was ever admitted to it.*

In the USSR as in East Germany, women were excluded from power, but benefited nonetheless from real advances. In Mao's China, female workers held subordinate, poorly paid positions, but they were integrated into the *danwei* ('work unit' of a state enterprise). In Iran, on the other hand, the betrayal was complete. At the call of Imam Khomeini, millions of women participated in the demonstrations of 1978–1979. A few weeks after his return to Tehran, Iranian women celebrated International Women's Day for the first time on 8 March 1979. But the new regime demanded that they go to work wearing a veil, without make-up, on the grounds that 'Muslim women are not dolls'. Women were forbidden to pursue certain professions. Sharia law henceforth governed the family, replacing the 1967 law that prohibited underage marriage and gave women certain rights in matters of divorce and parental authority. At a Paris rally held on 22 March 1979, attended by the American feminist Kate Millett, who had just been expelled from Iran, Simone de Beauvoir expressed her hope that 'this revolution would be an exception': if women's rights were not respected, the new regime 'would in its turn be nothing but a tyranny'.†

In the end, the Iranian revolution gave rise to an intrinsically misogynist state oppressing women in the name of Islam. In the following decades, men became the 'natural' holders of religious, political and family power, while women were subjected to dress constraints, legal tutelage, inequalities of inheritance, professional exclusions and prison rapes.

---

* Gisela Helwig and Hildegard Maria Nickel (eds.), *Frauen in Deutschland, 1945–1992* (Berlin: Akademie, 1993); and Valérie Dubslaff, 'Les femmes en quête du pouvoir? Le défi de la participation politique en République démocratique allemande (1949–1990)', *Allemagne d'aujourd'hui*, No. 207, January–March 2014, pp. 33–45.

† Chahla Chafiq, *Islam politique, sexe et genre: A la lumière de l'expérience iranienne* (Paris: PUF, 2011), p. 136 ff; and Marie-Jo Bonnet, *Mon MLF* (Paris: Albin Michel, 2018), ch. 47.

FROM SAUDI ARABIA TO ICELAND

Since the eighteenth century, women, men and state powers have all contributed to the victories of feminism. It is difficult to know which of these agents has played the most decisive role, even if it has clearly been women who instigated and won most of these struggles. The role of associations, labour unions, businesses and municipalities in which both men and women are found also has to be taken into account. However that may be, state powers are not simply a means of implementation: both the democratic welfare state and the revolutionary socialist state extended women's rights, while colonial and theocratic states limited them. To put it another way, the collective demands of women have (or have not) been transformed into statutes of law; the mobilization of feminists has (or has not) been followed by feminist policy.

State policy on prostitution provides an example. In the 1860s, the Italian state funded prostitution by means of a line item in the budget. In the Maghreb under colonialism, houses of prostitution were not just well established but the sanitary tax deducted from women's earnings also brought in large sums of money: 30,000 francs in Algiers, 90,000 francs in Tunis, 188,000 francs in Casablanca. The money was supposed to be used for improved medical monitoring and the fight against venereal disease, but that was not always the case, and in reality, prostitutes bore the burden of helping municipalities save money.* In twentieth-century Europe, the development of the welfare state combined with the rise in the standard of living made it possible to eradicate the mass prostitution that in the nineteenth century characterized the reality of women employed in a wide range of jobs, ranging from factory work to opera house dancing. In France, the closing of public houses of prostitution at the instigation of Marthe Richard in 1946 signalled the end of the state as a procurer of sex.

The state carries such weight that it is in a position to support or

---

* Christelle Taraud, *La Prostitution coloniale: Algérie, Tunisie, Maroc (1830–1962)* (Paris: Payot, 2003), pp. 258–260.

thwart feminist causes. In Great Britain, the model of the male bread-winner promoted by business and labour gave men a weapon to use against the demands of female workers, labour union activists and suffragists. In Germany, social democracy already included feminists in its ranks in the nineteenth century, but West Germany would offer less fruitful ground for that heritage than East Germany. Several decades after the fall of the Berlin Wall, the educational system of the *Länder* in East Germany and Eastern Europe have preserved traces of that state feminism, since the gap between girls and boys in the success rate in mathematics is as low as in the Scandinavian countries.*

Similarly, it was the former Soviet-bloc countries that provided the longest periods of maternity leave in the world in 2014: 18 weeks or more, or, in other words much more that the minimum of 14 weeks recommended by the ILO, and much more than the mean amount of time on record in Western European countries.†

In France, natalist familialism and the quality of services for early childhood have given women a certain autonomy, compensating for the weakness of nineteenth-century feminism, the sexism of the Republic and the misogyny of followers of Proudhon. Women have received from the state what they did not gain from revolutions. Except for 1789, the events of revolutions have not contributed much to women, either in 1792, 1830 or 1848, nor during the Paris Commune, despite the participation of Louise Michel, among others. From 1968 to 1972, revolutionaries displayed the same patriarchal convictions. Small groups of Marxist-Leninists, Trotskyites and Maoists squabbled about everything except the principle of masculine domination. While male activists prepared the revolution, female activists went back home to take care of the children: as Christine Delphy observed, the leftists defended their 'interests as men'.‡ A large number of women active

---

* Quentin Lippmann and Claudia Senik, 'Math, Girls and Socialism', *PSE Working Papers*, No. 2016–22, 2018.
† Laura Addati et al., *Maternity and Paternity at Work: Law and Practice Across the World* (Geneva: ILO, 2014), pp. 8–10.
‡ Christine Delphy, 'Nos amis et nous' (1977) in *L'Ennemi principal*, Vol. 1, *Économie politique du patriarcat* (Paris: Syllepse, 2013/1998), p. 151. See Ludivine Bantigny, Fanny Bugnon and Fanny Gallot (eds.), *Prolétaires de tous les pays, qui lave vos chaussettes? Le genre de l'engagement dans les années 1968* (Rennes: Presses Universitaires de Rennes, 2017).

within the extreme left would become feminists in the 1970s, and it was under this label that they would continue their struggle.

From the perspective of women's emancipation, the democratic welfare state and the revolutionary socialist state have allowed comparable advances, but the latter, as a result of both dictatorship and poverty, always ends up trammelling their rights: hence we can conclude that *freedom of expression associated with social safety nets* have proven to be globally more effective. These are the conditions that most often translate women's demands into concrete gains. In the twentieth century, democracy has been women's best ally.

The feminists' struggle, men's support and state involvement are collective actions that come into clear focus in the *Gender Gap Report*, which classes every country in the world with regard to the condition of women, taking into account various criteria such as health and educational environment, along with participation in political and economic life.* In spite of the criticisms that one can level against a worldwide classification established from heterogeneous data, its findings cannot be simply brushed aside.

In the first place, the emancipation of women does not directly result from a country's wealth. There would be no point in staging a competition between North and South, or between the West and developing countries. Rwanda, for example, has been ranked fourth, ahead of most of the European countries and far ahead of the United States, which is relegated to forty-ninth place. One can doubt whether the situation of Namibian women (ranked thirteenth) is really better than that of Danish women (ranked fourteenth), but the low ranking of Italy in eighty-second place, just ahead of Mexico and Myanmar, certainly reveals the weakness of the political and economic opportunities that country offers to women.

Most importantly, these rankings point to the role of the state in the emancipation of women. On that level, the Scandinavian model stands out: Iceland, Norway, Finland and Sweden figure among the five highest rankings. Western Europe posts good results, with France, Germany and the United Kingdom occupying eleventh, twelfth and

---

* World Economic Forum, 'The Global Gender Gap Report 2017', available at www3. weforum.org/docs/WEF_GGGR_2017.pdf

fifteenth places respectively. The condition of women in Iceland, ranked first out of 144 countries, reflects that democracy's political and social choices. The 'Icelandic miracle' is due to the educational success of girls, the massive presence of women in the workplace, the equal salaries that are guaranteed to them and their access to positions of responsibility. It also reflects political victories such as the feminist strike of 24 October 1975 and the 1980 election of Vigdís Finnbogadóttir by direct universal suffrage. As the female singer Björk, born in Reykjavík in 1965, explains:

> I am very lucky to have been brought up in this country. It was actually a shock when I experienced the rest of the world. All of a sudden, I was a woman, and considered as such, in this funny relation of the sexes that governs the rest of the planet... Up until the age of 27, I had lived as a man's equal. Living elsewhere, I understood that such was not the case everywhere.*

On the opposite end of the scale, one of the richest countries on the planet, Saudi Arabia, is ranked 138th out of 144. Not because it is a Muslim country, but rather because, beginning in 1932, the Saudi state made Wahhabi doctrine an essential component of its national identity. In other Arab countries, the national agenda was put together with women and in opposition to colonial powers. Saudi women, on the other hand, were sacrificed on the altar of a religious nationalism which aims to make Saudi Arabia into the most 'pious' country, the model of an 'immaculate' Islam. Hence the subjugation of women, placed under the tutelage of males in every aspect of their lives: the legal system of the patriarchal family, non-mixing of the sexes in schools and workplaces, the mandatory wearing of the burka and the omnipresence of the religious police. As hostages of a masculine dictatorship, Saudi women have many fewer rights than other Muslim women in the world.† After September 11 (2001), the Saudi state suddenly pushed women into the media and business, in order to boost its image on the international scene.

---

* Cited in *Télérama*, No. 3538, 1 November 2017.
† Madawi Al-Rasheed, *A Most Masculine State: Gender, Politics and Religion in Saudi Arabia* (Cambridge: Cambridge University Press, 2013).

Saudi Arabia, or state misogyny

1932	First appearance of Wahhabi-inspired religious nationalism.
1962	Abolition of slavery; the first schools for girls are opened, much to the annoyance of the conservatives.
1971	Patriarchal reforms in the Council of Senior Ulama.
1970s	Segregation-marginalization of women linked to oil revenue and the model of the male breadwinner; internationalization of Wahhabism.
2001	September 11 terrorist attacks in the United States.
2006	Mixed-sex workplaces are authorized.
2010–12	Arab Spring.
2011	Women gain right to vote in municipal elections.
2018	Women gain right to obtain a driver's license; feminist activists are tortured in prison.

THE EXTENDED PATRIARCHAL CIRCLE

With the full scope of human history in mind, the twentieth century stands apart, constituting a break, and its legacy inspires silent admiration: for the very first time, women benefited from rights, and freedom for women in all its forms was recognized. Added to a certain number of technical advances (obstetrics, baby bottles, household appliances, the pill), this revolution translated into the improvement of the lives of hundreds of millions of women throughout the world. One only has to take a look at one's own family and life to observe this fact. Feminist victories touch the lives of each and every one of us: women without exception, but also men, in that they have grandmothers, mothers, sisters, wives and daughters.

One nevertheless clearly senses that we are still only halfway there: while there is a widespread crackdown on sexual inequalities, particularly in Western Europe and North America, there remain a number of vestiges. Why has the revolution of rights still not demolished the patriarchal structures handed down from the Neolithic age?

The emancipation of women was carried out thanks to a widening of the patriarchal circle that allowed women to get out of their households, yet women were still burdened with the attributes of the woman function. In the nineteenth century, maternalist feminism demanded rights for women as women. In the twentieth century, the development of the welfare state extended the skills of the wife-mother out into society. That is what Jon Eivind Kolberg calls the theorem of the 'family turned public': what was formerly found within the family is nowadays obtained via the feminized public sectors of healthcare, education and social services. The same phenomenon has taken place in the private sector.

Despite their progress towards full emancipation, women in Sweden remain confined to the social and educational service sector linked to the welfare state. When they manage to get into the bastions of masculine industry, they only rarely gain access to technical professions (8 per cent) and almost never reach the managerial level (1 per cent). In France, women make up 98 per cent of secretaries, 97 per cent of domestic aids, 90 per cent of medical assistants, 73 per cent of sales associates, 70 per cent of custodial workers and 66 per cent of teachers. A hierarchy has been established even at the highest levels of the state: with the same level of university degrees, women are

The extended patriarchal circle

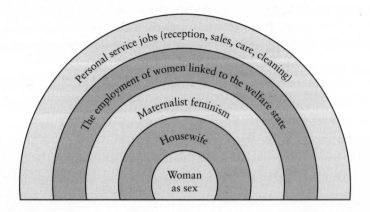

more likely to choose highly feminized 'social' ministries (Social Affairs, Health, Labour), whereas the norms of prestige and remuneration drive men to serve in the most eminent ministries of state power and authority (Finance, Interior, Foreign Affairs).*

Whether a mother in Athens, a citizen's wife in Rome, a servant in Renaissance Italy, the lady of the house in the Victorian age, a housewife in Kansas City, a secretary in the mid-twentieth century or a nurse or teacher today, the woman always provides for individual and collective wellbeing. She contributes maternal types of care for her family and society, and often for both at the same time.

Neo-patriarchal society entrusts responsibilities to each sex, on the one hand making the woman function into a profession, and on the other, making sanctuaries of the spheres of masculine power in the world of occupations. That explains why the emancipation of women coexists with the preservation of institutional sexism: it constitutes a final protection for men. In order to finish dismantling patriarchy, it is therefore imperative to continue to extend women's rights everywhere. However, it is also necessary to transform the masculine. This undertaking may well be Herculean, but it is not impossible, thanks to the strength of the global feminist movement. Besides, democracy is an asset; the state can be an ally in this endeavour. And not all masculinities are oppressive – some men fight alongside women for the cause of feminism.

* Observatoire des inégalités, 'Une répartition déséquilibrée des professions entre les hommes et les femmes', 11 December 2014; and Catherine Marry et al, *Le Plafond de verre et l'État: La construction des inégalités de genre dans la fonction publique* (Paris: Armand Colin, 2017), in particular pp. 56–57.

PART THREE

Deficiencies of the Masculine

9

Man in His Alienations

It may seem rather astounding to see newspapers increasingly speaking of masculinity in crisis. With all their prerogatives – their social privilege from birth, their habitual appropriation, their frequent recourse to violence – how could men possibly be in crisis? Are their crocodile tears not simply a ruse intended to elicit sympathy and discourage resistance?

Actually, this question stems from an erroneous definition of the masculine, which presents it as being synonymous with its patriarchal core. Not all men are tyrants, and not all of the masculine can be reduced to the desire for domination. Not only does some men's violence shatter other men, but the cult of authority also plunges the entire gender into anxiety. Moreover, the types of alienation commonly associated with masculinity are made worse – almost tragic – by the emancipation of women.

We must therefore take the crisis of masculinity (and even the sense of a crisis) seriously, because it represents a break, and through it, the masculine can escape from its own prison: reconstituting the masculine begins with a diagnosis of its fragility. That is why we must not only point out the deficiencies of the masculine, but even expand on them, deepening the doubts while upholding forms of masculinity that are least accepted, in order to shatter the monolith.

MASCULINITY HAUNTED BY FEARS

In Indo-European mythologies, the integrity of the hero (Indra in India, Tarquin in Rome, Gwynn for the Celts) is tarnished by 'three sins': one against the law (murder), another against honour (disloyalty) and a third against morality (rape).* It is not so much that heroism implies the possibility of failure; it is rather that the hero always turns out to be a giant with clay feet, a mere mortal who is fallible, which paradoxically heightens his prestige. It is no accident that the *Iliad* opens with the wrath of Achilles, the man of jealousy, suffering and tears, the combatant made vulnerable by the heel that his mother did not immerse in the Styx.

The hero's misadventures underscore an important characteristic of the masculinities of domination: a man must constantly prove that he is one. Masculinity carries within itself a fear, that of being unworthy of the male sex. It is therefore intrinsically fragile, self-doubting, afraid of not meeting the standard: hence all the provocations, ostentatious behaviours, sacrifices, all the 'fine deaths', which only raise the stakes even more.

The crises of masculinity have existed since antiquity, and *independently from any demands made by women*. Conversely, men have had to learn how to block themselves off from women, at the risk of their downfall. Greek and Latin literature contains many episodes in which the masculine is threatened from within by the feminine: Aristophanes' effeminate contemporaries are mocked for gossiping, Hannibal is scorned for having given in to the 'delights of Capua', the Hellenists' weakness and corruption are denounced by Cato, the ancient austerity of Mummius and Cincinnatus were praised and the 'decadence' of the Romans was lamented at the end of the Empire. In *The Quadrilogue invectif* (1422), written during the Hundred Years' War, Alain Chartier rebukes French knights for their love of finery, a feature blamed for the Agincourt debacle in 1415. In the mid-eighteenth century, Rousseau reviled the mollifying influence of the salons, in which each woman assembled her own 'private collection of men more feminine than herself'. In painting, the neoclassical rigour of the 1780s was both a response and an antidote to Boucher's Rococo frivolity.

In the first half of the twentieth century, fascism and Nazism

---

* Georges Dumézil, *Heur et malheur du guerrier: Aspects mythiques de la fonction guerrière chez les Indo-Européens* (Paris: Flammarion, 1985/1969), p. 114.

Crises and backlashes of the masculine

Period	Epicentre	Alleged cause	Virile backlash
2nd century BCE	Rome	Luxury, moral corruption	Cato's moralism
14th century	France	Defeat at the Battle of Agincourt (1415)	Chartier's pamphlet (1422)
18th century	France	Moral decadence under Louis XV	'Republican' current (Diderot, Rousseau, David)
French Revolution	France	Regicide and devaluation of the husband-father	Civil code of 1804
1830–1918	Western Europe	Peacetime softening; dandyism (Huysmans)	Imperialism and militarism; First World War
Interwar years	Germany	Defeat in 1918; the Weimar Republic	Rise of Nazism
End of the 20th century	Europe, the United States	Feminist victories	Masculinist reaction
2010s	Europe	Rise of Islam	Populism, re-virilization of the Church

constituted a response to an anxiety about a perceived loss of virility. In France, Mussolini and Hitler's admirers were haunted by the spectre of national decadence, which only added to their personal impotence. Drieu La Rochelle set the feminine (the bitter, passive, castrated intellectual) over against the masculine (the man of action): force was a remedy for the degenerative state of the old bourgeois society. For Drieu, as for Aristotle, the fear of becoming effeminate concealed the hatred of democracy: only 'real' men could save civilization. After the supposed weakening came the return swing of the pendulum, the virile backlash that put an end to this internal crisis of masculinity.

THE WARS OF THE MASCULINE

All we have to do to become aware of the scope of masculinity is to watch a western. No fewer than seven types of men interact in Howard Hawks' *Rio Bravo* (1959): Sheriff John Chance (played by John Wayne); Dude, his alcoholic sidekick; the lame grouch Stumpy; young Colorado; the latter's boss; the Mexican innkeeper; and the gang leader. There are males who are either good or bad, up and coming young men (Colorado), and old men on the decline (Stumpy). Needless to say, the hierarchical summit is occupied by the sheriff, a white man; he is wise, experienced, a representation of authority. It is he who 'wins' the pretty woman traveller at the end.

Other masterpieces feature a kind of secondary plot in which a masculine duo play on a system of opposites: a young, idealistic, untainted man has to team up with an older man with marks of virility (alcohol, a beard, sexuality, money). Tamino and Papageno in *The Magic Flute*, Tintin and Captain Haddock in *The Adventures of Tintin*, and Luke Skywalker and Han Solo in the *Star Wars* trilogy are all variations on this binary scheme. Within the very sphere of the masculine, the man who is an almost feminine virgin rubs shoulders with his mature male partner who, despite his many faults, happily connects with life's pleasures: the interaction of these two contrasting figures creates comical tensions and misunderstandings. In Fellini's *La Strada* (1954), the fairground entertainer, with his motorcycle, leather jacket and chains, and his brutish manners, kills 'The Fool', a young, mischievous, poetic, high-wire walker, with one blow of his fist.

We can understand why the flip side of the masculine's comic surprises is masculinity's tragic wars: the latter are a battle for legitimacy which results in the exclusion, or even the slaying, of the inferior man. For corruption always stalks the masculine: men who are like worms in the fruit, inner enemies. This threat is embodied by four figures: the loser, the Jew, the Black and the homosexual.

The loser is the man without any virile qualification, the one who has failed at one of the four masculinities of domination: he is cowardly, whining, nerdy, bespectacled and lame; he has neither courage, nor strength, nor sex-appeal. Because he brings shame to the gender in its entirety, he is despised by the 'real' men. Excluded from legitimate masculinity, he is the one unable or unwilling to fight: Leporello in *Don Giovanni*, the Mexicans and the Chinese in westerns, Yossarian in *Catch 22*, the hippies as seen by conservatives. The army itself admits this stratification: in the Israeli army, the combatants are superior to both the 'blue collars' (cooks, mechanics, drivers) and women

Charlie Chaplin, or the deficiencies of the masculine (1920s)

As a penniless tramp in ragtag clothes, clumsy, ridiculous, but always endearing, the character invented by Charlie Chaplin in the early twentieth century is the most universal of all anti-heros. He constantly runs up against the masculinities of domination: brutes, trappers, bosses, fat cats, policemen, and so on.

soldiers (instructors), such that, once returned to civilian life, a former fighter pilot will 'count' more than a former truck driver for a logistical unit.*

Excluded from legitimate masculinity are the men of few means: the poor wretches, the 'passive citizens' in Revolutionary France in 1791, the 'vile multitudes' in the France of 1850, *schnorrer* in the world of the Ashkenazim, landless peasants in Latin America – or 'white trash' in the United States, seen as backward and crude, their unworthiness an insult to WASP masculinity.

Anti-Semitism and racism make the Jewish man and the Black man foils of the virile white man. Their femininity is seen as a pathology. By his love of study and fondness for learned discussion, the Jew belongs to a type of 'unmanly' masculinity. In the 1930s, the French socialist leader Léon Blum was referred to as a 'courtesan' and a 'hysterical loudmouth'; the newspaper *L'Oeuvre* wrote that he dressed 'like a crazy virgin wearing a low-cut dress, with bare arms, lipstick, shaved legs, powdered, and perfumed'.† A similar hatred was directed against Black men, because they were seen as both non-virile and non-human. Racism was responsible for the frightful plight of African-Americans, from cotton plantations to Supermax penitentiaries.

The homosexual represents a twofold threat: not only does he have an 'abnormal' sexuality, but he is also capable of luring astray those of his own gender, which creates a wave of panic among all males whose honour is based on heterosexuality. As with anti-Semitism and racism, homophobia culminates in violence: rejection, stigmatization at school or in the locker room, insults, harassment, aggression, imprisonment and, in some countries, murder. The German penal code made homosexuality a punishable offence beginning in 1871. In Egypt, filmgoers at certain showings of *The Yacoubian Building* clapped when the homosexual journalist was murdered.‡ For its part, the Portuguese Church announced in 2017 that it would investigate the profiles of its

---

* Orna Sasson-Levy, *Identities in Uniform: Masculinities and Femininities in the Israeli Military* (Jerusalem: Hebrew University Magnes Press, 2006).
† Cited by Solange Leibovici, *Le Sang et l'Encre: Pierre Drieu La Rochelle, une psychobiographie* (Amsterdam: Rodopi, 1994), p. 281.
‡ Shereen El Feki, *La Révolution du plaisir: Enquête sur la sexualité dans le monde arabe* (Paris: Autrement, 2014), p. 256.

candidates for seminary, in order to reject both homosexuals and paedophiles.

Sociologist Raewyn Connell and historian George Mosse have shown how masculinity defined itself in terms of relations vis-à-vis a shameful feminine, but also with respect to the subordinate or marginalized masculinities of the intellectual, the homosexual, the disabled person, the poor man, the immigrant, and Jewish and Black people. In order for gender to be handed down from one generation to the next, certain groups of men had to be systematically disparaged. The masculinities of domination assert their legitimacy by ridiculing, even destroying the other masculinities.

The wars of the masculine have therefore preceded the war of the sexes and have been more violent. They must result in the victory of the 'real' man over the 'underling', whose anti-masculine character reveals the nation's decadence. In response to this peril, certain revolutions forge a 'new man', a virile hero heralding the future. During the French Revolution, King Louis XVI was accused of being sexually impotent, among other defects. Pamphlets and engravings depicted him in bed, a nightcap on his head, with a bare belly and a limp sexual organ: 'Sire was so soft that ... nothing pumped life into the royal sceptre.' Conversely, the patriot drew his citizenship from his seminal power and the rights of the man-phallus.*

While the citizen's vigour foreshadowed the Republic's victories, the toughness of the overman justified totalitarian crimes. The myth of the new man was one of the points that Bolshevism, Fascism and Nazism have in common. In the 1930s, these regimes disseminated a virile iconography linked to the regeneration of the state: athletes with the bodies of demigods, soldiers with invincible chests, Stakhanov looking off into the distance, statues of the 'Nazi nude' chiselled out by Arno Breker. The enemy, be he the Jew, the capitalist or the communist, threatened the vitality of the nation with his slimy femininity. Like the irregular forces of the *Freikorps* units after 1918, Nazi shock troops fought against the sickly, the weak, the soft, sensual laxity and the syphilitic Jew. Fascist aesthetics worshiped weapons and associated with

---

* Antoine de Baecque, *Le Corps de l'histoire: Métaphores et politique (1770–1800)* (Paris: Calmann-Lévy, 1993), pp. 73–75.

military dress: the kepi, the sword-belt and boots, with the soldier transforming into a creature of steel.*

The wars of the masculine unfold in such a climate of hatred that they incite their own victims to pattern themselves as counter-stereotypes. In place of the stooped, fearful 'Jew from the ghetto' there is Max Nordau's 'muscular Jew', the ploughman-soldier proudly working the land of Israel in a Kibbutz; instead of the 'queen', the macho-looking homosexual, with muscles, leather jacket, and a moustache, as in the sketches of the Finnish artist Tom of Finland, beginning in the 1950s. These were ways of being Jewish or gay without troubling the order of gender any further.

UPBRINGING AND SUFFERING

The masculinities of domination rule by overwhelming other masculinities, but their victory is a defeat for the entire gender. Shows of force, aggressive behaviour, the assignment of roles, the obligation to succeed and the culture of achievement are all traps that society sets for men, and those who have the strength to resist find their masculinity called into question. At the end of the day, this imperative virility is a burden, and those on top end up being dominated by their own domination. This mandate weighs on boys, young men, soldiers, lovers and fathers: all are victims of masculine alienation.†

The child is particularly vulnerable to macho culture. Rites of passage, 'educative' violence and domineering family fathers have the aim of making the little boy's gender coincide with his sex: hiding weakness, repressing his emotions, behaving 'like a man'. In numerous cultures, parents forbid their son from crying 'like a girl'. In Nigeria, boys are raised as future leaders with cries of 'Hard man!' as

---

* Klaus Theweleit, *Male Fantasies*, Vol. 1 (Cambridge: Polity Press, 1987 and Vol. 2) ; (Minneapolis: University of Minnesota Press, 1989).
† Joseph Pleck, *The Myth of Masculinity* (Cambridge: MIT Press, 1981); and Olivia Gazalé, *Le Mythe de la virilité* (Paris: Robert Laffont, 2017).

an encouragement.* Now, the more a man is taught to be tough, the more his ego becomes fragile. To humiliate a little boy in claiming to make him grow up is to make him believe that a man is someone who humiliates others.

Jennifer Siebel Newsom's documentary *The Mask You Live In* (2015) analyses the masculinity of American boys growing up under the tyranny of virility and performance. Why are they urged to curb their emotions and limit their calls for help? Why, so young, are they cut off from their feelings? In one scene, a teacher asks a group of eight Black boys what there is 'under the mask': on a piece of paper, they sheepishly write 'anger', 'suffering', 'sadness', 'fear' and 'tears', all that they had buried deep inside themselves because they did not have the right to mention it.

The educative and social harshness to which boys are subjected gets translated into violence, violence against themselves and violence against others, although only the latter attracts attention. Ever since the Revolution, French society has been obsessed with how to handle wards of the state: illegitimate, abandoned, delinquent children, and those at odds with society. Not all of them were subjected to penitentiary colonies aimed at straightening them out, but all were deemed to have been perverted by their families or by life on the streets: their unbridled, dangerous masculinity had to be filtered by an upbringing with a healthy virility able to transform the little savages into citizens. In the second half of the twentieth century, this model of social integration was applied in France to youth of North African descent in the housing projects, and in the United States to young Black men from the ghettos, 'bad boys' whose inadaptation to society only confirms their ethno-cultural deviance. In France, the result has been a cycle of riots and repression, and in the United States, mass incarceration.

The fear of juvenile deviance, which is linked to failure in school, together with the problems of street subculture and delinquency, all converge in making masculinity a problem of society. When they are old enough to go to school, boys are often accused of being disruptive.

* Chimamanda Ngozi Adichie, 'We Should All Be Feminists', TEDxEuston lecture, December 2012.

In the United States, boys are diagnosed as 'hyperactive' twice as much as girls, up to 20 per cent of a generation at the secondary school level. In France and Switzerland, medications such as Ritalin are prescribed for more than 3 per cent of boys, but only 1 per cent of girls.* Are boys really more hyperactive than girls, or do they prompt more intolerance from parents and institutions? Whatever the answer, society is missing something in respect of its boys, whose humanity is suffocating under such narrowly defined masculinity. A virile upbringing makes way for distress and rage, and society responds by making it into a pathology.

The model of the male breadwinner, defended by employers and the working class in the nineteenth century and subsequently adopted by certain welfare states, imposed physical ordeals on men in addition to a specifically masculine set of responsibilities: working hard, earning enough money to support one's family, and in all circumstances taking on the responsibilities assigned to one's gender. Obviously, working women also suffered from industrial jobs. In the coal mining areas of Scotland around 1840, women were toiling away in unhealthy mine shafts in water up to their knees even when they were pregnant. Respiratory ailments affected men much more, however, because they spent more time in the mines. The incapacitation of men diminished not only their ability to work, but also their social standing, precisely because they were expected to provide for their families.† Over the course of the nineteenth century, in both France and Great Britain, women were increasingly kept from descending into the mine shafts, and, in 1906, the catastrophe at Courrières in northern France killed more than one thousand male miners.

Such is the logic of the patriarchal circle as it applies to men. They can choose to get out of it, but, as is the case for women, they pay a high price: contempt, loss of status and accusations of not being up to the task. It is here that another crisis of manhood is visible. Since everyone commands him to hold up, what gives way in his place are

* Ryan D'Agostino, 'The Drugging of the American Boy', *Esquire*, March 27, 2014; and Sandrine Cabut, 'Hyperactivité: la Ritaline est-elle mal prescrite?', *Le Monde*, 18 June 2013.
† Angela Turner, 'Corps meurtris: Gendre et invalidité dans les mines de charbon d'Écosse au milieu du XIXe siècle' in Judith Rainhorn (ed.), *Santé et travail à la mine* (Villeneuve d'Ascq: Presses Universitaires du Septentrion, 2014), pp. 239–260.

his body and his mind, through workplace accidents, premature exhaustion, stress, burn-out and the feeling of not having seen his children grow up.

THE ABSENT FATHER

Ever since the French Revolution, thinkers identified to one degree or another as reactionary have worried about the disappearance of the father foreshadowing disturbances in a leaderless society. For the Catholic sociologist Frédéric Le Play, the elimination of the freedom to make a will in 1793 (a few weeks after the execution of Louis XVI) was a 'monstruous innovation'. Several psychoanalysts have expressed a similar fear: Paul Federn in *The Fatherless Society* (1919), Lacan in the 1930s in reference to the 'social decline in paternal image', and Alexander Mitscherlich in *Society Without the Father* (1963). Their idea is that revolutions and wars, and, more generally, social change as a whole, bring about symbolic parricides that make authority disappear. Boys no longer learn next to their fathers in the fields or at the workbench, but rather in schools where instruction is given by women.

The situation in which the man is incapable of being a father is a different story. Paternal defections arise from various catastrophes, including industrial exploitation, colonial society and slavery. In the nineteenth century, harsh work environments impacted masculine roles: 'the worker who drinks his pay in the cabaret' was a favourite theme of social reformers. Similarly, empires see increasing numbers of mixed-race children abandoned along with their mothers by fathers leaving for other horizons. The soldier conquers territories and hearts before vanishing. This phenomenon existed in Indochina as in Chile, and the opera *Madam Butterfly* by Puccini, which is set in Japan, echoes the pattern.

An abundant literature has been devoted to the challenges of the African-American father in the United States. In his controversial report on *The Negro Family* (1965), sociologist Daniel Patrick Moynihan established a link between the breaking apart of the African-American nuclear family and the permanence of racial inequalities. Between 1880 and 1960, Black children were deprived of one of their parents from two to three times more often than whites, and this parental absence increased again in the second half of the twentieth century, going from 32 per cent in 1960 to 53 per cent in 1980, as opposed to 9 and 16 per cent for white children.* In 1990, 46 per cent of Black families were headed by a woman, as opposed to 28 per cent twenty years earlier. Stigmatized as absent or immature, Black men as fathers participated in the Million Man March of 1995, in an effort to protect their children from drugs and violence in the ghettos. Various guides, such as *Black Fatherhood: The Guide to Male Parenting* (1992) and *Becoming Dad: Black Men and the Journey to Fatherhood* (2006), have been written in response.

Researchers have rejected racist hijacking of these statistics by showing that Black fathers were overwhelmed by centuries of slavery, discredited by endless unemployment, sequestered by mass incarceration or swept away by premature death. Conversely, other adults such as stepfathers, uncles, cousins, friends and pastors can act as paternal figures. What is important is to have a 'positive Black male role model' who spends time with the child, helping it confront problems.†

The break-up of the paternal figure can also be observed in the Caribbean area, particularly in the French Antilles, even if the resulting mother-centred family structure is not identical to that of single mothers in the United States.‡ Similarly, poverty, social humiliation and alcoholism take away the dignity of the white working-class father in the United States. Russell Banks' work, particularly *Affliction* (1989), elaborates on the idea that socio-economic downfall is passed down from father to son.

Once we put aside individual cases of irresponsibility or abandonment, the reality is that the difficulties many fathers face are linked to the violence of capitalism, slavery and colonization. It is society that has created the conditions for the failure of certain men – workers,

* Steven Ruggles, 'The Origins of African-American Family Structure', *American Sociological Review*, Vol. 59, No. 1, February 1994, pp. 136–151.
† Michael Connor and Joseph White, *Black Fathers: An Invisible Presence in America* (New York: Routledge, 2006), p. xii.
‡ Stéphanie Mulot, 'Redevenir un homme en contexte antillais post-esclavagiste et matrifocal', *Autrepart*, Vol. 49, No. 1, 2009, pp. 117–135.

soldiers, Black people and Caribbeans of African descent – from the nineteenth century on.

WHEN THE MAN DIES

In times of peace, as in times of war, men die earlier and more brutally than women. Since the end of the nineteenth century, this phenomenon has been observed everywhere and for all stages of life. In several countries, the risk of dying between the age of 35 and 65 is twice as great for men as for women. As far as life expectancy is concerned, the difference in favour of women in the 1980s was six years in England and Sweden, seven years in the United States and Italy, and eight years in France. Two decades later, it was seven years in Japan and thirteen years in Russia.[*]

The causes of men's higher mortality rate are not only tobacco, alcohol and an unhealthy diet, but also workplace accidents, diseases linked to their professions, violence, unnecessary risk-taking and a general reluctance to see a doctor or a therapist. One woman in New Guinea told an anthropologist the story of her three successive husbands dying one after the other: the first was killed by looters, and the second by a rival, who replaced the first husband before being killed in turn by his victim's brother.[†] In the United States, the National Center for Victims of Crime estimated in 2013 that 90 per cent of homicides were committed by men, who also make up 77 per cent of the victims. Highway death rates in Great Britain and the United States are twice as high for men, and three times higher in Sweden. In France, three quarters of people killed or injured in accidents are men: they represent 79 per cent of drivers and 96 per cent of motorcyclists killed. More than 80 per cent of those causing accidents are men, even though they do not drive much more than women.[‡]

Throughout the world, men commit suicide from three to four times

[*] France Meslé, 'Espérance de vie: un avantage féminin menacé?' *Population & Sociétés*, No. 402, June 2004.
[†] Cited by Jared Diamond, *Guns, Germs, and Steel: The Fates of Human Societies* (New York: W. W. Norton, 1997).
[‡] *Women's Issues in Transportation: Summary of the 4th International Conference: Proceedings 46*, Vol. 2, Washington, Transportation Research Board, 2011, p. 48 ff;

more often than women. From one country to another, young men take their own lives from three to seven times more often than young women. In the United States, white men have the highest suicide rate, followed by Black and Latino men, then white women. On the whole, American men kill themselves four times more often than American women (and ten times more often when they are elderly, since men make up 83 per cent of suicides of persons age 65 or older). White men commit 72 per cent of all suicides and 79 per cent of suicides by firearm.*

In the twentieth century, the percentages of children enrolled in school and the rates of professional qualification and employment for men and for women have come closer to each other, but not suicide rates. The gap even widened from 1970 to 1990 in the United States, Canada, Japan and several European countries, for all ages of males. Men are more susceptible to the ups and downs of the economic situation. Prepared to be family breadwinners holding social authority, they are shaken by unemployment and severe economic slumps, which devastate their expectations all the more, since they are less involved in the domestic sphere. Other factors come into play: the suicide risk is higher for young gay men, and elderly men are more sensitive to breaks in personal relations, to loneliness and to depression.

Men turn to more violent methods of suicide (by firearm or hanging), with a higher 'success' rate that women, a sign that masculinity continues to express itself even in dying with the qualities attributed to their gender: strength, decisiveness, rationality, courage.† So it is that, at the very moment when he seems defeated, the male triumphs by restoring his power, publicly resisting his loss of status. And death renders an ultimate dignity to the deceased, following the very logic of the masculinity of sacrifice.

This is the cost of collective alienation: violence directed against others, and against oneself. At the end of the day, excessive male

---

and 'Bilan définitif de l'accidentalité routière 2017', securite-routiere.gouv.fr, May 29, 2018.

* 'Gender differences in Suicide' and 'Males and Suicide' in Glen Evans and Norman Farebow (eds.), *The Encyclopedia of Suicide*, 2nd edition (New York: Facts on File, 2003), pp. 244–248.

† Katrina Jaworski, *The Gender of Suicide: Knowledge Production, Theory, and Suicidology* (Farnham: Ashgate, 2014), pp. 25–26 in particular.

mortality reveals a suffering that results from commands that men have internalized since childhood: displays of virility, the culture of excess, overinvestment in work, the refusal to complain, the choice of not opening up to others, the inability to express one's emotions. The model of masculine plight in patriarchal societies is to slave away for others and die before they do.

Not only are men vulnerable, but they also deny it, as do people in general. The sufferings of masculinity are based on gender inequalities: refusing to recognize this fact only adds a further injustice to the rest. No one wants to see that virility destroys men as much as it makes them. The masculinity of domination pays, but it comes at a high cost: an insecure ego, puerile vanity, disinterest in reading and the life of the mind, atrophied inner life, the narrowing of social opportunities (ranging from the choice of a 'masculine' occupation to the imbecility of misogyny and homophobia) and, to top it all, a diminished life expectancy. The higher death rate for males constitutes a tragedy on an individual and family level, but it also carries broader implications for society, concerning the matter of retirement, for example, since men pay their contributions for a lesser benefit.

It does not seem that public institutions devote much effort to fighting against this gender suffering. In 2018, a report from the American Psychological Association raised an alert about the physical and psychological damage inflicted by patriarchal masculinity: its toxicity affects all men. Launched in Australia at the end of the twentieth century, Movember is one of the rare organizations to concern itself with men's health. When will there be a campaign to raise awareness about premature deaths, which will declare, 'Dad, your life matters' or 'Men, we need you'?

Family, religion and society offer boys a rather paltry definition of masculinity: they adhere to it for lack of anything better. The real prison of gender is its mediocrity, compensated by endurance and intensity. The masculine can never prove itself enough: because one is a man, one must be one at every moment, and be ever more manly. Such blind fidelity has the effect of precipitating men into crisis, be it latent, individual or collective. For example, prostate cancer looms on the horizon as a dark cloud threatening the virility of men already facing the trials of old age: the collapse of narcissism drives some of the younger patients (under 60) to refuse treatment, as if it were preferable to die with a hard-on than to softly live on. These patients are much more afraid of losing their erections than of dying, whereas with the same prognosis for survival (almost 100 per cent for five years), patients suffering from kidney cancer fear for their lives.*

The masculinity of domination is therefore constructed as a three-fold violence against women, 'lesser men' and boys. Unbalanced, masochist, tortured, lacking confidence, it is by nature always in crisis: the man is never assured of his hegemony, never satisfied, always caught up in a struggle against women and 'inferior' men. Subordinate and illegitimate masculinities suffer domination, but masculinities of domination are themselves alienated: the man in power is a slave of his gender.

All of this makes it possible to throw patriarchy off balance. As bell hooks explains, 'inability to acknowledge the depths of male pain makes it difficult for males to challenge and change patriarchal masculinity'.† Conversely, some men in crisis, capable of self-criticism and of speaking their suffering, carry a 'will to change'. This personal inclination has to be converted into a collective movement. Thanks to their gains in the twentieth century, women have gradually freed themselves from servitude and stereotypes. We might dream of the same freedom for the masculine: the possibility of getting out of the obligatory model of virility without being exposed to either shame or ridicule.

---

* Anne-Sophie van Doren, 'Que reste-t-il de leurs amours? Étude exploratoire, clinique et projective de patients traités pour un cancer de la prostate', Doctoral dissertation in psychology, University of Paris-Descartes, 2017, pp. 28–34.
† bell hooks, *The Will to Change: Men, Masculinity, and Love* (New York: Washington Square Press), p. 139.

IO

Pathologies of the Masculine

In 2007, Carmen Tarleton was attacked in her home in Vermont by her former husband, from whom she had recently separated. Slipping into her house in the middle of the night, he beat her with a baseball bat before dousing her with an industrial cleaning agent. The liquid burned 80 per cent of her body, transforming her face into a mass of pulpy flesh and leaving her almost blind. A few years later, Carmen Tarleton received a face transplant. In the United States, one out of every four women has suffered serious acts of violence from her spouse and one out of every seven women has suffered harassment from a husband or an ex-husband.*

Such criminality shows to what degree masculinity is debased from within. That was the savage deed of one man in particular, but it partakes more generally of misogyny, *an ideology that postulates the inferiority of women and organizes their subordination by means of violence, discrimination and stereotypes.* These three forms of demeaning women correspond to three gender abuses: criminal masculinity, privileged masculinity and toxic masculinity. Misogyny has always existed. And yet, it does not constitute the essence of the masculine, but rather its perversion.

* Abby Goodnough, 'For A Victim of Ghastly Crime, a New Face, a New Beginning', *The New York Times*, October 25, 2013. Statistics for the United States as a whole can be found at https://ncadv.org/statistics

CRIMINAL MASCULINITY

Men's violence has been attributed to various factors, and it is not really possible to choose any one in particular to the exclusion of others: aggressive behaviour stemming from hormones or biological evolution, physical strength, upbringing, a fragile ego, the aggravating influence of poverty and alcoholism. For men, violent acts against women correspond to unilateral rights: a right to life, to physical integrity, to sexual satisfaction, to the fury of desire. Misogynist crimes can of course be collective, involving both men and women, as is the case with genital cutting and the selective abortion of girls, but they always aim to bolster the patriarchal order. Moreover, men sometimes lash out against other men, as do women against men or other women. Historically, feminine acts of violence have been perpetrated by women poisoners, female brothel owners, female 'kapos', certain spouses in heterosexual or homosexual couples, and mothers who kill their children or offer them to predators. There are no prize-winners for inhumanity.

In Roman and medieval law, in Christendom as is the lands of Islam, the husband can inflict punishment on his wife. That was one of his responsibilities: like a child, she was to be trained, by force if need be. In a village in the Italian Alps at the outset of the twentieth century, women were frequently beaten by men (fathers, stepfathers, husbands): one woman was lashed with a whip, another woman received a head injury from a bucket of frozen water.* A century later, 15 to 30 per cent of women in North America and Western Europe are victims of conjugal violence. In France, a woman is killed every three days by her husband or former husband. The situation is worse yet in Eastern Europe: Hungary and Ukraine have not ratified the Istanbul Convention of 2011 on domestic violence, and Russia even passed a bill decriminalizing acts of violence committed by 'near relatives'. Latin America and the Caribbean are also particularly violent regions. In Mexico, 43 per cent of women

---

* Serenella Noonis Vigilante, 'Tensions et conflits familiaux à Vauda di Front dans le Canavais (XIXᵉ–XXᵉ siècle)', *Le Monde alpin et rhodanien*, No. 3, 1994, pp. 111–124.

have been victims of their partners, and this figure is probably an underestimate.*

The statistics of rape are difficult to interpret, because the definition of the crime differs from one country to another and because an increase in cases filed can point to a greater combativity on the part of victims: so it is that Sweden has one of the highest rates of rape in Europe. In 2006, a survey of the 'context of sexuality in France' established that 7 per cent of women had suffered sexual assault and 9 per cent an attempted assault. In other words, one woman out of six had been assaulted, with minors and lesbians being the most affected. Sexual violence is endemic in several regions of the world, particularly in Latin America and the Indian sub-continent. In 2014, about one hundred women were raped each day in India, with Delhi holding the national record, followed by Mumbai, Jaipur and Pune.† In Malawi, men are paid to rape little girls and widows: this ritual, aiming to 'purify' women, was not officially abolished until 2013.

The murder of a woman as a woman is called femicide. It includes putting witches to death in Europe from the fifteenth to the seventeenth centuries; the infanticide of girls in Asia; the murder of adult women; 'honour crimes' in Southern Europe, the Middle East and the Indian sub-continent; and serial killings, beginning in the late nineteenth century. A huge number of young women have disappeared in the region of Ciudad Juarez in Mexico and among the Amerindian populations in Canada, where nearly 1,200 women were murdered between 1980 and 2012, constituting 16 per cent of the women murdered, although indigenous peoples only represent 4 per cent of the total female population.‡

Femicide is often accompanied by acts of torture. The horrific violence suffered by Elizabeth Short in Los Angeles in 1946, Mokhtaria

---

* 'Amnesty International Annual Report 2017/18: The State of the World's Human Rights', London, Index number: POL 10/6700/2018. Available at https://www.amnesty.org/download/Documents/POL1067002018ENGLISH.PDF.

† Christin Mathew Philip, '93 Women Are Being Raped in India Every Day', *The Times of India*, 1 July 2014.

‡ Jill Radford and Diana Russell (eds.), *Femicide: The Politics of Woman Killing* (Buckingham: Open University Press, 1992); and Gendarmerie Royale du Canada, *Les Femmes autochtones disparues et assassinées*, 2014.

Chaïb and Marie-Hélène Gonzalez in France in 1977 and 1998, and Lucía Pérez in Argentina in 2016 show that sexualized ultra-violence is a form of patriarchal terrorism. The murderer does not simply kill a woman; in her, he destroys all women. Misogynous barbarity can also manifest itself as a sort of vengeance in the face of feminine emancipation. The 'age of sex crime' was inaugurated by Jack the Ripper in 1888, after British women had acquired the right to divorce, vote in local elections and pursue their studies on the same level as men.* Certain femicides take on a political dimension: the 1960 murder of the Mirabal sisters, democratic feminists opposed to dictatorship in the Dominican Republic; the massacre of fourteen female students at the Polytechnique Montréal engineering school in 1989; the 2014 Isla Vista slaughter perpetrated by a man who could no longer bear being rebuffed; the ramming car attack perpetrated in Toronto in 2018 by an 'incel' – an involuntary celibate.

The most widespread cases of mass sexual assault are war rapes (modern examples of which were seen during the Second World War, in the former Yugoslavia, and in the Democratic Republic of Congo) and prostitution. On an international level, sexual trafficking afflicts 800,000 victims annually, 80 per cent of whom are women: the situation is the most disturbing in China, Nigeria, Russia and certain former Soviet countries. In Nepal, dire poverty, the weakness of the educational system and the absence of opportunity have profoundly worsened the condition of women: 20,000 are employed as sex workers in Kathmandu, 12,000 are sent to be sexually exploited in India and the Persian Gulf countries every year, and 300,000 are employed in quasi-slavery conditions in South East Asia and the Middle East.†

Though lesser known, selective abortion is frequent in China and India. A long tradition of infanticide and the abandonment of girls has led up to this 'gendercide', which has been modernized by the arrival of ultrasound in the late 1970s. It has also been spreading to places new to the practice, such as South Korea, Taiwan and countries in the Caucasus region. One of the key reasons for the termination of

---

* Jane Caputi, *The Age of Sex Crime* (Bowling Green: Popular Press, 1987).
† Neha Deshpande and Nour Nawal, 'Sex Trafficking of Women and Girls', *Reviews in Obstetrics and Gynecology*, Vol. 6, No. 1, 2013, pp. e22–e27.

girls before birth is that they are perceived to cost more than they bring in. Abortion, an instrument of women's liberation, has been turned back against them, denying them the right to live. In China and India, authorities are trying to fight this practice, but most often to no avail, although mindsets are changing. According to various studies, there is today a deficit of some 100 to 150 million women: as a result, Asia has become 'the most masculine continent in the world'. The consequences of this shortage of women are several: an impoverished human capital, a newly-appeared wives market, an increase in sexual trafficking and rape, and, in the future, additional military tensions as an outlet for frustration.*

Conjugal murder, femicide and gendercide stem from the notion that women are too free or insufficiently profitable: to remedy the situation, the masculine resorts to crime, as if women's deaths were their own fault. Whereas sex trafficking aims to fully exploit women's bodies, murder is the sign of the bloody failure of patriarchy, which usually obliges women to comply with the woman function. That is the reason why misogynist violence has been tolerated, even justified for so long: by an extensive conception of the husband's 'rights', by blaming and stigmatizing the victims of rape, and by leniency and indulgence for the 'natural' impulses of men.

The criminal is therefore excused. Cases of protection and complicity can be observed in highly masculine institutions such as the Church, the army and the intelligentsia. When Louis Althusser, the star of Marxist philosophy, strangled his wife Hélène Rytmann in 1980, his friends and former students went into action in order to clear their master thinker of responsibility: they spoke of a 'tragedy', 'depression', or 'suicide' by proxy, to the point of transforming the murderer into a victim.† The same solidarity went into play in the early 2010s, in support of socialist leader Dominique Strauss-Kahn, accused of rape in New York. The media treat the private life of male

---

* 'Gendercide', *The Economist*, March 6, 2010; and Bénédicte Manier, *Quand les femmes auront disparu: L'élimination des filles en Inde et en Asie* (Paris: La Découverte, 2008).

† Francis Dupuis-Déri, 'La banalité du mâle. Louis Althusser a tué sa conjointe, Hélène Rytmann-Legotien, qui voulait le quitter', *Nouvelles Questions féministes*, Vol. 34, No. 1, 2015, pp. 84–101.

politicians differently from that of women. They also report in a biased manner on acts of sexual violence. In the 1990s, for example, the daily newspapers of Montreal always viewed conjugal murders from the same angle: the crime story described as an isolated sensational event, thereby depersonalizing the victim while simultaneously minimizing the responsibility of the attacker.*

FROM DIRTY LAUNDRY TO THE MENTAL WORKLOAD

While serial killers are rare, men who take advantage of their masculinity are less so. That is why male privilege is more disturbing than acts of violence, especially since it is almost impossible to admit. Male privilege can be defined as the whole set of advantages conferred on men due to their gender: to the extent that men are for the most part unaware of these advantages, they give in to them without restraint or soul-searching. That is why any man who holds a position of power of any sort should always ask himself to what he owes this position. Led on by the model of the male breadwinner, he may point to his work and his merit. There are three other factors that often go unnoticed, however: male privilege, the domestic exploitation of women and workplace discrimination.

The masculinity of domination confers prestige and authority on men. Turn on the television, open the newspaper, study the organizational chart: there they are. Men can sometimes be co-opted by other men in executive committees or universities, and power as such is expressed and manifested as typically masculine. In day to day life, cooking, clothing and personal care remain the domains of women, while the 'exceptional' talents belong to the great chef, fashion designer or professor of medicine. Similarly, the rare men practising 'feminine' professions (nurses, elementary school teachers, social workers) benefit from the 'glass escalator', in other words, accelerated

* Ghislaine Guérard and Anne Lavender, 'Le fémicide conjugal, un phénomène ignoré: Analyse de la couverture journalistique de 1993 de trois quotidiens montréalais', *Recherches féministes*, Vol. 12, No. 2, 1999, pp. 159–177.

career trajectories. In schools for midwives, one of the most feminized tracks of French higher education with 95 per cent females, men are expected to assume their masculine prerogatives: they are called upon to take care of the few tasks involving physical labour, step forward to serve as class delegates and take their place in the Council of the National Order of Midwives.* Proof, once again, that patriarchy is not a plot, but a system.

This sexual division of labour was established in the Palaeolithic period: men were freed from the chores of mothering and nurturing that partake of the woman function. Is it possible that not much has changed ever since? In any case, many men feel that the anthropological destiny of women is to make sure that the fridge is full and the clothes clean: it's basically *their* problem. Such assumptions are so firmly anchored in age-old history that even women comply; if not, 'nobody would do it'. Why is washing the clothes the exclusive responsibility of the woman, even in young couples? 'That's the way it worked out,' in the unsaid workings of habit, under the influence of automatic reflexes, in response to men's willing incompetence and abstention.†

However, a fundamental break occurred over the course of the twentieth century: women entered the job market, mainly in the service sector. From that came the servitude of the 'double workday': salaried employment outside the home, unpaid labour within the household. In 1869, John Stuart Mill explained why women were still behind in the careers that were opening up for them: taking charge of the household absorbed a major portion of their time and attention. At about the same time, the French feminist Hubertine Auclert denounced the injustice of domestic labour: unlike women, men get paid when they sweep, clean, cook and do the dishes – that's called a job. A century later, Christine Delphy recalled that the tasks assigned to women in the area 'outside of a job' are in fact a job, just not one

---

* Christine Williams, 'The Glass Escalator: Hidden Advantages for Men in the "Female" Professions', *Social Problems*, Vol. 39, No. 3, August 1992, pp. 253–267; and Alice Oliver, 'Des hommes en école de sages-femmes. Sociabilités étudiantes et recompositions des masculinités', *Terrains & travaux*, Vol. 27, No. 2, 2015, pp. 79–98.
† Jean-Claude Kaufmann, *La Trame conjugale: Analyse du couple par son linge* (Paris: Nathan, 1992).

that is salaried. Women are therefore doubly exploited: by capitalism outside the home, and patriarchy inside.

Women thus have to pursue two 'careers' at the same time, as salaried employees and as mothers of families, in a 'supermum strategy'. At the end of the twentieth century, this 'second shift' makes for an increase of about 15 hours in women's workload, as compared to that of men. Only 20 per cent of couples function on a truly egalitarian basis, but in all cases, women are the ones who take on the great majority of routine daily tasks such as cooking, housecleaning and childcare, and do them all at the same time; whereas men take care of the car or home repairs and improvements when they have the time, doing only one thing at a time. The result for women is stress, frustration, increased illnesses and a decrease in libido: they come off as 'the villain', when in fact they are the victim.*

So then the patriarchal circle closes back up like a trap. Men 'don't know how to go about it', out of a well-calculated apathy; women 'know what to do', out of habit and obligation. At night, mothers are awakened by the crying baby, while fathers 'unfortunately' slumber on in deep sleep. In the interests of efficacy, women in the childcare centre call mums first. Among the working class, even the subsistence economy mainly involves the work of women, who have to take responsibility for buying groceries and basic household commodities, look for discounts or sales, fill out forms for governmental subsidies, take care of housekeeping chores, and maintain the network of friends and relatives. In the eyes of husbands, this work does not count: 'I do not have one minute to myself, but he does not see it, he is never there. He never understands why I am tired.'†

Women not only work more, taking on the combined responsibilities of their two jobs, they also deal with all family matters and the chores of daily life, including shopping, enrolments and registrations, appointments, reservations, planning everything from vaccinations to birthdays, a judo course to an end of the school year ceremony. All of this makes for a mental workload that does not make it into any

---

* Arlie Hochschild, *The Second Shift* (New York: Avon Books, 1989).
† Collectif Rosa Bonheur, 'Des "inactives" très productives: Le travail de subsistance des femmes des classes populaires', *Tracés: Revue de sciences humaines*, No. 32, 2017.

statistics. Mothers juggle several overlapping schedules at the same time: at the office, with the kids, with the family, and; when they can manage, their own – their own appointments with the doctor, the dentist, the hairdresser, and so on come last. The real revolution will occur when men share that mental workload in addition to household tasks.

DISCRIMINATION IN THE WORKPLACE

These familial servitudes are aggravated by discrimination in the workplace. As Arlie Hochschild points out, the professional world was conceived by and for men who had a wife at home. In addition to men's disinvestment from the household, business culture penalizes women, particularly when meetings are held at 8 in the morning or 7 in the evening. Gender conventions and career demands discharge men from family responsibilities; for example, it is almost always women who have to take over from the childminder in the evening or have to leave work in the middle of the day to care for a sick child. Because of that, the mental workload of the male employee is never weighed down by his other role – that of the father.

Men's overinvestment in work is therefore of a piece with their spouse's latent or explicit sacrifice of her career. This can lead to hypogamy, meaning the woman's job is less demanding and less lucrative than the man's. Either the marriage is non-egalitarian from the beginning (an executive married to a teacher), or else it becomes gradually imbalanced, with the wife giving up her professional ambitions when children arrive, putting her career on hold while she follows her husband in his different positions. The result is a negotiation within the couple whereby in a 'natural' way, the wife stops working when her husband is assigned to work abroad, or the wife of a high-level government administrator looks after the practical matters while her husband builds his CV within the cabinet of a government minister, and so on.

Now, the demands of a career crop up at the very time when women have to take care of their small children and infants. In the OECD countries, the rate of employment for mothers (65 per cent on average) is from 5 to 15 points lower than that of women in general. The gap is wider in Japan, Great Britain, Germany and Central European countries. The rate of employment for mothers everywhere drops – or even collapses – when their children are from nought to five years old (it goes from 79 per cent to 65 per cent in the United States). The arrival of a third child brings about a new crash: the rate of employment for mothers then decreases from 20 to 60 points, except in Northern Europe. Indeed, only when proactive policies of maternal and parental leave are in place can the employment rate for new mothers be maintained at around 80 per cent.*

In the nineteenth century, the prevailing view was that women could only bring in a supplementary salary because their primary obligation was to the household. Today, the causes of unequal salaries are much more diverse. Women are more often penalized by temporary, part-time or unstable employment, either by choice or necessity. The unfavourable distribution of income is also due to sexual segregation: women are concentrated in underpaid sectors (from cleaning services and personal care to teaching, publishing and administration), and are a minority in the most highly paid professions (in information technology, aeronautics, petroleum, banking and finance). Such is the post-industrial trajectory of the United States in the late twentieth century: women and people of colour are globally confined to menial jobs, while white men dominate management and professions in law, architecture and medicine.

Other factors can also come into play: career interruptions linked to maternity, lower salary demands at the time of negotiation, internalizing the idea that ambition is not becoming of a woman, inhibition when applying for a position, the imposter syndrome, and so on. On LinkedIn, women do not tout themselves as much, provide less information about their itinerary, and have a less extensive networks of contacts.† In France, the overall gender pay gap reaches 26 per cent.

---

* OECD, Social Policy Division, Directorate of Employment, Labour and Social Affairs, LMF 1.2, Maternal Employment rates, 2011. See also David Cotter, et al., *Moms and Jobs: Trends in Mothers' Employment and Which Mothers Stay Home* (Miami: University of Miami Press, 2007)
† Rachel Bowley, 'Women's Equality Day: A Look At Women in The Workplace in 2017', blog.linkedin.com, 28 August 2017.

It is reduced to 16 per cent for full-time employment, but men are still paid 12 per cent more than women who perform the same role, a discrimination that 'has not been explained'.*

Women hit a glass ceiling that keeps them away from positions of responsibility. All one has to do to understand that reality is to look at the leadership positions of business and industry. In the nineteenth century, the French glass firm Saint-Gobain was managed by men at all levels: glass plants, chemical production, factories, commercial affairs, management and board of directors. The first woman engineer, a graduate of the École Centrale, was recruited by the division of patents in the interwar period. At the end of the 2010s, Saint-Gobain's senior management team of fourteen executives included only three (or 18 per cent) women: the directors of human resources, communication and strategy.† In France, women made up 34 per cent of executives in 2011, as opposed to 23 per cent twenty years earlier. Men and women take on roughly the same responsibilities in their early careers, but the gap widens from the age of 35. In mid-career, 30 per cent of male executives have reached a leadership position, as opposed to only 14 per cent of the women.‡

In the United States, women have made dramatic progress in securing management positions, progressing from 18 per cent in 1972 to 45 per cent in 2000, but they remain under-represented at the highest levels of business and industry, and stock values drop considerably when a woman is named to the position of CEO, especially if she comes from outside the firm. At the 'C-suite' level (CEO, chief financial officer, chief operating officer and chief information officer), the only leadership position reached by more women than men is that of director of human resources. In the 500 companies making up Standard & Poor's index, women hold less

---

* François Dubet, Ce qui nous unit: Discriminations, égalité, reconnaissance (Paris: Seuil, 2016), p. 17.

† Jean-Pierre Daviet, Un destin international: La Compagnie de Saint-Gobain de 1830 à 1939 (Paris: Éditions des Archives contemporaines, 1988), pp. 231–233; and Saint-Gobain, 'Équipe dirigeante', at www.saint-gobain.com/fr/le-groupe/gouvernance/equipe-dirigeante

‡ Association pour l'emploi des cadres, Femmes cadres et hommes cadres: Des inégalités professionnelles qui persistent, March 8, 2011.

A conference of *Le Monde*'s editorial staff

In the second half of the twentieth century, the most eminent French daily newspaper had men at its helm. From left to right: an assistant chief editor, the chief of news reports, the chief of international news reporting, the chief of the economic section and another assistant chief editor.

than 5 per cent of CEO positions. In the 500 companies of *Fortune* magazine's classification, they represent 15 per cent of C-suite positions, but only 1 per cent of CEOs.*

The glass ceiling also restricts women's access to the highest echelons of the public sector, in the upper administration, public hospitals and universities. According to the Japanese Ministry of Education in 2018, three-quarters (and up to 83 per cent in national universities) of university professors were men. At a large hospital in Paris, women make up only 15 per cent of the university medical

---

* Peggy Lee, Erika James, "She"-E-Os: Gender Effects and Investor Reactions to the Announcements of Top Executive Appointments', *Strategic Management Journal*, Vol. 28, No. 3, March 2007, pp. 227–241, and Catalyst, 'Pyramid: Women in S&P 500 Companies', 3 October 2018.

professor practitioners (the highest-ranking group), even though their scholarly publications are equal to those of men.* In Spain, women achieve better results than men in their studies, and they are equally productive researchers, but their number decreases as one goes up the ladder of the university hierarchy. The tipping point is situated at the age of 34, connected to having children. At faculty level, one finds no more than 20 per cent women, and only 12 per cent at the University of Cantabria, 11 per cent at the Polytechnical University of Carthagena, 8 per cent at the Polytechnical University of Catalonia and 7 per cent at the University of Huelva. Parallel to this vertical segregation is a horizontal segregation concentrating women in certain fields such as the liberal arts, law and health.† The masculinity of privilege still has a long life ahead of it.

GENDER STEREOTYPES

Toxic masculinity disseminates a degrading image of women. Many books have been devoted to negative images of the feminine, from the myths of Pandora and Eve to Pierre de Coubertin's anathema, not to mention the seventeenth-century treatises *Les Singeries des femmes de ce temps* (The Monkey-Like Antics of Women of This Age, 1623) and *Le Tableau des Piperies des femmes mondaines* (A Tableau of the Stunts and Tricks of High Society Women, 1685). Here is a quick compilation of such stupidity.

First figure: the ravishing idiot, the dummy, the potted plant, the sex toy, the blonde. While La Bruyère, Nietzsche, Larousse and others have portrayed women as mindless flirts, feminists have shown how women get transformed into bunny girls or simpletons to whom one

---

* Charlotte Rosso and Anne Léger, 'Le plafond de verre dans les carrières universitaires au sein du groupe hospitalier Pitié-Salpêtrière', diploma in medical pedagogy, University of Paris VI, 2017.
† Esther Escolano Zamorano, 'Discriminación en un medio meritocrático: las profesoras en la universidad española', *Revista mexicana de sociología*, Vol. 68, No. 2, April–June 2006, pp. 231–263; and Marina Gama Cubas, 'La universidad española lejos de la paridad en las cátedras', *El Mundo*, 27 September 2017.

has to explain everything.* This presumption of stupidity explains why it was so easy in the twentieth century for women of science to be robbed of their discoveries by men, who alone received the credit and the honours. Among the victims were Cecilia Payne, who was the first to demonstrate that stars were composed of hydrogen, Rosalind Franklin, co-discoverer of the structure of DNA, and Marthe Gautier, whose work revealed the nature of Down's Syndrome.

Second figure: the devouring whore, the demonic female, the succubus, the Beautiful Jewess, the fatal seductress, the ambitious woman who sleeps with men in order to climb the career ladder. Men of all backgrounds desire and hate her, as if they expect to be corrupted by her. This is Daji, the perverse favourite of a king under the Shang dynasty; the 'demon who appears in the form of a young lady' in *The Tragic Stories* of François de Rosset; 'La Belle Dame sans Merci' of Keats, who subjugates knights; Carmen in the eponymass novella by Mérimée, who opens his story by stating that a woman 'has two good moments, one in bed, the other in death'; the 'slut' of the ghettos and favelas, a girl with no honour with whom anything goes. In an Internet forum frequented by economists in the United States, the words most often associated with their female colleagues are 'hot', 'lesbian', 'tits', 'anal', and 'slut.'†

Third figure: the emancipated intellectual, the woman who acts like a man, who has renounced her own sex, the untameable shrew, the 'troublemaker' who gets taunted, 'Are you on the rag?' Too free, too brilliant: she comes off as a denatured woman. The slur makes it possible to stigmatize women who challenge masculine monopolies in the domains of knowledge and professional success: the 'learned lady', the 'blue stocking', the 'killer' who climbs the company ladder. In the nineteenth century Gisèle d'Estoc played on all these clichés as a female writer, sculptor and fencing enthusiast who got into duels and was a transvestite and bisexual.

Sexism is not limited to stereotypes, however. It shows up in

---

* Gloria Steinem, 'A Bunny's Tale', *Show Magazine*, May 1963; and Rebecca Solnit, *Ces hommes qui m'expliquent la vie* (Paris: L'Olivier, 2018).
† Alice Wu, 'Gender Stereotyping in Academia: Evidence from Economics Job Market Rumors Forum', Working Paper, Princeton University, Princeton School of Public and International Affairs, August 2017.

families as well. When parents are asked to describe their newborn, for a boy they tend to speak of a big, strong, stocky baby, whereas for a girl, they describe a delicate baby with subtle features. In reality, there are no differences of that kind. Girls' fathers smile and sing to their child more often, using words related to the body and emotions, while boys' fathers more often horse around, having recourse to the vocabulary of success.* In the Santo Domingo quarter of Mexico City, people will say of a boy 'what a big boy', and 'what an intelligent face', but of a girl 'what pretty eyes she has', and 'what pretty legs she has'. On Mother's Day, the audience claps for a parade of four and five year-old children: miniskirts and fishnet stockings for the girls, black trousers and white shirts with braces for the boys.†

In *The Second Sex*, Simone de Beauvoir shows how children are brought up in a differential manner so that each will learn her or his gender: while the girl pampers her doll, parents invest in the boy. Coaxing, caresses and dresses for her, adventures and discoveries for him. By playing, she learns to become a doll, he projects himself into life. From the nineteenth century, toy manufacturers targeted children according to their sex: for boys, the world of war, transport, science, techniques, the vocabulary of speed and heroism. For girls, maternity, fashion, the emotional security of the household, the vocabulary of fairies and beauty. Publishers created collections intended for boys: the themes were exploration and conquest (the Landmark Books published by Random House in the 1950s and 1960s followed the same pattern).

Social activities are organized according to gender. In Europe as in the Maghreb, the flipside of boys' freedom is the close monitoring of girls. Boys in the rural areas of France in the 1950s were allowed to wander about, hunting snakes and catching birds, while their sisters stayed at home knitting: 'The girls sew, the boys run around.'‡ In countries like the Ivory Coast, Guinea, Mali, Niger, Senegal and Togo, from

---

* Katherine Karraker et al., 'Parents Gender-Stereotyped Perceptions of Newborns', *Sex Roles*, Vol. 33, No. 9–10, November 1995, pp. 687–701; and Jennifer Mascaro et al., 'Child Gender Influences Paternal Behavior, Language, and Brain Function', *Behavioral Neuroscience*, Vol. 131, No. 3, 2017, pp. 262–273.

† Matthew Gutman, *The Meaning of Macho: Being a Man in Mexico City* (Berkeley: University of California Press, 2007/1996), p. 105.

‡ Yvonne Verdier, *Façons de dire*, p. 176.

10 to 30 per cent of girls put in more than 28 hours of domestic labour, as opposed to 3 to 10 per cent of boys.* In the same era in France, boys took part in more sports activities than girls. Federations for dance, horse-riding and skating record about 85 per cent of their licences for females, as opposed to 5 per cent recorded by the federations for rugby and soccer. Does this have to do with what children want or what parents want, or is it an imperceptible social orientation?

And this lasts a lifetime: as a baby, child, teenager, student, employee, spouse or mother, a woman is treated in line with her predefined, conventional role until sex and gender coincide perfectly, according to the ideal set by each society: keeping her legs close together when seated, not speaking too loud, being pretty, being ashamed of bodily imperfections, never taking the first step in love, keeping her professional ambition in check. At the end of this long, silent instruction, women become creatures-for-others, empathetic oblates, painfully self-reflexive, deprived of the born legitimacy that the masculine confers on men. Even language incorporates the learning of gender: in the United States, women more often have recourse to protective expressions (I think, sort of, like), questions (isn't it?) and intensifiers (so, really, oh my God), such that their discourse seems both trivial and lacking in authority.†

SEXISM AND MASS CULTURE

Viewed from the angle of gender, popular culture (advertising, the cinema, video games) is a sexist bathing pool where everyone is splashing around. In the twentieth century, advertising perennially praised the woman function: the wife buys her husband his favourite beer, faithfully brings him his slippers and smilingly cleans the sink. Conversely, the products being sold are identified as a woman, a thing to possess. In the 1960s, a commercial for the Volvo 144 explained: 'There are some women who manage the miracle of being beautiful, pleasant and

---

* Christelle Dumas and Sylvie Lambert, *Le Travail des enfants: Quelles politiques pour quels résultats?* (Paris: Rue d'Ulm-ENS, 2008), pp. 64–67.
† Penelope Eckert and Sally McConnell-Ginet, *Language and Gender* (Cambridge: Cambridge University Press, 2013 / 2003), p. 38.

*Two sexist advertisements: Frigidaire (1954)
and Soli Dishwashing Liquid (1966)*

*Helpful and charming, like a wife who feeds her husband; delighted and
attentive, like a little girl who does the dishes.*

reliable: those are the ones that are chosen as wives. The Volvo 144 is like those women... A Volvo never divorces for assault and battery.' And the punchline: 'A Swedish woman whose curves you can regulate.'*

Towards the end of the twentieth century a new scenario was introduced: consumers were offered a gorgeous creature. Posing and smiling, femininity suggests sweetness, submission and sexual availability. The pornographic use of women has been used to sell anything and everything: beer, laundry detergent, perfume, cars, subscriptions. As an object of desire, ultimately a mere object, women become accessories of virile success.

In the early twenty-first century, progress in information technology made it possible to modify women's bodies at will. This third phase of sexism in advertising uses ever younger, ever more slender models, touched up to the point of anorexic 'perfection' in the form of clones without body hair or fat. In the end, advertising shows women two paths to follow: that of a scantily clad bimbo or of a housewife in charge of the laundry.

As is the case in the great epics, cinema offers variations on the theme of the hierarchical complementarity of the sexes. Men go on an adventure while women wait: as damsels in distress or the hero's ultimate reward (and sometimes both), they are placed in a position of passivity in relation to both the story's other characters and to cinema-goers. That is the basic structure of the *Odyssey*, *Reynard the Fox* and all the chivalric romances including *Amadís de Gaula*, *Peer Gynt*, *King Kong*, the James Bond series and dozens of other Hollywood films. When a (beautiful) woman is part of the story, she is there to be offered to the hero. A real male is characterized by his strength and aggression; a seducer never asks permission before pouncing on the object of his desire: a woman's resistance is a ruse signifying that she is in fact interested. These axioms govern the hero's sexual behaviour in westerns, as well as in the saga of *Indiana Jones*.†

* Georges Falconnet and Nadine Lefaucheur, *La Fabrication des mâles* (Paris: Seuil, 1975), p. 59 ff; and Erving Goffman, *Gender Advertisements* (New York: Harper & Row, 1979/1976).
† David Wong, '7 Reasons Why So Many Guys Don't Understand Sexual Consent', cracked.com, November 3, 2016. See also Laura Mulvey, 'Visual Pleasure and Narrative Cinema', *Screen*, Vol. 16, No. 3, October 1975, pp. 6–18.

These schemata have been passed down to the world of video games. In the beginning, information technology appeared to be like office work typical of a feminized tertiary sector. With the arrival of the personal computer in households in the 1980s, this changed and the secretary trained on office machines gave way to the computer programmer (and soon to the hacker), who withdrew from the world to live in the parallel universes that he could master. In France, 20 per cent of students earning degrees in information science in engineering schools were women in the early 1980s, but that number slid down and stagnated at around 10 per cent in the 1990s and 2000s.*

From the start, video games were flooded with gender stereotypes: a virile, muscular hero active in the midst of hyper-sexualized women, whose fleshy anatomy is revealed by ultra-short clothes. Like geek culture, the world of video games is androcentric, with a large majority of masculine characters (from 70 to 85 per cent according to the set studied). In Japan, the *bishōjo* games consist of seducing sexy young girls, in a school or a restaurant: this very popular genre includes pornographic variations. Nevertheless, female characters gradually started to appear. It was in the game *Metroid* (1986) developed by Nintendo, that the heroine Samus Aran, a bounty hunter seeking vengeance after the murder of her parents, appeared for the first time. In the arcade game *Street Fighter II*, Chun-Li was an aggressive combatant, whose flash kick was capable of taking out the most fearsome adversaries. As the figurehead of *Tomb Raider* (1996), Lara Croft gave rise to the 'Lara phenomenon', in which the female adventurer, as sexualized as ever, prevails through her blend of sensuality and violence.† Bayonetta, a heroine of an action game first commercialized in 2009, is a witch armed with four pistols and capable of sadistic attacks: she goes around nude, wrapped in her voluminous black hair. It is not the representation of woman that changes, but rather the fantasies of the players.

* Isabelle Collet, 'La disparition des filles dans les études d'informatique: Les conséquences d'un changement de représentation', *Carrefours de l'éducation*, Vol. 17, No. 1, 2004, pp. 42–56.
† Jeroen Jansz and Raynel Martis, 'The Lara Phenomenon: Powerful Female Characters in Video Games', *Sex Roles*, No. 56, 2007, pp. 141–148.

From the end of the twentieth century, measures have been taken against toxic masculinity. Relatively old agencies, such as the Advertising Standards Authority in Great Britain and the Conseil supérieur de l'audiovisuel (High Audiovisual Council) in France, work towards reducing sexism in advertising. Cinema has given life to increasingly complex feminine characters displaying intelligence, autonomy and courage: Clarice Starling in *The Silence of the Lambs* (1991), the two female fugitives in *Thelma and Louise* (1991), Buffy Summers in *Buffy the Vampire Slayer* (1997) and the titular whistle-blower in *Erin Brockovich* (2000) for instance. Even Disney, true guardians of gender conventions, seized upon Rapunzel, a bold princess who decides to set out and discover the world. In France, the heroine of *Julie Lescaut* (1992) is a police captain, a divorced mother who heads a team of inspectors and lieutenants. Such productions, particularly the televised series that make their way most easily into households, are seen by millions of people from all walks of life.

Likewise, the video game sector is creating more and more elaborate female characters that do not conform to the rules of gender. *Uncharted* (2007) features Elena Fisher, a reporter and archaeologist, as well as the adventurer Chloe Frazer and militia leader Nadine Ross. In *The Last of Us*, which came out in 2013 on PlayStation, fourteen-year-old Ellie is an orphan capable of breaking her jailer's finger and slaying her aggressor with a machete. With her ingrained toughness and an irreverent vocabulary, the young girl ultimately dominates her sidekick, an old backpacker who serves as a father figure.

Is this true progress? One could argue that these young women are portrayed within the logic of toxic masculinity. Either way, since the 2010s, videogame companies have opted to feminize their games, betting that girls will soon play as much as boys.

'COMPLICIT' WOMEN?

Misogynist men often achieve their ends by means of contempt and violence. There are some cases of women who withdraw their complaints about being beaten and housewives who think they are inferior to their husbands. Stereotypes produce their effects, but how? How is one subjugated by power? On a broader level, we have to wonder to what degree women consent to their own domination.

Pornography conveys a degrading image of women, reduced to their orifices. Yet it has not been proven that the millions of users of the site YouPorn are sexual predators, nor that rapists have been influenced by the pornography industry. In the area of prostitution, many men pay to be passive subjects, even punching bags: commercial sex allows them to escape from the conventions of the male heterosexual. One study dealing with 3,000 male fantasies showed that most were of a sadomasochist nature, with violence against women remaining the exception.* Men frequent pornographic websites and prostitutes much more than women, but their sexuality does not necessarily become more aggressive.

Certain women enjoy a soft eroticism in which, as in X-rated films, the feminine subject is reduced to an object of desire within a patriarchal framework. Romances often have the same structure: a rich man dominates a young woman of a modest background for the greater happiness of both. In the romances of Kathleen Woodiwiss or Celeste De Blasis, the hero sometimes rapes the heroine 'by mistake', because he believed her to be a prostitute. She gives in to him in the end, but with the benediction of marriage; in other words, without the guilt associated with a woman who asks for sex. These romances reassure female readers who live in a state of conjugal subordination. The heroine is first mistreated then protected by the hero: the initial act of violence was a sign of true love.

The lesson is clear: a woman must learn to trust a man, even if he does not appear to be worthy of that trust. Romances lead them to accept the inevitability of masculine power, but also of feminine know-how. In the end the heroine succeeds in making the hero love her, and forget all the women that he casually encountered and consumed without love. The heroine was therefore right to wait patiently for a long-term relationship, cemented by sexual pleasure and conjugal fidelity. Neither prudish conservatism, nor feminist revolt: by eroticizing the subordination of women, these romances perpetuate

---

* Lynne Segal, *Slow Motion: Changing Masculinities, Changing Men* (Basingstoke: Palgrave Macmillan, 2007/1990), p. 179 ff.

the female reader's investment in marriage and maternity. Phallic power is no longer threatening, but glamorous.*

There is nothing anecdotal about the success of these productions. Invented in Italy in 1947, the photo-novel met with astounding success in Europe and Brazil by making use of local stars. With twelve new novels per month, published in 'romantic' or 'steamy' collections, Harlequin have appealed to hundreds of millions of female readers since the 1970s. E. L. James's erotic novel *Fifty Shades of Grey* (2012) sold 150 million copies around the world. By their own admission, Harlequin's female readers indulge in such books as an escape from their everyday worries and to enjoy a moment to themselves. The fans of *Fifty Shades of Grey*, in general younger women with children, holding lower echelon unspecialized jobs, reject others' judgements that they are 'obsessed' or 'frustrated', insisting instead that they're simply setting aside moments of freedom within the constraints of gender and class.†￼ Popularized by pornography or pulp fiction, stereotypes bear patriarchy's imprint on men and women, who take active pleasure in it.

Janice Radway's analysis concurs with Gerda Lerner's: some women adhere to a patriarchal vision of society – that is, they acquiesce to their own subordination. Poullain de la Barre displayed this pessimism in the seventeenth century: imbued with such notions, some women can become misogynist, owing to ingrained prejudices, but also out of well-understood self-interest. For just as patriarchy sings the praises of docile women, so conservative maternalism reserves a special place for the mothers of male children. In the Maghreb, they indisputably hold power not only over their sons, but also over the entire household, and that is the way they become beneficiaries and guardians of the subjection of women.‡ In South East Asia, when three generations live together under the same roof, the mother-in-law

* Janice Radway, *Reading the Romance: Women, Patriarchy, and Popular Literature* (Chapel Hill: University of North Carolina Press, 1984).
† Delphine Chedaleux, 'Genre, classe et culture populaire: Enquête auprès des fans de *Cinquante Nuances de Grey*' in the colloquium on 'Croiser le genre et la classe', (Meetings, crossings, and intersections of class and gender) Lausanne, UNIL, 9–10 November 2017.
‡ Camille Lacoste-Dujardin, *Des mères contre les femmes: Maternité et patriarcat au Maghreb* (Paris: La Découverte, 1985).

sometimes bullies her daughter-in-law (providing an inexhaustible theme for televised series). In China's Forbidden City, the ladies in waiting for Cixi (1835) serve their mistress while obeying a very strict protocol, wearing a long black braid, using white powder make-up and a little lipstick, never showing their bare feet, never speaking or even whispering, sleeping curled up on their side, eating meagre portions.* By governing the lives of girls and boys, these women acquired bits of power in a society that ordinarily excluded them.

Throughout the twentieth century, feminine anti-feminism revealed, beyond the fear of change, an attachment to the ancient forms of prerogatives granted to women. In the Belle Époque, the novelist Colette Yver denounced the 'brainy girls' and other 'princesses of science', while Ida Sée restricted the role of women in *Le Devoir maternel* (The Maternal Duty, 1911). In Great Britain, the Women's Anti-Suffrage League was opposed to women voting in legislative elections. Their argument was that each sex had its mission, with women assigned to child-rearing and social functions, while the domains of politics and economics belonged to men: the complementary nature of the sexes was more important than their equality. Nowadays, some stay-at-home mothers have become the ardent defenders of 'domestic tranquillity'.†

In the business world, the dominant masculine norms (leadership, competition, toughness) become imperatives for women as they climb up the ranks. Female directors and bosses become 'accomplices' of the patriarchy that reserves a place for them. In one online sales firm, a thirty-two-year-old woman project leader harassed by one of her male colleagues went to inform the department of human resources, where women were also victims of this man. 'But the female boss closed the case. She explained to me that I was too friendly with my male colleagues and that my way of dressing caused problems. In other words, I had been asking for it. Her ultimate argument: "That never happened to me in my career." '‡ Other women testify to being subjected

---

* Yi Jin, *Mémoires d'une dame de cour dans la Cité interdite* (Paris: Picquier, 1993).
† Julia Bush, *Women Against the Vote: Female Anti-Suffragism in Britain* (Oxford: Oxford University Press, 2007); and Carolyn Graglia, *Domestic Tranquility: A Brief Against Feminism* (Dallas: Spence, 1998). See also https://ladiesagainstfeminism.com/
‡ Cited by Romain Jeanticou, 'La sex touch de la French tech', *Télérama*, No. 3541, 22 November 2017.

to harassment and moral violence from their female superiors (the female shop assistant forced to account for a variance of ten euros to her female boss at nine in the evening, for example). Whether due to widespread, ingrained patriarchal values, attachment to the father figure or a degeneration of the mother-daughter relationship, sexist ideology can be found among women themselves.*

Women too have converted to the patriarchal order. From the midwives complicit in gendercide in Asia, the mothers performing genital cutting in Africa, the women of the Rajput aristocracy glorifying sati in India, anti-abortion activists in the United States, the millions of women voting for Donald Trump, to the homophobic mothers of lesbian girls: stereotypes have colonized the feminine. Is it a choice or pure indoctrination? Individual freedom or the fate of the non-dominant gender? We can think that these subjugated women are also victims of the subjugation that they propagate. Passivity is their only activity.

Criminal masculinity, masculinity of privilege and toxic masculinity are the repugnant tentacles by which men seize upon women, degrading, destroying or discriminating against them. Their means are so powerful that many women have no choice but to submit. These forms of violence inflict damage on their self-esteem, dignity and integrity. That is why they constitute a tyranny in contradiction of women's rights and of human rights in general. We must get rid of the masculine's pathological tendencies. In the meantime, every man can ask himself how he partakes of such violence. If it appears that he has nothing to do with it – nothing at all – then it is his duty to take an active part in fighting against it.

* Annik Houel, *Rivalités féminines au travail: L'influence de la relation mère-fille* (Paris: Odile Jacob, 2014), pp. 74 and 110 ff.

11

The Decline of Virility

In the twentieth century, the rapid rise of feminism was accompanied by the decline of virility as a social value. This dramatic leap was less a reflection of the obsolescence of men in general than of masculine maladjustment. Indeed, certain masculinities were abandoned, while at the same time entire groups suffered from wars and crises.

THE SHATTERED SOLDIER, THE DONE-FOR WORKER

Men die in wars; those who come out alive are damaged. The records of admission to Les Invalides in Paris reveal the trauma of military life in the eighteenth century: 83 per cent of wounds were caused by fire-arms and bladed weapons. There were numerous men with crippled hands, arms, thighs, legs and feet, not to mention those suffering from digestive or ocular pathologies, who ended up joining the ranks of men 'out of service'.*

During the First World War, 9 million out of the 74 million men mobilized were killed. For the belligerent nations of continental Europe (Germany, Austria-Hungary, France, Italy, Russia), these losses represent from 13 to 17 per cent of their soldiers. France, for example, lost more than 1.3 million men out of the 8 million sent into action. Many veterans returned wounded, maimed or traumatized. In 1921, two of these veterans founded the Union of the Wounded in the Face,

---

* Elizabeth Belmas and Joël Coste, *Les Soldats du roi à l'Hôtel des Invalides: Étude d'épidémiologie historique, 1670–1791* (Paris: CNRS, 2018), p. 157 ff.

the 'broken faces'. Industrialized warfare led doctors to discover the phenomenon of 'shell shock' (today known as PTSD, post-traumatic stress disorder): they were victims of bombardments and horror, but also of the virility with which they had been inculcated.

The *rōnin*, or samurai without a master in feudal Japan, and the 'leopard', who sees the collapse of aristocratic values in Giuseppe Tomasi di Lampedusa's novel, are both in their own way fallen combatants. But World War I veterans were soldiers who had been wounded in their bodies and souls: for them, it proved impossible to return to normal in 1918. Having escaped a massacre and a world that had been swallowed up by the war, they struggled to once again find their place in society, particularly with women, who had become more independent. The interwar years in France bore the stigmata of their anxieties: slow demobilization, the election of a National Assembly predominantly made up of war veterans, the rejection of women's right to vote and the rise of the extreme right-wing leagues. The masculinity of sacrifice had turned out to be a fool's bargain.

In the United States, the Hollister riots of 1947 were caused by ex-servicemen seeking to remedy their wartime trauma through the thrills of motorcycling. A generation later, veterans returned from Vietnam with the shame of defeat, but most of all with a bitter sense of betrayal. Themselves victims of the war, of communists, of an unfair draft system, of an indecisive government, of pacifistic propaganda and of the American people's lack of gratitude, they became emblems of fallen masculinity. While they were risking their lives at the other end of the world, feminism and the civil rights movement were transforming American society: deprived of their status, they now found themselves competing with women and Black people.*

In the second half of the twentieth century, the long period of peace during the Cold War weakened the role of the soldier in Western societies. Having been the crucible of masculinity for centuries, the regiment disappeared as a virile body, as did the army in its role as an agent of socialization. In Germany, as in Latin America, the figure of

---

* Susan Jeffords, *The Remasculization of America: Gender and the Vietnam War* (Bloomington: Indiana University Press, 1989), ch. 4.

the soldier was discredited by dictatorships. France's 200-year-old obligation of military service was suspended in 1997.

Workers followed soldiers in their decline. In the nineteenth century, Marx's philosophy, Menzel's painting and Zola's literature had exalted the earth-shaking power of miners and rolling mill operators. Dire poverty was nevertheless accused of debilitating men, as shown by the description of one of the leaders of the 1884 Anzin strike as 'short, puny, lame, irritable, capable of all sorts of bad counsel', one poor specimen among the many other underfed, sickly men.* In the United States, the Great Depression of the 1930s dealt a blow to the virile dignity of the proletariat: cohorts of the unemployed could be seen at that time lining up in front of employment offices and soup kitchens. The titans had become tramps.

After the post-war economic boom, the crisis of the 1970s and 1980s struck at the very heart of industrial centres, hitting the Rust Belt in the United States, the old bastions of Lancashire, Glasgow and Newcastle in the United Kingdom, the coal mining and steel producing areas of north-eastern France, and the Sambre-et-Meuse coal mines in Belgium. The decline of shipyards, factory closures and mass unemployment resulted in a crisis of working-class masculinity. In families, the decline hit husbands depressed by long-term unemployment and immigrant fathers whose health had been ruined on construction sites. The virility of the male worker was also affected by the significant expansion of the tertiary sector. The arrival of white-collar operators and control monitors, 'competencies', and 'quality standards', overshadowed muscular strength. In Europe and North America, it was the end for male workers.

Of course, blue-collar workers have not disappeared. In France, they represent 20 per cent of the active population (as opposed to 40 per cent in the 1970s), and a number of them are still subjected to an infernal pace of work, with elevated levels of sound, smell and high temperatures. Workers of the few industrial sectors left over from the nineteenth century, such as the sewers and slaughterhouses, have the appearance of castaways fouled with blood and excrement. One man

* Cited by Michelle Perrot, *Les Ouvriers en grève: France, 1871–1890*, Vol. 2 (Paris: Mouton, 1973), p. 457.

Unemployed men in Chicago (1931)

During the Great Depression, men wait in line in front of a soup kitchen opened by the gangster and businessman Al Capone.

working at a water purification station testified: 'When I came home, my niece would tell me, "Uncle, you stink." . . . I was all sweaty and, nevertheless, I was not at the station.' The disgust for the masculine is even more humiliating when it is expressed by women and children. Other workers are 'elderly at age 50', with a body worn down by the weight of loads, repetitive gestures and professional illnesses.*

Everything nevertheless conspired to erase the visible presence of

---

* Agnès Jeanjean, 'Travailler à la morgue ou dans les égoûts', *Ethnologie française*, Vol. 41, No. 1, pp. 59–66; and Stéphane Geffroy, *À l'abattoir* (Paris: Seuil, 2016), p. 71. See also Thierry Pillon, 'Virilité ouvrière' in Jean-Jacques Courtine (ed.), *Histoire de la virilité*, Vol. 3, *La virilité en crise? XXᵉ–XXIᵉ siècle* (Paris: Seuil, 2011), pp. 303–305.

workers: the collapse of the Soviet Union, the loss of influence of both the French Communist Party and the stridently left CGT labour union, the closure of major industrial sites such as the Billancourt Renault factories, as well as the rise of industrial worksites scattered through rural areas. In the United States, working-class men have developed a masculinity based on morality and family values: uprightness, integrity, self-discipline, the sense of responsibility, the work ethic. Their 'dignity' has become a substitute for the 'American dream'. Contrary to what economic logic would lead us to expect, the lower their salary, the more they disapprove of their wife's salaried employment, by remaining the only breadwinners for their families, they still have in their private lives the status they lost in the workplace. The end of the metal worker has paradoxically favoured the return of the male breadwinner, only now as a kind of pauper.*

DEVIANCE AND REDEMPTION

In the suburbs of major French cities, the economic and urban crisis has fuelled the revolt of subordinate masculinities. Lower-class youths with little or no professional skills, stuck between a degraded model of paternity and a future with no horizons, maintain their identity by means of three virile redemptions: sport, religion and music.

The boxing ring in poor French areas is a space of training and regaining legitimacy. Open to both sexes, valuing technique over strength, it helps reorient the masculinity of 'macho' ostentation into a masculinity of 'respectable' control.† Similar motivations can explain conversions to a more or less rigorous version of Islam: religion serves as a lifeline. In the Paris of the 1990s, a youth who was failing in school

---

* Michèle Lamont, *La Dignité des travailleurs: Exclusion, race, classe et immigration en France et aux États-Unis* (Paris: Presses de Sciences Po, 2002); and Jane Riblett Wilkie, 'Changes in US Men's Attitudes Toward the Family Provider Role, 1972–1989', *Gender & Society*, No. 7, 1993, pp. 261–279.

† Akim Oualhaci, 'Faire de la boxe thaï en banlieue: entre masculinité "populaire" et masculinité "respectable"', *Terrains & travaux*, Vol. 27, No. 2, 2015, pp. 117–131.

entered into a mosque: 'Dumbfounded, the small-time thug discovered the majesty of his Creator.'*

Rap sublimates frustration through violent words, syncopated rhythms and self-exhibition: video clips in which singers show off jewels and race cars ward off the curse of society and race while at the same time glorifying consumer society. Some songs roll off a catalogue of clichés: Kalashnikovs, suitcases stuffed with bills, bigshots on jet skis, impressive 'balls', consumption of 'pussy', solidarity among 'buddies', hatred of 'fags', and so on. Poetic rage is accompanied by hints of misogyny.

In France, the rapper Orelsan, born in 1982, provoked an outcry with his song 'Sale Pute' (Dirty Whore), whose theme was borrowed from 'Kim' by Eminem. A young man, having caught his girlfriend with another boy, vents his hatred, expressed not only in the form of insults ('cunt', 'dirty whore', 'sow'), but also threats: he is going to unhinge her jaw, break her arm, impregnate and then abort her with a knife. Such physical destruction takes away all of the young woman's usefulness, since she was only meant to 'suck' or have 'her rectum blown up'. To top it all off, she is promised a violent death, like that of a demon on fire or an animal in the slaughterhouse. After other songs of the same ilk, feminist associations lodged a formal complaint against Orelsan in 2009 for inciting hatred and violence on the basis of sex. Convicted in a first trial, the charges were dismissed on appeal in 2016. According to the court's ruling, the rapper was depicting 'a disenchanted youth, misunderstood by adults, distressed and anxious about an uncertain future'. His characters were expressing the 'malaise of a generation drifting without orientation or guidance, particularly in the area of relations between men and women'.

Virility is expressed in an even more aggressive form by the occupation of public space, offensive public behaviour, petty delinquency, brawls and riots. This 'masculinity of protest', as Raewyn Connell put it, is a performance of gender in response to social impotency. It blends easily with anti-Semitism, homophobia and misogyny – three types of hatred used to reaffirm virile honour. In France, some youth from the housing projects distinguish between 'sluts' and 'good girls',

* Omar Benlala, *La Barbe* (Paris: Seuil, 2015), p. 9.

who must not live alone, nor be independent, nor agents of their own sexuality.*

Hooliganism pushes the masculinity of protest into bloody violence. Unlike the ultras who simply live for their football team, hooligans deliberately provoke incidents and brawls. The phenomenon appeared in England in the 1960s when bands of youths, adolescent subcultures and sports rivalries would clash together. It reached its peak between the 1982 World Cup and the Heysel tragedy of 1985 (caused by English fans at a match between Liverpool and Juventus), before finding a foothold in Italy, Serbia, Ukraine and Brazil. The violence of British hooligans corresponded to a strategy of visibility and social survival following the collapse of the working class brought about by deindustrialization, unemployment and Thatcherism. Hooliganism takes some of its codes from working-class culture: collective discipline, a mind for organization, physical engagement and virile solidarity.† The same is true of men filled with uncontrollable hatred such as neo-Nazi skinheads in Europe and white supremacists in the United States.

Working-class masculinities are now socially subordinate, except perhaps for when rap music manages to force open the doors of showbusiness. Public powers handle them with tough measures of law and order. One study conducted in French criminal courts shows that males judged in accelerated trials are more severely punished than women, protected by their attitude of deference and their status as mothers. Delinquent women have problems, whereas delinquent men are the problem.‡ In the 1990s, the increase in the price of tickets, the screening of fans and the installation of video surveillance cameras in stadiums put an end to hooliganism, which lost its desperate fight against the working class's loss of status and pride.

In another area, public health and road safety policies have struck

---

* Christelle Hamel, 'Le mélange des genres: une question d'honneur: Étude des rapports sociaux de sexe chez de jeunes Maghrébins en France', *Awal*, No. 19, 1999, pp. 19–32.

† Dominique Bodin, *Le Hooliganisme* (Paris: PUF, 2003), pp. 26–28.

‡ Maxime Lelièvre and Thomas Léonard, 'Une femme peut-elle être jugée violente? Les représentations de genre et les conditions de leur subversion lors des procès en comparution immédiate' in Coline Cardi and Geneviève Pruvot (eds.), *Penser la violence des femmes* (Paris: La Découverte, 2012), pp. 314–329.

a fatal blow to working-class virility. Messages warning of the dangers of alcohol and of eating too much meat and fatty foods, the banning of smoking in public places, as well as the regulation of hunting, have clearly resulted in greater well-being for the general population, but at the expense of traditional masculine identities. The familiar complaint, 'We don't have the right to do anything anywhere anymore,' can be understood as a cry of protest, once again in desperation. Similarly, the tremendous progress in road safety in France, thanks to the requirement to wear a seat belt in 1973, the creation of a point system for drivers licenses in 1992, the installation of speed cameras in 2002 and the reduction of the speed limit to 80 kilometres per hour in 2018, ran up against the masculine cults of speed and unlimited power.

In a world whose environmental problems are taking on tragic dimensions, the craze for SUVs and other high-emission 'status' vehicles has become a menace for everyone. Has the masculinity of ostentation, which is harmful to the individual and to others, become incompatible with modernity? In any case, male pride might well turn out to be a catastrophe for public health and the environment.

HOW WOMEN HAVE ADAPTED

To be sure, working-class masculinity is not in itself more misogynist that the masculinity of male intellectuals or politicians. However, deindustrialization did indeed widen the gap between men and women in the working class by differentiating the social trajectory of each sex. This distortion can be seen in the area of education.

In the early nineteenth century, the literacy rate for men was higher than that for women everywhere in the world. Two centuries later, girls are achieving globally better results than boys. In reading, the gap is huge: 38 points on average according to the 2012 PISA study, which is equal to a year of schooling. The situation is just the opposite in mathematics: boys do better, but the gap is much smaller (9 points), and even insignificant in several countries like the United States, Poland

and France. In Finland and Iceland, girls achieve better results than boys in all subjects.*

Since the 1990s, the underperformance of boys in Great Britain, the United States, Australia and China has been attributed both to mediocre results and problems with their behaviour. In American high schools, boys receive 70 per cent of Ds and Fs (the lowest grades), are more likely to be expelled and less likely to be at the top of their class. In France, girls over the age of 15 are more often enrolled in school than boys, who are more likely to end their schooling for an apprenticeship: this gap is the widest at the age of 18 and continues at the same level from then on. Girls have a higher rate of success than boys in all tracks of the *baccalauréat* exam.†

The same tendency can be found within universities. In France, female students outnumber males, with the widest disparity at the level of the master's degree. Several *grandes écoles* admit a majority of girls: such is the case for Sciences Po (with 60 per cent in 2017) and the National School for Magistrates. In the United States, 40 per cent of women have college degrees, as opposed to 31 per cent of men. In 2017, several institutions of higher education showed an imbalance in the number of males and females admitted: such was the case at Yale (with 52 per cent girls), the University of Wyoming (53 per cent), Southwestern University in Texas (54 per cent), Western Kentucky University (58 per cent), UC Davis (59 per cent) and Boston University (62 per cent). Should we conclude that boys have become the 'new minority' at universities?‡ The disaffection is actually more marked among young white men from rural areas in America, since universities are striving to attract women and ethnic minorities.

Be that as it may, boys remain in the majority in most elite schools and universities, as can be seen in the École Nationale d'Administration

---

* *PISA 2012 Results: What Students Know and Can Do*, Vol. 1 (Paris: OCDE, February 2014).
† Arlie Hochschild, 'Male Trouble', *The New York Review of Books*, Vol. 65, No. 15, 11 October 2018; and Stéphanie Durieux, 'Les femmes sont plus scolarisées et diplômées que les hommes, mais davantage au chômage', *INSEE Flash PACA*, No. 10, March 2015.
‡ Jon Marcus, 'Why Men Are the New College Minority', *The Atlantic*, 8 August 2017.

in France and Harvard Business School in the United States, and they are certainly more numerous in STEM subjects (Science, Technology, Engineering and Mathematics). Certain institutions frown on the increasing prominence of girls. In China, the foreign language department of the University of Peking and that of the University of Jilin accepted boys below the minimum requirements and deliberately rejected female candidates. Through the 2010s, the Tokyo medical school favoured male students by raising their scores on admissions exams, until they reduced the number of girls to 20 per cent (it had been 40 per cent in 2010).* Beyond their shockingly illegal character, these frauds are striking: by their very existence, they recognize the disparity of achievement between the two sexes. What if boys, poor readers, mediocre students, wrapped up in their video games, were increasingly incapable of confronting the world?

In the twentieth century, recessions were often 'mancessions' in that men represented the majority of those affected in the worst-hit economic sectors. During the Great Depression of the 1930s, which hit construction, industry and finance particularly hard, three quarters of the unemployed were men. Beginning in the 1970s, the sectors in decline – mining, steel-making, metallurgy, the automobile industry – were masculine. The same phenomenon can be observed in the United States after the 2008 financial crisis, in the sectors of real estate and finance. Industrial automation would make the situation worse: trades such as the metal worker, derrick operator, electromechanical technician, truck driver and train engineer will all be doomed.† Conversely, women became the majority in the expanding tertiary sector, either because deindustrialization had already ravaged heavily feminized sectors such as the textile factories, or because they were the first victims of lay-offs in industry.

The decline of workers stands in sharp contrast to the post-industrial success of women, who can take advantage of several assets in the new

* Sun Jiahui, 'Boys Won't Be Boys', *The World of Chinese*, 10 April 2018; and 'Une faculté de médecine accusée de discriminationn de genre', *Courrier international*, 9 August 2018.

† Carl Frey and Michael Osborne, 'The Future of Employment: How Susceptible Are Jobs to Computerisation?' *Technological Forecasting and Social Change*, Vol. 114, September 2013.

globalized economy: not only better training, but also traditionally 'feminine' qualities such as communication and cooperation acquired from childhood on. In certain American cities, the collapse of industry and the disappearance of dynasties of prominent men have paved the way for a 'new matriarchy': within the middle class, women are the ones who bring in money, pay the bills and leave Post-its to their husbands on the refrigerator. This feminization of society has led to the emergence of a new type of couple: 'Plastic Woman', with a university degree, holding a rewarding job, full of ambition, and 'Cardboard Man', fallen from his position as head of the family, paralysed in his archaic masculinity.*

The rise of women is even more pronounced in the working class. Up until the 1970s, physical strength alone was enough to be hired in the industrial sector, but now poorly skilled young men will have trouble finding employment. The masculinity of ostentation, with aggressive, tattoo-laden displays of virility, has become a disadvantage in the service industry, and it is even more of a drawback for boys from ethnic minority backgrounds. Women, on the other hand, can professionally implement traditionally 'feminine' skills (agreeableness, empathy, thoughtfulness, the propensity to assist) that they have acquired in their families and in school, and it is exactly that conformity to gender that enables their employability in the areas of food service, sales and personal care.

For the young women of the English working class, care is a social capital based on maternal knowledge and skill: it is valued in the job market in work with dependent persons, such as children, seniors, the disabled and the sick. Class solidarity, but also the feeling of being favoured because of their gender, explain the anti-feminism of working women, who are indulgent toward their brothers and boyfriends:

> what really disturbs me about feminism . . . is the way it's so anti-men. It just doesn't make sense, all this stuff about men as evil oppressors and that. I look at Kevin [her ex] and I think well, you know, my dad too and his brother: it's like what have they got going for them. They've

---

* Hanna Rosin, *The End of Men: Voici venu le temps des femmes* (Paris: Autrement, 2013).

no future. They've no job, they're miserable, they don't know what to do with themselves.

Kevin committed suicide after five years of unemployment.*

For the working class men without training or education, with an increasingly threatened social identity, the future appears grim. This feeling of decline was not irrelevant to the rise of populism. In the United States, Donald Trump was the spokesman for 'angry white men', looking for a new form of pride.

THE 'CASTRATED' MAN

In the era of the French Revolution, thinkers and artists worried by the new demands of women strove to revamp the image of the masculine: Burke in his *Reflections on the Revolution in France* (1790), Schikaneder in *The Magic Flute* (1791), the Baron Van Swieten at the end of Haydn's *Creation* (1798), as well as the legal experts of the French civil code whose influence was felt throughout Europe. The Napoleonic legend disseminated by paintings and Romanticism can be interpreted as a parade of virile pride.

In the late nineteenth century, the accession of women to the threshold of prestigious professions wounded the pride of upper-class men. Unable to prevent this evolution, they tried to slow it down. As women came nearer the masculine sanctuaries, the attacks became increasingly virulent. Secondary schools for girls? 'They will be taught everything, even rebellion against the family, even impurity.'† Women's suffrage? 'The day when they have the right to vote, elections will sink into ridicule or blood.'‡ Careers open to women? 'They speak to us about becoming judges, doctors, apothecaries, and prefects? And perhaps

---

* Cited by Beverley Skeggs, *Formations of Class & Gender: Becoming Respectable* (London: Sage Publications, 1997), p. 152. See also Linda McDowell, 'The Trouble With Men? Young People, Gender Transformations and the Crisis of Masculinity', *International Journal of Urban and Regional Research*, Vol. 24, No. 1, March 2000, pp. 201–209.

† Octave Mirbeau, 'Fleurs et fruits', *Le Gaulois*, 25 November 1880.

‡ Joseph Ginestou, 'La Femme doit-elle voter? (Le pour et le contre)', political science thesis, the University of Montpellier, 1910, p. 102.

An anti-feminist caricature (from the 1910s)

what else? State troopers and soldiers!'* George Sand elected to the French Academy? 'We men are henceforth the ones who will make jams and pickles!'†

Anti-feminism is not the grousing of old reactionaries, but rather a paradigm of thought that marshals arguments for refusing equality. That is why it is allied with other hatreds of the same origin. In *Sex and Character* (1903), a bestseller in Vienna, Otto Weininger denounced both women and Jews, demons of vitiated sexuality, inapt for genius,

---

* Pierre-Joseph Proudhon, *La Pornocratie ou les Femmes dans les temps modernes* (Paris: Lacroix, 1875), p. 171.
† Jules Barbey d'Aurevilly, *Les Bas-Bleus* (1878), XIXᵉ siècle: Les oeuvres et les hommes, Vol. 5 (Paris: Palmé, 1860–1902), p. 82. See also Annelise Maugue, *L'Identité masculine en crise au tournant du siècle, 1871–1914* (Paris: Rivages, 1987).

pure negativities of civilization: the same association of traits found in the works of Nietzsche and Schopenhauer.

The third outpouring of anti-feminist rants erupted in the United States in the 1970s, between sexual liberation and the defeat in Vietnam. Instead of denigrating women, men presented themselves as victims dispossessed by ambitious women, castrated by seductresses, excluded by matriarchs, persecuted by ambient misandry. For anti-feminists, masculine power was a myth, as was the oppression of women. Being a man had become impossible, even dangerous. Men were always in the wrong, criticized everywhere by everyone, automatically accused, discriminated against. Designated as the new enemy, he was becoming short-changed by the march of history. Rather than an oppressor, he was oppressed. Everything had been taken from him: authority, work, dignity, seduction, in other words, the right to be himself. After decades of frenzied feminism, the 'first sex' had ceased to exist.*

From John Updike to Michel Houellebecq, several novelists have joined the chorus of complaints of the white male pulled down the slope of decline, while women, the winners of social transformations, leap from one success to the next. What humiliates the loser are his amorous failures and his sexual impotence: he has been doubly devirilized by being rebuffed by brilliantly successful and beautiful young women. Similar to what we find in Aristophanes, a degenerate society arises from this reversal: women advance their pawns, men are turned into wimps, and so the Amazons rule over a lot of losers.

Roles have been inverted even within the couple: does a 'liberated' woman who earns her living, who knows how to change a tyre and assemble a piece of furniture, who knows her own body well enough to give herself an orgasm, still need a man? This is the twilight of the family man. What if it were women's independence that explained why men's sex lives were so impoverished and why they engage in massive consumption of pornography from adolescence on? A quadragenarian and former enthusiast of May 1968 observed bitterly:

Our generation has trouble accepting the castrating role of women. We have gone from a generation in which men dominated women,

* Herb Goldberg, *The Hazards of Being Male: Surviving the Myth of Masculine Privilege* (New York: Nash, 1976); and Éric Zemmour, *Le Premier Sexe* (Paris: Denoël, 2006).

preventing their sexual and social self-fulfilment, to a generation in which women are the ones preventing men from sexual and social self-fulfilment.*

These words show to what extent the feminist revolution of the twentieth century succeeded in unsettling the hierarchical complementarity of the sexes at the base of patriarchy. Deprived of their traditional power, men feel useless. And so the anti-feminists exhort rebellious women one last time: 'Don't insist on becoming our equals – you are making us miserable.' According to them, women have gone too far. It is time for men to regain their place.

THE MASCULINIST REACTION

In Europe, Asia and America, there are now countless books devoted to the 'decline' of men, who have become an endangered species to be protected, lest societies and nations lose their soul. This stereotyped drama is unfolding in four acts.

First act in the defence of the masculine cause: worrying about the feminist 'cabal', denouncing the 'gynocentric' society. Raising boys is supposedly in the hands of women, stay-at-home wives and female schoolteachers. In *Save the Boys* (2010), Chinese pedagogue Sun Yunxiao asserts that the educational system gives the advantage to girls and ignores the natural talents of boys, who suffer as a result. For the Canadian psychologist Jordan Peterson, misandry rules on campus and Marxist ideology have been recycled to overwhelmingly condemn the Western man. In France, the ideology of decline has rallied a few preachy middle-aged moralizers, convinced that everything is going downhill. As in the myths of New Guinea and of Tierra del Fuego, feminine power engenders chaos. Peterson's bestseller, *Twelve Rules for Life*, moreover presents itself as an 'antidote to chaos'.

Since the early 2010s, social media has served as an outlet for masculinist rancour, as shown by the cyber harassment campaigns on Reddit

---

* Cited by Christine Castelain-Meunier, *Les Métamorphoses du masculin* (Paris: PUF, 2005), pp. 113–114. See also Sally Robinson, *Marked Men: White Masculinity in Crisis* (New York: Columbia UP, 2000).

in the United States, the chatroom 'Blabla 18–25 ans' (Blabber For 18 to 25 year-olds) in France, and more generally on Twitter. In 2014, Gamergate provided another example in the world of video games. Cyber harassment is also a manifestation of masculine power. In the late 2000s, some young journalists grouped together in a 'Ligue du LOL' (LOL League), persecuting female bloggers, journalists and feminist activists on Facebook and Twitter via scurrilous messages or doctored pornographic photos. Such verbal violence, ranging from insults to calls for rape, is the white man's nemesis, as well as the rallying cry of the mob. There is no need to articulate an explicitly masculinist line of argumentation: it is sufficient to reduce women to silence.

Second act: restoring masculine honour. Chatrooms and support groups spring into action to come to the aid of men, seeking to determine what rights, reasons for pride and means of defence they may have. In *The Myth of Male Power* (1993), Warren Farrell wrote that men had become the 'disposable sex'. Since 2009, his disciple Paul Elam has offered a 'voice for men' on the Internet. The 'Red Pill' subforum on Reddit developed a strategy for affirming masculine identity: 'Wake up the alpha in you,' 'Invest in the ego,' and so on.

This diffuse network has also sprung into action to elaborate an art of picking up women, so that men can once again enjoy their power. Mastering seduction codes to the detriment of women in order better to 'screw' them (in both senses of the word) – the idea is not new. In the Greece of the 1980s, *kamaki* was a technique for 'harpooning' female tourists from Western countries, seducing them with a little English and a bit of cheap romanticism, taking advantage of them for a season, before discarding them like prostitutes. The *kamaki* champion was interested in sex, but his exploits also took on an aspect of social revenge at a time when Greece was seen as being 'behind': the female tourist became a chance for vengeance, and for social climbing as well.*

For the experts in picking up women in the 2010s, men were too often the playthings of women. They are enticed, pay for the movie

---

* Sofka Zinovieff, 'Hunters and Hunted: Kamaki and the Ambiguities of Sexual Predation in a Greek Town' in Peter Loizos, Evthymios Papataxiarchis (eds.), *Contested Identities*, pp. 203–220.

and dinner at a restaurant, and in the end, are not even sure of getting laid: she was just taking advantage of him. Internet sites teach how to up one's 'sexual market value': paying close attention to clothes and muscular appearance, using charm, displaying strength, being una-bashedly self-assured. Training workshops enable 'pick up artists' to regain the upper hand. In their reckoning, seduction is an art, and men must remain 'masters of the game', and 'regain ground' lost to women: they must be arrogant and funny, intersperse criticism with compli-ment, and always play hard to get.* Scoring with a woman in this way is a victory of masculine pride that benefits the entire community.

Third act: men are back! Humiliated, mocked, seemingly beaten, they return, stronger than ever. They are going to show what they are made of. Such is the cinematic narrative underlying *First Blood* (1982) and the other films in the *Rambo* series, as well as *Missing In Action* (1984): a traumatized Vietnam veteran reconnects with masculinity after horrific ordeals. Everything is there in the panoply of the newly reborn warrior: muscles, weapons, courage, sacrifice, a taciturn demeanour.

The thought conveyed by Robert Bly's bestselling *Iron John: A Book About Men* (1990) is more subtle. His basic idea is that men have been dispossessed of their masculinity. Estranged from nature after two centuries of industrialization, and influenced by the femi-nism and pacifism of the 1960s, men have been cut off from paternal models, from the sources of virile energy, from the deep forests and from well-tempered steel: they have excessively identified with the 'woman inside them'. Like the child in the tale *Iron John*, they must not fear to follow the untamed man of the wild, who will become their mentor in masculinity. The 'male deep inside' will be able to re-emerge through contact with nature, through new emotions, and through a regained familiarity with the body.

After women's liberation comes that of men, then. Initiation rituals make it possible to unleash contemporary masculinity. The remedy for macho rigidity is to follow one's primitive instincts. In the 1990s, the mythopoetic men's movement combined advice for well-being and

---

* Mélanie Gourarier, *Alpha Mâle: Séduire les femmes pour s'apprécier entre hommes* (Paris: Seuil, 2017).

personal development with the awakening of virility in order that men could once again dare to be men.

This trend of 'masculine awakening' spans out into support groups, retreats and fraternities, as well as sports clubs and concerts. At hard-core punk and heavy metal festivals, amid the decibels and the moshing, men show that they are capable of holding up. For a few thousand dollars in the late 2010s, businessmen took part in an intensive course in the framework of a *Warrior Week*. On a beach in the Pacific, they were subjected to ordeals, thrown into the sea blindfolded or plunged into a tank of ice-cold water, all while meditating on the meaning of masculinity, thanks to readings of 'Invictus' and anecdotes from antiquity. As explained by the founder of the *Warrior Week*, 'We teach them how to be a man ... There is a primal nature in men that has been completely castrated.'*

These themes of neo-virility have been exploited by certain churches, too. To be inspired by the strength of Jesus, to be willing to fight for a cause and live among brothers, to initiate one another from father to son: such is the message of John Eldredge in *Wild at Heart: Discovering The Secret of a Man's Soul* and of the Catholic communities that organize the Optimum camp and the 'In the Heart of Men' retreat in France. Under the cover of spirituality, the message is crystal clear: men must return to their position of authority, and women, to their place in the household. To each his 'nature'.

CHANGING MEN?

Final act: redefining masculine identity on new bases, and accepting the fact that the macho brute belongs to the past. To that end, one can borrow from a neo-Kiplinger ethic: discipline, moderation, elegance, in other words, the formula for a masculinity of control as opposed to the brutal and potentially worrisome masculinity of ostentation. In keeping with the etymology of the Latin word *vir*, the virile requires virtue of the self. The seducer's social class and refinement overshadow

* Dana Schuster, 'This Boot Camp for Men Claims It'll Revive Your "Primal Nature"', *New York Post*, 3 June 2017.

the mannerless boor. The feminists' criticisms can be cavalierly brushed aside: 'I cannot be a macho, since I am a gentleman.' The brute can also be furbished with the help of money and an Epicurean lifestyle: wearing a cashmere sweater, furnishing one's penthouse, enjoying jazz, being a connoisseur of whisky and making love with flair all serve to validate a 'sophisticated' heterosexual inner masculinity.

However, while some men allow their 'inner masculinity' to re-emerge, others denounce sexism and rape. The action of these pro-feminist men has taken various forms since the late 1970s: in the United States, the National Organization for Men Against Sexism, Michael Kimmel's work on masculinities, and the Men Can Stop Rape organization; in Canada, the White Ribbon Campaign cofounded by Michael Kaufman in 1991; in Australia, the Men Against Sexual Assault organization; in Great Britain, the magazine *Achilles Heel* (1978) and the conferences on 'Men Against Sexism'; in Norway, the movement of the 'gentle men' (*Myke menn*). Some initiatives appeared in France two decades later in connection with the association Mix-Cité (1997), and within the European network EuroPRO-Fem, whose message was to be relayed by Zéromacho in 2011.

As nice as they may be, the actions of pro-feminist men have not produced the results hoped for. Focused on the issue of sexual violence, these movements have stagnated, when they haven't worn themselves down with internal quarrels. Even at their peak, they had only a very limited audience. Mix-Cité, one of the very few organizations in France to combine reflection on patriarchy with concrete actions (against the world of models and sex toys, for example) suffered from the increasing power of men in its structures of leadership, compromising the original ideal of gender diversity. It was precisely in order to avoid such expansionism that French Women's Liberation Movement (MLF) feminists turned men away. Warren Farrell, one of the theorists of 'men's lib', close to the National Organization for Women and Gloria Steinem in the 1970s, drew close to the masculine group, reserving his criticism for 'discriminatory' feminism.

Most importantly, these movements approached the problem from an essentially psychological angle, urging men to gain greater awareness: women must be treated well, and violence and prostitution are

Hugh Hefner with two bunnies (2003)

Founded by Hugh Hefner in 1953, the men's lifestyle and entertainment magazine Playboy *offered its readers photos of nude women along with all sorts of articles on politics, culture and sport. In her eulogy, Camille Paglia wrote: 'Hefner reimagined the American male as a connoisseur in the continental manner, a man who enjoyed all the fine pleasures of life, including sex.'* On the contrary, Hefner reinforced the image of the white male surrounded by dolls, a conception perpetuated by Donald Trump*

odious. In Brisbane, Australia, the Men Against Assault centre organized an eight-week training session for Aboriginal men condemned for conjugal violence. In the same vein, the authors of *Feminism with Men* proposed that men take an oath reposing on six principles: abandoning their privilege; applying feminism in their personal lives; giving priority to the elimination of the oppression of women; promoting

---

* 'Camille Paglia on Hugh Hefner's Legacy, Trump's Masculinity and Feminism's Sex Phobia', *The Hollywood Reporter*, 2 October 2017; and Beatriz Preciado, *Pornotopia: An Essay on* Playboy's *Architecture and Biopolitics*, Zone Books, ch. 2. See also www. artofmanliness.com

social change, implementing non-hierarchical forms of communication; showing respect for women.*

But to get rid of sexism, it is not enough to denounce it. Before being a state of mind, patriarchy is a system of society. Goodwill alone, even within the context of group action, is therefore not able to block the mechanisms of domination that are holistic and centuries old. Moreover, pro-feminists have a very specific sociological profile: often coming from the middle and upper classes, highly educated, experienced with activism, they generally grew up in the company of a feminist mother, or far from their father.† And that is sufficient to make them an ultra-minority.

MEN IN THE FACE OF EQUALITY

How can we escape from the ridiculous masculinist surge and illusory activist energy? First, concrete initiatives must be fitted to accurate lines of reasoning. While anti-feminist men hide behind a more or less smiling mask, not all male allies of feminism are activists in left-leaning organizations. Condorcet's disciples are few in number, but they are spread throughout society: they prove to be the most effective not within associations, but in carrying on the struggle, at times alone, at their desk, in the National Assembly, in a business, a hospital or in a lawyer's study. The feminism of men does not proceed from a solemn promise, but first from revolt, and then a commitment to a new manner of governing and to structural reform. The institutions of the state or local administration therefore prove to be indispensable, as is the active involvement of the private sector.

Next, we have to analyse the crisis of the masculine with lucidity. Men's malaise has several causes: the inculcation of masculinities of domination, alienating by their very nature; the decline of virile values

---

* Steven Schacht and Doris Ewing, *Feminism with Men: Bridging the Gender Gap* (Lanham, Rowman & Littlefield, 2004), p. 200. See also Amanda Goldrick-Jones, *Men Who Believe in Feminism* (Westport: Praeger, 2003).
† Alban Jacquemart, *Les Hommes dans les mouvements féministes*.

owing to wars and recessions; the achievements of women in higher education and in the workplace; society's increasing ecological imperatives; the rise of feminism. Obviously, patriarchy is not destined to disappear simply because men are worried about themselves. Patriarchy has declined, but the numerous pathologies of the masculine are causing it to hang on in a sort of headlong flight forwards. That is why the male 'oppressor' nowadays coexists with the 'suffering' male. Masculinists have tried to take advantage of this duality: their victim's discourse is often nothing more than a strategy for conserving their privileges.

Finally, some men suffer from doubt. While many no longer see virility as mandatory, the ideal has still not disappeared. Some would like to 'do the right thing' with regard to gender equality, but don't know how; others feel that they are 'in the wrong', but without discerning the link between their personal situation and the organization of society. Amid this forest of contradictory injunctions, well-intentioned men can sometimes feel lost: they no longer know their proper place, role, status or function – in other words, what is expected of them. No one has of yet invented a feminist GPS system for men to follow.

Actually, men are less disturbed by the 'decline of authority' or the 'feminization of the world' than by the advent of an *egalitarian society*. The breaches in masculinity have been widened by the tectonic plates of gender whose movements have been shaking up our societies: a march towards the emancipation of women and their increased role in every domain. The solution is not to humbly recant virile values, nor to ostentatiously reclaim ownership of them, but rather to hear the criticism that feminism levels at democratic societies: that work in the areas of liberty and equality remains unfinished, and so perpetuates the denial of justice.

A political leader can no longer boast of being a misogynist with impunity; a 'hand on the bum' of a secretary or a nurse is now called sexual assault; almost all nations, regions and big cities, as well as major international organizations and NGOs, have inscribed equality between men and women on the first page of their agenda. Certain resistances can be felt everywhere, and there will still be Donald Trumps in places of power, but the revolution of rights has set into motion an irreversible movement. Despite swan songs and rear-guard fights, we are witnessing the disappearance of an 'innocent', visible patriarchy accepted as such. Inequality has ceased to be legitimate.

Seen collectively, this crisis is not a problem, but an opportunity: it makes it possible to create a new foundation for the masculine. On the scale of generations, the decline of virility might reinforce feminism's arguments. Once the end of men has been diagnosed, men can be reinvented as fair and just.

PART FOUR

Gender Justice

12

Masculinities of Non-Domination

In *Republicanism: A Theory of Freedom and Government* (1997), Irish philosopher Philip Pettit argued that institutions must maximize the freedom of individuals, in other words, protect them against all forms of domination. The problem is that the men who lead nations, regions, cities, armies and churches are often embodiments of patriarchy. Masculinity must therefore conform to the ideal of non-domination as defined by Pettit.

The masculinity of non-domination consists not only in refraining from interfering arbitrarily with women's will, but also in guaranteeing the social and political conditions making it possible for women to actually exercise their freedoms. A man conforms with a masculinity of non-domination when he implements mechanisms that prevent himself and others from imposing any constraints of sex or gender on women. Such a conception opposes the paternalism ruling the lives of women, and makes it possible to put feminist demands at the heart of democracy. Masculine power is completely capable of carrying out feminist policy, defined as *the entire set of actions favouring the emancipation of women to the detriment of the patriarchal system.*

FEMINIST LEADERSHIP

Theoretically, nothing prevents a male head of state from implementing feminist policy, since some men and some nations enacted feminism in the twentieth century. There is an important distinction between a personality and a mode of government: a traditionalist can very well fight against gender violence or the inequality of the sexes. However, women, like men, are victims of typically masculine scourges such as wars, dictatorships, fundamentalisms and the race for profits: in that sense, what feminist policies have to overcome is not men, but the masculine. And men themselves can fight against the monsters that their gender has created.

International organizations are actively working for women's rights and defending the equality of the sexes. UN Women sponsored the solidarity campaign 'He For She'. UNICEF, the WHO and FAO, as well as the World Bank, have developed similar programmes. The condition of women nevertheless differs enormously from one country to another. The areas that need urgent attention are sub-Saharan Africa (because of wars and poverty), China and the Indian sub-continent (because of gendercide and dire poverty in rural areas), Japan (because of archaic patriarchal practices), the Catholic Mediterranean world and Latin America (because of gender violence), and Muslim countries (because of *sharia* law and fundamentalism). The prime causes of women's oppression are poverty, war, and political or religious tyranny.

It is crucial not to confuse the pseudo-egalitarian whitewash of speeches, intended to burnish the reputation of the men who deliver them, and an authentically feminist agenda. Some politically correct formulas are in many cases only artifices of communication, and the enthusiastic slogans in favour of parity are forgotten when it is time to form a president's cabinet. Similarly, the revolutionaries and independentists of the twentieth century often betrayed the women who had supported them.

It is quite rare for a leader to proclaim himself a feminist, since power is so synonymous with the masculine. Canadian Prime Minister Justin Trudeau, born in 1971, has defended the equality of the sexes not only in his declarations, but also by the orientation of his government's budget. He has stated that he views each set of issues through a 'feminist lens': reduction of unequal pay, access for women to all professions, aid to female entrepreneurs, fighting against sexual violence, and even the construction of an oil pipeline, if it should pass through the territory of a community in which women find themselves in a situation of vulnerability.*

* Justin Trudeau, 'Je suis féministe et fier de l'être!' *Le Monde*, 22–23 April 2018.

Justin Trudeau is one of the very few statesmen in the world to take ownership of his feminism. In his case, it is not a generational difference, since none of his contemporaries, neither Alexis Tsipras in Greece, nor Emmanuel Macron in France, nor Volodymyr Hroisman in Ukraine, nor Tamin al-Thani in Qatar, all born between 1974 and 1980, speak like him. Even for Trudeau, however, it is more a matter of promoting women than of changing the masculine. But the reality is that equality begins by putting an end to privileges.

THE RIGHT TO POWER

The presence of women in places of power is no guarantee of equality. It is also necessary for them to make themselves heard. In West Bengal, there are only 32 per cent women in village meetings. When they come, they have the floor less often than men, and when they speak, they are less often heard. All in all, women pronounce less than 3 per cent of the words spoken; half the time, they do not say one word throughout the entire meeting; 40 per cent of the time, they get a rude or aggressive answer from the elected officials.*

Political parity begins with *women being able to take the floor*. Gender justice requires that men not only recognize women's legitimacy, but also listen to what women have to say. That means getting rid of the condescension that usually surrounds women in politics (as it does women writers and those in business and religion), and protecting their right to make themselves heard in the media, meetings and assemblies, soliciting it if need be, and shutting down men who try to delegitimate women who speak up. And if such men refuse to yield to women – which is what happens in most cases – they can at least learn to be quiet when women speak. A man should always ask himself if what a woman has to say may be more important that his own comments. However that may be, the effacement of the masculine would create an increased visibility for women.

A feminist policy consists of facilitating *women's access to power* in

---

* Esther Duflo, *La Politique de l'autonomie: Lutter contre la pauvreté (II)* (Paris: Seuil, 2010), pp. 80–81.

the same terms and the same spheres as men, particularly where they are often excluded: the executive branch, the government ministries embodying sovereignty (foreign affairs, justice, interior security, defence), courts of justice, constitutional courts, parliamentary committees, governmental agencies and central administrations. In post-genocide Rwanda, women have played an important role in the Parliament, where they are a majority, as well as in the gacaca courts established in order to judge persons suspected of having taken part in the massacres. On the other hand, in 2005, the Japanese Supreme Court validated Article 750 of the Civil Code requiring the husband and wife to have the same name (to the detriment of the woman 96 per cent of the time). Only two of the fifteen judges making up the Court were women, both of whom voted to abrogate this article.

Whenever gender justice is at stake, electoral freedom can be limited by a system of quotas. In Belgium, the Smet-Tobback law of 1994 stipulates that an electoral list may not include more than two-thirds candidates of the same sex. In Senegal, the parity law of 2010, adopted with the support of not only the caucus of women leaders, but also of the priests and imams favouring equality, led to the election of an assembly composed of 43 per cent women.* Since the 1990s, women in India are obligatorily represented in village councils (*gram panchayats*) on two levels: each council must include one-third women and a third of the councils must be headed by a woman. When the head of the council is female, women take the floor more often, speak longer and find their appeals taken more seriously: collective needs (the condition of roads and wells in West Bengal) are more often taken into account and men's prejudices end up being reversed, since the discourse of women in power is more favourably received than that of men.† In this case, gender justice reposes on three pillars: equal legitimacy, equal access to taking the floor and political parity. To put it differently, women have the right to power, whatever it may be.

---

* Fatou Sow Sarr, 'Loi sur la parité au Sénégal: une expérience 'réussie' de luttes féminines', *Passerelle*, No. 17, June 2017, pp. 119–124.
† Esther Duflo, *La Politique de l'autonomie*, p. 81 ff.

WOMEN IN WAR, WOMEN OF PEACE

The masculinities of domination have appropriated the handling of civil and military conflicts for themselves. But since conflicts are part of life, there is no reason why women should be excluded. Three figures undo the equivalence between the masculine and war: non-violent men, women in war and women of peace.

After the assassination of Jean Jaurès in 1914, pacifism was kept alive during the war by intellectuals such as Romain Rolland and Stefan Zweig, before it came to inspire sizable portions of European public opinion in the 1920s and 30s. Non-violence, adopted as a principle of political action by a few such visionaries as Gandhi, Martin Luther King, Nelson Mandela, the Dalai-Lama, is different. For Gandhi, *ahimsa* (absence of the desire to commit violence acts) involves not only humility and charity, but also the effort to discourage the violence of the other: in this sense, it is a strength, an act of courage requiring much more determination than passive resistance (abandoned by Gandhi in 1908).*

Men have kept women away from military operations, with gender dichotomy prescribing strength and courage for males, with gentleness and empathy assigned to females. It is precisely because they were intent on disproving these prejudices that the rare women of state were not particularly pacifist: Isabella of Castille expelled Jews and Muslims from the kingdom of Grenada, Maria-Theresa of Austria and Catherine II of Russia divided up Poland between them, Indira Gandhi engaged in war against Pakistan, and Margaret Thatcher made Argentina stand down during the Falklands War (while dismantling the 'feminine' welfare state). While the vast majority of sovereigns between 1480 and 1913 were men, European states led by queens were more often involved in armed conflicts. Among them figured several unmarried sovereigns, either because they seemed weak in the eyes of their neighbours, or on the contrary because they wanted to signal that they

---

* Ramin Jahanbegloo, *Gandhi: Aux sources de la non-violence: Thoreau, Ruskin, Tolstoï* (Paris: Le Félin, 1998).

were standing firm.* The study of military expenditures and actions from 1970 to 2000 in twenty-two democracies shows that women in legislative assemblies have a pacifying effect, whereas they are more hawkish when they lead the executive branch or the ministry of defence.†

Women have almost never been asked to go to war, and the rare female combatants had to sneak into the ranks disguised as men. In the twentieth century, a few armies accepted women in the middle of a war: the Red Army during the Great Patriotic War (as shown by Svetlana Alexievich in *The Unwomanly Face of War*) and Tsahal over the course of the Arab–Israeli wars. Since the 1960s, the Kurdish army has included a large number of women, up to 40 per cent of its troops, including infantry, snipers and commissioned officers, sometimes trained in feminine academies. They notably fought in Raqqa in 2017, within the Women's Defense Units (YPJ). In the northern Syrian region of Rojava, some Kurdish communes are experimenting with total parity, including equal feminine and masculine responsibility in the army, politics and administration.‡ Kurdish society nevertheless remains quite patriarchal, and when the female combatants return to the village, they are so 'virilized' that they cannot marry. In these three armies, women risk their lives on an equal basis with men: a disappearance of gender in the face of death, or admission of women into the masculinity of sacrifice?

Just as military command centres and regiments include very few women on a worldwide level, so peace negotiations take place among men. Since 1992, women have represented 2 per cent of chief mediators and 4 per cent of the signatories to peace accords. Certain peace processes completely excluded women: the Dayton Accords in Bosnia (1995), national reconciliation in Somalia (2002), the Linas-Marcoussi accord in the Ivory Coast (2003), the peace accords in Nepal (2006), the cease-fire agreement in the Central African Republic (2008) and the power-sharing agreements in Zimbabwe (2008). Out of the nearly

---

* Oeindra Dube, S. P. Harish, 'Queens', NBER Working Paper, No. 23337, April 2017.
† Michael Koch and Sarah Fulton, 'In the Defense of Women: Gender, Office Holding, and National Security Policy in Established Democracies', *The Journal of Politics*, Vol. 73, No. 1, 2011, pp. 1–16.
‡ Olivier Grojean, *La Révolution kurde: Le PKK and la fabrique d'une utopie* (Paris: La Découverte, 2017).

600 peace accords signed between 1990 and 2009, less than 5 per cent make reference to the equality of the sexes, the rights of women and sexual violence. UN Women, which works for female parity and autonomy, has developed a programme for including these two principles in peace processes.*

The stakes are not only moral: an agreement has greater chances of being long-lasting if women have participated in it. Indeed, they seem more honest and less threatening to belligerents, as was the case with Visaka Dharmadasa during negotiations between the Sri Lankan army and the Tamil Tigers in the 2000s. They help to promote dialogue and restore confidence. Most importantly, they raise questions vital for peace: about education, housing, food security and gender violence, as well as the reintegration of refugees and political prisoners.†

The masculinities of non-domination guarantee *the access of women to deliberations and politics, war and peace*, which amounts to sharing with them the responsibility for all civil and military matters. Men passionately committed to equality refuse to handle public affairs without the participation of women.

DEMOCRACY IN SERVICE OF WOMEN

Led by men, far right regimes glorify force, the army and obligatory sacrifice, while sending women back to their households. The state according to Mussolini, Hitler, Franco, Pinochet and Videla is also a gender dictatorship. In Japan in the 1930s, official organizations strove to rally women together under the banner of war nationalism through the Feminine Movement for National Defence, the Association of Patriotic Women and the Federation of Japanese Women, whose publication was called *The Household*.‡

---

* 'Women's Participation in Peace Negotiations: Connections Between Presence and Influence', UN Women, August 2010.
† Marie O'Reilly, 'Why Women? Inclusive Security and Peaceful Societies', Washington, Inclusive Security, October 2015.
‡ Yuko Nishikawa, 'Les femmes et la guerre, ou comment les mouvements féministes japonais en arrivèrent à collaborer à la Seconde Guerre mondiale', *Les Cahiers du CEDREF*, No. 4–5, 1995.

'Chief', 'guide' and 'supreme commander' are words that do not bode well in any way for women. With respect to gender justice, dictatorships and other juntas are by their very nature powers to be combated. So too are authoritarian states whose leaders need macho military displays to affirm their power, as in the case of Putin in Russia and Erdogan in Turkey. In China, Xi Jinping explained in 2013 that the USSR collapsed because it had not found any virile man within the Party capable of holding up. In Japan, imperial succession still excludes women, in spite of the controversy lasting throughout the 2000s.

Yet the emancipation of women has not been the preserve of democracies alone. An authoritarian, even dictatorial regime can promote the rights of women without respecting human rights. The examples of the USSR, Kemal Atatürk's Turkey and Bourguiba's Tunisia show that a social revolution can be imposed by exerting state power. In the late 2010s, the two countries with the greatest proportion of women in the National Assembly were Paul Kagame's Rwanda (61 per cent) and post-Castro Cuba (53 per cent), neither of which is a model of democracy. Sweden is in eighth place with 43 per cent, France sixteenth with 39 per cent, and the United States with 19 per cent far behind in 102nd position, between Indonesia and Kyrgyzstan.* Depending on whether civil society is in a position to resist dictatorship, the 'logics of depatriarchalization' (autonomization of educated women of the middle class in Iran) prevail over the 'logics of repatriarchalization' (nationalist rhetoric in Russia, reassertion of religiously oriented political authority in Turkey).†

Increasingly associated with video surveillance, the police state that reigns in dictatorships spares women from attacks in public places. The streets of Beijing and Doha are relatively safe, even at night. But it would be completely wrong to present these advantages as a pretext for claiming that the choice is between the security of a dictatorship and the disorder of democracy. An all-powerful police force in fact simply displaces the danger: women are victims of other forms of violence and abuse that do not incur sanction precisely because they are

---

* Inter-Parliamentary Union, 'Women in National Parliaments', 1 June 2018, available at www.ipu.org/wmn-e/classif.htm
† Éric Macé, *L'Après-patriarcat* (Paris: Seuil, 2015).

perpetrated by the forces of order. In Mexico, police frequently resort to sexual torture when women are arrested. Raped in 2006 by police agents in the state of Mexico, eleven plaintiffs testified before the Inter-American Court of Human Rights, without receiving much support from authorities in their own country, since President Enrique Peña Nieto was the governor of the state of Mexico when the crimes took place.

Social and religious conservatism, mixed with consumerism, also works against the rights of women. In Saudi Arabia, shopping centres have since the first decade of this century combined the segregation of the sexes with techniques for inciting people to buy. In the Al Mamlaka tower in Riyad, an exclusively feminine level houses the 'kingdom of woman', with stairs and escalators off limits to men. These are safe spaces made for consuming that which, while respecting the 'modesty' imposed by religion, allows Saudi women to parade their chic outfits, with jeans, high heels, Louis Vuitton purses and Gucci sunglasses.* In China, liberal reforms have since 1978 been accompanied by patriarchal discourse: the men at work, with their wives at home. International Women's Day, on 8 March, has become a marketing event halfway between Valentine's Day and Mother's Day, when the 'rights of women' are celebrated by way of special sales and exclusive offers in cosmetics and apparel.

The absence of public discussion makes it impossible to denounce the patriarchal order and the pathologies of the masculine. Not much gets said about the selective abortion of girls, conjugal violence or sexual harassment at the university or in the workplace in China. Since 1996, *The Vagina Monologues* have been translated and performed throughout the world, but it took seven years to be staged in China, at the Sun Yat-sen University of Canton. A theatrical troupe finally staged the play in Beijing in 2013 amid an atmosphere of reprobation, since women were not supposed to speak of sex in public. Public protest movements were immediately quelled by the police. In 2015, five feminists who were distributing tracts against sexual harassment were detained for a month. A large number of NGOs have

---

* Amélie Le Renard, *Femmes et espaces publics en Arabie saoudite* (Paris: Dalloz, 2011), pp. 118 and 265.

been banned. Social media campaigns on platforms such as WeChat and Weibo were censored before gaining influence, and the #MeToo movement has had a rather limited impact in China. Only a handful of female activists risking their safety have succeeded in publishing information: such is the case of the journalist Sophia Huang Xueqin in Canton, who in 2018 reported on sexual harassment in the media.*

Prohibited from speaking out in public and reduced to the 'freedom' to consume, women find themselves more or less helpless. Threatened by an oppressive police state, their rights are also at the mercy of a despot's sudden reversal (as in the USSR in the mid-1930s) or ideological tension (as in China in the 2010s). Democracy, however, offers a political and intellectual framework for the emancipation of women, even if it is sometimes instrumentalized by men. The quality of public life in a democratic society is the antidote to political and religious orthodoxies that enforce patriarchal order. Democracy is both the origin and outcome of the rights of women. The origin, because democracy bears the promise of equality among citizens who are all endowed with inalienable rights; the outcome, because the emancipation of all men and women is its reason for being.

Several conditions are indispensable, however. Unlike the Declaration of the Rights of Man and the Citizen of 1789, human rights must explicitly and systematically include the rights of women. For that reason, no European country was a true democracy before the establishment of universal suffrage in the first half of the twentieth century. Nowadays, there is a greater distrust of democratic institutions than of the masculinity from which they emanate. In this context *a counter-masculinity* can be established in the sense of the 'counter-democracy' theorized by Pierre Rosanvallon. Thanks to collective efforts at vigilance, surveillance and monitoring, women and men are capable of resisting the hypertrophy of the masculine. This counter-masculinity can take various forms: books, articles, testimonies, petitions, reports, observation committees, public demonstrations, protest campaigns and ridicule on the Internet.

* Gabrielle Jaffe, 'Performing *The Vagina Monologues* in China', *The Atlantic*, 29 November 2013; and Catherine Lai, 'No #MeToo in China? Female Journalists Face Sexual Harassment, But Remain Silent', *Hong Kong Free Press*, 5 December 2017.

And so the masculine must remain an area of debate, even conflict, a dissensus, like democracy itself, in order not to be a seizure of power. The masculine is an 'empty space' that no one has the right to appropriate.

FIGHTING AGAINST
THE POVERTY OF WOMEN

Women are massively afflicted by poverty and underdevelopment. According to the World Food Programme, they represent 60 per cent of hunger victims, or about 600 million people. Gender poverty is due to the precarious nature of feminine jobs and their low level of remuneration. In developing countries, three quarters of women work in the informal economy, often without any contract or social safety net. Because of discrimination when it comes to inheritance, women have little access to land: they represent 15 per cent of landowners in sub-Saharan Africa, 5 per cent in North Africa and the Middle East, and even less in Kenya and Northern India. However, they carry out most of the work in their households, without compensation. The supply of water used for food preparation, hygiene and irrigation depends essentially on mothers and daughters. In Guinea, women devote 5.7 hours per week to this task, as opposed to 2.3 hours for men; and for women in Malawi, the numbers are 9.1 hours, as opposed to 1.1 hours for men.* Associated with other tasks, the chore of fetching water results in fatigue and lack of schooling.

In 2012, about 500 million women in the world were illiterate: that is two-thirds of illiterate adults. The disparities between the sexes were enormous in several regions: in Southern and Western Asia, 74 per cent of men were literate as opposed to 52 per cent of women; in sub-Saharan Africa, 68 per cent of men as opposed to 50 per cent of women, though the number of literate women was even lower in certain countries of Western Africa such as Niger, Mali and Burkina Faso. In the rural areas of Cambodia, 86 per cent of men are literate, as

---

* Inter-Agency Task Force on Rural Women, 'Rural Women and the Millennium Development Goals', UN, 2012.

opposed to 52 per cent of women. In Ethiopia, 90 per cent of male city-dwellers can read and write, as opposed to only 30 per cent of women in rural areas. It is women who most often suffer discrimination: on a worldwide scale, their rate of enrolment in secondary education (39 per cent) is lower than that of boys in rural areas (45 per cent) and girls in urban areas (59 per cent).*

Illiteracy has a major impact on the health of women and their children, including poorly administered medicines, a persistently high rate of maternal and infant mortality and ignorance about AIDS. By contrast, just one additional year of schooling increases girls' salaries from 10 to 20 per cent, increases the age at which they marry and lowers their birth rates. Educating girls is in and of itself a policy conducive to health, because it results in reducing the number of unprotected sexual relations and premature pregnancies. In Kenya, distributing uniforms to girls beginning middle school and supplying them with a new uniform eighteen months later if they are still enrolled brings about a reduction in pregnancies (10 per cent as opposed to 14 per cent) in the three years that follow, and even afterwards.†

Women's lack of education, their poor health and their dire poverty not only constitute a moral scandal, but also paralyse the entire evolution of a country, resulting in less human capital, collective intelligence, talent, discovery and innovation. The cost of these gender inequities is enormous: 6 billion dollars per year in the Ivory Coast, 89 billion in Asia.‡

Men can choose any of several battlefronts. To support the emancipation of women, they can not only share in household chores, fight against sexism in small towns and cities, condemn genital mutilation and the marriage of underage girls, but also improve infrastructures of water supply and healthcare. In Burkina Faso, Thomas Sankara's 1984 agrarian reform facilitated women's access to land. In the Swat Valley of Pakistan, Ziauddin Yousafzai (father of the young Malala,

---

* Ibid.; and 'Teaching and Learning: Achieving Quality for All', Paris: UNESCO, 2014.
† Esther Duflo, Le Développement humain: Lutter contre la pauvreté (I) (Paris: Seuil, 2010), pp. 94–95.
‡ Gertrude Tah, 'And If the Emergence Was a Woman?' The World Bank, July, 2017; and William Pesek, 'Asia's $89 Billion Sexism Issue', The Japan Times, 24 November 2015.

A television series for women's rights (2015)

Several men, including the producer Moussa Sène Absa and showrunner Charli Beléteau, participated in the Senegalese series C'est la vie, *broadcast throughout all of Western Africa since 2015. By showing life in a health centre in a working-class area, it makes viewers aware of subjects concerning women's health and conjugal violence.*

winner of the Nobel Peace Prize in 2014) founded a school for girls. Karunachalam Muruganatham, an Indian entrepreneur and inventor of a machine that manufactures low-cost sanitary pads, enabled millions of women to lead a normal life during their menstrual periods.

Fazle Hasan Abed was born in 1936 in British India, now Bangladesh. He first worked as a financial director for Shell before founding the Bangladesh Rural Advancement Committee, an NGO aiding 140 million persons in twelve Asian and African countries. He builds schools and day-care centres, grants micro-credit, distributes chicks to women in agriculture, and fights against discrimination and sexual violence. Since 1993, one programme has enabled adolescent girls to participate in sport, meet in safe spaces in their communities and obtain information about their health and sexual rights. Within a few decades, Fazle Hasan Abed has managed to reduce extreme poverty and illiteracy, particularly among girls. In 2014, he was the first man to receive the Trust Women Hero Award for supporting women's rights. 'If we are capable of undoing patriarchy, there will be gains for men as well as women,' he said on International Women's Day, 8 March 2018.

Madhav Chavan, who was born in India in 1954, founded the organization Pratham, an NGO that takes care of millions of disadvantaged children. By means of a 'second chance' programme, Pratham brings young women throughout the world back to school, particularly in India, the United States and Great Britain. Like Fazle Hasan Abed before him, Madhav Chavan received the WISE prize for education in 2012. There are also ultra-rich businessmen who fund the fight against poverty on a worldwide scale. Examples include Bill Gates through his foundation and Mohammed Abdul Latif Jameel through MIT's Poverty Action Lab.

Female entrepreneurship must be supported beyond the fight against poverty. In Togo, the 'Nana Benz' did not need anyone's help to make a fortune in selling wax printed fabrics from the Netherlands. In a more or less patriarchal context, however, men sponsored some initiatives coming from women. In Saudi Arabia, female chambers of commerce were opened in Djedda in 1998 and Riyad in 2004; women were authorized to create an enterprise in 2018. In Bangladesh, an institution like the Grameen Bank, founded by Muhammad Yunus in 1976, has developed a system of micro-credit to assist women in investing in small businesses or collective projects, with the regularity of loan payments guaranteed by their women's organization (where groups meet regularly and collectively accept financial responsibility for each other's debt). The outcome of micro-credit has nevertheless turned out to be disappointing: in India and Sri Lanka, in Ghana and Burkina Faso, the productivity of capital invested in female-run businesses remains low, either because they function in largely unprofitable sectors of the economy, or because their activity benefits from fewer investments.

Regardless of their level of success, the NGOs, associations and philanthropists must not overshadow the state. Nothing can replace the role and function of the government in health, education and social welfare. However, men are the ones who often hold the key positions within the state. In 2009, the Ministry of Water and Irrigation in Kenya implemented a system of incentives for government employees, who were contractually responsible for realizing the objectives of gender mainstreaming each year. In one year, 100,000 dollars were allocated to government agencies to support gender equity and conduct awareness campaigns.* As the World Bank recommends, it is also important to bolster the training of police and magistrates by including women's rights (in particular property rights) and the repression of sexual violence.†

OPPRESSIVE RELIGIONS

Since it situates men as mediators between God and believers, religion has a problem with women. Every religion should question the masculine, that is to say, authority, power, orthodoxy and the family. Without such conscientious self-examination, religious conservatisms will obstruct equality between the sexes. Men of religion never openly say they are sexist: they claim to act out of respect for 'tradition', which intends for women to be virgins, then mothers. The contempt for women is concealed under the discourse of 'protection' that men owe to these weak, impure beings.

Literal readings of the Bible or the Quran are catastrophes for women's rights, enabling patriarchy to don the most disgusting cloak of respectability. Fundamentalists are misogynists by nature: they use the sacred to dominate women. A man of religion who does not challenge the power enjoyed by males is an unjust man. A believer who takes pride in his masculinity is impious, since on the contrary, the divine message prescribes equality and justice.

The Catholic Church is one of the most patriarchal institutions in the world. From priests to the Pope, its hierarchy is entirely masculine. Granted, women have been playing a larger role in dioceses,

---

* World Bank, 'Gender in Water and Sanitation', Water Sanitation Program, November 2010, p. 19.
† Amanda Ellis et al., *Gender and Economic Growth in Kenya. Unleashing the Power of Women* (World Bank, The International Bank for Reconstruction and Development, 2007).

chaplaincies, the preparations for marriage and reflections on bioethics, but they are still excluded from the sacred. Outside the ecclesial sphere, some people refer back to the story of the creation of Adam and Eve to denigrate what they call the 'theory of gender'. In 2017, a judge in the Portuguese city of Porto's appeals court excused conjugal violence by referring back to an obsolete penal code and the book of Proverbs, which condemns the adulterous woman. The same set of arguments can be found in the Hindu world. After the suicide of a young eighteen-year-old widow (possibly pressured by her in-laws) in the Indian village of Deorala in 1987, fundamentalists invoked religious customs. On 8 October of the same year, a demonstration in favour of sati drew 70,000 people, while at the same time in Jaipur a committee for the defence of religion was created and led by Rajput men aged between twenty and thirty.*

The *Gender Gap Report* shows that in the Muslim world, the situation of women is bad: the lowest ranking countries are Yemen, Pakistan, Syria, Iran, Mali, Saudi Arabia, Morocco, Jordan and Egypt. The first reason for this is the alliance of tyranny with religion, taking the form of theocracy in Iran, masculine dictatorship in Saudi Arabia, and Taliban obscurantism in Afghanistan and Pakistan. Furthermore, the absence of democracy makes it impossible to freely discuss the place of women in society without speaking of religion itself. Ranked the eighty-fourth country out of 144, Indonesia constitutes a notable exception thanks to its educational and healthcare systems.

In several countries, sharia law is one of the bases of the legal code, particularly concerning polygamy, repudiation, female adultery and inequality in inheritance. In Algeria, a Muslim woman cannot marry a non-Muslim; a woman must call on a guardian to end her marriage; wives are required to obey their husbands; and children are affiliated with their fathers. Over the course of the 1990s, Malaysia introduced various amendments to Islamic law governing the family, facilitating polygamy and divorce for men, and reducing their financial responsibility toward their wives. In case of rape, the burden of proof is incumbent

---

* John Stratton Hawley (ed.), *Sati, the Blessing and the Curse*, pp. 6–9, 105.

upon the victim.* In Saudi Arabia, certain conservatives claim that women are treated like queens: they have the 'right' to be chauffeured around in a car, not work, and receive religious instruction, which supposedly makes them luckier than Western women. Middle Eastern countries offer a maternity leave of less than 12 weeks, even falling to 6 weeks in Saudi Arabia and Bahrain.

Lastly, a powerful wave of sexism has swept through the societies of the Maghreb and the Middle East. The three reports of the United Nations Development Programme in 2002, 2005 and 2016 concerning the Arab world all arrived at the same diagnosis, pointing to a steadily high level of female illiteracy, discrimination integrated into religious beliefs and family traditions, an emphasis on the procreative role of women, a lack of equal opportunities and a low level of participation in political and economic life. In Morocco and Algeria, young women's sexual lives are tightly constrained by taboos, and the obsession with virginity has led to a boom in hymenoplasty surgery. Inequality is also visible in the frequency and impunity of rape, the persistence of forced marriages in rural areas and the belief in menstrual 'impurity'.

MUSLIM AND FEMINIST

Not long ago, dictatorial Arab states – along with the patriarchy on which they stood – were shaken by revolution. Between 2014 and 2017, Morocco, Tunisia, Egypt, Jordan and Lebanon abrogated the articles of their penal code allowing authorities to drop charges against a rapist if he married his victim, even if she were a minor. In Morocco, a law passed in 2018 punishes sexual harassment and violence perpetrated against women. It does not recognize conjugal rape, but a few months later the appeals court in Tangier sentenced a man to two years in prison for raping his wife. A similar law was passed in Tunisia, with the same lack of recognition of conjugal rape. Moreover, President Béji Caïd Essebsi launched two new initiatives – equality of

* Zainah Anwar, 'Négocier les droits des femmes sous la loi religieuse en Malaisie' in Zahra Ali, *Féminismes islamiques* (Paris: La Fabrique, 2012), p. 143 ff.

inheritance and the possibility of marrying a non-Muslim, before appointing a Commission on Freedom and Equality charged with making proposals. This undertaking was supported by the Syrian Mohamed Shahrour, a scholar of the Quran heavily influenced by Marxism.

A new masculinity is emerging in the Muslim world, the fruit of democratic activism and the freedom of social media. Thanks to the Tahrir Bodyguard and various movements against sexual harassment, some men in Egypt have denounced the violence to which women are subjected. In 2015, in Istanbul, a few dozen men donned skirts, appealing to the public with a hashtag translating as 'A Miniskirt for Özgecan', in order to denounce the rape and murder of a female student. In Iran, a few men snapped pictures of themselves with a headscarf after the hashtag 'Men in Hijab' had been sent out on Facebook and Twitter, at the initiative of the female journalist exiled in New York, Masih Alinejad: 'I challenged my readers to wear a hijab, even if just for a few seconds, and to send me their selfies. That resonated with men who reject the traditional model of virility, who are willing to stand up for women's rights.'* Women's freedom increasingly symbolizes the freedom of all, and certain men do not hesitate to play with their gender to defend it.

For each social function, there is a corresponding possibility of masculine justice: a father raising his daughters in the same way as his sons; a brother who does not believe that he has been allocated the role of monitoring his sister; a jurist striving to modernize the legal code; a chief of state with equal numbers of men and women among his staff and cabinet; an intellectual standing up against fundamentalism, as the Algerian writer Kamel Daoud has been doing since the 1990s.

Even men of religion could commit to action in favour of women. The notion of Islamic feminism arose toward the end of the twentieth century: that approach is useful, not to justify the veil or condemn the so-called 'Western model', but rather to show that the rights of women are not a priori incompatible with Islam. Such a reconciliation requires

---

* Nadje Al-Ali, 'Egyptian Sexual Harassment Activists Battle Growing Acceptance of Violence', *The Conversation*, 14 February 2014; and Pauline Verduzier, '"Men in Hijab": Des Iraniens se voilent en signe de solidarité avec les femmes', *L'Express*, 30 July 2016.

a critical approach: interpreting texts (*ijihâd*), fighting against literal readings of the Quran, reforming jurisprudence in order to promote equality within the family. Two movements of Malaysian origin, Musawah and Sisters in Islam, have been organized from that perspective. The Women Living Under Muslim Laws network was founded in 1984 and is present in seventy countries. It provides support to women whose existence is governed by laws and customs inspired by Islam. It condemns violence that women suffer in Senegal, Morocco, Algeria, South Sudan and elsewhere, and assists them in enforcing their rights, in particular the right not to be defined as Muslims.

Men of religion would bring themselves honour by joining these movements. Theologians could work at dissociating Islam from the masculinity of domination, ridding laws of all their patriarchal baggage, recalling that violence against women is anti-Islamic and that women are capable of being leaders of a nation or an enterprise the same as men. Some professors of Islamic law holding positions in Western universities have read with interest the book by Ziba Mir-Hosseini and her colleagues, *Men in Charge? Rethinking Authority in Muslim Legal Tradition*, first published in 2014. In the early twentieth century, Qasim Amin and Tahar Haddad showed that a man can be considered both Muslim and feminist: not that he would 'protect' women, but would on the contrary respect them. Muslim men can help women escape from the patriarchal circle.

These remarks apply to men of all religions, including, for example, an Orthodox Jewish man studying in a Jerusalem or New York yeshiva while his wife struggles frantically to handle their six children. Fundamentalists are ready to kill each other, but are together hand in hand when it comes to proclaiming the superiority of men. They agree on monopolizing transcendence, knowledge and morality, in the name of virtues they believe they share with God. Now, if the equality of human beings is inscribed in sacred texts, divine justice and gender justice are one and the same thing. If God lends His protection to all, no one can glory in their sex or gender. And if God is a woman, She can only be upset with the phallic arrogance of Her priests.

The masculinities of non-domination rely on a willingness to share speaking time, authority, knowledge, weapons, wealth and spirituality. They consist not only of recognizing the equality of the sexes, but

also of fighting against patriarchy, misogyny, discrimination and violence, and of *refusing to let masculinity be the expression of power*.
For all male leaders who might not have the courage of Justin Trudeau,
we can lay out a basic feminist agenda: democracy, peace, economic
development, healthcare and education policies, tolerance and religious liberalism. All of this would make it possible to improve the
condition of hundreds of millions of women in the world.

13

Masculinities of Respect

Love is not unrelated to the emancipation of women, since they have so often been reduced to sex objects or reproductive bodies. Masculinities of respect flourish in the context of a new sexual civility.

IN LOVE ALSO

Since the 1960s, feminists have demanded sexual rights and denounced violence. That is what their adversaries have not forgiven, labelling them with insulting terms characteristic of the misogyny greeting women who claim their rights.

As one of the organisers of the French MLF (Mouvement de Libération des Femmes) explained, feminism is not focused on sex, and the determination to 'enjoy unfettered sexual pleasure' is a masculine slogan: 'For us, the "sexual revolution" is something quite different. It's constructing egalitarian relations with the beloved.'* On the subject of the rape trial held in Aix-en-Provence in 1978, when three men were prosecuted for having raped two women, the paediatrician Alexandre Minkowski (prevented from testifying by the presiding magistrate) gave a very similar analysis: 'In this region of the Mediterranean, there is a consensus on the notion that one "pierces" women; in the end, this type of masculine complicity appears to me to be an insult for men and for the conception that we have of love.'†

---

* Marie-Jo Bonnet, *Mon MLF*, p. 73.
† Cited by Cédric Condon, Jean-Yves Naour, *Le Procès du viol*, documentary, France, 2013, 52 minutes.

Freedom to love, equality of desire, the dignity of each woman and each man. When it comes to love, the emancipation of women concerns ownership of their own bodies, guaranteed by three rights: the right to sexual activity, which includes pleasure; the right to sexual security, which demands consent; the right to sexual expression, whatever lifestyle she should choose. The masculinity of respect ensures the rights of women in three realms: the emotional, the legal and the social. In the formulation of Axel Honneth, this means the ability to be both a *desiring subject* (freely leading her love life), an *inviolable person*, protected against all assaults and damage to her honour, and a *valued being*, having the right to be respected by others. This is how we can conceive of gender justice in the area of sexuality. It is therefore not feminism, but rather machismo that is 'anti-sex', when it instils fear, violence, and contempt into the lives of women.

The Nigerian writer Chimamanda Ngozi Adichie and the Franco-Moroccan writer Leila Slimani associate feminism with sensuality, seduction with empowerment. In her TEDx lecture of 2012, Adichie defined herself as a 'happy African feminist, who does not hate men, loves gloss, and wears high heels for herself'. In the wake of the Weinstein scandal, Slimani claimed the right to 'wear a miniskirt, plunging neckline, and high heels' without being constantly bothered.*

Whether feminine or masculine, beauty admits no definition. One can be beautiful with or without make-up, through visiting or not visiting the beauty shop. The eroticization of the body does not run counter to the emancipation of women, as long as they are the ones who enact it, either for personal pleasure or in defiance of authoritarian patriarchy: from Saint Paul to Khomeini, fundamentalists have required women to wear a headscarf for the sake of 'modesty', since their hair, supposedly eroticized, could attract men's gaze or kindle their desire, and therefore 'disturb' the public order. To that extent, dressing freely can be a way of refusing the entire set of constraints that gender violence imposes on all women.

The two sexes not only find themselves side by side, but also seek

---

* Leila Slimani, 'Un porc, tu nais?' *Libération*, 12 January 2018.

I want to – you don't want to

The Bolt, *one of Fragonard's masterpieces, depicts a couple about to make love. The man bolts the door for more privacy, but the woman tries to escape his grasp. Is it resistance becoming of a lady or the resignation of a victim? A scene of libertine gallantry or of the culture of rape?*

each other in the desire for intimacy, for flirtation, romance, love and sex. It is sad to have to regulate these activities, but they can only thrive in the absence of violence. Legislators have no business intervening in dating or in S&M parties, except if someone's liberty is being violated. Indeed, S&M parties are highly codified spaces with numerous explicit rules, so that participants submit to constraints with full awareness of what is involved. It is, on the contrary, in contexts where the rules are neither precise nor, consequently, respected that the rights of women are no longer inviolable. The principle that all is permitted among consenting adults presupposes for that very reason that consent be defined. In love, as in sex, the masculine must be called into question.

SEDUCTION

Contrary to what we are led to believe about the alchemy of dating, seduction is a matter of highly codified social relations that vary with time and according to cultural context. This not only pertains to institutions such as the selectively organized gatherings called 'rallies' designed to induce youth from 'good families' to opt for endogamy. Other customs make it possible to impose family expectations while at the same time regulating adolescent sexuality. In Brazil, the *namoro* designates chaste, but exclusive meetings occurring after the families of a potential young couple have met each other. With family honour at stake, the young girl is closely monitored until she marries her *namorado*. In Brazil, a new relation appeared in the 1980s: two people engaging in a physical, even sexual relationship without the slightest commitment.*

Every culture allows demonstrations of sexual interest. Banter, flirting and dating make possible anodyne conversations and exchanged looks over the course of ever-closer relations that can lead to sex once those involved have confirmed their compatibility. In some countries like France and Italy, men are supposed to make the first move, from the first compliment to romantic gestures. Online meeting sites such as Meetic (created in 2012) and Tinder (in 2012), reset the balance in favour of women, placing them on an equal footing with men by giving them more romantic and sexual autonomy.

In Germany, seduction tends to depend on women, with men taking a relatively passive role: some women don't care for this, while others enjoy being able to go out in a miniskirt without men constantly gawking at them. In North America, approaching women in public places is much less acceptable than in Latin countries, and dating is designed to define the parameters of seduction. Hence this half-regretful, half-annoyed testimony from a female French expatriate: 'Over the course of twenty-two years in Quebec, I must have been approached twice. Here, it's odourless, without colour or taste. I don't

---

* Michel Bozon and Maria Luiza Heilbom, 'Les caresses et les mots: Initiations amoureuses à Rio de Janeiro et à Paris', *Terrain*, No. 27, September 1996, pp. 37–58.

know how they manage to encounter each other! In France, you get approached at the butcher's, in the street, everywhere.'*

The cultures of love are rarely egalitarian, and considerate gestures can be marks of a subtle gender inequality. In the twelfth century, the tradition of the courtly romance, in which the knight wins over his lady's love by proving his valour, is implicitly grounded on the social and military superiority of the man searching for a female trophy. The refinement of the culture of love in the arts of conversation and correspondence in the eighteenth century did not in the least forbid coercion and rape, as attested by the Venetian adventurer Casanova and the character Valmont in *Dangerous Liaisons* (1782). A seducer is a man who manages to overcome the 'resistance' of women.

For men, the tradition of gallantry consists in honouring women within the framework of a more or less eroticized civility: holding the door, offering one's seat in a restaurant, and so on. It can also be found in other forms, such as in the phrase 'women and children first' in times of shipwreck, from the 1850s on, and this masculinity of sacrifice makes the man into a saviour, a symbol of noble action and stoicism in the face of danger.† Like the courtly romance, gallantry can be interpreted in two opposing ways: it can mean either the man's submission to the woman (the lady of his heart) or the woman's submission to the man (her valorous knight). Already in the late eighteenth century, Mary Wollstonecraft criticized gallantry in the name of equality.

Why exactly would women specifically need to be assisted, or even rescued? If a man offers to carry the suitcase of an attractive young woman without being willing to assist a person in a wheelchair or an ailing homeless person in the street, there is nothing gentlemanly about him. Gallantry projects women into a sexualized relation in spite of themselves. Precious, ornamental, fragile, awkward, helpless when it comes to physical strength, mechanics, electricity, cars and

* Cited by Josée Blanchette, 'Noir désir', *Le Devoir*, 20 October 2017. See also Maurice Wojach, 'Bedienungsanleitung für den deutschen Mann', *Märkische Allgemeine*, 7 February 2018.
† Robin Miskolze, *Women and Children First: Nineteenth-Century Sea Narratives and American Identity* (Lincoln: University of Nebraska Press, 2007).

risky situations, they are perceived to be a 'disfavoured category' for whom men are supposedly responsible: the incompetence of young women has their sexual availability as its counterpart.* If men want to offer their seat to women, they should do so in government and big corporations.

The same line of reasoning applies to compliments. In order to know whether they are intended to give pleasure or to confirm gender identities, one has to determine their nature. Could the same word of praise be addressed to either a young woman, an elderly lady or a man? Does it concern the woman's appearance, or rather her intelligence, knowledge, humour or decision-making ability? Does it create a sexual atmosphere? Not all comments are equally desirable, desired or fitting.

Whoever pays a compliment is in a position of authority, since the other person is the object of their judgement. If they reinforce masculine authority, the chivalrous mindset, by overemphasizing women's appearance, polite gestures of protection partake of a benevolent sexism that complements hostile sexism.† It is doubtless pleasant to be told nice things, but it all depends on the moment, the tone, the frequency and the timeliness of the compliment and its hidden meanings. Men also have to be aware of the effects of various contexts: words do not have the same meaning when spoken at a gathering in a friend's home and on public transport. No legislator will ever stake out a position on the propriety of men undressing women with their eyes, but such stares amount to a visual or symbolic form of assault. Men don't have the right to gawk at a woman like a piece of sexual merchandise.

Romantic encounters are obviously part of life. Conversation, flirtation, desire: human relations have to remain free. One has the right to try to seduce someone, but imposing that seduction, bothering someone with persistent attempts, is a violation of the law. There is a difference in nature between flirting and harassment: what marks the

* Erwing Goffman, 'The Arrangement between the Sexes', *Theory and Society*, Vol. 4, No. 3, 1977, pp. 301–331.
† Peter Glick and Susan Fiske, 'An Ambivalent Alliance: Hostile and Benevolent Sexism as Complementary Justifications for Gender Inequality', *The American Psychologist*, No. 56, 2001, pp. 109–118.

passage from one to the other is the inability or unwillingness to acknowledge and respect the other person's refusal.

The ethics of compliments on looks consist in not bothering or disturbing, nor imposing a sexualized relation on the other person, for a catcall is nothing but a verbal act of violence. A woman walking down the street should not have to put up with the slightest remark of any sort. That is what can be called the right to tranquillity. Equality in relations of seduction involves an exchange, at the minimum a shared intention, attentiveness to signals of receptivity and non-receptivity – in other words, systematically respecting the other's desire.

'We won't have the right to flirt any more,' complained certain men and women soon after the Weinstein affair. That's not true. *Flirtation appropriate for gender justice* recognizes both the liberty of the other person (to say yes or no) and the equality of the sexes (each can express their desire).

THE CONDITIONS OF SEX

The sex life of adults is nobody's business but their own, but the state is authorized to define consent and punish those who violate it. The legislator's protective mission stops here, and that is why the law does not a priori prohibit relations between managers and employees, doctors and nurses, professors and students. But how to ensure that the hierarchical relation does not skew consent by the very fact that it involves a certain domination and a certain vulnerability? In the United States, many universities have rules forbidding sexual relations between professors and all undergraduates (between the ages of 18 and 22). One bill in California forbidding sexual relations between teachers and students was rejected in 2012: there again, it is for universities to decide.

How consent is to be expressed remains to be determined. First possibility: smiles, gestures, the eloquence of signals, tacit agreement, the surge of fervour in complicit silence, and so it is that the two hold hands, kiss and undress each other. In bed, it is easier to act than to speak, not to mention that desire is not always rational. But body language can lead to misunderstandings in situations of embarrassment, uncertainty, even panic, and can conceal forms of aggression where one acts as the other is subjected to those acts. There are women (and in particular young women at the beginning of their sexual life) who give in without having consented, who let themselves go because they do not dare to say 'no', because they are defenceless in the face of intense insistence. And the victim allows herself to be penetrated out of weariness, resignation, without a word, resisting in her mind but not with her body.

As a young summer camp counsellor in the late 1950s, the French writer Annie Ernaux allowed herself to be kissed by the head counsellor at a party:

> He goes too fast, she is not ready for such rapidity, such passion. She feels nothing. She is subjugated by this desire that he has for her, the desire of a wild, unrestrained man, unrelated to her slow, careful spring-time embrace ...
>
> 'Take your clothes off,' he says. From the time that he asked her to dance, she did everything he requested. Between what was happening to her and what she was doing, there was no difference. She lay down beside him on the narrow bed, naked. She did not have time to get used to his complete nudity, his naked man's body, she immediately felt the enormous stiff member that he pushed between her thighs. He forces. She feels pain. She says that she is a virgin, as a defence or an explan-ation. She cries out ...
>
> It was as if it were too late to back out, as if things had to follow their course. As if she did not have the right to abandon this man in the state that she had triggered in him.
>
> Subsequently, she seeks the presence of this man, she thinks about him all year and feels herself to be a woman via the sexual intimacy that he snatched from her.*

In an interview given after the publication of her book, Annie Ernaux refused to use the word 'rape'. The fact remains, however, that this scene resembles one, even though it was committed without physical

---

* Annie Ernaux, *Mémoires de fille* (Paris: Gallimard/Folio, 2016/2018), p. 46 ff. See also Dephine Dhilly and Blandine Grosjean, *Sexe sans consentement*, documentary, France, 2018, 52 minutes.

violence. Why do so many women sleep with a man without wanting to? For some, it is difficult to get off the 'sexual escalator' which is supposed to lead directly from the first date to physical intimacy: it is as if they fear upsetting their suitor. An aggravating factor may be the impression that saying 'no' would be useless. But why are so many men 'motivated', even excited by a refusal? A woman who does not speak, nor move, nor answer words and gestures is saying 'no'. This refusal, not utterable due to embarrassment, fear or mute astonishment, is the opposite of consent. The man who touches a woman who is reticent, passive, listless, frozen, petrified or dead drunk may not have any criminal record of rape, but he most assuredly does have the soul of a rapist. Body language harbours romantic passions, but also quasi-rapes in the 'grey zone'.

In the 1970s, feminists popularized the slogan 'No means no.' Making refusal explicit in this way enables women to ward off various advances to which they are subjected in the street, at work, and elsewhere. A man has a right to 'try his luck' with a compliment or a gesture until the woman in question gives the first expression of reticence. At that point, he is under the obligation to stop: failing that he becomes intrusive, an undesirable solicitor, even an aggressor. The German legal code has since 2016 defined rape as a sexual act committed against a person's will.

However, 'No means no,' as relayed by several public awareness campaigns throughout the world, is insufficient when the woman is not in a position to express her refusal, either because she is intimidated or because she is afraid or because she is unconscious due to alcohol or drugs. Fostering the culture of respect is all the more difficult since, for decades, Hollywood films and romance novels have conveyed the myth of the woman who says 'no', but thinks 'yes', expecting the seducer to bypass her semblance of resistance.

Which is why it is necessary to ask for explicit consent. That's what is meant by the formula 'Yes means yes.' Before engaging in sexual activity, there must be a clear and simple agreement on the part of each partner. The verbalization of consent moreover has the advantage of favouring sexual communication within the couple.

In the United States, the feminist perspective on consent has had an impact on college campuses. In 1991, Antioch College in Ohio was the first to promulgate rules on the matter, which were quickly mocked on television. After several cases of rape under intoxication with alcohol, however, affirmative consent became the norm in the second decade of the twenty-first century, for example at Yale, the University of Texas, the State University of New York and, for the first time statewide, in California. Without some expression of willingness from both partners, a sexual act is considered to be forced and therefore illegal. Neither indifference nor the absence of refusal are valid justifications: consent must be reiterated at each step of the sexual relation.

The University of Colorado's definition of sexual consent (2019)

Understanding Affirmative Consent

What is affirmative consent?

CU Boulder has an affirmative consent standard. This means that consent for sexual activity must be clear, knowing, and voluntary. Consent must include words or actions that create mutually understandable, clear permission conveying acceptance of the conditions of the sexual activity and willingness to engage in the sexual activity.

- Consent must be clearly established through words or actions.
- A person who does not want to consent to sex is not required to resist.
- Consent to some forms of sexual activity does not imply consent to other sexual activities.
- Silence, previous sexual relationships, or the existence of a current relationship do not imply consent.
- Consent cannot be implied by how someone is dressed or inferred from the giving or acceptance of gifts, a ride, money, or other items.
- Consent can be withdrawn at any time during sexual activity and need not be a verbal withdrawal, as long as it is conveyed clearly.
- Under Colorado law, a person under the age of 15 cannot legally consent to sex with someone who is four or more years older than they are. A person who is 15 or 16 cannot legally consent to sex with someone who is more than 10 years older.

When is someone unable to consent?

Incapacitation is when a person is unable to give consent due to effects of alcohol or other drug use, or other factors such as sleep, illness, or disability.

Incapacitation is a state where a person cannot make a rational, reasonable decision because they lack the capacity to understand the who, what, when, where, why, or how of a sexual interaction. The use of alcohol or drugs, in and of itself, does not render a person incapacitated, nor is it a defense against an allegation of sexual misconduct. The impact of alcohol and/or drugs varies from person to person. Someone who is aware or should know that an individual is incapacitated and engages in sexual activity with that individual, is in violation of university policy.

Office of Institutional Equity and Compliance, available at https://www.colorado.edu/oiec/policies/sexual-misconduct-intimate-partner-abuse-stalking-policy/understanding-affirmative-consent

---

As the woman in charge of the programme for the prevention of sexual misconduct at Antioch College explained in 1992, 'We are not trying to reduce the romance, passion or spontaneity of sex; we are trying to reduce the spontaneity of rape.'*

Over the course of the more than two decades that followed, numerous people in the United States spoke out against the affirmative consent rules. Here are a few of the criticisms:†

- The law depicts sex as something frightful. Men are supposedly predators in search of prey; women, defenceless victims; young people supposedly need government assistance to make love.
- The law encourages the misinterpretation of every attitude, every compliment, every gesture. Taking someone shyly by the hand during a first date is 'criminal sexual conduct' according to article 213.6(3)(a) of the law.

---

* Karen Hall, 'Antioch's Policy on Sex is Humanizing', *The New York Times*, 20 October 1993.

† See for example Laura Kipnis, 'Sexual Paranoia Strikes Academe', *The Chronicle of Higher Education*, Vol. 61, No. 25, 27 February 2015; Robert Carle, 'How Affirmative Consent Laws Criminalize Everyone', *The Federalist*, 30 March 2015; and Judith Shulevitz, 'Regulating Sex', *The New York Times*, 27 June 2015.

- Each new step in the relation requires an additional request for consent: 'May I take your arm? May I kiss you in the nape of the neck? On the mouth? May I caress your back? May I take off your T-shirt?' And there remain at least a dozen more questions before the end of sexual intercourse.
- Is the couple's checklist valid for all sex acts of the week, the month, the relationship, or only for one single time?
- It becomes possible to retrospectively denounce a sexual act, even the entire relationship, on the grounds that one was intimidated or manipulated. How is it possible to protect the male or female partner against later regrets, grudges or resentment?
- If, in order not to be accused of rape, one must be able to prove that there was explicit consent, do the partners have to sign a protocol, a release, a formally verified document, or do they have to fill out some form on the Internet, checking off the sexual practices that they accept?

The 'Yes to Sex' app was indeed created and made available via Apple Store and Google Play in 2016, making it possible to indicate one's excitement and consent on a secure server twenty-five seconds before sexual relations. However, users were advised to leave the app on in case they changed their mind in the heat of action. It would perhaps be simpler to record one's agreement on a smartphone before entering any new phase. But who would accept such a killjoy? How could one prevent a woman's affirmative consent from being broadcast on the Internet by an ex resorting to revenge porn?

In 2014, a student in California added the story of his romantic disillusionment to the debate. While they were in bed, his girlfriend raised her hands in disgust: 'How am I supposed to get turned on when you keep asking for permission for everything like a little boy? Just take me and fuck me already.'*

In conclusion, we can say that the three types of sexual consent – the eloquence of signals, 'No means no' and 'Yes means yes' – are not only valid, but can also be juxtaposed so as to combine their

---

* Cited by Conor Friedersdorf, 'Why One Male College Student Abandoned Affirmative Consent', *The Atlantic*, 20 October 2014.

advantages and neutralize their deficiencies: by words or gestures, an explicit agreement is necessary before any sexual relation; the absence of reaction is not an agreement; no practice can be required; the slightest refusal must be respected; dialogue enables the enrichment of sexual life. These clauses serve as so many guardrails for human sexuality, which clearly carries some irrational, instinctive, even impulsive urges, which one does not necessarily have to deplore. And it should not be feared that this civility will undermine desire: on the contrary, violence is what destroys eroticism.

Once these principles are established, people need to be left alone, particularly young people: the great majority of adults live their sexuality without a problem. Government does not have the right to invade individuals' private lives. In any case, we have to distinguish between educating about consent and paranoid repression: if not, love risks becoming an Orwellian nightmare.

EQUALITY IN PLEASURE, FREEDOM OF BODIES

Once there is agreement on the issue of consent, it remains to be seen what the masculine contributes to the sexual fulfilment of women. People used to say that a man 'possessed' a woman when he slept with her. 'There is not a single man who does not want to be a despot when he gets a hard-on,' wrote the Marquis de Sade in *Philosophy in the Bedroom*. So many men glory in their phallus – male prestige, triumphant heterosexuality, the culture of performance – that sex seems to be delineated according to the masculine. In the nineteenth century, the most subtle of writers, Hugo, Flaubert, Maxime Du Camp, kept count of the women they had 'screwed', in the manner of what Leporello did for his master Don Giovanni in Mozart's opera. Conversely, the wife had to 'offer herself' to her husband whenever he felt like it. Accordingly, in 1925, the feminist Louise Bodin deplored that the wife 'does not need to know what the husband did with her. That is none of her business.'*

* Louise Bodin, 'Prostitution et prostituées', *L'Ouvrière*, 15 April 1925.

Desire steers between power and tenderness, play and pleasure. If women consent to give their body over to it (as men consent to give theirs), this gift is at every instant revocable. However, for what reason should women 'give themselves over' to masculine gazes, desires, pleasures? In other words, what is a man good for?

In heterosexual love, the man is cast as the one who provides the pleasure, at least if he can. That obviously supposes not only the banning of sexual mutilation, but also a willingness to share. In France, during the 1970s, 74 per cent of men said they were satisfied with their first sexual relation, as opposed to 50 per cent of women (83 per cent and 55 per cent respectively among young people). At the beginning of the twenty-first century in the United States, 91 per cent of men were reaching an orgasm during intercourse, as opposed to 39 to 64 per cent of women. By masturbating, on the other hand, 95 per cent of women climaxed easily in a few minutes, while only 4 per cent cited penetration as the best means of attaining orgasm.*

This 'pleasure gap' stems from several things, particularly the lack of clitoral stimulation, out of ignorance or shame on the part of women. The behaviour of men also plays a crucial role. In *Frigidity in Woman, in Relation to Her Love Life* (1926), the Austrian doctor Wilhelm Stekel cites the testimony of women traumatized by their husband's brutality, sometimes beginning with their wedding night, which subsequently renders them incapable of reaching an orgasm. In the second decade of the twenty-first century, some Moroccan women deplored their spouse's selfishness: 'It's as if I were not there,' 'No man ever taught me to love myself or to know my own body,' 'For many men, a women is nothing but a vagina in which you masturbate.' Lacking verbal exchanges and caresses, 'A lot of women feel like they are being raped when they make love.'† The culture of performance, associated with the patriarchal vision of the woman-object, explains why some men are so totally insensitive and inept. But sex could on the contrary be considered as an area for learning and exchange for a lifetime.

* Pierre Simon (ed.), *Rapport sur le comportement sexuel des Français* (Paris: Julliard, 1972), p. 217; and Laurie Mintz, 'The Orgasm Gap: Picking Up Where the Sexual Revolution Left Off', *The Conversation*, 16 May 2018.
† Leila Slimani, *Sexe et mensonges: La vie sexuelle au Maroc* (Paris: les Arènes, 2017).

For millennia, the sexuality of women has been governed by masculine codes. Men's sexuality could nowadays be redefined in a way that gives due consideration to the interests of women. This is not just a matter of ridiculing the tropes of masculine braggadocio, penis marathons and the bedroom stud. It is above all about implementing a sexual education aimed at men and boys, breaking with the 'information' they receive from pornography. Vigorous physical expressions of passion are not in themselves to be condemned, as long as they correspond to the desire of both partners. However, gentle tenderness and laughter are also part of sexuality.

In most countries, secondary school students have courses on sexuality, but these deal more with reproduction and STDs than with sexual civility properly speaking. But sexuality is not just an individual practice: it is also a social bond. It therefore makes sense to talk about desire, consent and the right to pleasure, as well as the right to refuse. A truly educational course on sex must be able to deal with the question of orgasms by including masturbation and the anatomy of the clitoris. The respect due to each individual demands that the variety of sexualities be recognized: failing that, they will be reduced to scurrilous clichés.

In the Arab world, sex education runs up against the resistance of parents and teachers, as well as the prudishness of institutions, leaving the field open to the double standard that encourages boys to charge ahead with virility, but preaches virginity and fidelity to girls. Some progress has been achieved thanks to the Rabita Mohammadia des Oulémas in Morocco, and the Muntada Association in the Arab schools of Israel.* *The Big Talk*, a television programme created by Heba Kotb in 2006, follows in the tradition of Muslim sexology. She addresses the problems of the couple stemming from the husband's selfishness and the absence of communication, which are responsible for a large number of cases of vaginismus. Even though she sticks to a very moderate approach, advising women to be available to their

* Sami Abdelli and Pierre Clément, 'L'éducation à la sexualité: conceptions d'enseignants et futurs enseignants de trois pays maghrébins', *Review of Science, Mathematics and ICT Education*, Vol. 10, No. 1, 2016, pp. 65–92; and Anaia Lefébure, 'Au Maroc, l'épineuse question de l'éducation sexuelle', *Huffington Post Maroc*, 30 August 2017.

husbands so that they will not seek sex elsewhere, Heba Kotb encourages women to demand 'sexual rights', in conformity with the message of Islam.* Educating the body is a way of working for gender justice: asserting women's sexual rights breaks up men's monopoly over orgasms.

In *The Second Sex*, Simone de Beauvoir was one of the first women to write that a woman's orgasm does not depend on intercourse, while a 'normal' sexual relation makes her 'depend on the male of the species'. The heterosexual script is organized around penetration followed by ejaculation. The signifying power of this scheme of things, which is too favourable to men, explains the orgasm gap underscored by so many statistics. One survey in the United States showed that 86 per cent of lesbians climaxed during sexual relations, as opposed to only 65 per cent of heterosexual women.† Men do not necessary become superfluous as a consequence. However, their desires lose their centrality in favour of an *equality of sexual pleasure*. Ultimately, 'equitable' heterosexual intercourse should include clitoral stimulation by masturbation, caress or cunnilingus.

A sexuality passionately committed to equality might result in alternative scripts. Virile power defines itself by the refusal to be penetrated as by the desire to penetrate. It supposes the opening of the feminine body and the inviolability of the masculine body. But men might lend themselves to receptive desire as a sort of dephallicization, not to be 'sodomized like a homosexual' (the fear haunting the macho), but to be 'penetrated like a woman', in order to experience, if only once, what heterosexuality is like for women. While it is important, coitus has no intrinsic dignity. Other practices and acts enable the enrichment of sexuality. One of these is exchanging or sharing roles: the fluidity of gender exists in bed as it does elsewhere.‡

After sexual equality, sexual liberty: women's rights concern their appearance – make-up, hairstyle, manner of dress – as well as their

* Shereen El Feki, *La Révolution du plaisir*, p. 63 ff and p. 159 ff.
† David Frederick et al., 'Differences in Orgasm Frequency Among Gay, Lesbian, Bisexual, and Heterosexual Men and Women in a U.S. National Sample', *Archives of Sexual Behavior*, Vol. 47, No. 1, January 2018, pp. 273–288.
‡ Jean Markale, *L'Homme lesbien: Essai sur un comportement sexuel et affectif méconnu* (Paris: Rocher, 2008).

sexuality. Men have no business imposing their will on women who have chosen to enjoy themselves, their orgasms, or their life in general without them. Men have no authority over women. For that reason, abortion is not their exclusive purview. Although women's liberty includes the willingness or refusal to procreate, abortion is completely banned in several countries, including El Salvador, Honduras, Nicaragua and Haiti, even in cases of rape or danger to the life of the woman. In 2017, President Trump prohibited American funding of NGOs in favour of abortion. In Poland, threats hang over abortion rights, already strictly limited since 1993.

Patriarchy offers men only a very limited range of feelings: respect for the woman function, contempt for the impure woman. It is up to men to break away from such poverty of the soul. Century after century, the masculine has imposed on the feminine a self-hatred that even struck Simone de Beauvoir, for whom the vagina was 'concealed, troubled, mucous, moist; it bleeds every month, it is often soiled with secretions, it has a secret and hazardous life'.* We can better understand why, beginning in the 1960s, artists such as Judy Chicago, Valie Export, Paola Daniele and Maël Baussand glorified menstrual blood: not only were they refusing shame, but also striving to express feminine pride, leaving nothing out.

In this area, as in others, men have no business 'helping' women to be free, but they can break with the misogynist culturalization of the female body that surrounds it with mysteries and superstitions. The taboo on menstruation must come to an end not only for women, but also for boys, brothers, husbands and fathers. In Sweden, a children's video showing a dance of tampons disguised as kings and pirates has been created by a young 23-year-old television announcer, Alex Hermansson, singing and playing his guitar. As he explains, 'We have to be able to talk about the most natural thing in the world, since it concerns half of humanity.'† Menstruation belongs to the private realm, but it concerns everyday life as well. Men should know how to speak of it, not with embarrassment or irony, but instead with

---

* Simone de Beauvoir, *The Second Sex,* II, 147.
† Maddy Savage, 'Dancing Tampon Song to Teach Kids About Periods', *The Local,* 14 October 2015.

simplicity and as much empathy as the situation requires. After all, they are not suffering abdominal pain or headaches; the women whom they live with are.

THE SCOURGE OF SEXUAL HARASSMENT

Harassment must be treated separately, as a criminal offence. What defines this act is the will to humiliate, or what the European Parliament and Council's directive characterizes as the 'violation of the dignity of a person' through the creation of a hostile or degrading environment. French law is behind the curve on the matter, since dignity loses its centrality, becoming merely one circumstance among others. Moreover, while the French penal code prohibits sexist or obscene utterances, it does not sanction them from the outset, since they have to be repeated in order to be legally classified as harassment.*

In the workplace, harassment can take several forms: direct aggression, via an undesired sexualization of the relationship (remarks about dress, invitations to dinner, the sending of pornographic photos, sexual blackmail), or indirect aggression via the creation of a sexist atmosphere (making misogynist jokes, displaying photos of scantily clad models, visits to a red-light district during a trip abroad). While these practices by their very nature take on a humiliating character, a whole range of excuses are used to justify them: 'it's just good fun', 'it binds the group together', 'nobody died', 'women lack a sense of humour', and so on.

Sexual harassment is endemic wherever power is exercised. In France, one in five women are victims of it at work, and 40 per cent of those who lodge a complaint suffer reprisals. Only 18 per cent of businesses have taken measures against sexual harassment, even though the laws governing the workplace require them to prevent this risk to women. In the legal system, 94 per cent of complaints fail to

---

* Nicolas, Chaignot-Delage, 'Pour une véritable justiciabilité du droit en matière de harcèlement sexuel au travail', *Revue de droit du travail*, No. 1, January 2018, pp. 17–20.

result in any conviction.* In hospitals, 9 per cent of female interns have been harassed with physical contact, and 61 per cent have suffered from everyday sexism, the operating room being a risky place owing to the all-powerful status of the surgeon and the absence of witnesses. The aggressions can occur during training periods for resident or non-resident interns, sometimes from the lead physician himself, amid widespread apathy.† In 2016, one year before the Harvey Weinstein scandal, television broadcast journalist Gretchen Carlson, followed by several other women, filed a complaint against the chairman and CEO of the Fox News network, Roger Ailes. Fox News is of course one of the institutions of cultural patriarchy, embodying and broadcasting its values: female journalists must wear tight-fitting dresses openly displaying feminine availability, denounce the right to abortion, and so on.‡

In public places, harassment consists of bothering a woman by commenting on her appearance, asking for her phone number, calling her names or following her. Such aggressive behaviour characterizes the masculinities of ostentation and of protest, and is therefore not correlative to social class. In the Arab world, unemployment and a lack of future opportunities delay boys' entry into adult life. In Egypt, the great majority of single men live with their parents. This lack of privacy is not unrelated to the epidemic of sexual harassment and assaults that are hitting the country, particularly in Cairo. The rash of these incidents points not only to frustration, idleness and misogyny, but also to the political oppression driving men to take it out on these female 'inferiors'. In Algiers, the young *hittistes* (literally, those leaning back on the wall) call out to women using words that animalize them as 'gazelles', 'cats', 'hogs', or 'wasps,' all while turning the assailant into a valiant warrior. Women accordingly hasten along their way,

---

* Maude Beckers, 'La lutte contre le harcèlement sexuel dans l'entreprise: d'un dispositif muselant à des protections vacillantes', *Revue de droit du travail*, No. 1, January 2018, pp. 13–17.

† Valérie Auslender (ed.), *Omerta à l'hôpital: Le livre noir des maltraitances faites aux étudiants en santé* (Paris: Michalon, 2017), p. 191ff.

‡ Laura Kipnis, 'Kick Against the Pricks', *The New York Review of Books*, 21 December 2017.

head down, reduced to their condition of stalked animals or consumer items.*

Institutions rarely warn their female students, interns, collaborators, custodians or directors about the harassment to which they might be subjected in other countries. Similarly, men in power, in business, higher education and politics, as well as men without power in the street, are largely insensitive to the matter of sexual violence. The easiest step to take is to warn women who travel abroad about the potential poor behaviour of men from other cultures. It's exactly this that the following excerpts from guidebooks show.

Advice to Western female tourists in order to avoid harassment (2019)

Wear loose-fitting clothes, covering the shoulders and knees (avoid transparent garments!)
Say that your husband is waiting for you down the street.

Guide du Routard, Maroc (A Hitchhiker's guide to Morocco)

The first precaution is to avoid all crowded places.
Your manner of dress should be relatively 'cloaked'. Your attitude must never be friendly. No kiss on the cheek, friendly touch, steady gaze. Be mindful to always maintain a certain barrier in relations.
In order to travel in serenity, it is better to go unnoticed: it's the rule! Don't pay any attention to whistles in the street, to stares that undress, or provocative little calls.
Don't hesitate to raise your voice and call people to witness what is taking place.

Guide du Routard, Égypte (A Hitchhiker's guide to Egypt)

Avoid wearing short skirts, T-shirts with plunging necklines, or tight-fitting trousers. Conversely, sunglasses have the great advantage of making you inaccessible.

---

* Shereen El Feki, *La Révolution du plaisir*, pp. 132–142; and Djamila Saadi-Mokrane, 'Petit lexique du dragueur algérois' in Fethi Benslama and Nadia Tazi (eds.), *La Virilité en islam*, pp. 261–270. Concerning France, see www.stopharcelementderue.org/.

[Say] that you are married and that your dear husband is waiting for you at the hotel.

Guide du Routard, Inde du Nord (A Hitchhiker's guide to North India)

Don't respond to stares. Dark glasses, a phone, a book, a tablet, or earphones help to keep your distance.

Women who travel with a male companion are much less bothered. Arrange things so as not be waiting in a train station or arriving late in the evening.

Cut short conversations with strangers. Silence can be very effective. Some women wear a ring or mention that they are married or engaged (whether or not it is true).

Give the impression of being sure of yourself in public; avoid looking lost (and therefore vulnerable); consult maps at your hotel or in a restaurant rather than in the street.

Banish sleeveless tops, shorts, miniskirts, and all tight-fitting or transparent clothing.

Lonely Planet, South India and Kerala

ERADICATING SEXUAL VIOLENCE

For certain men, aggressive behaviour is but the extension of their desire or the expression of their masculinity. For others, it is an unbearably abusive behaviour. In any case, we are able both as individuals and a collective to push back against everything that our sex and our gender prescribe. It is therefore false (and insulting) to say that men are supposedly violent 'by nature' or intrinsically imbued with a 'culture of rape'.

As Steven Pinker has shown, violence, and in particular violence against women, has declined since the eighteenth century, thanks to the revolution of rights, humanitarianism, the strengthening of governments and of the penal code, as well as the decline in wars on a planetary level. The police, the criminal justice system and social workers have been taking increasingly better care of victims. In the United States, the annual toll of rapes fell by 80 per cent from 1973 to 1980, and domestic violence (generally due to men) dropped by two-thirds from the 1990s on. The same pattern can be observed in England and Wales. It is on the contrary when government fades into the background – in the context of a war, for example – that women find themselves threatened by physical and sexual violence on a daily basis.*

In the early twenty-first century, the problem of violence against women is far from being solved. Criminal masculinity exists in every country of the world, including affluent democracies such as France and Japan. It remains a particularly serious problem, however, in regions where it takes the generalized form of gendercide, genital cutting and human trafficking. Although the patriarchal mindset does not directly produce violence, it justifies such acts as soon as women refuse to serve. That is why the rise of feminism and the increasing presence of women in positions of responsibility are conducive to amending masculine cultures. We cannot count only on education, information and awareness campaigns: the law must also be used to combat misogyny.

Latin America and China have made notable progress in fighting against gender violence. The charge of 'femicide' has been integrated into the penal code of Guatemala, Chile, Argentina, Mexico and Peru. Infractions such as domestic violence and conjugal rape have been legally defined and prosecuted in court. Some thirty countries have ratified the Belém do Pará Convention concerning acts of violence against women, which was signed in 1994. At the end of the first decade of the twenty-first century, Argentina implemented a National Plan of Action for the prevention and eradication of violence against women. In Brazil, the struggle against masculine violence has become a national priority. It has resulted in the 2006 Maria da Penha law, the creation of an emergency hotline, awareness campaigns and programmes of assistance to victims, as well as the recognition of femicide in 2015. For its part, the NGO Promundo is working with men to promote a model of active paternity and reduce violence against women and children.

After hosting the fourth World Conference on Women in 1995, China passed a law on domestic violence that requires the police, businesses, doctors and social workers to intervene. Several provincial

---

* Steven Pinker, *The Better Angels of Our Nature: Why Violence Has Declined* (New York and London: Penguin Books, 2011), p. 394 ff.

governments have issued directives encouraging the police to warn violent husbands in writing. However, most infractions are only punished with fines. Women's rights figure in the 'high-level dialogue about human exchanges' that China and France have maintained since 2014. Despite their obvious shortcomings, these initiatives provide evidence of a new awareness.

New technologies have increasingly been used to counter sexual violence. Free-to-call hotlines have been supplemented by systems making it possible to respond quickly to emergency situations: alert terminals in the metro and on college campuses, panic buttons in taxis and buses, cell phones directly linked to the police. The Internet has widely democratized these protective means. Thanks to a geolocation service, the South African app Namola makes it possible to be rescued by police and loved ones. In Egypt, sites where assaults have taken place are signalled on the interactive HarassMap.

Though it is sometimes used to vent misogynist resentment and aggression, the power of social media can also be harnessed in the service of women's rights, as shown by the #MeToo campaign in 2017. The aggressors are individually accountable in court, but multinational corporations and governments are sensitive to the immanent justice meted out by people on social media, who have the capacity to use criticism, boycotts and ridicule against them.

Masculine violence is far from having disappeared: however, it is increasingly less tolerated by national and international public opinion, and more and more subject to government sanction. Men are taking part in this fight alongside women. Among them, legal experts, elected representatives, police officers, judges, developers, artists and intellectuals are all trying to eradicate the misogyny that rapes and kills. Fathers, brothers and spouses are participating in demonstrations in favour of women's rights. Others intervene or notify the police when they witness sexist violence. Men have a thousand ways of fighting against the pathologies of their gender.

To the extent that desire is both of an instinctive and intellectual nature, sex will never be 'pure'. It is nevertheless possible to have seduction without violence, a mixing of the sexes unadulterated by any contempt, a desire that would not be sullied by an urge to destroy – a sexuality better suited to the post-Weinstein world.

14

Masculinities of Equality

Paris, the Arc de Triumph: from the Place Charles-de-Gaulle one can go down avenues Victor Hugo, Foch, Carnot, Mac-Mahon, Hoche, Marceau or Kléber. One has, then, the choice between a male writer, two field marshals, and four generals. Above the Tomb of the Unknown Soldier on the Arc de Triumph are engraved the names of some thirty French military victories, from Valmy to Dresden.

The walls of our cities exude testosterone. In Paris, half the streets bear the name of a man, less than 5 per cent, the name of a woman. The avenues, monuments and statues recall the grandiose actions of statesmen; men of war, law, religion, science and letters. Everywhere in the world, the urban landscape displays masculinities of domination.

Equality in the polis does not imply taking down statues and repenting, but rather more reflection, being keenly aware of the asymmetry of gender; not only lifting up new models of femininity, but also reconsidering things taken for granted, reflecting on the access of every woman and every man to urban spaces, power, money and free time. This is not about denying physical differences between women and men, but rather about organizing these differences such that they do not lead to any social inequality. In this way, gender justice demands a certain type of relation between the sexes, a certain quality of social bonds, as much as it does women's rights. This relation between men and women can be gauged by a twofold criterion: the distribution of material wealth (who does what, who earns what) and the distribution of symbolic value (how men treat women). A masculinity of equality supposes that men should learn to *live as equals* in the polis as well as within the couple.

CITIZEN CITY DWELLER

The equality of the sexes is as necessary for the quality of life in democratic society as freedom of expression or social safety nets. In this respect, we must recognize that men have not fulfilled their roles as citizens in these early years of the twenty-first century.

One of the most neglected topics is the sharing of public space. The patriarchal system settles the matter with simplicity: women inside (in the kitchen, their separate quarters, a harem), men outside (in the street, the agora, the café). Cities were designed by and for men. Women had no business being outside: going out without a husband or a chaperon was at their own risk. Since it was difficult to enforce such separation in every circumstance, certain exceptions were allowed: women could go to the market, visit friends and relatives, attend celebrations. This solution has been institutionalized in Saudi Arabia: since women cannot be locked up all their life, they have their own spaces, with guards at the entrance to university campuses, cafeterias, parks, shopping centres, and so on.

Democracy cannot be based on segregation: it has to find ways of ensuring both the mixing of the sexes and their security. Movements created in the 1970s – Take Back the Night (in Philadelphia) and Reclaim the Night (in Leeds) – have condemned sexism's limitation of time and space for women. One exhibit displayed in Lille in 2014 brought to life individual and collective acts of resistance prompted by violence.* Gender justice requires men to respect the right of an unaccompanied woman to frequent any public place, at any time of the day or night, with the certainty that she will not be bothered. The last point is crucial: this is not only about banning actual assaults, but also eliminating the fear of being assaulted, with all the strategies of discretion, caution, flight, self-censorship and self-defence that such fear entails. For women, *the very possibility of some arbitrary interference* is a factor contributing to vulnerability. Making oneself

* Camille Guenebeaud, Aurore Le Mat and Sidonie Verhaeghe, '*Take Back the Night!* Une exposition pour combattre les violences sexistes dans l'espace public', *Métropolitiques*, 11 October 2018.

invisible therefore constitutes a form of protection. Putting an end to such anxiety supposes the implementation of a certain physical and spatial morality: a man cannot hinder a woman in going anywhere she chooses. As we have seen, amorous encounters – even those involving 'love at first sight' – have nothing to do with the so-called 'freedom to bother'.

Because women's right to circulate freely in cities is not respected, certain municipalities have had to create safe zones, particularly on public transport. The Rio de Janeiro, Mexico City, Tokyo and Osaka, subways have women-only carriages for certain hours of the day and night. 'Pink taxis' for women driven by women are available in England, Egypt and India. In Toronto, the Metrac agency has since 1989 offered 'audits for women's safety' to help local authorities reduce the risks of assault in public places (squares, parks, streets, mass transit, car parks, schools, university campuses).

Men can help make cities more inclusive. The first actions can be undertaken on the political level, which remains largely masculine. The European Charter for Equality of Women and Men in Local Life was drafted in 2006 with the goal of achieving balanced representation of the sexes in decision making and integrating gender into the entire set of public measures. Twelve years later, it had been signed by more than 1,500 territorial bodies, 274 of which were French. In Germany, 'women's representatives' (*Frauenbeauftragten*), task forces for equality of the sexes, have existed not only in most cities, but also in businesses and universities since 1949 in the former East Germany and 1980 in the Federal Republic of Germany. A National Association of Municipal Services for Women (BAG) links federal policy with local initiatives.

Gender mainstreaming means accounting for equality of the sexes at all levels of municipal policy, in budgets, bids, calls for proposals and programmes of urban development. In Austria, the city of Vienna began to reflect on these issues towards the end of the twentieth century, ordering a study of the over-representation of boys in parks and playgrounds. Two pilot parks, Einsiedlerpark and Sankt-Johann-Park (now Bruno-Kreisky), have applied the findings of that study by installing mixed playground equipment, a covered stage and grassy knolls. In addition, day-care centres offer children open play areas instead of arranging 'doll' and 'car' corners: boys are taught to change nappies and girls to build skyscrapers. Recesses are designed to have all sorts of games, and not just football. Sports such as volleyball and badminton are encouraged. Lighting in public spaces is egalitarian too, since it serves to improve security .*

In other parts of the world, most playgrounds and sports fields are adapted to boys' activities. Indeed, certain municipalities implicitly design their equipment that way in order to avoid acts of juvenile delinquency or summer outbreaks of violence. Collective public space accordingly becomes masculine, while girls go off to play elsewhere, or else stay at home. On school playgrounds, lines on the ground mark off football pitches and basketball courts: boys occupy the centre, while girls gather on the side, in little corners or on benches. Boys 'take the field', while girls try to 'find their place'.†

Some municipalities are striving to correct such spatial embodiments of gender inequality. In Malmö, Sweden, the Rosens Röda Matta play area was specifically designed to be mixed. In France, the Peyrouat school in Mont-de-Marsan has since 2011 undertaken a project aiming to establish a culture of equality and respect by means of a plural approach, with dance, theatre, song and cooperative games. Other experiments are underway in Trappes and Rennes.

Women driven by feminist ideals are the ones who have made such progress possible, while men have remained a minority in these initiatives which are themselves exceptions to the general rule. This masculinity of equality could be expressed in the very conception of the cities, public spaces and their facilities. The matter is in the hands not only of elected officials, but also urban planners and architects. Once men have taken responsibility, we will be able to teach boys that they are not the owners of the city nor the guardians of the street.

---

* 'Gender mainstreaming in Wien', available at www.wien.gv.at/menschen/gender mainstreaming.
† Édith Maruéjouls-Benoît, 'Mixité, égalité et genre dans les espaces du loisir des jeunes: Pertinence d'un paradigme féministe', doctoral thesis in geography, University of Bordeaux III, 2014. See also the Plateforme d'innovation urbaine at www.genre-et-ville.org.

THINKING WITHOUT SEXISM

Since the 1970s, feminists have been fighting against the biases conveyed by language. In the United States, the National Council for Teacher Education formulated instructions for a 'non-sexist use of language' which has been used by universities and publishing houses. In Quebec, reflections on the feminization of ranks, titles, public offices and job functions began in the mid-1970s. It was only ten years later in France that government minister Yvette Roudy appointed a commission on terminology presided over by Benoîte Groult. Despite linguistic conservatism, terms such as *directrice* (director/school principal), *avocate* (lawyer), *magistrate professeure* followed by and *autrice* (principal private secretary) author or *(cheffe de cabinet)*, have become common usage.

To fight against the masculine view of the world in English-speaking countries, textbooks recommend the use of 'business executive' rather than 'businessman,' 'salesperson' instead of 'salesman', 'fire fighter' instead of 'fireman', 'flight attendant' rather than 'stewardess'. 'Woman' can also be substituted for 'man', as in 'policewoman' and 'chairwoman', so that the feminine becomes associated with authority, competition and success. To dissociate nurses from women in German, *Krankenschwester* (literally 'patients' sister') will be replaced by *Krankenpflegerin* ('woman caring for patients'), along with its masculine counterpart *Krankenpfleger*.

The generic use of the masculine conveys the notion that the ideal person is a man and that it is therefore superfluous to mention women. Whenever he spoke of equity in *A Theory of Justice* (1971), Rawls used the expression 'rational men' and the masculine pronoun, 'his place in society, his class position'. The systematic use of paired words (she/he, her/his) makes it possible to avoid such bias. In an institutional setting, in job announcements, for example, such formulation has the advantage of eliminating the underlying preference for the masculine: 'The position is intended for a person holding a PhD. The person recruited will be responsible for . . .', and so on. Patterned after the Finnish *hän*, which neutralizes the third person singular, gender-neutral pronouns (called 'epicenes') were introduced at the end of the twentieth century, such as the Swedish *hen* and the English 'they' when used for the singular. In Spain, certain parties on the left have recourse to the feminine plural to designate the entire body of citizens (the 'Unidas Podemos' coalition in 2019).

'Inclusive' writing often proclaims the equality of the feminine and the masculine, a fundamental ideal in every democratic society. But it all depends on what one has to say. By depicting his hero in *Atomised* in the act of 'ejaculating in the female researcher's vagina,' Michel Houellebecq feminizes an intellectual profession for the misogynist pleasure of reducing it to a sex organ open to a man: the attack is aimed at the emancipation of women after May 1968. Similarly, inclusive writing and epicenes risk being little but futile mechanisms, refuges for the politically correct, if they are not accompanied by an effort to introduce gender justice into the entire range of intellectual activities.

This is not simply a matter of putting more girls in STEM and achieving gender balance in disciplines such as astrophysics and information technology, where women are conspicuously under-represented. Men must also be encouraged to break out of the 'androcentric illusion' which leads them to believe that their opinion represents all of humanity.* That can be achieved by respecting the principle of parity not only at events, but also by radically reconfiguring analysis in such a way as to integrate the entire set of human experiences, understood as a range of necessary and equally valid viewpoints.

Agnotology, the scientific field dealing with the causes of our collective ignorance, shows that it often stems from social belief: for example, white men's scorn for women, Africans, Native Americans and Asians. This phenomenon of disregard explains not only why the clitoris was for centuries shrouded in indifference, but also why botanical knowledge of the 'peacock flower' (*Caesalpinia pulcherrima*) and its use as a method of abortion – first noted by Marie Sibylle Merian in 1705 – were subsequently forgotten: they seemed to hold no interest for the learned men of Europe.† In the field of medicine, including women in clinical trials makes it possible to avoid the presumption that the specificities of masculine physiology are

* Gerda Lerner, *The Creation of Patriarchy*, p. 220.
† Londa Schiebinger, 'West Indian Abortifacients and the Making of Ignorance' in Robert Proctor and Londa Schiebinger (eds.), *Agnotology*, pp. 149–162.

universal. For the past few years, the European Commission and the National Institutes of Health in the United States have subordinated the funding of medical research to consideration of sex and gender as well as the participation of women in research.

In history, an academic discipline that men have dominated like all the others, women were for a long time ignored, reduced to the figures of a few queens or royal mistresses. Pioneering works such as Léopold Lacour's *Les Origines du féminisme contemporain* (The Origins of Contemporary Feminism, 1900) and Léon Abensour's *Histoire générale du féminisme* (A General History of Feminism, 1921) helped widen the field. At the Collège de France, Jacques Flach, the father of three girls, gave a course on the feminine condition based on legal documents and literary works in 1897, and then went on to link 'the people's sovereignty and the political suffrage of women' in his lesson of 1909.

The work of other pioneers was added to theirs: the first volume of *Women's History*, published in Japan by Takamure Itsue on the eve of the Second World War, Gerda Lerner's seminar on the history of women at the University of Wisconsin in 1963, Michelle Perrot's course 'Do Women Have a History?' in 1973, not to mention *Hidden From History*, published that same year by Sheila Rowbotham, who surveys three centuries of the oppression of women in Great Britain. In 1979, Marie-Jo Bonnet, formerly active in the Women's Liberation Movement in France and the Gouines Rouges (Red Dykes), defended a doctoral thesis in Paris on the 'love relationships between women from the sixteenth to the eighteenth century'. Women were beginning to be subjects of study in their own right. Feminism is not only demands and action: it is a willingness and determination to think differently.

And yet, it is not certain that this historiographical revolution has changed men's way of seeing things. In Europe and the United States, virtually all books on gender in the human sciences are published by female researchers. This desertion on the part of men has several causes: a feeling of incompetence, respect for private preserves defined by university mindsets, but also a deep disinterest in these 'others' who are women. This is compounded by a male love for great events and deeds of history accomplished by great men, and a fascination with war, discovery, conquest and revolution; in other words, with the glorious things that 'we men' are capable of doing. Indeed, the positions of power occupied by figures such as Napoleon, Lincoln and Churchill have similarities with the positions that their male biographers enjoy in the university.

There are solutions that can bring academic patriarchy to an end: prohibiting faculty from holding both executive and honorary functions concurrently, mandating parity in selection committees and editorial boards, incorporating gender into the researcher's toolbox, continuing to develop the history of women as a subject. The hubris of method must also be relinquished. That means replacing the hyper-specialization of mandarins with multidisciplinary research; getting rid of ironclad certitudes in favour of the flexibility of those who dare to doubt; favouring the integration of specifically situated viewpoints over that of the narrator-God (another name for the abstract masculine) looking down from on high.

The academic norm favours habitual topics and non-writing. To be an institutional man, a specialist on a subject, a historian in the masculine sense of the term, men reject the 'literary' by setting it against the 'scientific', avoid experimentation and adhere to their academic positions and the discourse of authority that these positions enable. Gender equality would involve studies based on a plural 'I' with its visible imperfections, being open to emotions that lead to understanding and a willingness to create new forms. This is how *history and the social sciences can truly be demasculinized.*

THE MANAGER'S RESPONSIBILITIES

As far as women are concerned, the business world has over the course of the twentieth century gone from policies of protection (maternity leave, reduced workdays, prohibition of night work) to policies of equality (access to leadership positions, affirmative action). This trend has favoured highly skilled women employees in the tertiary sector more than unskilled female workers. Having the same level of education as men, women lay claim to the same responsibilities. There has been notable progress in two areas: the highly feminized sectors such as culture and publishing, in which the work environment is overall good (the horizontal model); and big business, which is more competitive but strives to promote women to the upper levels of management (the vertical model). The fact remains, however, that the level of active engagement varies considerably from one business to another. Some companies initiate good practices, but most are only adapting to changes in society.

We can see this ambiguity in the French media, where women are grossly under-represented. Female press executives, heads of television networks, chief news editors, lead reporters and expert commentators are rare. Women were given less than one third of the speaking time on radio and television in the first two decades of the twenty-first century, and that share was even lower during prime time.*

There are powerful strains of sexism in the audiovisual world. Some progress has nevertheless been made. In 1981, Michèle Cotta was appointed to preside over Radio France, then over the Haute Autorité de la Communication Audiovisuelle (the agency with oversight for audiovisual communication), before becoming news director for the TFI television network in 1987 and CEO of France 2 in 1999. A graduate of the prestigious HEC business school and a specialist on economic matters, Claire Chazal was the news anchor for TF1 on Friday evenings and weekends for almost twenty-five years, from 1991 to 2015. Late in the second decade of the twenty-first century, 36 per cent of journalists and 44 per cent of executives of France Télévisions were women. According to the company charter, France Télévisions wishes to develop the mixing of the sexes, favour women's careers, guarantee equal salaries and make it easier to combine professional with private life. Michèle Cotta was appointed by Prime Minister Pierre Mauroy with the approval of President François Mitterrand in 1981, while Claire Chazal was recruited by TF1 at a time when the network was headed by two men.

In the second decade of the twenty-first century, Japanese Prime Minister Shinzo Abe embarked on economic policies favouring women, at a time when the country was ranked 111th in the Gender Gap Report. Privileged by a highly sexist business culture, men were monopolizing

* David Doukhan, 'À la radio et à la télé, les femmes parlent deux fois moins que les hommes', INA, March 4, 2019.

management positions, while numerous women were being subjected to moral harassment in conjunction with a current or future pregnancy (*matahara*). Despite the 1997 law on equality in the workplace, discrimination remained rife. Shinzo Abe's ambition was to transform business culture so that women could gain access to leadership positions and benefit from modified work schedules. The result of 'womenomics' has been mixed: the rate of professional activity for women has increased since 2012, but 96 per cent of executives are men and three quarters of all businesses cannot count a single woman in a leadership position. In 2017, Japan even slid back to 114th place in the rankings.*

There are actively committed men within big companies, even if they do not publicly speak out in favour of feminism. Danone, the Société Générale, Coca-Cola, and Randstad have implemented policies in favour of their female employees. Lowell McAdam, the CEO of Verizon, and Guillaume Pepy, president of the French railway SNCF, have praised diversity in the business world, while at the same time fighting against sexual harassment. Reid Hoffman, the founder of LinkedIn, denounced the ambient misogyny that reigns in Silicon Valley businesses: to improve workplace relations, he put forward the idea of an 'oath of decency' that entrepreneurs should take with investors.

Obviously, one cannot simply count on the goodwill of men in power. The law has a more extended range that makes it possible to fight against the various pathologies of the masculine: discrimination, sexual harassment, exclusive control over leadership roles. In France, the Copé-Zimmerman law passed in 2011 mandates a proportion of 40 per cent women on boards of administration and oversight: thanks to that legislation, the proportion of women reached 44 per cent in the 120 largest businesses at the end of the second decade of the twenty-first century. In Iceland, businesses with more than twenty-five employees must reach equal pay by 2022. It would be judicious to introduce a system of fiscal incentives for businesses to assist their employees, both women and men, in reconciling their professional and family lives.

In a market economy, certain domains remain out of legislative purview. We can hope that business feminism and the increasing power of

---

* 'Has Shinzo Abe's "Womenomics" worked in Japan?' BBC News, 17 February 2018.

women will make it possible to achieve goals to the benefit of all, such as the sharing of responsibilities at all levels. We are still far from it, which is why it is necessary to implement an agenda for men in positions of power (team leaders, executives, directors, presidents) so that business will cease to be a patriarchal space. This agenda is built on three main ideas:

- sensitizing men to gender stereotypes
- developing management as a model to be followed
- creating quotas as a means of accelerating change

Road map for equality between women and men in business

BECOMING AWARE
Ask questions about equality between the sexes:
- Among managers, what is the proportion of white, heterosexual men from dominant religious groups who are fathers?
- What proportion of managers have a spouse who works less than they do? Is the couple organized according to hierarchical complementarity of the sexes, with the man earning most of the money, the woman having supplementary employment while taking care of the children?
- How many managers work an extended schedule, to the point of 'spending their lives' in the office? Among factory managers, how many are at work as early as 7 in the morning? Among the executives in the central office, how many stay on the job until 9 in the evening?
- Are women in charge of departments other than marketing, communications, and human resources?

TRAINING
Sensitize men to forms of machismo in order to help them interpret their own behaviour, such as:
- monopolizing the floor during meetings
- interrupting women who take the floor (manterrupting)
- forms of aggression or condescension towards women
- the 'transparent woman' syndrome: she is not introduced or spoken to, and is present as a mere stand-in

---

Organize periodic training for all employees about masculine domination, gender stereotypes and everyday sexism.
This will lead to create a more polite, kindly and respectful culture of listening.

WORK PRACTICES
Grant flexible work schedules to fathers and mothers of young children.
Prohibit meetings before 9 am or after 6 pm.
Develop work-from-home strategies for men as well as for women.
Give men and women equal speaking time at meetings; solicit input from women and men who speak less than others.
Find alternatives to company leisure activities such as dinners with alcoholic beverages and games of golf that tend to exclude women.

CAREERS AND REMUNERATION
Make mixing of the sexes mandatory in executive and managing committees, based on the principle that best practices are spread from the top down, by those who lead by example.
Use charts to organize hiring in managerial positions to avoid male domination of command structures.
Seek out women and encourage them to apply for openings; mandate a minimum number of women on lists of applicants.
Evaluate managers on the basis of what they accomplish for the equality between the sexes.
With the assistance of the director of human resources, underscore cases of unequal pay for employees holding the same responsibilities; commit to the equality of salaries on the managerial level and throughout the company.
Facilitate women's return to work after maternity leave.
Make it mandatory for men to take their days of rest and their paternity leave; offer them part-time positions.

ZERO TOLERANCE
Make sure the director of human resources and the heads of other departments are sensitive to matters of sexual harassment.
Provide a special channel for reporting violations that protects the anonymity of victims.
Create a task force to conduct an internal investigation in cases of suspicion or rumour.
Form partnerships with relevant associations so that problems may also be handled with outside assistance.
Fire harassers, even if they help the company make money.

MIXED LEADERSHIP

The business workplace continues to be the domain of the masculinities of domination: aggressivity, competition, the rule of money, sacrifice for the company. In order to assert themselves in a world of men, some women have adopted these virile behaviours. Convinced that the culture of testosterone on Wall Street and in the City of London leads to disasters, the female co-founder of Audur Capital, an Icelandic financial services company, has tried to introduce what she calls 'feminine values': always telling the customer the truth, never forgetting the human factor, reconciling profits with social and environmental principles.* Such an approach is commendable, but it has the disadvantage of reinforcing stereotypes that have purchase within business entities. In the United States, one study showed that, when it comes to management, men 'take charge', while women 'take care' of things. The former supposedly excel at solving problems, using their influence, and delegating responsibilities; the latter are supposedly better at assisting, supporting, consulting, inspiring, encouraging and motivating.†

The business world offers women an extremely limited range of options: either a 'masculine' (tough, competitive) attitude, or a 'feminine' (insightful, understanding, empathic) approach. This pathetic alternative forces women to choose between the tools of 'strength' or the strategies of 'weakness': combined with the different tracks of study followed by women and men, it results in a highly gendered distribution of responsibilities. Confined to a few leadership positions such as directors of human resources or of communication, women rarely lead laboratories and factories, and remain under-represented in technical professions, operational sectors and logistics. The French electrical power company EDF has focused its efforts in this area: in

---

* Halla Tómasdóttir, 'A Feminine Response to Iceland's Financial Crash', TED Woman talk, December 2010.
† Jeanine Prime et al, 'Women "Take Care," Men "Take Charge": Managers' Stereotypic Perceptions of Women and Men Leaders', *The Psychologist-Manager Journal*, No. 12, 2009, pp. 23–49.

2018, its executive committee included only two women, or less than 15 per cent. From 2010 to 2015, the number of women in the crews running France's nuclear reactors went from 13 to 17 per cent. Since women made up only 23 per cent of executives, the company decided that women would constitute one third of those recruited to operational leadership positions.*

Organizations throughout the world are helping women build their own projects. Founded in San Francisco in 2007, and now present on every continent, Girls in Tech supports female entrepreneurs in the digital sector and new technologies. Over the last twenty years, France has created similar networks, from Femmes Business Angels (2003) to Femmes@Numérique (2018), with the ability to fund start-ups and innovative projects. Other mutual aid groups such as InterElles, founded in 2001 at the initiative of leaders with France Télécom, IBM, Schlumberger and GE Healthcare, encourage women's careers in the industrial sector. Since 2010, the programme EVE, first conceived by women executives at Danone, has organized at Évian an inter-company seminar aimed at inventing a 'feminine leadership' capable of bringing change to the business world. The goal of SNCF au Féminin (the French National Railway in the Feminine), the first company network in France with over 6,500 members, is to favour women's careers and transform the managerial culture within the company.

These business clubs are also open to men, but they do not have many members, so gatherings and training workshops take place almost exclusively among women. In general, the coaching provided responds to two questions: the use of personal assets (knowing how to assert oneself, highlighting one's competencies, widening one's network) and with groups (motivating one's team, developing team members' potential, learning to negotiate with customers). As pointed out by Susan Colantuono, the CEO of a management consulting company, there is now a third dimension, the 'missing 33 per cent', which is much more important in order to climb to the upper levels of management: financial competence and knowledge of company strategy. It is precisely that aspect that is missing from the coaching session offered

* Tristan Hurel, 'FEM'Energia 2017: le nucléaire au féminin à l'honneur', *Revue générale nucléaire*, 17 October 2017.

to women, not because they would be incapable of benefiting from it, but because they are not supposed to have this sense of business.*

It is unfair to advise a woman to gain confidence while helping a man do business. A strategically guided training programme can just as well be conducted by women as by men. Mentoring that can really teach women to compete with men would make it possible to give women access to positions in management, finance, technology and logistics now monopolized by men. The problem is therefore not that women lack ambition: it is rather that we lack ambition for them. With equal qualifications and motivation, they experience discrimination in advancing their careers. An executive hesitates in promoting a 35 year-old female manager, since she 'risks' getting pregnant and going on maternity leave. Another problem is the 'boys' club' phenomenon, the 'good ol' boy' network that, in addition to sexist jokes and alcohol-laced parties, keeps women out of the inner circles of power.

The sisterhood of feminine networks is effective, except when it corroborates gender stereotypes. Instead of guiding women to positions that supposedly correspond to their 'assets', we can break up certain associations commonly taken for granted, between men and entrepreneurship, men and business, men and innovation, men and start-ups, men and authority. Rather than create new myths of feminine leadership, it is preferable to practise mixed and inclusive leadership that does not automatically tie power to masculinity. Women are leaders like others, capable of leading a team, being role models, and building the future.†

THE 'DIVERSITY FACTOR'

Early in the second decade of the twenty-first century, several studies established a correlation between 'feminine' values and company performance. The presence of women on administrative boards and on

---

* Susan Colantuono, 'The Career Advice You Probably Didn't Get', TEDxBeacon-Street talk, November 2013.
† Valerie Petit, 'Pour en finir avec les mythes du leadership féminin', Forum JUMP, Paris, 2017.

the C-level has an appreciable impact on a company's social and environmental responsibility, since women are more mindful of reducing the carbon footprint, protecting biodiversity and building human capital in developing countries.* Even investors have an interest here: in the United States, Great Britain and India, the presence of women at a company's highest echelons increases its profitability and potential for innovation.† That is hardly surprising: eliminating women from the race spares men half of the competition that they would otherwise have to deal with. Do the men populating executive committees throughout the entire world owe their positions to merit, masculine connivence, or structural exclusion of women?

This profitability remains difficult to quantify. The 'woman factor' as such probably matters less than the 'diversity factor': including not only women, but also younger people, members of ethnic minorities, those representing minority cultures, people from different universities, and so on. Promoting women is an excellent antidote to the domination of white, well-to-do males of Christian culture, but this is not the only remedy.

Business feminism has another blind spot: working conditions for non-specialized female employees, workers, secretaries, checkers, sales associates, housekeepers and cleaners. The objective of these workers is not to shatter the glass ceiling, but to clean floors at a sustainable pace and with better pay. In 2016, top management was earning up to 347 times more than entry-level employees, which included millions of women in the United States. Among working women in Europe, one in four earns a low salary and 9 per cent are poor. In France, 63 per cent of non-specialized jobs are held by women: more than a quarter of single mothers, one million persons, are impoverished workers.‡

Now the stakes of feminism are situated on that level as well.

---

* Kellie McElhaney and Sanaz Mobasseri, 'Women Create A Sustainable Future', UC Berkeley Haas School of Business, Center for Responsible Business, October 2012.
† Nancy Carter et al., 'The Bottom Line: Corporate Performance and Women's Representation on Boards', *Catalyst*, 19 October 2007. Available at https://www.catalyst.org/research/the-bottom-line-corporate-performance-and-womens-representation-on-boards/; and Francesca Lagerberg, 'Women in Business: The Value of Diversity', Grant Thornton, September 2015.
‡ 'Travailler et être pauvre: les femmes en première ligne', Oxfam, 17 December 2018.

Gender justice can be translated into principles of equal opportunity, creating conditions such that women's ambitions have no limit other than the sky. Such is the feminism advocated by Sheryl Sandberg, director of operations for Facebook, in her bestselling book *Lean In* (2013). While there is still much to be done in that regard, public institutions as well as business are generally aware of the stakes. However, gender justice can also be translated into the principle of an equality of positions, reducing inequalities between the various socioeconomic statuses.*

In this area, the silence is deafening. Very few corporate charters deal with unskilled jobs held by women, considering a wage hike, for example, or shorter workdays, schedules better adapted to family life, or training programmes. The high marks for feminism that large corporations give themselves do not seem to include female workers. An executive woman will not cross paths with a female cleaner employed on an interim basis any more than a male executive, because that working woman arrives before dawn, disappears during the day and returns after night has fallen. From October 2017 to February 2018, the women working for the company in charge of cleaning a hotel in Clichy-la-Garenne in the Paris region went on strike to protest against their working conditions and harassment from their female supervisor. They were immigrant women living alone, housed far from their job site, with a part-time contract of only a few hours a day, subjected to a hellish pace of work, since they were paid on the basis of the number of rooms cleaned.

HOUSE HUSBANDS

From the introduction of a monetary benefit for taking care of a child at home in 1986 to the 2005 Borloo plan, France has through the second decade of the twenty-first century continually provided support for personal care jobs, which represent 1.2 million employees, 96 per cent of whom are women. Several European Union countries have

---

* François Dubet, *Les Places and les Chances: Repenser la justice sociale* (Paris: Seuil, 2019).

implemented similar policies, in keeping with the strategy laid out in Lisbon in 2000: domestic service jobs provide employment for women without specific training, while at the same time increasing the productivity of more highly trained and educated women. This agenda with a feminist slant has greatly increased the number of low-level, low-paying and poorly protected jobs, therefore giving rise to 'subsidized precarious employment' benefiting upper-class women and men.*

This new paradigm of women working as domestic servants was created by and for the same elites who say they are committed to equality between the sexes. Have the women in the highest echelons of the business world led by example and worked for the emancipation of all women, or have they joined forces with a neo-patriarchy that henceforth farms out domestic chores? It seems more accurate to speak of a twin alienation: that of unskilled working women serving the richest, and that of the highly trained serving their family. Indeed, the latter group's careers depend on delegating domestic and maternal chores to an army of nannies, babysitters and housekeepers: that lightens the physical labour, but weighs on their minds. Whether it concerns household chores, childcare or handling everyday life, the domestic imbalance shows to what extent all women are still far from attaining equality.

One way of looking at it is to say that the problem stems from women: too demanding, too pernickety, incapable of letting go. In *Lean In*, Sheryl Sandberg argues that men should assume more 'power at home', so that women can cease serving as 'maternal gatekeepers'. There is a whole list of tips for avoiding the responsibility for everything that happens in the household: know how to delegate and encourage, stop trying to control everything, be indulgent with a spouse who is a novice at cooking and ironing, and so what if the task is 'poorly done'.

Another way of looking at it is to say that women are 'lucky' when their spouse stoops to take care of a few chores, which sets them apart from all the men who do nothing at all (or beat their wives, come home drunk, and so on). Such minimalist participation, always overrated by the man who agrees to it, enters into an 'economy of gratitude'

---

* Clément Carbonnier and Nathalie Morel, *Le Retour des domestiques* (Paris: Seuil, 2018).

in which, since the husband starts from zero, the wife is supposed to cheer the slightest little signs of progress. As we have seen, that is the strength of the patriarchal circle, which ensures that each woman and each man have their place. It is true that hundreds of millions of couples live peacefully following the traditional model, but gender justice is also related to individual happiness.

Men sharing household chores

Masculine rhetoric	Argument	The couple's compromise
'I shouldn't have to do anything – it's not my job.'	Power	Patriarchal circle
'Count yourself fortunate – I am doing more than my friends/father.'	Comparison	'Supermum-ing' Reproaches/resentment
'I don't know how to do it.'	Ignorance	Voluntary inertia
'Tell me what you want me to do.'	Effort	Division of labour Negotiation
'Let's hire a maid.'	Money	Externalization
'Let's go 50–50, because it's only right.'	Equality	The model of parity
'You have your career, so I'll take care of everything.'	Sacrifice	Matriarchal circle

Several criteria can enable us to assess the moral validity of a couple's compromise. Did the wife choose this lifestyle? Is she fulfilled? Does she have the impression that she is sacrificing herself? What role model is she for her children, girls or boys? Is she free to go, like Nora in Ibsen's *Doll's House*? To sum it all up, does the woman love a man who is doing much less than she is in the household, or does she love a man despite the fact that he is doing much less than she is in the household? Men have a whole range of solutions available for working out responsibilities in the household.

Inegalitarian couple models are based on the same 'blackmail' found with mammals, when the male can abandon the female at will, knowing that she will take care of the offspring in which she has invested much more than he has. On the level of domestic chores, it is once again the female who yields. Because of her spouse's inertia, she ends up taking care of what cannot be farmed out: filling the fridge, buying the children's clothes, making paediatric appointments, and so on.

Men could carry out the only revolution they have never thought of: that of adapting to family realities. In other words, sharing, planning, anticipating in order to comply with the ideals of liberty and equality that bring gender justice into the home. To make the masculinity of equality a reality, we can choose to trust that new generations of men will be more invested on the home front than their predecessors. That is indeed what can be observed in several countries since the end of the twentieth century, and not only in North America and Western Europe.

In Vietnam, fewer and fewer couples are living with parents-in-law: as a result, men are (partially) compensating for the chores previously covered by the grandmother. In affluent circles, it is customary, with the arrival of children, to hire a maid-nanny, often a poor woman from the country who lives in the young couple's household. In Mexico, caring for children is part of working-class masculinity, and some men do not hesitate to carry their children in public, either in their arms or in a kangaroo pouch. Women holding salaried employment still have to endure the double workday, but young men often insist that they are doing more than their fathers, which leads to an impression that they have been 'emasculated' because they cook and do a few household chores.* We can therefore sometimes count on the evolution of mores and the willingness of men, but it is wiser to encourage them by means of public policy.

In many countries, the spirit and goal of marriage is explicitly laid out in the law. In France, Article 212 of the Civil Code and those that follow recommend respect, fidelity, mutual assistance and consideration of the children's interests, as well as contributing to household needs 'in proportion to their respective faculties'. It would not be

---

* Matthew Gutmann, *The Meanings of Macho*, pp. 58 ff and 149 ff.

incongruous for legislators to add to these principles the values of equality that must govern the organization of everyday life: 'The spouses shall commit to sharing equally in raising children and in the material and mental needs of the household.' As we know, formally reading these articles during the civil marriage ceremony gives them an additional solemnity.

In welfare states, two types of family models have prevailed. The first, 'universal family support', supposes that both women and men have access to employment, with domestic chores – except for pregnancy and parental love, which cannot be delegated – transferred to hired labour. This system assumes the equality of the sexes, but women have to conform to a masculine lifestyle, thereby reinforcing society's androcentrism. The second model, 'compensation for care', remunerates the mother through a number of arrangements (maternity leave, childbearing benefits, part-time work, flexible work schedules). This system eliminates the cost of the difference between men and women, but it leaves the gendered distribution of chores unchanged and encourages women to remain confined to the domestic sphere.

That is why Nancy Fraser has come out in favour of a third model: the 'universal caregiver model', which consists of making the current life of women the norm for everyone. Women would work as men do, but men would take care of the household and children as do women. This system offers several advantages: it emphasizes the value and dignity of care and eliminates androcentrism, while also providing a better balance of careers, family life and leisure time, along with a greater proximity of children to the elderly, with civil society become the very site of caregiving.* This new state feminism would be an extension of the results collectively achieved over the course of the twentieth century and would make it possible to call a halt to the mechanisms that inject injustice into conjugal and parental love.

A society could set the goal of creating not only a balanced division of chores, but also of their symbolic value, such that a man can declare himself to be in charge of the household, while a woman could with

---

* Nancy Fraser, *Fortunes of Feminism: From State-Managed Capitalism to Neoliberal Crisis* (Brooklyn, NY.: Verso Books, 2013), ch. 4.

no difficulty declare herself to be in charge of matters outside the domestic realm. All roles are worthy of respect, particularly caring for children and elderly parents: what is demeaning to both men and women is confining one gender or the other to a particular role.

'NEW FATHERS'

Much has been said about the need for fathers to be present and care for their children. This duty does not simply concern the baby. We can define the masculinity of pregnancy as the solidarity that a man displays for his companion before and after childbirth, even in the most prosaic aspects of maternity: transformations of the body, psychological and physical fatigue, the constraints of breastfeeding.

Nevertheless, the involvement of fathers follows more of a political than a psychological logic. There is a measure that can encourage them to assume their responsibilities as soon as their child is born: paternity leave. In Iceland, the mother and the father both receive three months' leave, and they have another three months to share between them while receiving 80 per cent of their salary. In Sweden, parental leave has included fathers since 1974. The maximum number of days of paid leave has been regularly augmented, reaching a total of 480, including sixty reserved for fathers, late in the second decade of the twenty-first century. Indemnities amount to 80 per cent of the covered parent, up to 3,000 euros per month. Fathers also have the possibility of taking conventional leave at the birth of a child, as well as days off (up to 60 days per year per child) to take care of an ailing child.

In Norway, a quota of leave intended for fathers has been implemented since 1993: it now extends over fifteen weeks without loss of salary, with twenty more weeks to be shared with the mother. Beginning in 2007, the quota became more flexible: the father can break his leave up into segments or take it on a part-time basis until the child is three years old. This reform has not only made it possible to bolster fathers' involvement with their children, but has also made them more aware of all the work carried out by mothers. During their leave, they not only take care of their children, but also do housework and cooking.* It remains to be seen if these reforms will lighten women's domestic and psychological burden over the long term.

In 2009, Portugal implemented an original system: fathers benefit from four weeks of paid leave (two of which are mandatory) and the possibility of extending it for several months after the mother's return to work, with the couple also receiving a bonus of 30 paid days if the father has assumed his responsibilities. As in Norway, fathers in Portugal have had an eye-opening experience. 'It was a very trying month. It was really very tiring to take care of a baby all day,' admitted one father, while another discovered what every mother of a newborn knows: 'Your focus is on the baby, and you cannot do anything else.'† Since 2018, mothers and fathers in Spain have each been entitled to sixteen non-transferable weeks of paid leave at full salary. It was a man, Pablo Iglesias, who championed the law: after it was passed, he paid tribute to the women and associations who had been fighting against workplace discrimination.

Other systems are less generous. Numerous European countries offer fathers only one or two weeks of leave for the birth of a child: fathers can take several months of parental leave, but with a low level of compensation. Neither fathers nor mothers benefit from paid leave for the birth of a child in the United States. Social programmes are aimed at men caught up in an at-risk fatherhood made fragile by conjugal instability or extra-marital births; hence the emphasis on values of responsibility and involvement. While Northern European countries offer fathers incentives to get involved in family life, the United States expects them to cover their financial obligations. Unlike the paternity of care, however, the paternity of cash changes nothing in the traditional division of gender roles.‡

In spite of these initiatives, leave time linked to the birth of a child remains very unequally distributed. In Germany, three quarters of the beneficiaries of parental leave are women. In Sweden, mothers took

* Elin Kvande and Berit Brandth, 'Les pères en congé parental en Norvège: Changements et continuités', Revue des politiques sociales et familiales, No. 122, 2016, pp. 11–18.
† Karin Wall and Mafalda Leitão, 'Le congé paternel au Portugal: une diversité d'expériences', Revue des politiques sociales et familiales, No. 122, 2016, pp. 33–50.
‡ Barbara Hobson (ed.), Making Men into Fathers: Men, Masculinities and the Social Politics of Fatherhood (Cambridge: Cambridge University Press, 2002).

77 per cent of available parental leave in 2009. Despite the 60-day requirement, fathers were taking less than a quarter of their leave days. One study dealing with 27,000 newborns showed that the increase in paternity leave days had only had a limited effect on the division of household labour, with fathers not taking care of their sick children any more often.*

Several measures offer men incentives to take or prolong their parental leave. In Sweden, social welfare offices send notices to fathers informing them of how many days of leave they have remaining. In addition to information campaigns, there are brochures reminding the public that leave has beneficial effects for both father and child. In Denmark, a national campaign with the support of the government, labour unions and large businesses was launched in 2017, with the slogan: 'Take it like a man!' The same year in France, forty prominent personalities signed a petition in favour of a mandatory paternity leave of six weeks (as opposed to eleven days at present).

Paternity leave goes well beyond those nice little illustrations picturing a smiling young father nose to nose with his baby. Indeed, leave plays a fundamental role in winning men over to the masculinity of equality, for more than the young couple's moving in with each other, the birth of the first child constitutes the moment when chores are 'naturally' divided: in other words, when inequalities are put in place, after which women's careers often come to a standstill. For the sake of equality between the sexes, we should implement mandatory, non-transferable paternity leave, with indemnities of at least 80 per cent of salary over three months. It would, as recommended by the European Union, also be possible to create a system of quotas with months reserved for each parent, as well as a system of bonuses doubling the number of days' leave if the couple's sharing of duties is egalitarian.

* Sara Brachet, 'Retour sur l'exemple suédois: Les pères et le congé parental: l'égalité en marche?' *Cadres CFDT*, No. 442, December 2010; and John Ekberg et al., 'Parental Leave: A Policy Evaluation of the Swedish "Daddy-Month" Reform', *Journal of Public Economics*, Vol. 97, January 2013, pp. 131–143.

STRONG GIRLS AND FEMINIST BOYS

To achieve equality between the sexes, we have to challenge discourses valuing the mother to the detriment of the father in infancy and early childhood. We can promote the benefits of breastfeeding without seeing it as the doctrinal symbol of motherhood. On the unlikely day when it is proven that a child needs his mother more than his father, we would have to return to the model of the male breadwinner and provide incentives for mothers to assume the woman function.

For the same reason, no divorce should deprive a child of a stable relationship with his or her two parents. Perhaps one day we will dispassionately take stock of the life of divorced fathers in France over the last three decades of the twentieth century, at a time when the default regimen consisted of entrusting them with their children on only one out of two weekends and for half of school holidays and vacations. In 2012, the model of custody most often requested by separated parents was residence with the mother. In cases of disagreement, moreover, judges ruled for residence with the mother for two-thirds of children. When the father requested alternating residence and the mother asked for custody, the judge ruled in favour of the mother in three-quarters of cases.*

All around the world, alternating custody of children should be the default legal arrangement; that would give both omnipotent mothers and indifferent fathers something serious to think about. In case of conflict, custody could be given to the parent best at sharing, that is to say, the one who commits to being the most conciliatory towards the rights of the other. Similarly, the parent having custody should be prohibited from moving to a distant region or other country, unless she or he receives the other parent's consent. In the absence of the most serious of reasons, it is the duty of the courts to prevent one or other parent from being evicted when the divorce is conflictual.

From one era to another, various modes of conduct have been prescribed for fathers: authoritarian, stern, gentle, and so on. In his

---

* Maud Guilloneau and Caroline Moreau, *La Résidence des enfants de parents séparés: De la demande des parents à la decision du juge*, French Ministry of Justice, 2013.

Memoirs from Beyond the Grave, Chateaubriand recalls just how cold and distant his father (born in 1718) had been, a man with little desire to kiss his children goodnight. After centuries of paternal rigour, European and American societies tend to value fathers who are understanding and affectionate and who have fun with their children. There is much

The little girl who wanted to go bike riding

In Born to Ride *(2019), Kelsey Garrity-Riley and Larissa Theule tell the story of a little girl born in the late nineteenth century who decides to go bike riding in spite of prejudices and obstacles. Meanwhile, her mother engages in activism so that women can gain the right to vote.*

less emphasis, however, on being a role model for equality. Egalitarian gender roles are best taught by example: a father who does his share of domestic chores sends a message to his children.

What is a good father in terms of gender justice? How to break out of patriarchal paternity? The reason why some women lack self-confidence and are haunted by the imposter syndrome is that they have been delegitimated from childhood. Parents have a role to play here. A father can raise his daughters as both princesses and fighters by arming them against the pathologies of the masculine and teaching them that they should never doubt their own abilities, because they are intelligent, courageous, strong and admirable. As girls, they can speak in public, venture out into the world, assert themselves, command respect, drive off an aggressor, take up challenges, hold leadership positions, achieve all their ambitions. They must aim high: that is the 'girl power' message that fathers, just as much as mothers, can convey.

It is nice to take one's son to a football match, but it is also important to teach him that a boy is not destined to be callous, violent, taciturn and stoic, nor heterosexual. A boy has the right to play with dolls, dance, read, cry, express his feelings, lavish care and love, and have female friends; he has the duty to learn to vary his perspectives, get the other person's consent to touch their body and remember that women are individuals before being women. If fathers do not know how to talk about equality with their children, they can begin by reading Anthony Browne's masterpiece *Piggybook* (1986). The book tells the story of a mother whose husband and two sons treat her like a servant. One day, she disappears: the three machos turn into pigs.

Masculine supremacy asserts itself not only through the humiliation of women, but also through how children are raised. To raise a boy in the tyranny of the father is to prevent him from finding his place in the new society, preparing him to be an unadapted man. A feminist upbringing does not transform boys into 'wimps', but rather into trustworthy and respectable partners.

15

Undoing Patriarchy

Defending women's rights, fighting for equality between the sexes, achieving parity and breaking the patriarchal circle are not all equivalent missions. Feminism can take pride in having won key victories since the nineteenth century. Thanks to those achievements, our nations have become true democracies. Women have subsequently been able to contest male monopolies and gain access to all spheres of power in many countries.

As we know, there is still a long road to follow. Now, it will not be possible to achieve equality without fighting patriarchal culture, in other words, without challenging the masculine as the criterion of the superior and benchmark of the universal. The masculinity of domination is rooted partly in biological phenomena (the 'monkey within', as Frans de Waal puts it) and partly in age-old institutions. That is why patriarchy cannot be abolished by fiat, nor by some massive protest: it can only be contained, delegitimated and disrupted, like a train that gets derailed. As for the masculine, it can be redefined in such a way as to become compatible with the emancipation of women – it can produce emancipated men. We can thus conceptualize gender justice.

In the twentieth century, women won rights in societies where they had previously suffered domination. In order to further shake up the patriarchal system, men have to participate. We will not be able to emerge from the masculinity of crisis by reinforcing male authority, but on the contrary by enriching the definition of masculinity, making it more complex to the point of marginalizing the posture of virility, the masculinity of privilege and toxic masculinity. Because feminism needs men, they must not be held up as either foils or enemies, nor as models. We must therefore avoid three dead ends: pro-women romanticism, belief in a masculine conspiracy and parity as the sole end.

WORKING FOR AN INCLUSIVE FEMINISM

In *A Different Voice: Psychological Theory and Women's Development*, Carol Gilligan attempts to rethink morality on the basis of sexual difference. The philosophies of Aristotle, Kant, Rawls and Kohlberg promote abstract morality, based on universal principles and legal rules, but these are incapable of taking women's experience and point of view into consideration. In contrast, women practise an 'ethics of care' anchored in everyday life, respectful of others and driven by personal commitment. While masculine ethics are contractual and legalistic, feminine ethics are relational and understanding. Care gives meaning to justice, whereas impartiality feeds indifference to the world. Feminine morality offers others the care and consideration not offered by the Kantian absolutes of truth and justice.

Studies have shown that the greater empathy of female primates – assistance, consolation, sharing, facial communication – resulted from evolutionary pressure linked to their maternal role, which obliges them to be attentive to the needs of their offspring.* Fortunately, human beings are hostage neither to their biology nor their gender, and we can easily find counter-examples to theories as ahistorical and anti-sociological as Gilligan's. In the eighteenth as well as the twentieth centuries, women of state were quite capable of waging war; businesswomen are, contrary to what the Fathers of the Church say, not particularly altruistic; there are women that subject other women to genital cutting and prostitution; some women are selfish, violent, intolerant, racist. But that is not the main point.

If care for others is the business of women, if their morality (not to mention their psychology) turns them toward human relations, they do not need to get out of the patriarchal circle that destines them to

---

* Leonardo Christov-Moore et al., 'Empathy: Gender Effects in Brain and Behavior', *Neuroscience and Biobehavioral Reviews*, No. 46, 2014, pp. 604–627.

fulfil the woman function. They excel in assisting their husbands, loving their children, taking care of their loved ones: their virtue lies there. The hierarchical complementarity of the sexes comes creeping back in. The ethics of care constitutes a regression compared to the feminism of the Enlightenment, which enables women to become subjects endowed with rights. Today, women need instead to distance themselves from the relational world of the family, while men need to take on more of that responsibility. That is why, for her part, Nancy Fraser proposes to make care into a universal principle.

Carol Gilligan's theory elaborates on the belief that women are supposedly progressive by nature. Granted, one side of their upbringing aims to convince them that they must be attentive to others and at their service. But is it really necessary to transform this biased socialization into a positive ethic? All things considered, it is better to be a male feminist ally than a female accomplice to patriarchy.

From the very beginning, feminism has been the struggle of women, both as victims of inequality and as founders of gender justice. It is revolting that they so often fought alone. Just as anti-Semitism is not just the problem of Jews, so feminism needs men as reinforcements. When Steven Pinker writes 'We are all feminists from now on,' it is not with the intention of usurping the glory of women pioneers and the gratitude we owe to female activists: he simply intends to recall that women's rights constitute a democratic goal par excellence.* A feminism that speaks to everybody, both men and women, would be the pillar of morality for our time.

To make men more conscious of the stakes, we can conduct a very simple moral experiment: a 'life swap'. Several ancient myths invert gender roles, but with the intention of stigmatizing the 'bearded women', the ones who think they are going to be in command of men. There are also fictions that urge men to put themselves in women's shoes, in order to gain an awareness of their servitude. One of the first to propose this exercise is the Chinese man Li Ruzhen: his novel *Flowers in the Mirror* (1825) leads the reader on a trip to the 'country of women', where men live cloistered at home, with bound feet and make-up on their faces, while women take exams and hold official positions.

* Steven Pinker, *The Better Angels of Our Nature*.

The female Japanese feminist Kanno Suga (who was executed in 1911) reversed the adage 'good wife, wise mother', suggesting that men should be 'wise fathers and good husbands.'* This pedagogy of reversal is also one of the principles of the 'He For She' campaign sponsored by the UN in the second decade of the twenty-first century.

We must not expect too much on the level of individual psychology, even if it may occasion a new awareness. But the moral fable is not without interest: men could experience the condition of women from within, not by wearing a flowery dress and lipstick, as if in a carnival, but by learning to *become a minority*. It would be their turn to be constantly reduced to their sex, perceived through their corporal embodiment, doomed to utilitarian functions. They would get interrupted in meetings, have their testicles groped in the subway, be followed on their way home in the evening, and see the little power they would hold being disputed; under the pressure of stereotypes and prejudice, they would have to put up with remarks about their physical appearance and jokes about their legendary stupidity, and people would time after time softly tell them not to be too ambitious. Being subjected to the lot of minorities would give men incentives to try to *live out gender justice*, instead of distractedly glancing at it from afar.

At that point, it would be possible to reinstate the common dignity of both women and men as equal human beings, subjects seeking to live together in a balanced relations, sharing rights as well as duties. The universal would no longer be represented by the masculine, but by gender justice, and such inclusive feminism – a feminism for all – would be the opposite of a war of the sexes.

GENDER ETHICS

'What must I do?,' asked Kant abstractly. Let's put this question to men as if they constituted a sexual minority.

In order to ground masculinity in a morality, we need to return to the

---

* Cited by Sharon Sievers, *Flowers in Salt: The Beginnings of Feminist Consciousness in Modern Japan* (Stanford: Stanford University Press, 1983), p. 149.

same premises that guided Gilligan: the autonomy of the individual subject, defined as a competent, active adult – a category that has been tacitly refused to women, children and non-Europeans. The sexism of Aristotle, Rousseau and Kant leads them to consider women as passive beings determined more by nature than by reason. By coming out in favour of patriarchal marriage, refusing to let women enter into contracts and identifying the feminine with the 'fair sex', fond of gossip and frivolity, Kant reserves moral will for men.* In that regard, the *Groundwork of the Metaphysics of Morals* (1785) and the *Critique of Practical Reason* (1788) present the same ambiguities as the Declaration of the Rights of Man voted by the Constituent Assembly in France in 1789: one never knows whether the topic is a human universalism, or just that of males.

Isabelle de Charrière's novel *Three Women* (1797) depicts women facing moral dilemmas (owning an ill-acquired fortune, choosing between their personal happiness and civic duty), at a time when they do not have the legal autonomy necessary to deal with these situations. Can one act morally when one is subordinate to a father, a husband, a master? Is it possible to lead an ethical life in spite of the laws of men? In posing these problems, Isabelle de Charrière deals with an issue that Kant neglected: the role of gendered difference in moral autonomy.† In the absence of any answer from men, there would be nothing more than a single 'morality' for women in the nineteenth century: femininity. Whether she were a young girl or a family mother, concern for others, charm, gentleness and kindness made up for woman's moral and civic incapacity.

Let's reverse the perspective: can we define a masculine morality for gender relations? Kant writes: 'Act in such a way that at the same time you always treat humanity as an end, and not as a mere means.' Applied to gender relations, this maxim immediately shatters the patriarchal circle. For the very principle of patriarchy is to tie women to their usefulness, treating them 'as a mere means'. In *Psychologie de*

---

* Sally Sedgwick, 'Can Kant's Ethics Survive the Feminist Critique?' in Robin Schott (ed.), *Feminist Interpretations of Immanuel Kant* (University Park: The Pennsylvania University Press, 1997), pp. 77–100.
† Carla Hesse, *The Other Enlightenment*, p. 119 ff.

la femme (Psychology of Woman, 1900), Henri Marion admits that a woman 'can perhaps never be treated by man as an "end in herself". Until now, her destiny has been and is still in most cases to be treated like a simple means.' Her function: to serve, perpetuate the family, the nation, the species.

A woman, on the contrary, can not possibly be defined by the woman function in the realm of ends. She is no longer 'useful' by virtue of her sexual organs, womb or breasts: she is her own end, which makes her *inviolable*. A moral act with respect to gender justice consequently consists in putting woman's freedom above function, that is, placing the human being before sex. From this principle follows a feminist conduct: if I see my equal in woman, and if I observe that she is in a situation of subordination, then I can only try to bring that to an end. A just man is one whose masculinity is consonant with the rights of women.

Kant never explicitly mentions relations between the sexes, however, because for him, women do not partake of humanity endowed with moral will. We therefore need to take practical reason out of its ambiguity, articulating its maxims in such a way as to make them universal.

Several religions are founded on the ethics of reciprocity. The Eternal in Leviticus and Jesus in the Gospel issue the commandment in the same terms: 'You shall love your neighbour as yourself.' The French Constitution of 1793, which professes belief in the Supreme Being, asks citizens not to do to someone else 'what you do not want done to you'. If we transcribe the ethics of reciprocity into gender relations, we get a first maxim: *Conduct yourself with a woman as you would want people to act with your own daughter.*

This rule promotes respect and condemns most of the pathologies of the masculine such as violence, discrimination and stereotypes. In addition, it has the advantage of showing men that they have a personal (and not only moral) interest in supporting the masculinities of equality. Nevertheless, it does not make it possible to completely escape from the patriarchy's grip, for certain fathers choose a forced marriage and a life of submission for their daughter out of masculine connivence with their gender. It is in this way that injustice would successfully pass Kant's universalization test: because he loves for women to be subordinate in every way, a dominant male will follow a maxim contrary to women's interest while wishing that 'at the same time, it should become a universal law'.

The principle of reciprocity must therefore be reinforced by safeguards. A moral act is one that respects the autonomy of the other person, woman or man, by recognizing their humanity, that is to say, their absolute freedom and equality. To do that, we can have recourse to the 'veil of ignorance' experiment that Rawls borrows from Rousseau and Kant: the principle of the action must disregard the characteristics (in this case, the sex and gender) of the person who is the object of that action. And so we get the second maxim: *Conduct yourself with a woman as you would act if you did not know her sex*. That makes it imperative to see not her sex in a woman, but the human being holding equal rights with all others. It makes it possible to neutralize aspects of a man's behaviour that stem from his masculine self-interest. For example, it enables us to solve dilemmas of gallantry: would you systematically invite a man to the restaurant?

But that is exactly why this rule of sexual anonymization is not suitable for all gender relations, beginning with seduction, for example, for heterosexual love involves the erotic attraction of difference. More generally, relating to another person means respecting them in their sexual identity, because it is part of the human condition. In order to recognize the other person as a fellow human being, one has to be able to put oneself in their place, in the other's particularity as in their universality. To that extent, one cannot pretend that a woman is not also a woman. Since sex is a given and gender a construction, it is possible to attack the hinge that serves as a joint between them. We then get a third maxim: *Conduct yourself with a woman in such a way that her gender and your own could be inverted*. This principle of conduct prevents manifestations of masculine authority, while at the same time encouraging exchanges and hybridizations that can enrich the definition of masculinity.

In the end, gender justice demands that men follow *a triple rule of reciprocity, impartiality and reflexivity*. This universal feminism based on an ethics of gender makes it possible to involve men and avoid romanticizing women.

GENDER DISOBEDIENCE

According to a Cambridge history professor, hardships encountered by female students can be attributed to an environment dominated by men, whose portraits hang on the walls of the university, and whose books are featured in bibliographies, while their words ('brilliant', 'genius') convey the inequality of the sexes.* Such statements depicting women as vulnerable little things surrounded by rapacious intellectuals and sexual predators, victims condemned to a life of danger, lead to a dead end.

Nobody has the right to lash out against radical feminism: every feminism is good in itself, and it is the radical nature of their commitment, their refusal of propriety, that made it possible for Hubertine Auclert, Qiu Jin, and Emmeline Pankhurst to drive back the forces of domination. However, certain currents of feminism are haunted by two old spectres: class struggle and conspiracy theory. Far left reflexes join with extreme right fantasies in constructing a Manichean world view: good and evil, victims and perpetrators, women oppressed by male oppressors, resistance fighters pitted against a universal machismo propagated by leaders, capitalists, doctors, judges and police. Instead of class enemies, there are enemies of gender, whose power is all the more invincible in that they stick together. The condition of women has experienced no progress, and all change is nothing but a mystification designed to hide the persistence of male domination. Men are the Adversary.

Over the course of its history, feminism has carved out safe spaces, listening zones where, sheltered from patriarchy, women could share their experiences and express their solidarity. From the International Conference on Women's Achievements and Institutions in 1900 to the Women's Art Colony Farm founded by Kate Millett in 1978, along with talking groups for abused women, the choice of non-mixing of the sexes comes from the need for protection from violence, mockery and voyeurism. There is also a desire for freedom; freedom of the

* Camilla Turner, 'Don't Call Students "Genius" Because the Word is Associated with Men, Cambridge Lecturers Told', *The Telegraph*, 12 June 2017.

body, freedom of speech, freedom of creation, and freedom to be far from the gaze of men. Beginning in the second decade of the twenty-first century, fitness centres, travel agencies, festivals, shared rentals and co-living projects combining work and habitat have opened for women who want to spend time together.

To what extent is it possible to live without men? In her utopia *Herland* (1915), which imagines a society composed solely of women, Charlotte Perkins Gilman envisages the possibility of an amorous relationship with a man; even the community of 'women guerrilla warriors' invented by Monique Wittig at the end of the 1960s admits a few male companions. The question is actually not to find out whether separatist feminism is legitimate, but if it is viable. The answer is no. Millions of women desire to live with men, to work or enjoy themselves in men's company, to have children with men – yet they are not nefarious agents of patriarchy. Since men can't be thrown in the bin, it is better to make do with them. The challenge is to live together in a just society, rather than in an oasis of pseudo-purity.

But before condemning non-mixing, men have only to look in the mirror. In what does their masculinity consist? Considered in a democratic framework (and not in the imagery of the overman characteristic of totalitarianisms), this question leads back to how boys are raised, socialized, granted resources and exclusive privileges, and allowed to get away with abuses. Perhaps the day will come when, thanks to scientifically calculated doses of testosterone, oestrogen and oxytocin, we will be able to nullify the differences between male and female *sapiens*, or even create new sexes. Or else, in order to eliminate inequities within couples, societies may prefer to transplant a uterus into men and activate their mammary glands. While waiting for that worrisome new era, we can *politicize the masculine* along two lines: subverting masculinities of domination and encouraging dissident masculinities.

Masculinity deserves to be consigned to oblivion if it only equates to aggression, violence, sexism and homophobia. Chivalrous gestures justifying the protection of women are retrograde. Worshipping the leader presages male oligarchy, even dictatorship. It is delightful to ridicule postures of masculine authority: the monarchical head of state, the media guru, the alpha male on top of the food chain, the seventy-year-old CEO who refuses to pass the baton, the young billionaire from Silicon Valley symbolic of the geek neo-patriarchy that dreams of colonizing space. It is good to mock extreme right-wing rabbis, prelates full of compunction, thundering imams, because 'Laughing is indispensable for feminism.'* Let's parody the man of power in what he holds most sacred, his authority and his transcendence. Let's be wary of the masters who adhere to their role. Let's be capable of renouncing the brawny male, the brute, the swine in us. We must practise gender disobedience. We must lose respect. And when we have made cracks in the masculinities of domination, out of them will come men, human beings rid of their little game of virility.

Thoreau went to live far away, and Gandhi and Martin Luther King rose up against violence, but they understood their weakness to be a strength. Let us value degraded, off-beat, fragile masculinities. In the wars of the masculine, let's be on the side of the weak. The gay man who is bullied. The secondary school student who dances or writes poems to girls. The boy who can't manage to learn his role: 'He makes an attempt at virility, but it's like an act that he can't really get into... As for boys who are violent, wild, crazy about football, handlers of chainsaws, quick to fight, he avoids them.'† Franz Kafka, the characters of Philip Roth, the neurotic plagued by doubts, capable of self-deprecation. Offenbach putting to music the ridicule of power, the whims of the powerful, the vacuity of honours, General Boum in *The Grand Duchess of Gerolstein*, the mythological heroes in *La Belle Hélène*.

Before the foundation of Israel, it was possible in Ashkenazi Jewish culture to project oneself into masculinity as an intellectual, a speaker, a reed, not as an athlete or a macho. In the Bible, the ones who fall are the strong men like Samson and Goliath, while weak men are raised up: the sterile Abraham and the blind Isaac. In the Roman era, Jews preferred to philosophize rather than to fight, and the first Christians would inherit this deliberate weakness: their effeminacy was a distinction that lifted them above Rome's brutality. There is a feminist potential in this attitude. Men of Yiddish culture took pride in studying. Violence was not part of their personality. The only jousting they accepted was pilpul, through which they made commentaries on the

---

* Judith Butler, *Gender Trouble* (Paris: La Découverte, 2006/1990), p. 352.
† Jérôme Meizoz, *Faire le garçon* (Genève: Zoé, 2017), p. 56.

Talmud, and their nobility carried an idea of gentleness. The Jew of the ghetto was a man who refused to be a man like others.*

As long as it has not condemned its position of power, derided its arrogance, masculinity is unjust, and the men who transgress the masculine break with that iniquity. That is why we can integrate not only feminism, but also the feminine into masculinity. There are men who are sensitive, who like to listen, who are attractive because they are gentle. The pacifism of their mores is the opposite of phallic aggressivity. The masculine opens itself to the feminine not to rule, as in the masculinity of ambiguity, but on the contrary to abdicate.

Politicizing the masculine can be accomplished in several steps:

- support women in all their struggles, for pragmatic reasons (they are our mothers, our sisters, our spouses, our daughters) as well as for moral reasons (this is a matter of democracy and human rights)
- identify and fight against pathologies of the masculine
- transform virility into a simple component of sociability among men
- refuse the tyranny of norms in order to complicate the masculine
- cultivate the feminine in ourselves
- promote masculinities of non-domination, respect, and equality

ALL THE MASCULINITIES
OF THE WORLD

The patriarchal system demands the concordance of sex, gender and desire. Women are submissive and feminine, men virile and dominant: both are complementary, in love as in the family. Now, just as the feminine is not inherently specific to women, so we can break the notion of a direct link leading from the male to the masculine and heterosexuality. By sowing 'gender trouble', we widen the field of possibilities. That's the major lesson from Judith Butler.

---

* Daniel Boyarin, *Unheroic Conduct: The Rise of Heterosexuality and the Invention of the Jewish Man* (Berkeley: University of California Press, 1997), pp. 6–11.

Trans identity, sex diverging from gender, is attested in Islamic lands as early as the seventh century. Sometimes sought as entertainers and go-betweens, sometimes banished as sinners, the *mukhannathun* were men who act like women. In ninth-century Baghdad, the *ghulamiyyat*, women impersonating men with moustaches, watch dogfights and horse races in the company of men. A millennium later, the transgendered in the Middle East are considered to be mentally ill or criminals. Similarly, the *yan daudu* of Nigeria, men who dress like women, are associated with prostitutes and homosexuals, and therefore persecuted in the name of Islamic 'morality'.

Intersexuality, whereby an individual escapes binary modes, can be defined as a sort of third sex. The androgyne is a still feminine

Faultless makeup, explosive outfits, elegant hairstyles, dapper beards and, of course, giant silver earrings: through a turn toward androgyny, men can break new ground by defying predominant codes of virility and machismo.

adolescent, an ephebe before puberty, sexually indeterminate, and has inspired an art of ambiguity leading to the Louvre's *Sleeping Hermaphroditos* and Girodet's *Sleep of Endymion* (1791). In India, the hijras, castrated males, hermaphrodites or asexual persons take on a sacred character that sees them invited to celebrations and marriages. In 2018, Germany recognized the existence of a third sex, inscribed on the birth certificate upon the presentation of a medical statement.

With its representations of deviant masculinities, art upsets the patriarchal order. Nan Goldin's photos show men with make-up, drag-queens, homosexual couples separated by AIDS. With his faces in the form of screaming skulls and crossbones baring their teeth, Jean-Michel Basquiat gives a bodily representation of the Black man's revolt in the United States. The figure of the young homosexual from the provinces rejected by his family, wishing yet unable to renew contact with them, appears throughout the works of the playwright Jean-Luc Lagarce and sociologist Didier Éribon.

Africa and Asia are the new pioneering fronts of the masculine. In Lagos, Richard Akuson has created the magazine *A Nasty Boy* featuring sensual, flamboyantly eccentric men posing in skirts or dresses, with flowery tops, tights, feathers and high heels. As a product of a new masculine creativity, this fashion is a response to the boorish behaviour of males, the brazen vulgarity of petroleum magnates and the homophobic legislation passed in Nigeria in 2014. In South Korea, the young boys dressed in flowers in the 'boy band' BTS efface the boundaries between feminine beauty and masculine sex appeal, as in their music video 'IDOL', in which, with make-up, costumes and dyed hair, they dance in a fluorescent psychedelic setting. In China, influencers sport an effeminate look, with make-up, earrings, frilled panties and pink toys, in tribute to the icons of K-pop and J-Pop.*

This scrambling of genders can be interpreted as a demand for freedom, in opposition to the virilist model provided by the authorities.

---

* Sophie Bouillon, 'Nigéria, sapés comme jamais', *Gentlemen's Quarterly*, March 2018, pp. 122–129; and Jack Kilbride and Bang Xiao, 'China's "Sissy Pants Phenomenon": Beijing Fears Negative Impact of "Sickly Culture" on Teenagers', ABC, 14 September 2018.

An increasing number of young people on all continents are declaring themselves non-binary, gender-fluid or neutral, regardless of their sexual orientation. These new identities go beyond politics and fashion. They express a distrust of patriarchy.

A French rapper against 'abusive virility' (2017)

You will hold the iconic heritage of Apollo in your hands
And like all boys, you will run from football to champion
And will become my little historic hero
Abusive virility
Abusive virility
You shall be virile, my boy
I want to see your pale complexion get blackened from fights and forge your mind
So that none of these ladies lead you to pink lands
Deadly to gloriously strapping young men
You shall be virile, my boy
You shall hoist your masculine power
To counteract that sensitive essence that your mother dishes out to use as a family
She wears down your invulnerable Achilles
You shall be virile, my boy. . .
You shall shine by your physical strength, your dominant look, your boss-man posture
And your triumphant sex for despising the weak
You will enjoy your raw spark
Abusive virility

Eddy de Pretto, 'Kid' (2017)

Numerous homosexuals, such as Charles de Villette or Edward Carpenter have been feminist fellow travellers. As Allen Young wrote in *Out of the Closets* (1972), 'Gay liberation is a struggle against sexism.' From the 1980s on, men have become icons within the LGBT community, along with actresses and female singers:

among international performers, Boy George, George Michael, and Elton John, and, in the former Soviet world, the Russian singer and dancer Boris Moiseev and the Ukrainian singer Verka Serduchka – dressed in his glittery silver suits.

Gay culture, which is strictly speaking distinct from homosexuality, is fought by the dictatorships of the Middle East and North Africa, as well as by the authoritarian governments of Eastern Europe. In 2000, Belarus legalized homosexuality, but not gay and lesbian organizations, which were unable to organize a Gay Pride in subsequent years. In the post-Soviet era, Belarus' homophobia fitted into a nationalist discourse aiming to restore the honour of the humiliated homeland: thought of as a traditional family, the nation is strong as long as it is led by men. The official media strove to discredit opponents by tying them to 'pederastic' sexual minorities.* The opposite to this movement can be seen in then-Mayor of San Francisco Gavin Newsom's 2004 decision to authorize same-sex marriage, despite this contradicting California's legislation.

The entire life of Chelsea Manning, born in 1987 as Bradley, and imprisoned after having leaked thousands of classified documents to WikiLeaks in 2010, reveals a malaise vis-à-vis the world of virility. She had been subjected to her father's exhortations to act 'like a man', the mockery of her classmates after coming out, the insults of other soldiers in the army, and a culture of obedience and sacrifice. After her conviction in 2013, the United States Army authorized Private Manning, now called Chelsea, to dress like a woman and begin hormonal sex-change treatments. Chelsea Manning was freed in 2017 after her sentence had been commuted by President Obama.† As a homosexual, a whistle-blower in the US Army, a man having become a woman, Chelsea Manning thrice betrayed the order of gender: it took these three transgressions for her to reinvent masculine – or feminine – heroism.

New figures are emerging: not only the stay-at-home husband, the

---

* Almira Ousmanova, 'Pouvoir, sexualité et politique dans les médias biélorusses', *Raisons politiques*, No. 31, 2008, pp. 47–63.
† Matthew Shaer, 'The Long, Lonely Road of Chelsea Manning', *The New York Times*, 12 June 2017.

male nurse, the son caring for his parents, but also the homosexual soldier, the homosexual father, the transgendered hero, the Black American president, the androgynous star – all holders of a masculinity that enrages some men. In such diffractions, masculinity loses its centrality: it is no longer the abstract and therefore universal norm, but a body expressing a lifestyle choice. Man is no longer the invisible centre from which everything else stems, around which the world turns, but one human category among many others. This scrambling of identities leads less to the equality of the sexes than to their disequality, an asymmetry in which masculinities are enriched by the recombination of sex, gender and sexuality. Masculine minorities demand another 'right of man': the right of every man to embody the masculine. These dissidences contribute to breaking with the fantasy of the Great Conspiracy.

Women also have the right to participate in the definition of the masculine. The lesbian butch identity is a critical reappropriation of virility fit for redrawing the boundary between genders. It implements not only an appearance, but also forms of the body, voice, movement and desire.* In another realm, Candace Kucsulain, the singer with the Walls of Jericho, an American hardcore punk group, reshuffles the standards of masculinity: she is tattoo-laden, has large muscles, a bristling physical and vocal presence, and makes use of the lexicon of anger. Accepting these varied choices makes it possible to diversify the masculine, and that is a form of liberation.

DUMB AS A MAN?

Given our current situation, the strategy of 'gender trouble' cannot be generalized: the violation of norms comes at a steep price, except when one is an international star, and not everyone has the desire to fight against patriarchy by becoming a gender renegade. It is therefore necessary to turn to state feminism translated into laws and public policy. The example of Northern Europe and the memory of the USSR and its satellites attests to its efficacy.

* Sally Munt (ed.), *Butch/Femme: Inside Lesbian Gender* (London: Cassell, 1998).

Nowadays, most democracies are taking action in favour of the equality of the sexes. We should salute that as a tremendous achievement, since it displays a break with the state patriarchy that arose in Egypt and Mesopotamia around 3000 BCE. Gender justice demands that women have the same rights as men. This ideal is far from being achieved everywhere, but it has been accepted by a great number of women and men throughout the world. The question remains: how can we know that this equality of rights has been reached? Is it by parity, the arithmetical equality underlying democracy?

Absolute equality is neither possible nor desirable when it comes to maternity, since women are the ones who bear children and, in many cases, breastfeed them. One male employee in Great Britain filed a discrimination complaint in 2018: during his shared parental leave, he had been paid less than a woman during her maternity leave from the second to the fourteenth week. In keeping with national and European law, the court ruled against him on appeal, because maternity leave protects the health and wellbeing of pregnant people, who for biological reasons happen to be women, whereas parental leave makes it possible to take care of a child.*

Egalitarian feminism does not particularly require women to share in the chores that are incumbent on men in armies, oil drilling platforms or construction sites. We might take offence that women only represent 2 per cent of construction workers in France.† Why are there not more women handling jackhammers? Just as Olympe de Gouges demanded the right to take the podium in exchange for that of climbing up the scaffold, we might, for the sake of equality between the sexes, demand that women share in the hardest, most thankless and dangerous work that men alone take on, sometimes at the risk of their lives. But we sense the absurdity of such a manner of thinking: gender justice consists in lowering the mortality of men on construction sites and theatres of military operations, not in increasing the mortality of women. Feminism does not in fact demand absolute equality between the sexes, but rather *progress in the feminine condition.*

---

* Employment Appeal Tribunal, *Capita Customer Management Ltd v. Mr. Ali,* 11 April 2018.
† Observatoire des inégalités, 'Une répartition déséquilibrée des professions'.

Should we protest because women are the majority in certain professions (teachers, professors, magistrates) of the upper socio-economic
echelons? It is good that qualified women hold an increasing number
of leadership positions in the highest levels of administrations and
businesses. But when they manage to compete with men in the latter's
sanctuaries, it is often the masculine model that prevails: working
long hours, greater competition, power over others. Since the 1980s,
women have adopted the same risky behaviours as men, and their
regimen has become equally unhealthy. Poor eating habits, sedentary
routines, stress and addictions have translated into an 'epidemic' of
heart attacks in women of all professions, particularly the highly
active from forty-five to fifty-four years of age, with an increase of
hospitalizations of 5 per cent by year. Cardiovascular diseases have
become the number one cause of death among women.*

There again, we see the absurdity of this line of thinking: true progress does not consist in preventing women from shattering the glass
ceiling under the pretext that it would be bad for their health, but in
seeing to it that everyone should benefit from better living conditions.
We can make notable improvements in cardiovascular care for
women: contraceptives containing synthetic oestrogen have highly
negative effects on their health, prescriptions for medicinal treatments
are issued in insufficient numbers, and so on.

Achieving equality 'like men' is good, desirable and just, and gains
in this area brought about an anthropological break over the course
of the twentieth century, in the laws and institutions of society as well
as within families. However, it has not been shown that men's way of
life is always good, desirable and just. Nancy Fraser rejects the 'universal family support' model because women's careers are then in part
patterned after the masculinities of domination. The 'Amazon syndrome' consists not of being 'like men', but rather like the worst of
them: harsh, aggressive, vain and exploitative. That is less a matter of
shaking up the patriarchal system than it is of taking one's place in it.

But is becoming as dumb as men an objective? Is adopting the masculine as a universal model progress? Is it preferable to create alpha

---

* Claire Mounier-Vehier, 'Santé cardiovasculaire des femmes', *Bulletin épidémiologique
hebdomadaire*, No. 7–8, 8 March 2016.

females compatible with alpha males, or rather to fight against the so-called model provided by men? We need men, not their authority. It is just that women get as much as men and that men lose their privileges. It is just that masculinities of domination are no longer the norm and the model of the good life. It is just too to support subordinate and marginalized masculinities. Feminism cannot be limited to defending white educated women while leaving others to suffer their own fate.

Achieving parity, with 50 per cent men and 50 per cent women everywhere is not a panacea: the glaring problems of lower level injustice, the concentration of power and wealth at the top and the preponderance of the masculinity of domination remain in place. This reinforces the idea that the inequality between men and women is a problem of sex, whereas it is in fact a problem of gender. After romanticizing women and the belief in some great masculine conspiracy, parity as the be-all and end-all is the third impasse.

It is, of course, legitimate to demand parity in constitutional courts, executive committees, editorial boards, expert commissions, and so on. When such sexual democracy has been achieved, however, we will only have travelled a quarter of the way to our goal. What remains will be to deconstruct the masculine, dismantle patriarchy and work for the equality of all the other men and women who, owing to their lack of specialized skills or discriminations that people refuse to see, remain sidelined.

All these examples show that parity as an end in itself does not coincide perfectly with gender justice and that the latter is more ambitious than the former. Here is what a gender justice agenda might consist of:

- Reaching parity in government, media, and top levels of business and administration
- Improving living and working conditions for women with low levels of education and training
- Fighting against the under-representation of women from lower socio-economic backgrounds and ethnic minorities in politics, the economy and the media
- Reducing the number of boys from the lower classes and ethnic minorities who drop out of school
- Lowering the excessive mortality rate of males

Upper-class feminism counts on the equality of opportunity and lower-class feminism on the equality of positions held, but a reform of the educational system would come to the aid of marginalized masculinities. It is easy to see that in almost all democratic societies, the only priority is upper-class feminism: most efforts are devoted to the executive woman. But it is not right to confine gender justice to the benefit of already advantaged women.

The fight for women becomes universal through working-class feminism and intersectionality. In order to bring about emancipation for everyone, we must improve schooling for socially disadvantaged girls and boys, even if that means implementing the same measures of affirmative action for them as for highly educated women in politics and business.

FEMINISM AND THE COUPLE

Partisans of the French Republic in the nineteenth century believed that 'equality in difference' was more suitable for women than mere equality. The expression was just as hypocritical as the 'separate but equal' doctrine of racial segregation in the United States: it had no purpose other than to set each sex's destiny, with power on the one side and the woman function on the other. That is why equality between the sexes is not negotiable. It will remain at the core of gender justice as long as patriarchy exists. Until then, we will need a feminism that is a radical as possible.

In the eighteenth century, feminism arose from a demand for equality: to live 'like men', having the same rights. But women are not relative beings defined in comparison with a masculine norm, merely worthy of 'catching up' with men. Just as men have no authority to direct the lives of women, determining how they dress, act, and so on, so the masculine is not the template for every human life. Otherwise, in love as in law, the existence of a woman would be a 'realization for man, in all and at all times'.*

* Alexandra David-Neel, *Le Féminisme rationnel* (Paris: Les nuits rouges, 2000/ 1909), p. 61.

A new stage of the struggle is in sight: gender freedom, which ensures women's independence from men; a free and, consequently, a good life. Autonomous women; women over whom men have no hold; women unavailable for the needs and desires of men, except if they give their explicit consent; absolute, intransitive, non-instrumental persons, free to choose everything that concerns them and to rule the human species on the same basis as men. The woman-subject of equality, polarized by the masculine, is fading into the new model: the *woman-subject of freedom*.

Monique Wittig feels that in a world that subjugates women, lesbians are like runaway slaves who have taken the risk of fleeing. Freed from the heterosexual institution, 'lesbians are not women,' and that is why they can welcome men as brothers in the fight. The experience of lesbians is valid for all women who want to escape from patriarchy, in other words, from being at the service of men, providing them with sexual, maternal or domestic amenities. There are women who do not need men, or need them only intermittently – at work, in friendship, for sex, on trips and for procreation.

But how about the women who want to stay at home with their husband and children? During the 1980 sovereignty referendum campaign in Quebec, Lise Payette, Minister of the Feminine Condition, compared the partisans of the 'No' to 'Yvettes', heroines of textbooks full of sexist stereotypes: whereas Guy dreams of becoming a champion athlete, his little sister Yvette pleases her parents by serving food, drying the dishes, sweeping the floor.* Lise Payette's words unleashed a torrent of outrage among federalists about whether or not they were conservative, and stirred up a debate over the role of women. Is staying with one's children worthy of contempt? Is an Yvette not an over-active woman?

As Marguerite Yourcenar recalled in a 1981 interview, women have no need to feel diminished because they give birth to babies, nourish and dress them, surrounding their loved ones with tenderness and care. The patriarchal circle is not bad in and of itself, as long as one has the possibility of getting out of it without shame or guilt. The

* Stéphanie Godin, 'Les Yvettes comme l'expression d'un féminisme fédéraliste au Québec', *Mens*, Vol. 5, No. 1, 2004, pp. 73–117.

demand for dignity on behalf of the Yvettes is absolutely legitimate, but can be made universal on one condition only: every mother and housewife must at every moment be able to go back on her choice at every moment, to work, pursue a career, travel, begin another life. That supposes at the very least having obtained an education, a driving licence and a retirement fund, without which the domestic investment will have only produced the comfort of servitude.

On that indispensable condition, we can accept arrangements in which for a certain time, depending on career demands, one spouse can be less invested in the family than the other. This arrangement must not benefit only men. When a woman holds a lower paying position than her husband or one with a more flexible schedule, they each may find it advantageous, but that does not justify an uneven distribution of household chores. Feminism must respect a couple's compromise, but the couple's compromise must also respect feminism.

FREEDOM BETWEEN WOMEN AND MEN

Gender justice is based on rights, freedom and equality, an agenda for complete emancipation. Women have the right to higher education on the same basis as men, to work, earn money, divorce, be respected in their bodies, choose their sexuality, circulate freely in public, speak out, vote, be elected and be taken seriously. They have the right to security, knowledge, a voice in all matters, legitimacy, expertise, authority and power, and the right to not be incessantly reduced to their sex or gender.

Equality between the sexes is included in the freedom of women's relations with men, defined as the total freedom conferred by rights. For millennia, men have restricted women's freedom while at the same time abusively exercising their own, proclaiming themselves 'free' to dominate, strike, rape, exclude, silence or efface. The masculine can by no means serve as a model of freedom, because it is stained by its own injustice. A man who would like to break away from the tyranny of his gender, who would like to enter truly into the universal, can start by being a feminist. He who wants to be free must himself recognize women's freedom. It is up to men to bow to the rights of women as long as these rights do not deprive them of their own. Men's duty consists in not prohibiting anything; women's is not to forbid anything for themselves. Neither censorship nor self-censorship: gender justice requires *respecting the independence of women as an absolute.*

It can be objected that women are far from enjoying such freedom everywhere. That is tragically true. A just society has the duty to protect the choices of individuals in order to prevent the freedom of women beginning only where the power of men ends. By the variety of their active engagements in careers, families, communities and public affairs, women are generally more useful than men, and their lives are richer and more balanced. Instead of glorifying women as mothers while demonizing men as aggressors, we can conceive of the feminine as a guidepost, a newly desirable role model for men to define themselves in society. In the twentieth century, feminism consisted of living 'like men'; one day, it will help men live 'like women'.

This model is not based on the values traditionally associated with the feminine – tenderness, comprehension, altruism, empathy – even if, like Romain Gary who deplored the 'absence of femininity in our civilization,' we are entitled to prefer them to the braggadocio of virile chauvinism.* In this case, we are dealing with another type of universalism, feminine this time, that welcomes the wealth of the human adventure and its possible freedoms: the freedom to choose one's lifestyle according to one's own individual awareness, to exercise power at all levels, to be like men, alongside men, with men or without men, to think differently, and to create new forms, new conceptions of life in society.

Gender justice is the best antidote to mere democratic parity, and it is the characteristic of systems in which *sex is not correlated to any social inequality*: its best weapons are mutual respect and the freedom of women's relations with men. Gender justice is inseparable from social justice, and the emancipation of women portends the emancipation of all.

It is a good thing to be a feminist; it is better to fight against patriarchy. In that way, we prohibit the domination of sexes and genders,

---

* Romain Gary, 'Je suis victime de ma gueule' (1975) in Jacques Chancel, *Radioscopie* (Paris: Sous-sol, 2018), p. 186.

particularly women whose femininity is deemed compliant and men whose masculinity is deemed non-compliant. Broken up into masculinities, the masculine becomes one experience among many others. The day when men are capable of defending equality will be the day they emerge out of the archaic and become modern. It is now their turn to fight against the patriarchy – which is toxic for them as well.

What is a just man? One who acts in solidarity with women, while at the same time breaking off from solidarity with patriarchy. One who respects not only equality between women and men, but also between the feminine and the masculine, as well as among the various masculinities. A man who recognizes the liberty of the others. This is clearly a matter of refusing a certain state of the world: violence, partiality, absolutism, privileges, monopolies, connivance. For men, gender justice stems from a threefold determination: to *call oneself into question* as an individual and as a group; to promote, but above all to *live out the ideal of equality* within one's own couple, in one's family, at work, in the street, on public transport, in gatherings; and *to build new alliances* in view of future activism. To put it another way, being a just man means coming out of silent complicity and speaking out for the rights of all women and men.

Epilogue:
What Unjust Men Can Do

'Men, are you able to act with justice? This is a man's question to you.' I have paraphrased Olympe de Gouges here to remind us that these reflections by a man are indebted to the feminism of women.

Twenty years ago, I had the honour of working for Simone Veil, when she was president of the French Foundation for the Memory of the Holocaust. She was seventy-five, I wasn't even thirty. She could have been my grandmother. This exceptional woman, an orphan, was for me the link between Auschwitz, the integration of Jews, and feminism. She was obsessed by the passing of witnesses, the eternal silence of the women and men who had seen, suffered and resisted. She had survived Auschwitz, lived her life, and has now passed away.

This book is the product of personal and family history, of my journey through the generations. I am the son of a father, but the father of daughters; son of a woman, husband of another woman. My parents and my maternal grandparents followed the traditional distribution of chores. As for myself, I try to be a good father, but I am not sure of being a good husband. In the nineteenth century, a European would have found it silly for a household to be ruled by equality between the sexes. Today, a Scandinavian would find it foolish for it to be otherwise. I place myself between the two. For me, born and raised in France in the last three decades of the twentieth century, it is not easy to share chores. I do it, thanks to my wife who has educated me at the cost of discussions, tensions and sometimes arguments.

As a fairly egalitarian husband, a father who raises his daughters, I do not claim to be a model. It seems obvious to me that at certain times in my life, I have benefited from advantages tied to masculinity. I am not engaging in repentance: rather than posing as the ideal man,

I struggle with my contradictions. Moreover, by revealing this inner conflict, I am also doing my job as a historian, which consists of tracing particular troubles back to the tectonic plates of society in order to understand the history that is passing through us.

Writing this book has been a way for me to break with myself. To live well, one needs to have a clear conscience, to believe that one is siding with the good. But working on the masculine, I suddenly found myself among the dominant, the privileged, the freeloaders. To argue for gender justice as a man is to fight against oneself. Counter-masculinity, a virtue of democratic vigilance, is first of all a counter-self. One has to be capable of undoing the upbringing that one has received, the reflexes that one has acquired, the gender ideology that one has forged, the atmosphere of tolerance that surrounds us, until one renounces the person that one has always been.

It is not easy to confront a way of functioning that has existed even before we were born. It is no easier to break loose from a world in which women are exploited by housework and underpaid jobs, but also by advertising, pornography and prostitution. And then, one quickly realizes that it is hard to give up one's privileges. To be a just man represents one of the great challenges of the future. It requires at the very least an individual and collective will, for the efforts of all must be backed up by systemic change.

Is it possible to fight patriarchy as a man? What am I doing here, amid the feminist struggle? Men have a habit of intruding into everything, getting into every area of discussion and confiscating women's turn to speak. And here I am, with my ruses, appropriating for myself words that are not mine. What if I made it clear that this book speaks first and foremost of the masculine, a man speaking to men? Will people reply that I am in the process of constructing a new 'hegemonic masculinity'?

Karl Marx was not a proletarian, nor John Stuart Mill a woman, nor William Garrison a slave, nor André Gide a forced labourer in the Congo plantations. They nevertheless chose to side with those who were unlike them. Césaire, the poet from La Martinique, was grateful that Rimbaud, a poet from the Ardennes, had written: 'I am Black.' And I who am not a poet, am grateful to Césaire for having written: 'I am a Jewish man, a man of the pogroms.'

Today, accusations of cultural appropriation may deter men from speaking about feminism, white people from talking about slavery. This is a terrifying regression obliging everyone to remain within their niche under the pretext that they would be unqualified to understand oppression that they had not suffered. Such a ban, moreover, condemns the whole of social science: for example, all historians who have not rowed in the galleys, nor fired a machine gun from the trenches. I am proud to have reconstituted in *Laëtitia, ou la fin des hommes* (Laetitia or the end of men) the life of a young girl who had been abused and murdered: it was published in 2016, one year before the Weinstein affair. I deserve no credit for that, but I claim the right to speak, as a man, about feminism and gender justice.

'I revolt, therefore we are,' writes Albert Camus. The dignity of the masculine comes from the awareness of the injustice on which it reposes. Men could draw from that a sentiment of belonging more powerfully than locker-room jokes. The just are first of all those who revolt, capable of protesting against themselves and the lot they have reserved for themselves, before participating in common struggles. And so it is that, as a social democrat, I strive to invent a utopia called gender justice.

Whatever my limits may be, I am committed. I am not an activist, nor an apostle Paul on the road to Damascus, but I try to be a 'good guy'. While I have sketched the portrait of the just man, I know what sets me apart from it. That does not prevent me from taking sides. I am a man against masculine power. I am a feminist.

It would take another book to recount my youth, the way that I very early on felt out of step with the habits and customs of virility in sport, friendship and love, at both school and university. My intelligence is not as keen as my sensitivity, which borders on anxiety. For me, cynicism and violence are abhorrent. I do not believe that my wife chose me for my physical force or for my psychological solidity. I prefer camper vans to SUVs. As a man without qualities, I feel at home when I stroll through a museum. As a historian, I dialogue with the dead, not knowing how to deal with the living. I am learning to take stock of my weaknesses. I prefer the child in me to the adult, the wanderer to the professor.

I have pursued a career in academia and I contribute to its production of knowledge. I work in the social sciences. But my research also concerns social science methods and forms: investigation, multidisciplinarity, reflexivity, narration, structure, atmosphere, emotion. My writing tells the truth because it is based on evidence. My sensitivity is a methodological rigour. I upset the order of knowledge just as I contest the order of gender. So while I am a man in my body, heterosexual in my choices, a professor in my career, I feel uncomfortable in the masculine. I am not inclined to become a woman, but I gladly switch genders.

Becoming the father of my girls has been the greatest thing that has happened to me. There are still a few more years left for me to be near them, intent on putting into practice what I profess. Before I leave this world, I will perhaps have the good fortune to see our sons becoming just men, and our daughters, free women.

Picture Credits

pp. 15, 21, 59, 104, 181, 265. © Bridgeman Images.

p. 110. Courtesy of Dr David Shields, University of South Carolina. Photographer credit – Andre Bartalier. From *A Daughter of the Gods* (1916).

p. 204. © Getty Images.

p. 209. Courtesy of Kharbine-Tapabor.

p. 255. Courtesy of Mbathio Diaw. From *C'est la vie* (2015), RAES Productions.

p. 311. Abrams, *Born to ride*. Text copyright © 2019 by Larissa Theule. Illustration copyright © 2019 by Kelsey Garrity-Riley. Used by permission of Abrams Books for Young Readers, an imprint of Harry N. Abrams, Inc., New York. All rights reserved.

p.324. Courtesy of Jamal Nxedlana.

Index

Abe, Shinzo, 294–5
Abed, Fazle Hasan, 255–6
Abensour, Léon, 292
abolitionism, and feminism, 132
abortion, 113–14, 147–8, 165, 279, 291; selective, 196–7, 251
absent father, 187–9
Adams, Abigail, 94
Adams, John, 94
Adichie, Chimamanda Ngozi, 264
Adventures of TinTin, 180
advertising, sexism in, 208–10, 212
Aeschylus, 7
Afghanistan, 162
African-American fathers, 187–8
agnotology, 291
agriculture, invention of, 15–17
Ailes, Roger, 281
Akan people, 4
Akuson, Richard, 325
Alexievich, Svetlana, 248
Ali, Safiye, 163
Alinejad, Masih, 260
Al-Tahtawi, Rifa'a, 144
al-Thani, Tamin, 245
Althusser, Louis, 197
Altmann, Anna, 164
Amaterasu (goddess), 22
Amazons, 18, 133
American Declaration of Independence, 90
Amin, Qasim, 144
androgyne, 325

Anne of Austria, 85, 86
Anneke, Mathilde, 103
Anomalies Act (1931), 154
antifeminism, 215, 227–31, 228–30
Antioch College, Ohio, 271, 272
anti-semitism, 182, 222
Anzin strike (1884), 219
Aquino, Cory, 107
Arab Enlightenment (*Nahda*), 144
Arinna (goddess), 22
Aristophanes, 178
Aristotle, 22, 40, 67, 314
Aruru (goddess), 23
Assyria, 75
Astarte (goddess), 23
Astell, Mary, 84, 96
Atatürk, Mustafa Kemal, 162, 250
Athens, sexual segregation, 22
Atlantic revolutions, 90–1, 97
Auclert, Hubertine, 105, 129, 130, 142, 152, 157, 199, 320
Audur Capital (company), 298
Austen, Jane, 49
authoritarian states, 250

Bachofen, Johann-Jakob, 3, 132
Baez, Joan, 115
Balabanoff, Angelica, 126
Balzac, Guez de, 84
Balzac, Honoré de, 48
Bandaranaike, Sirimavo, 107
Bangladesh, 255, 256
Banks, Russell, 188